Curtis Guild

Abroad again

Or, A fresh Foray in foreign Lands

Curtis Guild

Abroad again
Or, A fresh Foray in foreign Lands

ISBN/EAN: 9783337140519

Printed in Europe, USA, Canada, Australia, Japan

Cover: Foto ©ninafisch / pixelio.de

More available books at **www.hansebooks.com**

ABROAD AGAIN;

OR,

A FRESH FORAY IN FOREIGN LANDS.

BY

CURTIS GUILD,

EDITOR OF THE BOSTON COMMERCIAL BULLETIN, AND AUTHOR
OF "OVER THE OCEAN."

BOSTON:
LEE AND SHEPARD, PUBLISHERS.
NEW YORK: CHARLES T. DILLINGHAM.
1877.

Copyright,
By CURTIS GUILD,
1877.

Electrotyped at the Boston Stereotype Foundry,
19 Spring Lane.

PREFACE.

Such of us as have longed to "go abroad," remember, in our young days, and, it may also be said with equal truthfulness, in maturer years, that we have sometimes promised ourselves a good thorough gossip and chat with friends who had just returned from foreign lands; and that we were disappointed, even after most laborious effort, in obtaining the information which we expected familiarly imparted, or, in fact, any except what we knew before, and which anybody that had perused a reasonable portion of the current literature of the day would have been able to impart, without having crossed the ocean.

This sort of people have been to Rome.

"O, yes! It is a fine old city, and full of interesting ruins, you know."

"The Vatican? Certainly. The Pope lives there, and the works of art there are truly wonderful."

"How did the Colosseum look?"

"Why, it is oval in form, you know, and a large portion of it is ruins — a most interesting place."

Such are samples of the information you may get from your travelled friend, who, you fondly imagined, would describe to you his experiences and sight-seeings so much more intelligibly than it is done in the books. Those interesting trifles which the untravelled are so fond of reading about, it must be remembered, become so much a matter of course, so familiar to the traveller abroad, that he can hardly bring himself to believe they are of importance enough to allude to, or of interest enough to put in print. But in these days of abundant newspaper correspondence, and epistles from every part of the globe by those trained soldiers of the press who have tested every phase of popular taste, even that for trifles above mentioned, it is hardly to be expected that such an exhausted hunting-ground as Europe will yield at this late day much that has not, in some shape, been previously presented to the reader.

The author, on his first visit abroad, notwithstanding his journey was over fields that had been trodden and retrodden by American tourists, in his investigations for his own information, and his foraging for facts that he himself desired to obtain, found, upon presenting them, that they possessed a sufficient degree of freshness and importance to be most acceptably received by the reading public.

In this record of a second tour abroad, the reader is taken through an entire new series of scenes and experiences from those described in "Over the Ocean." Some time is spent in visiting curious historic localities in London; a pen-picture of English home life is given, and some of the modern wonders of the great metropolis are described more minutely than perhaps has previously been done.

To Rome, that ever fruitful field for historian, antiquary, and novelist, considerable space has been given in these pages, although no author can reasonably expect to present much that is new from a field that has been so industriously gleaned. If fresh interest can be excited with regard to those wonders of art and classical scenes of antiquity already familiar from frequent description, by a new presentation, possessing sufficient originality to command attention, it is all that at this time can be reasonably expected.

Although the gayeties of that paradise of many American travellers, Paris, are not described, nor the magnificent scenery and mountain-passes of Switzerland, or picturesque beauty of the river Rhine, as in the author's former volume, yet the reader is taken to quaint old cities like Verona and Innspruck, and among the lofty peaks and glaciers of the Tyrol and Upper Engadine, through the great art galleries of Dresden and Berlin, and into that curious country so much of whose territory has been wrested from the sea, — Holland.

Allusions are frequently made in these pages to information sought, but not found in the guide-books. While it will be admitted that if those publications gave everything everybody desired to find in them, they would become encyclopedias, yet to many tourists a portion of the information furnished by some of them is unintelligible. This arises from the fact that the compilers seem to have assumed that all tourists have a liberal, or university education. As regards American tourists, a large majority of those able to travel abroad have only enjoyed the benefits of a common-school education, hence copies of inscriptions in antique Latin without translation, names of buildings, statues, antiquities, public resorts, &c., given in the foreign vernacular in an English guide-book, or sentences in Greek, Latin, French, or Italian as the last words of great men, or descriptive of paintings, or, in fact, for any purpose of illustration, are to such majority not only an annoying puzzle, but a constant reminder of their lack of that knowledge possessed by others who have enjoyed more advantages. Even the savant and student prefer the most direct and simple style of information to any other.

With this in view, the author has sought to present his thoughts, impressions, and descriptions, not only in a graphic and interesting, but in a straightforward and simple manner. His foray for fresh material in foreign lands for readers at home, resulted in the discovery of an abundance of supplies; whether the selections therefrom were skilfully made, or are properly presented, it is for the reader to determine. C. G.

CONTENTS.

CHAPTER I.

Unpleasant Recollections. — Doubts Dispelled. — Why Americans go Abroad. — The Voice of Experience. — Sharp Practice. — Picture Marts. — Union Stores. — Tricks upon Travellers. — Hints about Shopping. — Prenez-Garde. — Notable Exceptions. — Bugbears of Travel. — Foreign Physicians. — Planning the Tour. 1–18

CHAPTER II.

Excursion Parties. — A Specimen Character. — A Yankee Inquisitor. — Turning the Tables. — Representatives of America. — "Most Interesting Thing in Europe." — Experts in Travelling. — Inexperienced Tourists. — Hotel Impositions. — Servants and Sovereigns. — Accepting the Situation. — Letters of Credit. — Bankers' Courtesies. — Seasoned Tourists. — A True Sailor. — Catechizing the Captain. — Steamship Experiences. — Pleasant Days at Sea. — Liverpool. — Hotels. — Torments of Tantalus. — The Circumlocution System. — Every One to his Calling. 19–47

CHAPTER III.

English Custom *vs.* American Requirements. — Behind the Age. — The Wonders of London. — Old Smithfield. — Historic Ground. — Wonders of a London Market. — The Strand. — Temple Bar. — Chancery Lane. — Realizing Dickens's Stories. — Historic Landmarks. — Classic Ground. — The Knights Templars. — Temple Church. — Scene of Initiation. — Templar Effigies. — Refinement of Cruelty. — Grave of Goldsmith. — The Thames Embankment. — London Bridges. — The West End. — Restaurants. — The City. 47–75

CHAPTER IV.

Well-bred People. — English Home Life. — English Servants. — Lunch. — English Stable-Yard. — Dressing for Dinner. — An English Dinner. — The Dessert. — "We will join the Ladies." — Finale of the Feast. — An Amusing Blunder. — An English Breakfast. — Taking Leave. — English Domestic Service. 76–92

CHAPTER V.

Catching a Train. — Against Regulations. — The Policeman in Plain Clothes. — Under Surveillance. — An Uncomfortable Position. — Five-Pound Penalty. 92–97

CHAPTER VI.

A Ride in London. — Old Holborn Bars. — Bowbells and Old Jewry. — The English Guilds. — Beckett's Birthplace. — Ballad of Beckett. — The Business Centre of London. — A Cheap Neighborhood. — Five Miles from Charing Cross. — Bethnal Green Museum. — An Admirable Institution. 98–108

CHAPTER VII.

Royal Albert Hall. — Grand Auditorium. — Well-planned Interior. — Costly Monument. — Superb Statuary. — Effective Groups. — Statue Group of America. — Art and Poetry. — Prodigality of Decoration. — Elaboration of Art. — A Costly Tribute. 109–119

CHAPTER VIII.

Rome. — The City of our Dreams. — First Sensations. — Reality vs. Romance. — Sight-seeing in Rome. — Tomb of Hadrian. — Magnificent Mausoleum. — St. Peter's. — The Grand Pavilions. — The Great Obelisk. — The Vestibule. — First View of the Interior. — Beneath the Dome. — Vast Proportions. — Kissing the Toe of St. Peter's Statue. — The Tribune. — Tombs and Monuments. — Marble Miracles. — How to visit St. Peter's. — A Village in the Air. — A Dizzy Promenade. 120–141

CHAPTER IX.

The Pantheon. — A Glorious Pagan Temple. — Vandalism. — The Capitoline Hill. — Legends and Localities. — The Square of the Capitol. — The Wolf of the Capitol. — Capitoline Museum. — Hall of the Emperors. — Portrait Busts. — Sculptured Stories. — The Endymion Sarcophagus. — A Youthful Prodigy. — Preservers of Art. — Hall of the Centaurs. — The Dying Gladiator. — Marble Faun. — Classic Ruins. — Roman Forum. — The Rostrum. — The Nameless Column. — The Arch of Titus. — Arch of Septimius. — Arch of Constantine. — Borrowed Sculpture. — The Mamertine Prison. — Trajan's Column. — Unearthing Old Rome. — A Pillar of History. — An Egyptian Relic. — Convent of the Capuchins. — Capuchin Church. — Ladies not Admitted. — A Hall of Horrors. — Suppression of the Convent. 142–179

CHAPTER X.

The Vatican. — The World's Art Museum. — Obstructions to Visitors. — The Pope's Guard. — Costumes in Rome. — The Last Judgment. — A Great Artist's Great Work. — Museum of Statues. — The Athlete. — Grand Army of Statues. — Priceless Art Wealth. — Tiberius Cæsar. — "A Mass of Breathing Stone." — Reading Up. — Sarcophagi of the Scipios. — The Boxers. — The Laocoön. — A Story in Marble. — Apollo Belvedere. — Lord of the Unerring Bow. — A Menagerie in Marble. — Hall of Statues. — Nero as Apollo. — Hall of the Muses. — The Muses in Marble. — A Suspected Character. — Sala Rotunda. — Hall of the Greek Cross. — Magnificent Mosaic. — Hall of the Chariot. — The Quoit Throwers. — Fatigue of Sight-Seeing. — The Etruscan Museum. — Ancient vs. Modern Workmanship. — Etruscan Art. — Ancient Vases. — The Egyptian Museum. — The Vatican Library. — Literary Wealth. — Raphael's Masterpiece. — Gallery of Vases. — Notable Art Treasures. — Hall of Maps. — Hall of Tapestries. — Grand Pictorial Effects. — Obstacles to Enjoyment. — Advantages of Preparation. . . . 179–228

CHAPTER XI.

The Colosseum. — Relics of the Past. — The Giant of Roman Ruins. — The Colosseum described. — Roman Vandalism. — The Royal Road. — Architectural Skill. — A Dream of the Past. — Exploring the Colosseum. — Behind the Scenes. — The Christians to the Lions. — Horrors of the Arena. — An Imperial Joker. — Systematic Sight-Seeing. — Caracalla's Baths. — Ancient Popular Resort. — Palace of the Cæsars. — Streets of Ovid and Virgil's Time. — House of Livia. — The Appian Way. — Tomb of Cæcilia Metella. — Roman Aqueducts. — Picturesque Views. — St. Paul Extra Muros. — Constantine's Cathedral. — A Struggle with Time. — Royal Chapels. — The Santa Scala. — Ascending the Holy Stairs. — Temple of Vesta. — Bridge of Horatius. — Guido's Aurora. — Guido and Raphael. 228-262

CHAPTER XII.

The Pincian Hill. — Farewell to Rome. — From the Sublime to the Ridiculous. — Venice. — Exploring the By-ways. — Gondoliers. — Scenes on the Grand Canal. — Italian Music. — Heart of the Venetian Republic. — The Voice of the Bells. 253-272

CHAPTER XIII.

A Singular Story. — The Fearful Three. — Ghosts of the Past. — Terrible Dungeon. — A Dangerous Experiment. — Venetian Prison. — Mysterious Visitors. — Prisoner of the Inquisition. — A Terrible Situation. — A Dash for Liberty. — A Chamber of Horrors. — A Desperate Struggle. — The Foe in the Dark. — A Puzzling Position. — Leaden Moments. — Trapped in a Prison Cell. — A Terrible Night. — Daylight at Last. — Vain Efforts for Freedom. — Starvation in Prospect. — Exhaustion and Despair. — Succor at Last. — The Luxury of Liberty. — "Such Stuff as Dreams are made of." — The Lady in the Case. 273-297

CHAPTER XIV.

The Arsenal at Venice. — Remnant of a Great Power. — Maritime Importance of Venice. — Ancient Armor and Wondrous Weapons. — The Bucentaur. — Verona. — Street Scenes. — Roisterers of Verona. — Montagues and Capulets. — Juliet's Balcony. — Tomb of the Capulets. — The Verona Amphitheatre. — Modern Performance in an Ancient Circus. — Della Scala Family Monuments. — A Murderer's Mausoleum. — Scenic Streets. — Relic of the Middle Ages. — Cathedral at Verona. — Church of St. Anastasia. — The Tyrol. — A Night in Botzen. — Tyrolean Scenery. — The Alps again. — Innspruck. — An Amphitheatre of Alps. — The Golden Roof. — Historic Beauty. — Royal Felicity. — Ambras Castle. — Andreas Hofer. — Spider-Web Pictures. — The Court Church. — Giants in Bronze. — The Silver Chapel. — A Grateful Picture. 298-337

CHAPTER XV.

Seeking Companions. — Post Horses for St. Moritz. — Memorable Mountain. — Perilous Position. — Route to the Engadine. — The Finstermünz Pass. — "The Day we Celebrate" in the Alps. — Hoch Finstermünz. — Wonders of an Alpine

viii   CONTENTS.

Pass. — Tarasp Springs. — The Engadine Valley. — Samaden. — Hans Christian Andersen. — St. Moritz. — A Fashionable Resort. — Crowded Out. — A Miniature Hotel. — Scenes at the Springs. — Study of Characters. — Improving an Opportunity. — Romantic Ride. — Bernina Brook. — The Morteratsch Glacier. — The Albula Pass. — From Mountain to Valley. — The Schyn Pass. — Gate of the Via Mala. — The Splugen Road. — Arrival at Prague. — A Hurried Visit. 338–373

CHAPTER XVI.

Dresden. — Protection of Art Treasures. — Japanese Palace. — Museum of Porcelain. — Streets in Dresden. — The Dresden Gallery. — Raphael's Madonna. — The Holbein Madonna. — Masterpieces of Great Masters. — Old vs. New School. — Art Treasure House. — The Tournament Hall. — Historic Armor Suits. — The Saloon of Costumes. — An Aladdin's Cave. — The Green Vaults. — Costly Burlesques. — Jewels sown broadcast. — Court of the Great Mogul. — Dresden Beer Gardens. — Americans in Dresden. — Berlin. — Unter den Linden. — Statuary in Berlin. — Old Friends in a New Place. — The Brandenburg Gate. — The People of Berlin. — Public Buildings. — Streets and Shops. — Thiergarten. — Mausoleum at Charlottenburg. 374–407

CHAPTER XVII.

The Museums of Berlin. — Allegorical Illustrations. — Gallery of Gods and Heroes. — Hall of the Emperors. — The Antiquarium. — Classic Antiquities. — Ancient Gems. — Antique Coins. — Picture Galleries. — A Wealth of Art. — Kaulbach's Frescos. — The Reformation. — Tower of Babel. — Battle of the Huns. — The Greek Saloon. — Unknown Antiquities. — A Monarch 1200 B. C. — Egyptian Historical Halls. — "In Thebes Streets Three Thousand Years Ago." — Prussian Historical Relics. — Frederick the Great. — Glass and Enamel Work. — Curiosities of Art. — Potsdam. — Sans Souci. — The Orangery. — A Monument of Justice. — Inside Look at Royalty. — The Five Palaces. — Berlin to Hanover. — House of Leibnitz. — A Beautiful Drive. 408–443

CHAPTER XVIII.

Amsterdam. — Dutch Windmills. — Dutch Characteristics. — Canals of Amsterdam. — Drawbridges and Canal Boats. — Peasant Women. — Commercial Importance. — Canals to the Sea. — Magnificent Public Work. — Dutch Agriculture. — The Palace. — Rembrandt's Night Watch. — Old Dutch Masterpieces. — An Excursion to Brock. — A Cow Saloon. — Dutch Cheese-Making. — Dutch Farm-House. — An Immaculate Village. — The Hague. — Statues and Monuments. 443–463

CHAPTER XIX.

Rembrandt's School of Anatomy. — Paul Potter's Bull. — Gems of Art. — Dutch Historical Relics. — The "House in the Woods." — Schéveningen. — A Dutch Watering-Place. — Magnificent Railway Bridge. — Back to Paris. — Guide-Books. — Good-bye to the Reader. 463–474

ABROAD AGAIN.

CHAPTER I.

ABROAD again! What! have you forgotten all those wretched days on shipboard, when, stretched out in your state-room, weak from sea-sickness, you longed so much for the comfort of your sweet chamber at home, where there was no mingled perfume of ocean and oakum? Home, where you could put your foot down with a certainty that the floor wouldn't reel away from you; where wash-bowl and pitcher and towels would stay in their places, and where everything on the floor didn't slide about, and everything hung up didn't swing back and forth till the sight of it produced nausea?

Have you forgotten that vow you registered, that, having seen Europe once, you were satisfied, and that books, and engravings, and lectures, and descriptions would satisfy you in future?

Do you remember telling friends that the best thing to make one appreciate a good home was to be away from it for six or eight months, and that one of the most agreeable sights you saw on your last journey was the spires of your native city on your return trip? Do you call to mind those wretched days in the cabin of the steamer, during the gale, when no one of the passengers went on deck but an old sea-captain, who was going to Liverpool to take command of a ship, the travelling agent of an English mercantile house, who had crossed twenty times, and the young American who had served in the navy; and how we all thought if we only got ashore safely this time, we never would be caught in such a predicament again?

Do you know how wretched it was to be ill at a Tyrolean inn, with no one nearer than a hundred miles who spoke your native language, and a doctor, whose French was worse than your own, to attend you?

Have you forgotten the swindles of hotel-keepers, the fatigue of *diligences*, the brevity of German beds, and the liveliness of Italian ones; the indigestible messes on some inn tables, and the garlic flavor of others; the bother with luggage, quarrels with couriers; the back-aching inspection of picture-galleries, the lies of the *valet de place*, and the omissions of just what you wanted to know in guide-books?

To be sure you have; but, like those bitter tonics which we swallow with a shudder, these memories only serve to rouse a fiercer appetite than ever.

The memory of sea-sickness exists but as a disagreeable dream, and you feel confident now that your knowledge and experience will make you to combat it successfully. The humdrum life of home has become monotonous. You feel that the first journey to Europe was merely preliminary — necessary to teach how you ought to travel to see it sensibly. And now you know how to travel abroad, how much better and more thoroughly will you see everything! Books, engravings, lectures, forsooth! What are they to seeing the place itself? What scores of interesting things you saw in Westminster Abbey, old St. Paul's, the Venetian palaces, St. Peter's, among Roman ruins, and even on the Parisian boulevards, that the letter-writers and the book-makers never think of writing about.

Appreciate a good home? To be sure you do. And the very thing you mean to do now is to buy something abroad to decorate it with and show your appreciation. The were those bronzes in Paris that you always regretted not taking; there was that picture in Florence that you find, after all, you might have afforded; and those Roman mosaics and antiquities, which, if your trunk had only been larger, you might have bought; and then, those — Ah! but next time you will look out for all those things. You mean to do good shopping as well as sight-seeing.

The gale? Well, that was only two days' discomfort, after all; and how pleasant were the next three days after it! How everybody was on deck, and how the ocean seemed to have got smoothed down as flat as a table-cloth! All the passengers were at the cabin-table, and several young men, who had been sick till then, absolutely smoked cigars after dinner; and the deck was steady as a rock.

How the old sea-captain, when asked if we had been in any danger, said, "Not to such a ship as this;" and how the agent of the English mercantile house told the lady who had vowed "if she only got on shore this once, she never would go on the ocean again — never!" the story of the Irishman on shipboard in a storm, who vowed a gift of twenty pounds to the Virgin Mary if he was permitted to reach land safely, and, being reminded some months after of the nonpayment of the vow, shrewdly remarked that "the Vargin wud niver" catch him "on the say agin."

What was two days' homesickness at a Tyrolean inn? One must have a bilious attack somewhere. As to hotel-keepers, let them try any of their games on *you* now — old, seasoned traveller as you deem yourself! You know more of *cafés* and restaurants now, and can avoid garlic messes without difficulty. Couriers you will have none; and galleries and museums you will inspect more leisurely, and *valets de place* shall be made to know their place.

In fact, when one has set his heart upon doing a thing, especially if it be something that he has thought he should not do, it is really astonishing what a number of reasons he can bring forward to sustain his change of opinion.

To one fond of travel, or to a person of any degree of education and culture, the European tour is a source of never-ending enjoyment, months and years after it is over. With how much more interest do you read of events that transpire in the old world, that are enacted in the very streets or in the historic buildings that you have visited and fixed in your mind while sight-seeing! With what new beauty do copies of statues, pictures, and busts become imbued, after you have seen the grand originals! With what fresh attraction is history invested, or even novels, the scenes of which are laid in those countries, cities, or very spots that you have crossed the ocean to see!

Enthusiasm in the returned tourist should never be mistaken for snobbishness, as it sometimes is by those who have never been abroad. I confess, before having travelled abroad, to have sometimes thought of those who had, and who were eloquent over the artistic beauty of foreign pictures, the magnificence of ancient architecture, and the grand conception that created celebrated statues which they expatiated most eloquently upon, over some wretched and familiar plaster model, — that their admiration might be affectation, and their expatiation but a parade of where they had been and what they had seen more than their less travelled listeners.

On the other hand, there are foreign-travelled snobs who are as amusing to sensible persons as the home-travelled members of the same genus. The latter will be readily recognized as those who are continually telling when they were last at Saratoga; or that General Bustah remarked to them in Washington; or that " our carriage was ordered in season for Senator Swyndell's reception." They ask you if you don't think Sharon Springs a prettier (!) place than the White Sulphur, and if you have many friends at Long Branch. "Chawming place, Newport; but, if you'll believe it, we took a cottage at Niagara Falls last season."

The foreign-travelled snob is fond of referring to when

he was in Vienna, or Paris, or London; and how much it cost for the opera; and of his having a courier; or being in Rome with the Highbreds; or "Came down to Geneva with Finifines;" or of the ride he took in the "Bowar des Bolone" with Colonel Throdice. He never refers to libraries, statues, museums, or pictures, except that he may halt opposite one, perhaps, in your drawing-room, squint knowingly at it through his closed fist, and ask where you "picked that up." This class of snob, male and female, travels and visits celebrated places, as it does at home, not to perfect itself in knowledge; not from a desire to see localities and historic places of which it has read and studied; not from any admiration of sculpture, painting, fine arts, or natural scenery: but because it is the fashion; or, rather, it thinks it out of fashion not to have been in Europe.

The lady snob of this class is better posted on dressmakers and milliners in Paris than she is on the natural scenery of Switzerland, and will be better able to tell you of her reception at a royal "drawing-room," — for which she obtained tickets through the moneyed influence of her husband, and which cost her no end of expense, — than to describe an Alpine mountain pass that she has journeyed over, an Italian picture gallery that she has sauntered through, or a cathedral that she only remembers from having lunched with a party with whom she went to see it.

Another class of travellers are those whom you would say, were it not questioning the inalienable right of the universal Yankee, had no right to be abroad. And, indeed, it might be better for our country if they had never been permitted to travel. These are a class of people practically ignorant of their own country and its institutions, and whose only knowledge about others is that they are "foreign parts," that "Queen Victoria lives in a palace, and the Pope of Rome in St. Peter's," and who are amazed to find that the people of Italian cities are not dressed like the brigands in the picture-books, and those of Switzerland like the characters they have seen represented at the circus or on the theatrical stage.

The annual spring and summer rush of tourists from America to Europe has now come to be almost an American fashion, and doubtless there are many who make the trip simply to be in the fashion; but we are not at all inclined to join with the opinion of some of our American journalists who ridicule and scold their countrymen for spending money abroad, laboriously figuring up statistics, showing how much American gold is disbursed by American tourists to English and Continental hotel-keepers and merchants, and lamenting that so large a portion of our means should be expended for foreign luxuries instead of articles of domestic production, and condemning the moneyed American because he does not expend all his money in his own country.

Americans who have money to spend and time to spare like to go to Europe, because there are more historic, artistic, and natural sights to be seen, and more easily seen there, and also because they can obtain some things which are utterly unattainable at home.

If the American in his own country desires to spend the summer at the sea-shore or a watering-place with his family, owing to the shortness of the season and the determination of landlords to make a handsome profit each season, he finds the expense very nearly as much as a three months' trip in Europe would cost him. And what has he had for the money at home? Small, inconvenient rooms in a great caravansary of an hotel, where the attendance is abominable, the extra charges frightful, the place noisy with brass bands, "hops," and various fashionable excitements from picnics to prayer-meetings, to make the blood more fevered in the heat of summer; while ill-cooked food, the confusion of constant arrivals and departures, and the utter absence of any of that restful quiet that the body craves, cause him ere the season is over to long for the quiet of his own home, and wonder why he deserted it. It is not to be asserted by any means that there is no discomfort in European travel or hotels, for off the great lines of travel routes the same annoyances exist as in America, but, as a general thing, at the great popular resorts a far more satisfactory return may be had for the money expended than in this country.

There is so much useful information that can be given by one who has been "over the route" to those who are about to start, and, moreover, as every one who has travelled abroad knows, there are so many dearly bought experiences that might have been avoided had the advantage of a little instruction from an expert been enjoyed previous to setting out, that the author feels warranted in commencing this work with a few hints to travellers upon minor matters. They are the results of his own personal experience, and may be of value to those who visit the localities here referred to. First, on the ever prolific subject of shopping abroad. Jewelry and pictures, to those who have the money to spend, are generally among the most attractive objects that claim attention. The price of jewelry in London is frightfully high. Geneva is the place for that article: first, because of your surety of getting the genuine 18-carat gold; and next, because they are a community of jewellers there, and labor and living are cheaper. It should be understood, however, that watches can now be made better and cheaper in America than in Switzerland.

Diamonds the Parisian jewellers think they can sell as reasonably as any dealers in Europe, but I rather favor the honest Dutch dealers of Amsterdam, the headquarters of diamond-cutting in the world, and where I have seen the finest diamonds — not in the royal treasuries — I ever looked on, and where diamond-cutting and dealing is as much a specialty as watches in Geneva or gloves in Paris. Here at Zenten & Jouen's, a solid old jewelry house at 438 Herrengracht, as their Dutchy old card says, I looked on diamonds that were as dewdrops upon the velvet into which it seemed they would momentarily sink and disappear. So charmed was an American senator with these gems and the quiet courtesy of the dealers, that a few thousand dollars gave his wife that coveted possession, a pair of solitaires, which the Parisian jewellers were compelled to admit they could not excel in purity or compete with in price.

Beware of gold-mounted coral ornaments or gold jewelry in the Piazza St. Marco in Venice. The former, which are palmed off on the unsuspecting buyer, are often not over three or four carats fine; but you will buy pounds of glass beads at the bead factories of the Queen of the Adriatic, recollecting, however, that the ivory inlaid furniture, at the old bric-à-brac stores that guides entice you into, that looks so pretty there, will drop to pieces in your own drier climate or furnace-heated house.

London can hardly be said to be a desirable place for an American to purchase oil-paintings in. Good ones bring higher prices there than in any other city on the habitable globe. It appears to be headquarters for water-color pictures, which are just now in high favor, and, if the lovers of that style of art wish to have their very hair stand on end with astonishment, let them ask the prices of some of the productions of artists of acknowledged celebrity in this line of their profession.

I am inclined to believe that Americans find Brussels and Florence more profitable picture marts than any other cities in Europe. In London the wealthy tradesmen and the nobility never seem to question price, if the painting is by a known artist, and they want it; and the prices obtained when some well-known collector's gallery is sold, are positively astonishing.

Care should be taken by inexperienced purchasers of pictures on the continent, to make their agreement to include packing and delivering on board steamer at Liverpool, Bremen, or whatever port they intend their purchase shipped from, and free of all consul, port, or express charges; otherwise he may receive his purchase in America with a very handsome charge of extras for boxing, bill of lading, consul's certificate, insurance, and even, as in the author's case, from a Hebrew merchant, of five per cent. on the value of the painting for "reimbursement" or guaranty of the sight-draft's passing through his hands, and a few francs more for postages. It is almost useless to attempt to purchase any good picture that is exposed at the exhibitions in Paris at anything like a bargain, as sharp picture-dealers, always on the lookout for any painting that is likely to sell, or that is from the pencil of any artist of reputation, purchase them of the artist, or arrange to take them as fast as produced, or to sell all his works through their house. The purchaser is thus forced to pay a round sum to the middleman, unless he has some friend, familiar with the artists in Paris, who will go with him personally to their studios, and find some who are not hampered by any such conditions.

French artists who have pictures at the exhibition are also very much like their shopkeeper countrymen, thinking that if a visitor, having seen their production, has thought enough of it to come to them with a view of purchasing, especially if the visitor be an American, he will pay a high price, and therefore often lose a sale by the extravagant figure which they put upon their productions, or make one to an experienced purchaser at a third or perhaps half the price originally charged.

One sees in Paris, though, it must be confessed, some of those superb specimens of the modern school of French art that cause him to think that the price which may be demanded is none too great a reward to the genius that created them. However, let the inexperienced purchaser engage the service of a trusty friend and expert in purchases of this kind, unless he is so abundantly supplied with cash as to render price no object.

In Dresden, the beautiful paintings on porcelain and an

elegant description of water-color, are sold. "The Chocolate Girl," "Rembrandt and Wife," Raphael's "Madonna," "Cherubs," "Madonna and Child," and other familiar masterpieces, are copied upon porcelain with that beautiful finish for which this style of painting is noted. All along a street called the Prager-Strasse are porcelain-picture stores, some of them kept by decorative artists themselves, who will copy paintings for you to order, or copy miniatures from photographs in the beautiful style of porcelain painting, if you give the color of the eyes, hair, and complexion of the subject, — at a price ranging from fifty to one hundred marks each. But beware of paying in advance for any such orders, as the promises of a Dresden porcelain painter are as "false as dicers' oaths."

Rome is so well understood to be a city where pictures of artists and works of sculptors, of different nationalities, who are sojourning there, may be purchased, that I will not go into details. The tourist, if he be an expert in pictures, and has an eye for an opportunity, will often find excellent ones in cities not specially noted as art centres, but where artists live or go, who send forward their works for sale. Düsseldorf, Hamburg, Antwerp, Verona, Amsterdam, The Hague, Munich, Bremen, and other cities, some of which might sound more oddly to experts as places to find good pictures, nevertheless produce and contain them, and many is the good and rare one picked up off the beaten track of fine-art travel.

English shopping I have pretty thoroughly discussed. Although the co-operative stores have not been referred to, they deserve brief reference. They are, it will be remembered, establishments where those belonging to the union or society may purchase at retail at a small percentage over wholesale prices, and the system has been so far extended and perfected that, with some of the most powerful unions, large dealers have made arrangement that all members of the co-operative body may call at the dealers' regular retail stores, and, on presentation of the card of the union with which each member is provided, have a discount of, in some instances, as large as twenty per cent. immediately taken from the usual retail price.

By this arrangement the union is saved the expense of transportation, handling, and storage of the goods, and its members enjoy the same benefit as though purchasing at the co-operative salesrooms. The dealer, on the other hand, is insured a quick cash trade of such magnitude, from the number of members of the union, that he can afford to sell at a very small profit; the aggregate being a handsome quick return, and very much larger than he might have expected in the ordinary course of trade at five or ten per cent. higher prices. These co-operative unions, be it understood, are not trades-unions, but simply an association of persons who begin by a contribution to start the enterprise, hire a store, and employ clerks. Then goods of the best quality are bought in large quantities for cash, and sold to members of the association only at the smallest possible profit necessary for running expenses, and if profit beyond this is made, of course it goes back in dividends to the members of the association. The plan has been found to work well, and the successful stores are such good and prompt-paying customers that the great food manufacturers especially are more than ready to make the most advantageous terms with their managers.

Shopping in London is, on the whole, more satisfactory to the purchaser than in any other city in Europe, from the fact that all respectable shopkeepers believe in the value of reputation, and where competition is so close, wisely believe that it will not pay to imperil their business by any dishonorable act.

The Viennese completely overreached themselves on the occasion of their great exhibition in 1873 In their grasping eagerness to make as much money as possible out of the whole world that was to visit the Austrian capital, they crowded up prices to such a fearful advance that strangers and foreigners utterly refused to buy; so that, with a city full to overflowing with visitors, the shopkeepers were actually complaining of dull trade. The hotel-keepers took such advantages of strangers, in the way of charging treble and quadruple rates for rooms, and putting on extra charges generally, that government was compelled to step in and establish a tariff which the landlords were obliged to have printed and posted in every room, under penalty of the law, and even then they contrived to evade it. The fact, however, of the impositions and high prices upon strangers became thoroughly known, and there seemed to be a freemasonry among travellers to resist it, to such a degree that, although, after a while, many shopkeepers put prices down, the travelling public actually refused to buy, or to be tempted to purchase even real novelties, and stayed in the city as brief a period as possible, and then left it, shaking off the very dust from their sandals at its gates.

It is now pretty generally known that honesty and fair dealing on the part of Parisian shopkeepers, milliners, and dressmakers, in fact all tradespeople in that gay capital, are the exception, and the American who trusts to their word, their honor, or even their expressed word of honor, will lean upon a broken reed.

Let ladies, if they buy a piece of silk, always take a sample of the piece, a bill of the number of yards, and be sure not to pay unless it is measured under their own eyes and taken home by themselves, till they have examined it after it has been sent home and compared with sample. *Beware of ever paying in advance for anything*, as it insures your being cheated. Those verdant and simple-minded American ladies who go into Paris shops, and, with their imperfect school-girl French, inspect goods, select what pleases them, and pay what is asked, or, worse than that, do as they would at Stewart's in New York, or Hovey's in Boston, order ten yards of this, a dozen of that, and a piece of the other, are received by obsequious shopmen and cringing clerks with an excess of civility, and swindled without mercy, — served with short measure, charged double price, goods inferior to those selected sent home, and every possible advantage taken.

I might enumerate dozens of instances of the swindling of American ladies by dressmakers and milliners, their changing of trimmings furnished them for others of inferior quality, scrimping out from one to three yards from dress patterns; but let ladies beware how they furnish dressmakers with materials according to their demand, lest they furnish a third more than required; and always keep a bit of the material furnished, that they may compare with the garments when made up. Never pay for a package of goods when received at your hotel without opening it and carefully verifying the contents, and ascertaining that the goods are exactly the same in quantity and quality that you purchased. No matter how late the hour in the evening, or how far the messenger has come, if he brings you short quantity or measure, or inferior quality, and promises by all the saints in the calendar to bring the remainder in the morning, *do not trust him.* His promise is but mere breath, and French tradesmen are so thoroughly accustomed to this sort of detection that they make any deficiency good without a murmur, and meet you again without a blush or with some trivial excuse for their rascality.

If you are ordering goods made up, or purchasing just prior to leaving the city, always, if possible, name three or four days previous to the day as the latest you can wait, as those dealers who intend to impose on you will contrive to send at the latest possible moment before your departure, in order to prevent the very examination recommended above, and will have the silk dress, or handkerchiefs, or embroideries, or whatever it may be, packed up very nicely for Madame's portmanteau, and regret that they are so very late, so that you may thrust the package into the last trunk or portmanteau and pay for it without inspection, as they have contrived that many careless Americans should do.

Ladies who make the rounds to fashionable modistes, milliners, and others, should bear in mind that most of these people have one of their number certainly who speaks and understands English, and they themselves, from their constant contact with English-speaking purchasers, either speak it or understand it tolerably well. It is a common practice at many of these places, when a shopping party of Americans come in, if any of them speak French, for the milliners and their assistants to feign an ignorance of English, in order that they may get at the minds of their customers and use them accordingly.

Thus, I have seen a party ask in the French tongue through one of their number the price of an article, and on being told, confer with each other in English, supposing that they were not understood, and agree it was better than that they saw elsewhere, or not so good, or if they couldn't make the seller take twenty francs off the price, they would take it at any rate: every word of which was understood by the shrewd but apparently unconscious saleswoman, who made use of the knowledge thus obtained to her best advantage.

A common trick in Paris is to have costumes in the shop-window labelled at a very low figure, tempting the purchaser to step in, only to find that that is but a sample, but that one can be made precisely like it in a day or two. Of course, when the costume comes home, it is of inferior quality, or imperfectly made, or the trimmings not equal to the sample, in fact, an egregious imposition. But there is no remedy: you ordered the goods; the costume is cut and made to your measure; you have no sample, or witness of your agreement; and, "rather than have a fuss," the bill is paid, and the tradesman reaps a round profit by his deception; for this is just what they rely upon, that American ladies or tourists about leaving the city will pay, rather than "have a fuss made about it."

NOTABLE EXCEPTIONS. 15

There are, of course, notable and honorable exceptions among Paris trades-people ; certain establishments who actually seem to have, by some means or other, learned that dealing decently fair with American purchasers will insure a steady, profitable, paying business worth catering for. In fact, they have probably been surprised at the appreciation of Americans of a virtue (honesty) which their countrymen seem to have no conception of. Encouragement of such rare instances may lead others to follow their example.

Beware of the Hotel Bellevue in Brussels, or, if stopping there, be sure and make bargains, and have a thorough understanding respecting price of rooms beforehand. *En passant*, the Grand Hotel, *ci-devant* Hotel New York, in Venice, is an admirably kept house, and in 1873 so honorably managed, free from imposition, and so much effort made to please American guests, that it was really an agreeable relief to have found such a place after the many perplexities one necessarily encounters with unscrupulous hotel-keepers in various other foreign capitals. Its situation is on the Grand Canal, just far enough removed from the Piazza to be quiet and comfortable, and within easy access to all the points of interest in the city.

But to return to Paris, which is the great stamping-ground for American shoppers. I have tried all the three methods of purchasing, and have learned, from practical experience, which is the best for one not thoroughly acquainted with Paris and not speaking the French tongue as his own. The first method is shopping by yourself, by which you are sure to make mistakes, take double the time necessary, and get very much fatigued and dissatisfied. The next method, of taking a guide or *commissionaire*, insures you more convenience, and also that he will cheat you instead of the tradesman. The third and only thoroughly satisfactory method is through a reliable American commission merchant, of which there are several in Paris established for just this kind of business, and through them tourists may do better than by any other method.

The European tourist, it may be *apropos* to say here, will encounter many bugbears in his travels. At Liverpool he will learn that London is too full or too empty, unhealthy, owing to the fog, or damp, owing to the rain. Scotland is raw or chilly, or it's too early or too late in the season. Rome? The malaria is very dangerous there; never go out after sunset. Going to Florence? It is full of diphtheria. Vienna? Heard there was cholera there. Venice? Mosquitoes; or don't drink the water, it's sure to make you sick. Munich? The regular fever city of Europe; badly situated; everybody has typhus fever that stays there over a week. Geneva? Hottest place in Europe in the summer season. Paris? Never drink Parisian water; or they are on the eve of another revolution: look out not to get shut up there. Naples? Drainage is atrocious, breeds disease; take care not lodge in the city. Amsterdam? Yes, very interesting city, but the sheets are often put on the beds damp. Going through Switzerland? Look out they don't give you glacier water to drink, it is very unhealthy. Italy? Yes, Italy is a pleasant country to travel in if it were not for the fleas. The Tyrol? Very difficult place to get along in; they speak neither German nor French, and who can understand their Tyrolean?

These are only specimens of the consoling assertions that I have received, and doubtless others will receive, from fellow-countrymen abroad who have been to the places they ascertain you intend visiting, and who seem resolved to give you all the disagreeable rumors respecting them which they can collect together, and which in nine cases out of ten will be found to be either exaggerations or merely the fruit of too vivid an imagination. There are certain precautions, of course, to be taken during the rapid changes that the tourist may make from one climate to another, or from one style of food and methods of cooking to another, if his digestion is not perfect; but these his guide-books and his own judgment will suggest, without his permitting himself to be made wretched by the doubts and fears or continuous phantoms which are so easily conjured up.

In the great capitals of Europe it is a comparatively easy matter to obtain the most excellent medical attendance and pharmaceutical preparations. Physicians' fees in London and Paris are: five dollars a visit, payable at the time of the visit, in the former city, and four dollars in the latter. The same price is charged in Rome, that is, by the best physician, a gentleman well known to Americans, whose name I cannot refrain from mentioning here — Dr. Valery, whose good offices every American who has occasion to require them speaks of most gratefully; and in Venice, if the tourist has occasion for medical advice, let him secure the services of Dr. Ricchetti, a most skilful member of the medical profession, who speaks English perfectly, and is moreover a kind-hearted and liberal-minded gentleman.

No one can tell, except he who may have the misfortune to be suddenly prostrated upon the bed of sickness in a foreign land, how grateful and soothing, as well as reassuring and strengthening to the patient, is the presence of a physician whose voice is gentle, whose knowledge, as a native, of the effects of his climate upon you, as a foreigner, is perfect, whose very questions show him to be a man of professional skill, and who scorns to make the least pretension of a mystery of medical treatment, or of the science of the profession to patients. Of Dr. Ricchetti's possession of the above characteristics, and his skill and success in quite a serious case of a dear friend in Venice, I have had practical demonstration. In Innspruck Dr. Berreiter, and in Paris Dr. Accosta, are physicians whom Americans can have every confidence in, if they have occasion to call one.

One favorite plan of American tourists who have but from three to six months to spend abroad, is to start immediately for Rome, and leave England, to many the most interesting of European countries, for the last portion of their visit. The consequence is, that, sated with sight-seeing, fatigued with travel, and their last experience the gayety and glitter of the French capital, on arriving in England, as the majority of three and six months' tourists do, late in the fall, when the air begins to be chill and damp, the contrast is unfavorable; while, mayhap, they have lingered so long on the continent that but a fortnight or three weeks remain to see that which as many months would not exhaust. London is then merely raced through; flying trips to Edinburgh, York, and one or two other places made; an imperfect or erroneous impression obtained; enough seen to make one regret more time had not been devoted there, and the tour wound up with two or three weeks of such hard work as neutralizes all pleasure of travel, and leaves the tourist in ill condition for the return voyage.

The European travelling season commences with Americans early in April, and tourists who arrive in England then have time to go direct to Rome, and stay from a fortnight to a month before hot weather sets in; whereas, if they commence with England in the middle of April or May 1, a longer stay abroad than three or six months must be made, to bring Rome into the catalogue of places visited, if one wishes to avoid the summer months, and have sufficient time to see even the principal sights of the city.

CHAPTER II.

Foreign travel is doubtless a most valuable instructor, and few Americans of average common sense can travel to any extent, either at home or abroad, without adding to their stock of knowledge and receiving a certain amount of practical instruction of real value. But certainly I have met American parties abroad as unfit for foreign travel, and who would receive as little intellectual benefit from it, as a student in mathematics, who has advanced no further than simple addition, would from a week's instruction in a calculation of logarithms.

The cheap excursion system has enabled a large number of this class of travellers to visit Europe; and, although not for a moment denying that it has enabled many worthy and well educated persons of limited means an opportunity for foreign travel and sight-seeing which they might never have been enabled to enjoy, yet many of the most *outre* and verdant specimens of humanity that even in our own great cities would have excited observation from all, and even ridicule from the unthinking, attracted by the wonderfully low figure of a Cook excursion ticket to Europe and the Vienna Exposition, scraped together their three or four hundred dollars, or withdrew it from the country savings-banks, and swarmed into the old country like crusaders after this new Peter the Hermit, who preached the attraction of the distant capital to them which they were to advance upon, and painted the journey in glowing colors. There were men from Vermont who had never seen the Green Mountains; from Western New York who couldn't tell you the height of Niagara Falls; an Illinois farmer who had never been in any city in his life but Indianapolis, and that only twice, till he started on the European excursion trip. Great tall fellows, with mourning-clothed finger-nails, who chewed tobacco and spat on the marble floors of cathedrals, and were the very types of characters which English writers have described in their books on America as representatives of our country; descriptions which may have vexed us and caused more than one to avow them to be caricatures, overdrawn sketches, or malicious misrepresentations. Yet here they were in *propria persona*, stalking through the Vienna Exposition, sticking their boots up on railroad-car seats, or stumbling over kneeling worshippers in St. Peter's.

One of this class came into our railway carriage between Munich and Vienna, a tall, somewhat ungainly-looking man, with the national characteristics of the American countryman as prominent as if the word had been painted upon his forehead. In the railway carriage, besides ourselves, was an Englishman and his daughter, our pleasant travelling companions, on both whom the new-comer soon opened fire, beginning with the usual fusilade of questions.

"You ain't an American — are ye?"

"No, sir, I am not."

"English, I s'pose?"

"Yes."

"Going to Vienny?"

"Yes."

"I s'pose ye mean to go to the World's Fair there — don't ye?"

"I think we shall go to the Exposition while we are there."

"What hotel shall you put up at?"

"We shall go to the Hotel Metropole."

"Haow?"

"The Metropolitan Hotel," I volunteered, in explanation for my English friend, who was beginning to be amused. The dialogue was resumed.

"O! ah! Yes; I don't understand French; but our

party — we're the eddicational excursion party — hev an interpereter, who goes 'long with us all the time, and translates everything."

Englishman. "Sir, you are very fortunate."

Yankee. "Yaas. Whole trip from Amerikee and back only four hunderd dollars."

Eng. "Very reasonable."

Yan. "Big pile o' money fur some on us; but I was bound to come. Ever been to Vienny before?"

Eng. "Yes."

Yan. "How big a place is it?"

Eng. "It's a city of six hundred thousand inhabitants."

Yan. "You don't say so! By the by, Vienny is the capital of Orstrey — ain't it?"

Eng. "It is."

Yan. "Which way are you goin' when you leave Vienny?"

Eng. "North."

Yan. "Travellin' for pleasure or business?"

Eng. "Principally for pleasure."

[The reader will please to recollect that this is no fancy sketch, but a report of a conversation which actually occurred as here set down.]

Yan. "What part of England do you come from?"

Eng. "The city of London."

Yan. "In business there?"

Eng. "No, sir, I am not."

Yan. "Carryin' on any business out of town?"

Eng. "No, sir."

Yan. "What *is* your business when you are to home?"

Eng. "I am not in any business."

Yan. "O! Retired?"

Eng. "Yes."

[One would have thought that the American, having now run his quarry completely down, would have "retired" also; but no, he returned to the charge again.]

Yan. " What business was you in before you retired ? "
Eng. " I was a book publisher."
Yan. " In business long ? "
Eng. " Forty years."
Yan. " Wal, you've got some time yet to enjoy yourself. How old do you call yourself ? "

[At this point the good-natured Briton, who had been more amused than vexed by this impertinent catechism, changed his tactics, and replied to his interrogator's last question in the true American style, by asking another, and continued to follow him up after the same fashion he had been attacked himself, as follows :]

Eng. " How old should you think me ? "
Yan. " Wal, about a marter of sixty-five or seven."
Eng. " How old are you ? "
Yan. " Give a guess."
Eng. " Forty-two. Are you an American ? "
Yan. " Yes, sir ! " straightening up.
Eng. " In what part of America were you born ? "
Yan. " Wal, I was raised in Vermont, but I moved to Elmiry, New York."
Eng. " Married ? "
Yan. " Yes, sir ; merried when I was twenty-five."
Eng. " Any children ? "
Yan. " No, sir ; never hed none."
Eng. " Wife travelling with you ? "
Yan. " No, sir. I'm a widower."
Eng. " Ah ! Excuse me ; but what's your business when you are at home ? "
Yan. " I'm a milkman — I carry round milk."
Eng. (smiling). " But what will your customers do for milk while you are away ? "
Yan. " O, I sold out my route, which was a good one, fur five hunderd dollars, and took four on't and bought one of them Cook tickets to come out here to the Vienny Exhibition."

This milk revelation was too much for me, who had been stifling my laughter by every possible device, as the unmerciful Englishman went on with his quizzing of the enemy, and at this point I was compelled to seek relief in an explosion of laughter, in which he joined, and, to our no small astonishment, the milkman also, who remarked that it *was* a good joke, and he " guessed the feller that bought the route would hev easier work deliverin' milk to some of his customers than collectin' their bills."

The above dialogue was no fancy sketch, and its hero was an actual sample of an American excursionist, and it is not the only one of this description either, that the facilities of travel, the cheap ticket system, and Vienna Exhibition attracted from their native land; for I have encountered several others equally amusing. One who rushed up to the carriage of a party of us who were leaving the hotel, to say that he was going to travel with a *currier*, and, so far from seeing the point when asked by a gentleman if he wanted to improve his acquaintance in the leather trade, seriously replied he never had any dealings in that line. Another, in Rome, on being asked to join a party to visit the Colosseum, replied, " Colosseum, what's that?"

" Why, the old Roman circus, you know."

" O, yes! Is there a performance this evening? What time does it begin?"

An explanation that the circus referred to was unlike the modern one with horses, clowns, and acrobats, had to be gently hinted to this ambitious sight-seer, to prevent misapprehension and disappointment.

The author may be permitted, perhaps, to cite another case, more mortifying because of its prominence. The daughter of an American official at a *soirée*, and in presence of several English people of high social and official position, upon being asked how she liked England, replied that " the country was well enough, but the people were not polite." Regret was expressed that the young lady had been disappointed in this particular, when she continued:

"Why, I've been in England all through May and June, and *never been bunched once!*"

Some, even of her American auditors, were taken aback by this, to them, untranslatable expression; and the good breeding of the English ones could scarce repress a smile.

It transpired, however, that being "bunched" signified, in western or southern parlance, the reception of a bouquet or "bunch" of flowers.

I would not speak thus in mere ridicule of many of these my countrymen, knowing that at home they are the bone and sinew of the country; but it is sometimes annoying that educated Englishmen, and men of high position and culture even, who have seldom met Americans, take such as above described to be the representatives of our American ladies and gentlemen of culture, and have the impressions that have been created by the stories of satirical or scurrilous travellers crystallized into absolute faith by these examples.

Is it any wonder that after meeting a few such people as these, besides innumerable Americans in every foreign capital; finding your countrymen rushing from a train or a *diligence* in Switzerland for the best rooms at an inn, as summer tourists do at home; or the meeting of persons whom you hardly thought could afford to visit Washington or the White Mountains, meandering about the streets of St. Petersburg, or staring at statuary in the Vatican, that you begin to think that going to Europe isn't so great an undertaking after all?

And, really, with such almost guaranteed safety as is now given by the excellent management of the principal steamship lines, it is *not* such a formidable undertaking as many think it, by any means.

Then, if you don't practise it yourself, you may have occasion to smile at the affectation of the young lady at the party, who says she got the bracelet when she was last in Paris, or who, in reply to your inquiry about her visit abroad, says that she has never "crossed" but twice, when you learn that the *last* was the only time that she was in the gay capital, and that "crossing twice" means once over and once back, a piece of fashionable deception supposed, perhaps, if successful, to add to the reputation of the utterer as an extensive traveller, and arguing a thorough familiarity with foreign lands. Then there are others who have been over the same route as yourself, eager to compare notes, and you will find anxious to impress you that they have seen something that escaped your notice, and that that one especial object, in their opinion, is the only one worth crossing the ocean to see. You are put through the usual round of questions by these newly-returned ones, such as, —

"Did you go to Edinburgh Castle?"

"Yes."

"See the room where Rizzio was killed?"

"Yes."

"You went to Dresden, I suppose?"

"Certainly."

"Saw the green vaults — didn't you?"

"O, yes; we visited them several times."

"Did you see that ostrich-egg cup set in jewels?"

"Remember it perfectly."

"Rome is an interesting city — isn't it?"

"Indeed it is."

"Did you go into the catacombs while you were there?"

"But a short distance; we had not time."

"O! you don't know what you missed. It's the most interesting thing in the whole city; there's nothing like it anywhere in Europe. Why, I'm astonished you didn't see all the catacombs," &c.

I used to feel somewhat mortified at my omissions when I first heard remarks of this kind, till I found that the utterers of them were the most superficial of travellers, and only laid these traps to discover something with which I was not familiar, in order that they might expatiate and enlarge upon it freely and with perfect safety, so that, while they maintained a discreet silence upon what we both acknowledged to have seen, they were more eloquent upon that which had escaped the listener's notice. This may be the safest course, perhaps, with some travellers.

If one has had much experience as a tourist, and has any habits of observation, he soon begins to study character, not only in the peoples of foreign countries, but in those of his own countrymen with whom he is thrown in contact in the great travelled routes abroad, now so thoroughly traversed by Americans. The old and experienced traveller is detected at a glance by the matter-of-fact way in which he takes all inconveniences, and the readiness with which he adapts himself to any unavoidable exigences which may arise. He is slow to find fault, but quick to check or avoid imposition; ready to adapt himself to the customs of the country as far as possible, and does not expect that everything will be arranged by hotel-keepers, railroads, and shopkeepers abroad according to the custom of his native land.

Much of the misunderstanding, difficulty, and discomfort of foreign travel with many tourists abroad arises from the fact that they expect, although manners, customs, and methods of transacting business are different from theirs, that they have only to pay money to cause an entire change of those methods to their own, or that the difference which they observe is an evidence of a lower scale of intelligence of the people.

There are also certain people who fancy that the payment of a sum of money not only entitles them to the most comfortable seat in a railway carriage, the best place at the hotel table, the first choice of apartments, the most convenient stateroom on board ship, and the first and exclusive attention of conductors, landlords, captains, and officials, but that it makes them of better clay than ordinary mortals, who should stand aside in deferential awe until their superior wants have been satisfied.

This class are also the most persistent of fault-finders.

They go abroad with the expectation of being more comfortable than at home; are unwilling to encounter even the necessary discomforts of travel, and not only fret, fume, and worry themselves into a state of unnecessary discomfort, but are annoying to all with whom they come in contact.

There is another class of Americans who seem to have an idea that, having a certain amount of money to spend, they should disburse it in the most expeditious and lavish manner possible. For the reason, may be, that having hoarded or striven for years for this dream of their life, — a visit to Europe, — they are determined to make up for a long period of abstemiousness, in the matter of expenditure, by a short and merry one of unrestrained extravagance. This last class take life pretty much as it comes, scatter their money right and left, are an easy prey to swindling couriers, grasping landlords, cheating shopkeepers, and the horde of different grades of *chevaliers d'industrie* who have come to look, and with good reason, upon the American tourist as their legitimate prey, and who feed fat upon the credulity and simplicity of the swarms of fresh innocents that each succeeding year fall into their clutches.

These two classes of travellers, the one arrogant and self-sufficient, demanding more than he is entitled to, the other lavish and careless, and actually not receiving what he more than pays for, have made the great travelled routes of Europe somewhat less pleasant to the average man of the world, travelling for recreation or instruction, who desires a fair value received for his expenditure, and who will in no case suffer the attempted imposition of any class of officials to pass unheeded or unrebuked, lest by so doing they may be repeated upon those who come after him.

American tourists, as a class, are generous in expenditures; and this is thoroughly understood by the shopkeepers of Regent Street, the cringing cheats on the Boulevards, and the brazen liars of Vienna and Venice, so that it has come to be a proverb with them, "As rich as an American."

Indeed, a friend has told me that in a little French reading-book, or primer, which he examined, one of the sentences or exercises read, "The Americans are very rich." The newly fledged tourist, on his first visit to Europe, endeavors sometimes to assume the *blasé* air of one who is "used to all that sort of thing, you know;" pays always what is charged, — sure sign of an American, — and believes, until taught by bitter experience, that Frenchmen tell the truth.

Many of our well educated Americans, people of culture and thorough understanding of the world this side of the water, can hardly bring themselves to the "beating down" process so generally expected in Paris and Italy, or to believe even that great hotels, like the Bellevue of Brussels, the L'Athenée of Paris, and the Hotel Metropole of Vienna, would imperil their foreign business by descending to absolute and positive imposition, as both have done to English and American travellers. The impositions of the latter were brought before the police of Vienna, and also extensively published through the English press; and those of the Bellevue at Brussels are pretty generally known among tourists of both nations.

The fact is, writers, correspondents, and book-makers do not like to be considered fault-finders. Americans especially had rather pay a five or ten dollar swindle than "make a fuss," or bother themselves about it.

Not so the Englishman. Be he ever so wealthy, he is never rich enough to pay an overcharge even of a shilling; and as it has been said that, whenever an English subject in any port in the world is imprisoned or maltreated, an English man-of-war steams into the harbor of that port, and anchors with her guns bearing on the town, within twenty-four hours after the occurrence, so whenever an Englishman is overcharged five francs on his room or his dinner, at a foreign hotel on any of the grand tour routes, and writes (enclosing his card of reference) to the *Times*, that journal prints his communication, champions his cause, and the offending landlord has a very wholesome lesson given him in a stigma that he finds attached to his house, which it requires no common effort to remove.

Again, Americans allow themselves to be imposed upon in a manner that English people would not submit to for an instant, probably from the fact that class distinction is so much greater in England than here. In America, those occupying positions of porters, railroad conductors, ticket-sellers, baggage-masters, salesmen, or hotel waiters even, conduct themselves as though they were, as a general thing, too good for the position, and those whom they were serving should be gratified at the condescension shown them, even though they pay liberally for it.

To be sure, it is a laudable ambition; and one great element of the strength of our nation is that these people may, by force of brains, elevate themselves to the position of merchants, railroad presidents, treasurers, and hotel proprietors; but we know that "every man a sovereign" feeling crops out quite frequently here, for instance in the lordly hotel-keeper who permits you to remain instead of welcoming you into his house, the railroad president who considers the public of no account, and the merchant who serves you indifferently or patronizingly.

How many Americans are there that will insist that a horse-car conductor shall do his duty; that a railroad president shall attend to the business of the road they own stock in; that city officials shall understand they are the servants of the public; that hackmen and express drivers, or baggage porters at railroad stations, shall do the duty they are paid for doing; that if they have paid for a place, or a seat, or a performance, or a railroad trip, they shall have it? It is "too much trouble," and cheaper to submit to an imposition, than to contend about it.

The difficulty this side of the water is, that many who occupy the above positions are not willing to accept and perform the duties of the situation. In England, the prompt measures which are taken with regard to the shortcomings of ticket clerks, railroad porters, cab-drivers, and railway guards, are such that one seldom receives anything but polite treatment and a prompt performance of duties belonging to the position.

There is a marked difference from our own country in the deference the traveller receives in every direction in travelling in England, from the landlord and landlady, who cordially welcome him in with smiles upon their broad and ruddy faces as though they felt honored by his being their guest, the obsequious alacrity of the brisk waiter, the courtesy of the white-aproned chambermaid, and the untiring devotion of the polite shopman. Then the politeness of the railroad ticket-sellers, the touch-hats of the porters, and the quiet performance of duty of the railway guard, impress the new traveller.

I am sorry to say, however, that the conduct of many American travellers towards these very officials is such as to give them a very unfavorable opinion of us as a class; indeed, it has been such with some as to cause them to say that there are no gentlemen in America. This conclusion may have been reached, perhaps, from the restiveness of Americans under the antique, slow-coach, old-fogy style of doing business by the mercantile houses in London, especially those on whom their letters of credit were drawn.

The American going abroad for the first time with a letter of credit in his pocket is told that, on presenting it to any of the "bankers" of the list printed upon the back, he can *draw* any sum within the full amount named in the letter. This means, that any of these parties are ready to buy his drafts, by which they make a small percentage and charge interest from the moment the amount is paid; therefore, instead of "letting you have money," as is said, they simply buy exchange of you at a small profit, according to the size of your draft, but still at a profit. Your letter is a written indorsement of you, showing that you have credit and actual funds to protect your drafts, and that you are therefore a perfectly safe person to buy a draft of, which draft is to be indorsed on the said letter. You are a far safer person to buy of than the stranger who comes in with no letter of introduction to sell a bill of exchange, which must be bought to a certain extent because of the presumable value of the names upon it, and because it will probably be promptly honored.

Letters-of-credit drafts, that is the amounts drawn by holders of letters of credit, bankers know to be against actual sterling, and that they will be promptly honored, no days' sight, protesting, or any hitch; so that, though in small amounts, they are the very best kind of bills of exchange. The profound ignorance of some of the tourist holders of these letters, is amazing, and their wonderment at "brokers" in Germany, France, or Italy "letting them have money" on them is amusing. Ladies, for instance, travelling with couriers, walk in and ask an Italian banker, perhaps:

"Could you let me have three hundred francs on this?" (showing her letter of credit.)

The banker looks at the letter, finds it drawn by a well-known strong banking-house of New York, Boston, or London, and replies in the blandest of tones:

"Certainly, Madam."

He takes the letter of credit, and shortly returns with two printed slips filled out for Madam's signature. These two slips are bills of exchange, or checks at sight on the deposit which her letter of credit represents. The check or bill is made in duplicate in case one should be lost in course of mail, and they severally read, "Pay this (original), second unpaid;" and "Pay this (second) bill of exchange, original unpaid."

The lady signing this has signed a check for some of her own money, and the banker or broker, after indorsing the amount on the letter of credit, in order that others may see how much she has drawn and how much is left that she has authority to draw for, proceeds to cash it, or, as she calls it, lets her " have three hundred francs."

This he does as follows : He pays for this cash draft the lowest figure the exchange on London or Paris is worth. The three hundred francs on Paris may be worth in Italy three hundred and thirty to three hundred and forty-five francs in the market. He pays, then, three hundred and thirty Italian francs, or lire, and charges Madam, besides, from one-half to one and one-half per cent. commission for cashing the draft, and "lets her have" the balance !

The broker or banker, who is generally doing a business with merchants and others having a continual demand for funds to place in Paris or London, turns these sight drafts right over to the said merchants, who buy them of him, as a general thing, at a good profit on what he paid when he let Madam have some money. That is, if he gave her three hundred and twenty-five francs (Italian) for her sight draft (authorized by the letter of credit), it may be pretty certain gets three hundred and thirty-five for it, — a profit of ten francs. A small profit, for the draft is small. But in the travelling season, in many localities, the aggregate of tourists' drafts amounts to quite a respectable sum of money.

The drawing of money upon a letter of credit is merely a mercantile transaction for which no favors can be expected on either side.

On the continent, where bankers do not despise small gains, even this business is fostered carefully. All bankers on the continent receive tourists politely, have withdrawing room and English and American papers, English-speaking clerks, and a register of tourists in town, for the convenience of those whose drafts they cash. They also receive the letters and papers of the tourist, of course charging sufficient postage to save themselves from any loss. Many, in Italy, for instance, receive from art dealers and others handsome commissions on purchases by buyers whom they recommend, or will purchase and ship home pictures, statuary, wines, jewelry, or articles of *virtu* or curiosities for the tourist, by which means they carry a very respectable sum to the profit side of their ledgers.

In fact, as a general thing, the bankers on the continent, whose names the tourist will find printed on the back of his letter of credit, and who will promptly cash his drafts and deal with him honorably, are courteous and civil, especially to Americans, having learned that the American, if humored, and if some of his peculiarities are borne with, will spend money liberally, and they can even find it profitable to transact business with him in *his* way, especially if he pays for it so to be done.

Hence many American tourists who have had no previous acquaintance, even by correspondence, with foreign banking-houses, and whose names have never been known on a bill of exchange, find some of them very pleasant places of resort from the courtesy of the officials upon any and all occasions.

In France, Germany, Italy, and other countries on the continent, it is customary to order packages sent to your bankers, you having shown by your letter of credit that you shall do business with them, they will take care of any such merchandise.

Thus you buy a picture in Rome, perchance, and cannot take it with you; but knowing that you shall want it in Florence, and knowing no one there, order it sent to the care of the banking-house on your letter of credit, the bankers receive it for you, subject to your disposition. I mention this, which is by no means information to any person who has travelled abroad, but to caution those who do not know, that the English " bankers," or merchants, as a class are a very different set of people, and that the tourist should beware of taking any such liberty (for so they consider it) with them.

They are perfectly right, according to their style of doing

business, which is simply to buy and sell bills of exchange and merchandise in bulk. They are not *commission* merchants, and do not expect pictures, ladies' dresses, or statuary consigned to their care, even if you pay storage charges and commission. They do not wish to be bothered with that class of business. In this a certain class of British merchants and bankers are right, and the fault lies in our great bankers here in America in not providing that their tourists' letters of credit shall be drawn on a house to whom American business shall be desirable, and who shall be ready to transact business with Americans, and yield a little something of the stiff buckram British style if it can be done without detriment, to the better accommodation of the American customer. It may be that there are such houses now in London, but it has been the author's fortune to have his "letters" on great banking and mercantile houses who seem, like the Chinese, to consider all who are not English, "outside barbarians," and that, the English system of transacting business being perfect, there should be no change in it, even if it were more convenient to foreign customers, and assured themselves increased profit. Hence the difficulties of which we speak.

There exists in London, as almost every American tourist will bear witness, the necessity of an American commission or banking-house of undoubted financial strength, which, besides the sufficient capital that some that have failed did not have, should also possess the spirit of accommodation, knowledge of human nature, and American human nature in particular, which those that failed *did* have, and the practice of which drew to them a large amount of business, some of which, though even in small amounts of letter-of-credit drafts, might, with careful fostering, have, in not many years, from the very nature of them, and the progress of American business, grown to heavy bills to purchase cargoes of merchandise instead of funds to pay hotel bills.

The banker in England is considered of the highest grade in the business social circle; only the true blood of nobility is above him. 'Indeed, some of his class, we know, are of the nobility, such as Baron Rothschild, Lord Ashburton, and others. They look down upon the merchant, still more on the tradesman, metaphorically, and doubtless there is an impression among them, as among many of the more wealthy English people, that the Americans are an inferior race, and should be treated accordingly. It may be judged from some specimens already described that they have some reason for this latter opinion.

Baring Bros. & Co., and MacCalmont Bros. & Co., especially the latter, are not the houses that should be selected by our American bankers for tourists' letters. They may "place" a government or railroad loan, advance on a cargo, or contract for a whole crop of merchandise, and do business in immense stocks of tens of thousands; and therefore the business of a letter of credit is so comparatively insignificant that they only treat it with the barest civility, out of consideration to their correspondents, certainly with but little to the holders of the letters.

The latter English banking-house, upon which the author held a letter, he found to be located in a filthy alley, so narrow that barely one cab could pass between the two curb-stones. The building, after getting inside, was fairly fitted up, but the space for customers in the banking-house outside the counter was not ten feet square, and all these bankers, or rather merchants, would do was to give you a check on a banking-house, in another street, where you were compelled to go yourself and get it cashed.

There was no relaxation of British stiffness, no American newspaper, no proffer of courtesy, no more effort to put the raw, inexperienced tourist at ease on the part of the managers, than there would have been towards a tramp buying a pound of bacon. The author writes this thoughtfully, and after months of cool reflection on the subject. And it does seem amazing, considering the enormous amount of American travel that now exists, some one of our great banking-houses does not make an arrangement with a house in London that will meet the requirements of Americans. Such a house would be sure of a profitable business; it is a want that every American tourist feels, and has long been the burden of American tourists' complaints, so that the American banker who will let it be known in America by advertisement that he can draw on such a house, may be sure of a handsome amount of business.

The traveller on his second trip abroad provides for many exigencies that, with all his advice from friends and study of guide-books, were not considered on the first voyage. He begins to feel like the seasoned traveller, and "knows the ropes," i. e., the customs on board ocean steamships. He does not on his first visit aboard address himself to members of the crew or some of the cooks, and ask the way to the cabin; four weeks' previous living on board a steamship make him a little familiar with its accommodations, and give him some knowledge of what to expect and what to demand.

The steward detects your cool, old, seasoned rover of a dozen passages in a moment. His battered sole-leather trunk, serviceable wraps, and his business-like way of "stowing his traps," distinguish him from the new tourist with his fresh clothing, all sorts of straps, spy-glasses, cushions, fashionable caps, and perhaps semi-nautical costume, in which he hopes to make an impression, little thinking oftentimes, poor soul! what misery is before him.

To be acquainted with the captain seems with many voyagers to be a great card, judging from the way they play it, in conversation, — somewhat as follows:

"When I went over long ago with Judkins, he used to say to me," — or, "Macaulay's a clever fellow, and I made two voyages with him," — or, "Did Moody ever tell you that story of the lady passenger and the custom-house officer?"

The captains on the great steamship lines appear to be thorough seamen, and to consider their first duty to carry their ships safely from port to port; but some passengers, by their acts, seem to think that a part of their duty should be similar to that of the skipper of an excursion steamer on a trip down the bay on a moonlight night. To walk arm-in-arm with young ladies, stand about in nautical uniform, and hold a spy-glass for them to peep through, tell them how he can tell anything by the compass, or whether he thinks it is going to be fair weather to-morrow.

Some of these captains I have heard accused of being reticent or surly, simply for the reason that they couldn't spend time from duty to answer an avalanche of silly questions. This was illustrated to me once quite forcibly during a voyage in the steamer Parthia, of the Cunard line, commanded by Captain Watson, said to be a very reticent man, and slow to make acquaintances.

For the first few days out all of us were good sailors, for it was delightful weather, and the sea was smooth. The captain minded his own affairs, and it was evident that the quiet man knew his business, and that his officers and crew knew that it would have to be done in a thoroughly seaman-like manner, with no "sogering." His ruddy cheek and sparkling brown eye told of health and humor, but "on duty" with him was a serious matter. The ladies, however, failed to make an idol of him, or the men to vote him a clever fellow, for the reason that they didn't understand the difference between a sailor and a society man.

Fancy a keen, bright-witted, practical seaman, fully realizing the importance of his position and responsibility as commander of an ocean steamship, being badgered by the gentler sex in this manner when he made his appearance on deck in fine weather:

"O, Captain! what was that horrid jar in the machinery about twelve o'clock last night?"

"I can't say, Madam; perhaps the engineer can tell you."

"Do you think, Captain, it will be as fine weather as this all the way over?"

"Certainly, Miss, if the weather does not change."

"Captain, tell me where is the most dangerous place one can be in on the whole passage?"

"Overboard at night, I should think, Madam."

"O, Captain! don't you sometimes get awfully frightened in a storm?"

"If it is much of a storm, Miss, we don't have time to be frightened till it's over."

Many observers will bear witness that similar questions were asked on voyages they have made, and are a fair sample of the feminine style of interrogatories. Hardly less ludicrous and absurd was that of some of the male sex, one of whom comes along, and squinting knowingly aloft, says:

"Ain't you carryin' sail pretty strong this mornin', Cap'en?"

"Perhaps we are."

"How much sail will she stan' in a breeze like this?"

"O, all that we make."

"Wind is changin', I see," says another, looking aft.

"Indeed!" says the Captain, for it was news to him.

Another comes along, perhaps, with an idea of doing the agreeable.

"Good morning, Captain."

"Good morning."

"Won't you go down and take a little suthin afore breakfast — cocktail or a little bitters?"

(Sententiously.) "No, thank you."

"O, Captain," says another, "I wish you'd see that I hev a napkin put to my plate at dinner; thet waiter forgets it."

"If you will speak to the chief steward, he will accommodate you."

Think of people, who ask a steamship captain questions like these (and these are no inventions), complaining that he is "reticent," or "plaguy short in his answers."

A great many ocean-steamship passengers cherish a kindly, and we might say reverential respect for some of these steamship commanders, somewhat for the same reason that a man does for a good family doctor that has successfully battled with disease for him, or a good family lawyer that has faithfully guarded his property. It is a recognition of their professional skill as sailors, and of the fact of their own utter helplessness in a position where the other was at home and master of the situation; and if ever there is a position where the man should be the master of the situation, it is as commander of an ocean steamer.

The life on an ocean steamer has become familiar from frequent description, to those even who have not experienced it; but it is astonishing how much more practically you take it after a trip or two across the Atlantic, and, if anything of a student of character, how much, even in the temporary misery of sea-sickness, there is that one sees which is ludicrous and amusing. The everlasting setting of tables and eating and drinking is nauseating until you get your appetite on; then it is interesting. A pale-faced passenger, on the sixth day out, once came to me with a triumphant countenance, saying, "I am all right now for the rest of the voyage, for I can stand right over the kitchen in the full steam and scent of Welsh rarebits and fried bacon." Those who know the sensations caused by the scent of cooking on a thoroughly sea-sick man will appreciate the strength of stomach implied by this boast.

But the sea-voyage is not always the disagreeable experience that is pictured. Between the months of May and September a reasonably pleasant trip may be expected across the Atlantic, and we must also recollect that everybody is not sea-sick, and that there are comparatively few but recover after two or three days of illness. There are the glorious days when the ocean air seems like a cordial draught, the blue sky above an azure never before so heavenly, and when the translucent green waves, fringed with white crests, as they bend in broad, graceful scrolls away from the ship's prow, seem to be molten and polished metal rather than the colorless fluid.

The great steamer, with all sails set and the wind directly aft, bends to her work like a yacht; steadied by the sails, the ship cuts through the water without a jar, nor sways from the side towards which she leans. We feel scarce any breeze, but the big-bosomed sails tell how it chases us, and the humming cordage overhead sounds like a great Æolian harp.

Not only the wind is sending us onward, but the chained giant below works untiringly at piston-rod and wheel, his ravenous and fiery appetite fed constantly by attendant slaves, and the monotonous, regular throbs of the machinery he keeps in motion becoming so much a part of our existence, that, let it but stop for an instant, and curiosity, not to say anxiety and alarm, is immediately expressed.

But these pleasant days, when the sea is smooth, the sky clear, and the system steady,— there is not enough said about them. Each one must, of course, give his experience of the discomforts of the voyage, as though there were no enjoyments in it, and there were none who enjoyed it. Can there be any better place for quiet thought, for grand meditation, or luxurious, lazy dreaming, than on the great boundless ocean at midnight, beneath a cloudless sky, and the moon and whole train of heavenly constellations looking indeed like golden lamps hung down from the blue dome above?

There is just movement enough of old Ocean's breast to seem like the regular inspirations of its life; the innumerable train of sparks from the steamer's chimney are like a flaming troop of elves flying off on a midnight revel, as they whirl and waltz and float far astern, till they seem to alight at some trysting-place behind a silver-edged wave in the distance. The great concave above rims us in upon a vast tremulous expanse of steel and silver, with a broad shimmering pathway stretching across it, made by the moonlight; the sound of the waves, or the plash of water that strikes the ear as you lean over the bulwarks, is like a liquid whisper, and caresses the side of the ship like a lover stroking the curls from the brow of his mistress; a distant sail, with the moon-beam striking on it, creeps like a phantom in its white robe hastily across the horizon.

Save this ghost-like vision, the broad expanse heaves, "boundless and sublime," far as the eye can reach, sending up here and there frosted frontlets of foam that shine for a moment like fretted silver, and then sink from sight. Then it is that the landsman begins to feel the inspiration of the ocean, and can realize how men may have written grand poetry about it, and applied those poetic terms that in his days of wretchedness in a close cabin seem misnomers and a mockery.

Perhaps he may realize also, during the voyage, what influence the salt songs of opera and concert-rooms might have been composed under, if the authors indeed ever had any such experience as the inspiration of a sea-voyage, as he steams up the Mersey of a glorious May morning. Watching rocky shores and green slopes, he meets out-coming ships spreading their great white wings for their ocean flight, hears the sailors' chorus softened into music by distance, or notes the great waves afar off rush and leap up against the rocks on which the warning light-house is perched as if in vain endeavor to overtop it; or sees that oft-quoted and really splendid sight, a full-rigged ship under full sail riding over the waves with graceful swing, and the glitter of her copper sheathing shining amid the dark waves, and flashing foam like the gold bracelets upon the ankles of a Hindoo woman in a white robe.

The breeze is fresh; a fountain of spray springs from the prow of the great ship as she rushes through the brine, and falls in the morning sunlight like a cataract of diamonds on either side.

Up goes the flag of Old England to the masthead, and up, too, go three or four colored pendants, the ship's signals, fluttering in the air, and hours before we reach our port of destination not only will the news of our coming have been told, but it will have, with magic speed, conquered in a few seconds the space that required of us weary days to overcome, and have told loved ones at home that we were fairly over the ocean and sailing into port as surely as though we were actually beneath their own anxious gaze.

Here we are on the pier, at the big shed under which the custom-house officers are waiting, and who make, as usual, short work with the trunks of American tourists. Here let me advise the new tourist *not* to leave his trunks to be sent up by the regular porters to the hotel, — "it'll be all right, sir, an' save yerself the trouble," — as it gives opportunity for a swindling charge, notwithstanding there is a regular price. If you have but little luggage, after it is examined have it carried up by a porter from the landing-stage to the street, where he will place it on a four-wheeled cab for sixpence, or at most a shilling, and you can then drive at once, "bag and baggage," to your hotel.

Hotels in Liverpool I have before alluded to, and will touch upon them again, as here is where the newly-arrived American gets his first experience of English hotel-keeping, notwithstanding he will probably stop at one which owes no small part of its patronage to American travellers beginning or returning from their European travels.

Since I was first abroad, the old Adelphi Hotel in Liverpool has been handsomely remodelled, its little box of a coffee-room enlarged to reasonable dimensions, and many other improvements made in deference to the numerous Americans who frequent it.

The Adelphi, Washington, and other houses, will be observed by the traveller; but the great Northwestern Hotel is *the* house at present in Liverpool, and one in which an American may be as comfortable as it is possible for him to be, under certain customs which the English people doggedly adhere to because they *are* English, no matter if the whole civilized world does not practise them, and, in the case of an hotel, no matter if the majority of their patrons are foreigners, to whom the custom may be positively annoying.

The Northwestern Hotel is at the terminus of the Northwestern Railway, which takes you to London, and is so near that you walk directly into the station from its hall or office to take the train, without leaving the shelter of the roof. It is owned, I think, by the railroad company. It fronts St. George's Hall, and the front outlook is light and pleasant. The beds are excellent, the rooms good and well kept, prices high, — about four dollars and a half, gold, per day, — drawing-rooms, halls, and public rooms quite convenient, food good, *when you get it*, and attendance in the dining-room execrable, and annoying to an American to the last degree.

In the first place, the proprietors seemed, when I was at the hotel, to have adopted the plan of a great many English hotels to get cheap waiters, namely, that of taking a large number of Frenchmen, Italians, and Germans, who had left their native country either to escape the usual military service, or else to learn the English language sufficiently to enable them to be polylingual waiters at continental hotels. The stupidity of these men, from their imperfect understanding of the English language, customs, cooking, &c., added to the English system of serving guests, which in itself was one of the most prodigious bores that can possibly be imagined, was very aggravating.

I have in a former series of sketches ("Over the Ocean") told the reader that every meal at an English hotel must be ordered in advance, and that nothing is ever "ready." Here at the Northwestern Hotel was a most ludicrous example of it. Placards posted in the reading-room informed "guests desiring dinner" that twenty minutes notice, at least, was desired. It was an absolute impossibility here to get dinner without paying twenty minutes of time, besides the money value of it. I personally tried .it, by coming at the hour the hot joints were announced to be "ready," and which stood smoking on the carver's table, within ten feet of where I sat.

Fortunately, I got an English waiter to attend me.

"Give me," I said, "a slice of that roast-beef," pointing to it. "I wish for no vegetables, but only a slice of the beef, and a bit of bread."

"Yes, sir." And the waiter left me, returned in two or three minutes with a little ticket for me to fill out, number of my room, name, and what I would order. I did so, and he retired again.

There I sat, the aroma of the beef saluting my nostrils, as its juice oozed out, and it slowly baked in its great chafing-dish over gas-heaters; but never a slice got I.

Five minutes passed; nearly as many more; and then knives and forks were placed, napkins ditto.

"Can't I have my beef *now?*"

"Yes-ir, d'reckly; 'ot plates here d'reckly, sir."

Then water was turned out in the goblets, the waiter left, and in a short time reappeared with plates, proceeded to the beef dish, cut off my modicum, and placed it before me in just eighteen minutes, by the clock, after I had ordered it.

It was no use. I, like all other Americans, was compelled to pay this eighteen to twenty minutes to the hotel proprietors, besides the money price charged, *nolens volens.* No matter if the beef stood at my elbow, and a waiter could have served me in ten seconds; there was the old English roadside-inn system of charging at the bar each item, to be gone through with just as was done to their great-grandfathers, and that must be followed out; and here is a description of it, and what caused the delay.

We will suppose that, as a genuine American, you come home at half past two, or five, P. M., to dine, and had not left written instructions with the head-waiter in the dining-room, when you went out in the morning, that you should be home at the hour, nor what to provide for you.

You find dinner going on, and sixty or eighty persons may be dining at the tables, and naturally suppose, as, per bill of fare, dinner is announced as "ready" at those hours, it is an easy matter to get it. Let us see.

In the first place, if you are a stranger, it is difficult to get a waiter. There is no polite head-waiter, as in America, to step forward, conduct you to a seat, and assign one of his subordinates to attend to you. The head-waiter, as you will see, is tremendously busy with his book and figures, and, owing to the English system, the number of subordinate attendants appears, to the inexperienced American's eyes, to be lamentably insufficient.

Finally, after finding for yourself a seat, you succeed in getting the attention of a waiter from the next table, from which he has been going, and to which he has been coming, with all the different courses, to a party of four or five. You begin to order from the bill of fare. He presents you the inevitable blank ticket to fill out. We will suppose that you wish neither soup nor fish, so that, after writing your name and number of your room upon the ticket, you write roast-beef, potatoes, peas, bread, lettuce.

The waiter takes this to the head-waiter at the further end of the long room; he copies it into a book, checks it, and sends it out across an entry to the bar-maid; she charges it, passes it back, and it returns the length of the hall and goes down to the kitchen, where a regular requisition is made for it, and in *twenty minutes* is placed before you, if there are not too many orders ahead of you; but frequently, if you have not ordered in advance of your coming, and "fixed things" with some waiter, you may wait for thirty minutes, or three quarters of an hour, before a morsel passes your lips, and yet dinner is "all ready."

American readers, who are so promptly served at their

own hotel-tables, will appreciate the annoyance of this circumlocution, and can imagine what a hurrying to and fro, and tremendous fuss generally, there is at the usual dining-hour.

An amusing illustration I must relate, of the utter ignorance of an English employé of any detail of business outside of his own particular department, although the fact is frequently commented on by Americans. One would suppose that the clerk in this Great Northwestern Railway Hotel, whose duty it was to register each guest's name on arrival, assign him a room, and receive payment on departure, would insensibly acquire, from the very fact of observing arrivals and departures of guests, a knowledge of the hours of arrival and departure of trains, and more especially as her constant position (the clerk was a woman) was within a dozen feet of the great entrance-door of the hotel into the station. But no; it was not her business to know, and she really knew nothing of the matter, as appeared by the following dialogue:

"At what hour does the train from Chester arrive?"

"If you ask the porter, he will tell you."

"But the porter is not here at present. Don't you know whether there are any trains that arrive in the forenoon?"

"I'm sure I can't tell you; for trains be coming and going all day, and my business is to take travellers' names on the book, and assign them rooms. It is the porter as knows the trains' time."

"But the incoming trains stop within a dozen rods of where you stand, and the travellers coming to the hotel from them come first directly to you; you surely recollect whether you are accustomed to see any from Chester by morning trains."

"Beg your pardon, I never took notice when they come. I knows there *is* gentlemen from Chester comes here often. Sir Henry Bowring was 'ere once from Chester, but whether 'twas in the morning or afternoon, I quite forget. The porter will tell you."

I turned to the porter, who had now arrived, with the same question, and got the following reply:

"Chester, sir? Tell you in one minute." And he took down a well-thumbed Bradshaw's Guide, and after consulting its pages about five minutes, continued, —

"Yes, sir; three trains in forenoon, two in afternoon;" giving the hour.

Now the bar-maid, to whom I first applied, acknowledged that she had held her position "a matter of eighteen months," and the incoming trains from Chester actually jarred the room in which she stood, and yet she had not the slightest knowledge of their hour of arrival, "because it is the porter's business, do you see?" The porter himself was not up in the time-table sufficiently to answer without refreshing his memory; and yet this is a very large and generally well-kept house.

CHAPTER III.

The Langham Hotel, in London, affected by Americans generally on their first visit, seems to have been built for the express purpose of showing how much could be done in the exterior and two lower stories, and how little real comfort could be provided the ordinary practical traveller.

Imagine an hotel with the lower halls those of a palace in extent; lavatories, smoking-rooms, &c.; furnished with brilliant and expensive tiles and porcelain; dining-room Englishly luxurious; drawing-room elegant, lofty, and well-lighted; and one story of great hall-like rooms extravagantly expensive, and hundreds of other rooms without wardrobe or closet, and only three hooks for clothing, and those placed on the chamber-door. These rooms, (and be it known they are not third or fourth rate, but considered very desirable,) when a gentleman and wife get into them, with two trunks, are so crowded that there is scarcely room to move about to the two chairs, wash-hand stand, and dressing-table, which, with the bedstead, constitute the furniture.

Fancy how an American tourist ejaculates compliments against "the directors," when he goes down and tells the "gentlemanly clerk," in his little corner den, that he has unpacked his clothing, and there is no closet in his room in which to put it, and no pegs on which to hang it; and the aforesaid gentlemanly clerk "tells him the same complaint had been made hundreds of times before by Americans, and the directors of the hotel company have had their attention called to it; but, as they are Englishmen, they cannot be made to see the necessity of closets, hooks and pegs, in a room that is to be occupied by travellers only a few days!"

Is there any use arguing against such pig-headed conceit as this? The fact is, one hundred years ago an Englishman travelled with a portmanteau and one change of clothing; he "took a bed," — that's the way the English novels have it to this day, — "a bed at an inn," not "a room at an hotel," and consequently the three pegs for his top-coat, hat, and wrapper were all-sufficient. Inns were built to accommodate that style of travel; and we may hope that in fifty or one hundred years more, if the thousands of American travellers continue to go to London, the idea will penetrate the London hotel-keeper's brain that it will pay to have convenient, well-fitted rooms *all over the house,* and that the return for such needed conveniences will be a lengthened stay and more liberal expenditure by the guest.

The plan seems now to be, to make a portion of the rooms as inconvenient as possible, in order to drive the tourist into the very high-priced ones; but as these at the Langham are generally crowded during the season, it only has the effect of rendering tourists, who are charged enough for good rooms, vexed at the great pretensions, wretched accommodations, and utter lack of proper attention that they find here. It is impossible, also, to get good service except through extra feeing of the servants.

There is need of a large, well-kept American hotel in London. The Langham pays an enormous return to its stockholders, and, having the field to itself, makes comparatively little effort towards any innovations for American comfort. The very clerks argue that "it is no matter if the Americans *do* swear at the 'ouse going away; there is allers others as takes their room soon as they leaves 'em; so, what's the hodds?"

Around in this part of London — the West End — are numerous comfortable English hotels, nearly every one of them remodelled from former aristocratic dwelling-houses: the Edwards House, a handsome and expensive, well-kept one; the Brunswick, and several others, where rooms may be had for from two to twenty guineas a week; and the Queen's, on Cork Street, Bond Street, a small, but an exceedingly well-kept and reasonable priced one, with a landlord who caters to American notions. It has the old-fashioned rooms of a fashionable dwelling of fifty years ago, with that air of solidity, old-fashioned clumsiness, and inconvenience, that makes you, as an American, long to put in an army of carpenters, painters, gas-fitters, and plumbers, and utilize the waste space, raise the ceilings, and lighten up the whole affair from sombreness to cheerfulness.

As a general thing, the American, on his return to London, after a few years' absence, seems to find everything just as he left it: the same sign-boards, same streets, same buildings, and same shopmen; the latter a trifle older, perhaps; but nothing seems to have been moved out of place, especially in the older part of the city. So unlike our American cities, over which, perhaps, a fire may sweep, levelling entire districts, and upon the ruins of which, in another year, would rise stately edifices of increased architectural beauty, upon newly laid-out avenues, so that he who has been but five years absent, on his return absolutely loses his way in streets bearing the names, and in that part of the city he had been familiar with all his life before.

But while Regent and Oxford Streets, Trafalgar Square, Temple Bar, and the Strand wear the same familiar aspect, there has been a startling change at the foot of Holborn, for at the point where the street used to run down to Farringdon Street it has recently been bridged over with a broad and splendid viaduct, and the last vestiges of the inconveniences of climbing Holborn Hill have been removed.

To show the amount expended on this grand improvement, which really connects what is known as "the City" with those great main thoroughfares, Holborn and Oxford Streets, it is only necessary to state that the cost of it was about two million pounds, about five hundred thousand pounds being obtained back by sale of land on the sides of the viaduct after completion.

The American reader must understand that this great bridge, or viaduct, was to obviate the inconvenience and difficulty of descending one declivity and ascending another, in going from one part of the city to another, and, high above the street dividing the two parts, Farringdon Street, which covers what was once the old Fleet Ditch. Residents of Boston may fancy a broad and splendid avenue running from the head of Hancock or Temple Street, on Beacon Hill, high above Cambridge Street, to the brow of another hill opposite, and they may get a tolerable idea of this great work.

The difficulties in the way when this work was begun may easily be imagined. Portions of whole streets in the oldest and most crowded part of the city had to be pulled down; travel and business in some of the most crowded streets diverted; twelve thousand bodies removed from old St. Andrew's churchyard, which was cut through; and an inconceivable amount of litigation, references, and other difficulties to be encountered. But here it is, finished, and one of the greatest and most successful public works ever undertaken in London, and one which every citizen of an American city ought to visit and examine carefully as one of the sights of London, and as an illustration of the thorough, complete, and magnificent manner in which any great public work of this kind is performed in England.

The length of this great street in the air — that is, from the brows of the two hills, from Holborn to Newgate Street — is fourteen hundred feet, and its width, exclusive of the space occupied by buildings, is eighty feet. Of this space, fifteen feet is used each side for side-walks, leaving a fifty-feet granite-paved roadway in the centre. At the four principal points on the bridge over Farringdon Street are colossal statues of Commerce, Agriculture, Science, and Art, and at the four corners of the bridge, elegant edifices in the Renaissance style have been erected, the fronts of which are ornamented with statues of several of London's eminent lord mayors. It was opened for public travel in November, 1869, by Queen Victoria, with great parade.

So the improvements in what was the old Smithfield Market are wonderful; the new Albert Memorial and monument gorgeous; and the new Bethnal Green Museum interesting; but the old streets of London seem to resist the march of progress and improvement much more successfully than those in our American cities, where buildings half a century old are considered antiquated.

The sights and wonders of London, as they are called, are pretty thoroughly known to everybody who reads, — the Tower, Westminster Abbey, St. Paul's, Houses of Parliament, British Museum, galleries, Exhibition, and places of amusement. But, besides all this, the city itself is a wonder; scarce a street but has its history, like an ancient city. Hunt up its record, and you find that old authors, whom you have read with delight, lived in it, monarchs had ridden through it, tyrants were killed in it, or battles fought through it; or that its very name is linked with the historic records of hundreds of years ago; or has been so gilded with interest by the novelist that it is almost the realization of a dream to walk over the very ground and among the very scenes that your imagination has so often pictured and populated.

So when I walked down Holborn and over the great viaduct, and looked down upon Farringdon Street and over to Smithfield, I couldn't resist going down through Giltspur Street, and over to the magnificent new meat market in old Smithfield. What an historic spot it is! Here I remembered what horrors had been enacted under the reign of Bloody Mary, for it was here that the fagots blazed and the fierce flames consumed the martyrs of whom we have all read in schoolboy days.

The first who perished here under the reign of the bloody papal queen was the noted John Rogers, who was burned at the stake, and at the last moment refused pardon at its price — recantation. The picture of his martyrdom at the stake, in the midst of the flames, "with his wife and nine small children, with one at the breast," looking on, — a rude woodcut in our fathers' schoolboy days, — is familiar to New England boys.

Here Anne Askew suffered for her Protestant opinions at the dawn of the Reformation in 1546, and for denying, on examination, her belief in the doctrine of transubstantiation, after having been subjected to frightful tortures on the rack, was burned, with three other persons, opposite St. Bartholomew's Church. She, too, had a paper handed to her, while chained to the stake, promising royal pardon if she would recant her belief and pronounce it error. But, like the rest of the noble army of martyrs who were the victims of the merciless cruelty of the Romish Church, she refused to listen to it, and perished rather than preserve life at the expense of conscience.

I had curiosity to inquire where the spot was where the burning of heretics took place, and learned from a good-natured Englishman that it was supposed to be opposite the entrance of the Church of St. Bartholomew-the-Great, which is a fragment of the ancient Priory of St. Bartholomew, founded in the time of Henry I., in the year 1120 or thereabouts, and which contains some fine old Norman columns and arches.

In the year 1849, near the spot pointed out in Smithfield by my informant, some workmen, who were digging to open a new sewer, came upon a heap of rough stones and ashes. The stones were blackened with fire, and beneath them were found charred human bones; and this, from the best accounts of antiquaries and old documents, was decided to have been the site of the stake at which heretics were burned in Smithfield.

That hero of the romance in schoolboy days, "The Scottish Chiefs," — William Wallace, — was barbarously butchered — it could not be called executed — at Smithfield, by order of Edward I., in 1305. Here, also, in Smithfield, and opposite old St. Bartholomew, it will be remembered, fell the rebel Wat Tyler, in 1381, stabbed by Walworth, lord mayor, while dictating terms of greater freedom for the people to the king, Richard II., then a boy of fifteen.

Executions of criminals, as well as the burning of martyrs, took place at Smithfield, or Smoothfield, as the old historians tell us it was called, and one John Roose, a convicted poisoner, was boiled to death there in a caldron, in 1530. Grand tournaments were held in old Smithfield, in 1374, by Edward III. Here is where the Bastard, brother of Charles, Duke of Burgundy, and Lord Scales, brother-in-law to Edward IV., fought in single combat, in presence of the king, in 1467.

Smithfield was the tournament field of old, the place of the gibbet, the knightly duelling-ground, and the field where, in the reigns of the Norman sovereigns of England, citizens, artisans, and soldiers contended in manly exercises.

And here in Smithfield, for hundreds of years, was held

the celebrated Bartholomew's Fair, that we all have read about, and which Ben Jonson has written of and Hogarth pictured. The great caricaturist, by-the-by, was baptized in this very church of St. Bartholomew-the-Great.

Smithfield is always associated in the minds of American readers with a cattle-market, and no wonder, for it was used for that purpose continually for several hundred years. Some idea of the amount of business that used to be done here may be gathered from the fact that in 1846 there were two hundred and ten thousand, seven hundred and fifty-seven head of cattle, and one million, five hundred and eighteen thousand, five hundred and ten sheep sold here. The sales used always to be for cash. When seller and purchaser closed a bargain, they shook hands, and no papers of any kind, other than bank-notes, were passed in this way. According to the statistics, over seven million pounds sterling were paid away annually in this market. It was abolished in 1852, as a nuisance, and removed to Islington, as the mud and filth used to be often ankle-deep, and the smell and noise of live-stock intolerable. Smithfield, however, is really one of the most historic points in Old London.

The Great Metropolitan Meat Market, that has now supplanted the crowded cattle-pens, is a wonder of its kind, a huge structure of red brick, with conspicuous towers, and its great iron entrance-gates of wrought scroll-work, twenty-five feet high, nineteen wide, and fifteen tons weight. Inside, and there is a bewildering scene of trade and traffic in every species of meat and poultry. And such a market! Only think of three acres under roof, and the roof a graceful structure of iron and glass, thirty feet above the pavement, through which abundant light and air are let in upon the busy scene below.

The dimensions of this great market are six hundred and thirty feet in length by two hundred and forty-six feet in width, and its conveniences the best of modern times; for underneath the market proper is a complete railway depot, from which run tracks communicating with the underground or metropolitan railway, with every part of London, also with the cattle market at Islington, and indeed the country round. Occupants of the market have also cool cellars beneath for the storing of their meats, and attached are elevators or dumb waiters by which the merchandise can be lowered or raised at pleasure. Thus the market-man can receive his meat fresh from the country or the cattle market by rail, store it in his cellar, raise it from the railway-car by elevator, or expose it for sale; and, having sold it, place it once again on the railway-car, and send it to any part of London or the suburbs.

Not only has the Metropolitan (or Underground, as we call it) railroad communicating tracks in the depot under this market, but the Midland, the London, Chatham and Dover, and the Great Western; and a train of one or the other line passes through it every two minutes.

The shops or stalls of the market are ranged on each side of the principal passage of the immense parallelogram, and on the sides of the cross passages or streets intersecting it, and are one hundred and sixty in number. The great central avenue is nearly thirty feet wide, and the six side avenues about twenty feet.

The *coup d'œil* — looking through this huge glass-roofed structure, with its beautiful arched roof of ornamental iron arches, pillars, and scrolls, and row of huge glass globes for gas-lights stretching far away in the distance — is beautiful in the extreme.

But then the wonders of the stock exposed for sale! Mountains of beef, hills of mutton, whole serried ranks of carcasses hung up, game by the cartload, and eggs by the chaldron. Besides these I saw here some curious things brought to market, which, if they did not disgust, as did the heaps of live snails and frogs in the French market, none the less excited astonishment, - because it never occurred to me that they were used for food. Plovers' eggs, for instance, for which there is a large demand at this market; Egyptian quails, which are brought alive from that ancient country by thousands; and a sort of eatable eagle from Norway; French geese, American grouse, and Belgian pigs.

The conveniences and desirability of stalls here are fully appreciated, and there is always great competition to obtain them.

Great attention has been paid to ventilation, and it appears with success, as has been tested during the heat of summer weather. The roof is so arranged as to let in an abundance of light without any sunshine, and all the air desired without any rain. Twelve great hydrants supply an abundance of water for purposes of cleanliness and safety against fire.

This new market was opened to the public with grand ceremony in November, 1868, by the Lord Mayor of London, the Building Committee on Market Improvements, and other officials. Over the principal entrance an orchestra was erected, in which Dan Godfrey flourished his baton and led his famous band of the Grenadier Guards. Ten thousand feet of gas-piping were laid to illuminate the building, and twelve or fifteen hundred people partook of the grand banquet prepared for the occasion.

It will be remembered that Smithfield has been the market-place since the year 1150, for over seven centuries, and as I take leave of this splendidly designed and convenient structure, I recall the remark of an American, whose national pride, and perhaps national envy, were excited by the encomiums of his friends, their invidious comparisons, and moreover their praise of its completeness.

"Complete? Yes it ought to be, considering they have been seven hundred years completing it."

I found myself one pleasant day, — they do now and then have pleasant days in London, notwithstanding all the talk about rain and fogs, and Englishmen always carrying umbrellas, — I found myself sauntering down the Strand, looking in at the shop-windows, and approaching Temple Bar.

The Strand! I often used to wonder why they called it so, and supposed, and correctly, the reason to be that it *was* the strand on the river's bank, as it really was in ancient times; but the street which, even until the time of Henry VIII., was a grass-grown way, is now a broad thoroughfare, of course changed in all save name, and separated from the river by houses and streets that occupy the space that was once the green banks of the river, or the gardens that extended to the river-banks and belonged to those who dwelt here in pleasant view of the rolling Thames: Now it is a broad avenue, known as the thoroughfare that connects "the City" with what was once Westminster, and all that remains of the residences of the ancient nobility who used to live in this once charming location on the river-bank, are the names of the streets that are called after the estates they were laid out over.

Thus we have Northumberland Street, Villiers Street, Buckingham, Salisbury, Essex, and others of names familiar in English history; and I turned down one little coal-smoke smelling street of monotonous English regularity, called Craven Street, to read on a slab inserted in front of one of the "lodgings-to-let" looking houses, that Benjamin Franklin, the American philosopher, resided there during his stay in London; passed Wellington Street, very appropriately leading to Waterloo Bridge, then the elegant St. Mary-le-Grand Church, and then St. Clement's-Danes Church, where a son of old Canute is buried, and at last arrived at the ancient barrier between Westminster and London, — an ugly, unsightly barrier, too, even if it was designed by Sir Christopher Wren.

Old Temple Bar, a clumsy structure, which ever and anon there is a stir about, and dark hints that it shall be taken down, for it is a bar indeed to the enormous tide of travel that surges about and around it where the Strand debouches into Fleet Street. Through its narrow arches the whole tide of travel must be compressed, and, clumsy old barrier as it is, it is one of the antiquities that we Americans all like to look upon, associated as its name is in our minds with many events in the most interesting portion of England's history. But its days are numbered, and although Englishmen will preserve it as long as possible, it has been declared unsafe, and it will probably be razed to the earth ere these lines reach the reader's eye.

Through Temple Bar, and you are in "the City," and you need not go a dozen paces for historic points or for old landmarks that are fraught with interest to the historian, the antiquary, and the scholar. A gossipy investigating saunter in this vicinity, with a London friend well read up on the different points of interest, or, perhaps still better, alone or with a friend who only knows of them as you yourself do, by historic account, and the searching of them out yourselves, has quite the charm of antiquarian research and discovery.

I remember I had brushed up my recollection of old London, and fortified it somewhat by digging into a friend's library for some hours, so that, on passing through Temple Bar, I at once began to recall the celebrated dwellers in Fleet Street, that figure in the biographies of English writers, and the actors and authors that are identified with English history itself. All around here you may find the names of streets, remains of celebrated resorts that you have read and re-read of in the writings of the oldest and the wisest of England's authors. The quaint antiquities of old London are on every side. Through the Bar I went on my first stroll, but got no farther than a street on the left, where the well-known name "Chancery Lane" arrested me as if by a command.

Halting on the corner, while omnibuses and drays roared past, and standing oblivious to drivers of Hansom cabs, who drove close to the curb in expectation of a customer, I began to think of poor Miss Flite, in Dickens's story of "Bleak House," especially as a little bent old woman, bag on arm, shambled along directly up the street as if to show the way. Ah! now I remember. It was "on the eastern borders of Chancery Lane, that is to say, in Cook's Court, Cursitor Street, Mr. Snagsby, law-stationer, pursues his lawful calling," — according to the "Bleak House," tenth chapter, and first verse, — and I wondered if there was a Cursitor Street, or a Cook's Court, where Mr. Snagsby kept his stationer's store, and Krook his rag-and-bottle warehouse, that looked as if it were a place where "everything was bought and nothing ever sold."

A penny to a street-boy quickly solved this mystery, so far as the streets were concerned; for I was piloted up through Chancery Lane — occupied chiefly by lawyers' chambers, and with dozens of law-stationers' shops, where blank forms, pencils, pens, sealing-wax, law lists, inkstands, and bunches of quills, with the old-fashioned binding of cord about them, and cutlery, and all that sort of thing, were sold, — into Cursitor Street, of somewhat similar character; and out of that ran Tooke's (not Cook's) Court.

What a halo of interest a novelist will throw around a narrow old alley! Ragged, shirt-sleeved men stood at the corner, and slatternly women were sauntering here and there, as I entered the confines of Tooke's Court; a bloated-faced lounger now and then looked at me curiously as I passed. Tooke's Court evidently don't have nowadays a prejudice in favor of decently-dressed people, or as respectable ones as Mr. Snagsby. I couldn't see in the little narrow place any store that looked like the successor of " Pfeffer and Snagsby," but I did see " Mrs. Perkins and Mrs. Piper," or their heirs, assigns, or representatives, although I think one, if not both, was of the Hibernian persuasion, and one stood in the middle of Cook's (Tooke's) Court, "having it out" in a war of words with the other in the second story of a house, under which onions and other fragrant green-groceries were sold.

Then, near by, was a house with two stone door-posts, upon one of which was inscribed that "wines and spirits" were sold, and against both of which leaned three or four seedy, beery-looking men, one of whom, a short fellow in a cutaway coat, dirty plaid trousers, and a battered white hat, and with a red kerchief about his neck, I set down at once as "Little Swills," and the door the entrance to "The Sol's Arms." There isn't any rag-and-bottle shop here now, but here must be the very place Old Krook moved out of, for here there are shops hard by where one would think "nothing was ever sold." And this is the scene of the inquest, and here's where Miss Flite lived, and Tulkinghorn came, and —

"Vas you lookin' for any von, guv'ner?"

I looked down; the fellow whom I had set down in imagination as "Little Swills" stood beside me, and an unmistakable odor of gin and onions flavored the atmosphere.

"Yes, I was looking for Mr. Krook."

"In the green-grocery line?"

"No; the rag-and-bottle."

"Rag-and-bottle, guv'ner? Vell, I don't mind showin' yer a 'spectible ole lady as keeps marine stores over by Fetter Lane; but Mr. Crook, in the rag-and-bottle, I doesn't know 'im."

"Very well, it's of no consequence;" and I turned to go, when, as usual, touching the brim of his battered old hat, he said:

"I don't s'pose you'd mind the matter of sixpence, guv'ner, for the hinformation."

I saw one of his friends drawing near to assist in the conversation, and therefore dropped the coveted coin into his hand, and passed on, not, however, without overhearing him communicate to his companion that I was "a bloke as was lookin' up rag-and-bottle shops — a gen'leman as stood two drains — come along, Bill."

I got out into Chancery Lane again, and met English-looking lawyers, with "fair round bellies," gray side-whiskers, respectable black suits, gaiters, and fob chains with big seals; one was getting into a trim-looking brougham, and giving the driver, who was dressed in livery, some directions; and the other was glancing at his watch, and telling a Hansom cab-driver he had just called that he had just time to catch the train. Then there were the unmistakable lawyers' clerks, and lawyers' boys, besides the stream that had other business, and took the cut of Chancery Lane to get from Holborn to the Strand.

Here in Chancery Lane is the entrance to the law buildings known as Lincoln's Inn, a fine old gateway adorned with coats-of-arms in antique carving. We might look in at the garden and over at Lincoln's Inn Fields, and while wandering round among this dreamy old pile, wonder where Sir Thomas More used to live, or Coke, the great lawyer, and Pitt, Canning, and Bishop Heber. They point to the wall next to Chancery Lane, and tell you that Ben Jonson worked there as bricklayer, and actually laid part of it before his wit and brightness were discovered.

Here I was told, in chambers in the square leading out of Chancery Lane, was the room where Cromwell came to meet Secretary Thurloe, and to lay a plan for the enticing of Charles the Second and his young brothers, the Dukes of York and Gloucester, from their exile in Bruges into his power,—a plan which was frustrated by a clerk who was thought to be asleep in the office, but who overheard the whole and warned Charles in time. Here also King Charles the Second, and, in 1661, with Lord Clarendon and others, had a jolly good Christmas revel; and here also the noted Nell Gwinne lived.

Out through the old gateway and into Chancery Lane again, — for I was really on the way to the Temple Church, the lodge of the old Knights Templars, — when the Chancery Lane signboard had caught my eye and led me mousing round its legal and historic intricacies.

Just out of Chancery Lane and standing in Fleet Street, I look at old Temple Bar again, which seems to have little that is of great historic interest in itself to render it worthy the jealous preservation with which it has been guarded. It was built in 1670, by Sir Christopher Wren, soon after the great London fire, and its chief celebrity seems to be that the heads of people executed for high treason used to be stuck up on it. It was, in fact, the dividing line or barrier of the city of London from the city of Westminster, or city from Shire, — a fact to be remembered by the curious American tourist who wishes to note "how London has grown." The room over the arch is hired by Messrs. Child and Co., a banking firm, for the storage of their old account-books, and contains two or three tons of them.

But the spot on which Temple Bar stands is inseparably connected with the historic events of England, for here passed Edward the Black Prince in triumph after the battle of Poictiers. Henry the Fifth made his triumphal entry through the old Temple Bar, or former structure of wood, after his great victory of Agincourt in 1415. Here Anne Boleyn, Henry the Eighth's beautiful queen, was welcomed, and also his daughter, Queen Bess, passing to her coronation in 1558. Through Temple Bar Edward the Fourth conducted the beautiful Elizabeth Woodville as his bride to her coronation; and here also passed the wife of Henry the Seventh to a like ceremony.

It is, perchance, because the clumsy old pile marks the spot of so many interesting events, and that it is a landmark from which so many others can be located, that London hesitates to level it to the ground.

That gentle old fisherman, Izaak Walton, lived near the corner of Chancery Lane and Fleet Street, "on the north side of Fleet Street, two doors west of the end of Chancery Lane," just about where I was standing, said one old history; and another puts him down as living in Chancery Lane, seven doors from Fleet Street, from 1627 to 1644.

On the north side of Fleet Street stands St. Dunstan's Church, near Temple Bar. My earliest recollection of the courageous saint for whom this church is named, is of a spirited picture of him, where he was represented in the act of holding his Satanic Majesty by the nose with a pair of red-hot tongs; for Dunstan was a famous worker in iron and brass, and was, it will be remembered, forging iron work in his cell when the Evil One appeared to him. Much to my chagrin, however, I found that Dunstan neither built nor founded this church, but that it was built on the site of an old one, in 1829. And the old one was built about the year 1200, over two hundred years after the devil-seizing saint had been laid comfortably away to rest under the high altar of Canterbury Cathedral.

But it is worth while to remember that all around the old St. Dunstan's were some of those famous Fleet-street publishers who printed the earliest editions of some of the most celebrated books in the English language: John Smethwicke, "under the dial," who printed "Hamlet" and "Romeo and Juliet;" Richard Marriott, who published Quarles's "Emblems," Butler's "Hudibras," and Izaak Walton's "Complete Angler;" and Mathias Walker, who printed Milton's "Paradise Lost."

All around here, within a few rods of the corner of Chancery Lane and Fleet Street, every street and alley is celebrated. Sam Johnson, Ben Jonson, Goldsmith, Cowley, Michael Drayton, Shenstone the poet, and a host of others, have made it classic ground. Here is Fetter Lane, the next street to Chancery Lane, that runs up to Holborn, and where Dryden used to live; and here is the house, which is pointed out to you; and Dr. Johnson is also said to have lived in this lane. Indeed, all the streets in this vicinity seem to have some reminiscence of the great lexicographer, so much so that, one dreamy summer's day, when I was prying around in some of the quiet, clean, enclosed courts, surrounded by quaintly furbished-up old buildings, whose rooms were lawyers' offices, it seemed as though the huge bulk of the old fellow might very naturally shamble across the pave in his cocked hat and knee-breeches, as he had done when living.

But I came down through Temple Bar to visit the old Temple Church, the famous church or asylum of the Knights Templars from 1184 to 1310. This ancient order first established themselves on High Holborn, but after a time, increasing in strength and riches, purchased a large tract of land extending from Fleet Street to the river. The Temple was in ancient times really a large monastery of military monks, arranged for the residence of the abbot, or prior, as he was called, brethren, knights, and serving brethren. It consisted of a church, for worship and the religious ceremonies attending the admission of approved candidates into the ranks of the brotherhood, a council-chamber, rough quarters or barracks, and humble fare for the knights themselves; cloisters, and the beautiful field and garden extending down to the river-banks, in which horses were exercised, and the knights themselves had opportunity for military exercise.

The fame of this order in the crusades, their original humility, their days of proud magnificence, their vows of chastity, to devote their entire energies to wresting the Holy Sepulchre from the hand of the Saracen, their progress from rigorous military monks to proud knights with regal possessions, their power and influence from embracing the most powerful nobles of the land among their numbers, and their unquestionable valor, render them among the most prominent figures in history.

For two hundred years all Europe rang with their exploits, and it was not until their wealth became so great as to excite the greed and cupidity of pontiffs and sovereigns, that the charges for monstrous crimes were brought against them by their accusers. The Templars, as time rolled on, doubtless were less rigorous with regard to their vows, and perhaps were somewhat arrogant; but after all, their great crime in the eyes of their ancient accusers was their wealth, and the charges brought against them were in many cases absurd and ridiculous.

To-day their memory is perpetuated by a Masonic order, who profess to have certain rites and ceremonies similar to those of the ancient knights, and to " work " somewhat as did these mail-clad warriors, in the initiation of candidates into their order.

Passing through Temple Bar, I turned into a little court or alley, which brought me to the old edifice, rich in historical associations, shut in by surrounding dwellings, and apparently sunken somewhat below the present level of the street. Around nearly all very old buildings the earth seems to have gained additional crust during the hundreds of years they have stood, and they have not risen, like living and moving things, to its surface; for, according to antiquaries who are interested in the exhumation of ancient Roman remains beneath the surface of modern London, the soil rises one foot every century.

But as we stand in this inclosed space, hemmed closely in by surrounding buildings on every side, we can hardly have a correct idea of what this beautiful house of the Templars was over six hundred years ago, when this grand round lodge, — for the old part of the church that remains is circular, — with the splendid colonnade of pillars, and lofty, grooved roof, which still remain, stood rich in architectural splendor upon the banks of the river Thames, commanding a pleasant view of the rolling stream beyond the space of ground between church and river.

The Temple Church, which is one of the most interesting historical edifices in London, is at the same time one of the most chaste and beautiful in its architecture. I was struck with this at the very threshold, where I halted beneath the old semicircular arched Norman doorway, to reach which I had to descend a few steps, and the deep recess of which was superbly ornamented with sculptured ornaments, elaborately carved pillars, foliated capitals, and twisted, carved work overhead. Passing the leaves of the old Norman door, which closed behind me with a clang, as of the fall of a portcullis, I was within this ancient structure, beautiful in its effect and majestic in its simplicity.

The Temple Church, it should be understood, is really two distinct churches. The first, or Round, in which I stood, is the older, having been consecrated in 1185, and was built by the Knights after a model of the Church of the Holy Sepulchre at Jerusalem. The other portion of the church is square, and of different style of architecture. It was finished in 1240. The great fire of London, in 1666, rushed up almost to the very walls of the old Temple Church; and another, in 1678, destroyed a greater part of what were known as the "residential buildings" of the old Temple. The ceiling of the interior is richly frescoed and decorated with the lamb, Templars' cross, and other emblems of the order — of course, modern restoration. In fact, the arrangement of the interior, with the exception of walls, pillars, and pavement, has been changed very much since the days of the old crusaders.

The round church remains in form as originally built, on the exterior, except that it has been re-faced with stone. The diameter of the round is fifty-eight feet, and there are said to be but three other churches in England of this form. The architecture is one of the earliest specimens of pointed arches intermingled with round arches. The walls are five feet thick.

No one who has read of the tremendous struggles of the crusades, when from time to time, during one hundred and seventy years, with a valor amounting to religious frenzy, the whole of Christian Europe sought with unflagging energy to redeem the Holy Sepulchre from the hands of the Moslem, but has recognized the Knights Templars foremost in every onset, and bravest in every battle; and it is interesting to stand here in the very centre of their ancient home; here, where they were charged to be brave, honorable, and true as a duty; to stay not for mountain, sea, or desert, and spare not even life in the effort to reclaim the birthplace of Christianity from the grasp of the infidel; here they knelt and pronounced their vows, and from here went forth on campaigns against the infidel.

As I stood in the centre of this renowned temple, and looked up to the ring of Romanesque windows above the old Norman arches, and upon six clustered pillars, with their sculptured capitals upholding the vaulted roof, I could not help thinking that here might have been the very spot where, when with doors closely guarded, and brethren ranged around in the robes and badges of the order, was the altar at which the novice knelt, and, after having pronounced his vows, and being instructed in his duty, with impressive ceremonies by the Grand Master, received arms and equipments, and a lecture with each, and lastly his sword, and the celebrated white mantle with the red cross.

Here in this circular sanctuary have stood some of the bravest hearts that ever beat beneath a steel corselet; here have been raised some of the stoutest hands that ever swung mace or battle-axe, in solemn oath to fight for the Christian religion, and to wrench the Holy Places from the hand of the Mussulman; here have stood princes, kings, potentates, monks, priests, knights, — all men whose names and deeds are imperishable in history; aye, and here at our very feet rest the ashes of those who have marched over the blinding sands and under the burning sun of the East, beneath the banner of the cross, or ridden with the stalwart Richard at the battle of Acre, and fronted the forces of Saladin himself.

Here rests one of those who forced King John at Runnymede to sign Magna Charta; and here, under the protection of the knights, dwelt John himself for a time, many of his public documents being dated from this place. After a look around at the beautiful pillars, the lofty arches, and pictured windows, the eye falls to the most interesting objects, the monumental effigies of Knights Templars that lie in groups in the central aisle.

First, in full Templar's costume, with sword at side, right arm on breast, and the left supporting his long shield, lies Geoffrey de Magnaville, who, it seems, had rather a difficult task of it in getting his mortal remains into the sacred spot; for, having rebelled against King Stephen, and committed various bad acts, he died excommunicated and forsaken by all save his Templar brethren. They clothed him in full costume, and, fearing the wrath of the Church if they should bury him in consecrated ground, rolled him up in a winding-sheet of lead, and hung him suspended in a leaden coffin from a tree in the garden, till they were able, several years afterwards, to soften the papal heart, and inter him and his leaden hammock beneath the portico of the western door of the Temple, where even the iron tramp of his brethren of the order over his head failed to disturb his sleep.

Next we stand beside the effigy of the bold and faithful Earl of Pembroke, who served his royal master, Henry III., so faithfully, and was indeed well worthy the title of Protector during that monarch's minority. He died in May, 1219, and his effigy represents him with his feet on a lion and hand on his sword. Next comes the sculptured figure of Lord de Ros, one of the leaders of the barons, but no Templar, for he has no beard and wears long hair, which the rules of the order did not permit. He was one of Cœur-de-Lion's knights, however, and one of the barons who forced King John to sign Magna Charta. This effigy is one of the best of any in the church.

Among the others, we are told, is another baron, who married King John's daughter; while William Plantagenet, son of Henry III. (marked by a rigid stone coffin), Gilbert Marshall, and other forgotten knights of olden time, mingle their dust together, and, although wrought with so much care, the remainder of these sculptured mementos but perpetuate the military costumes of those they represent, not even marking the spot beneath which they were buried, or recording those names with which doubtless their country rang in their day; for inexorable time, in a few centuries, obliterates all except "there lived a man."

This fine old church passed into the hands of the Knights Hospitallers in 1324, till that old tyrant, Henry VIII., abolished that order, and they leased it to the students of law, in whose possession it has ever since remained.

It is a step downwards, somewhat, to come from the time of mail-clad knights, whose armed tread made these old walls ring with their clang, to what we are wont to call old times, and might make one think "to what base uses," &c., when we find that this very part of this old historic spot was formerly a place of rendezvous for lawyers of the Temple, with their witnesses; for old Hudibras tells of them —

> "That ply i' th' Temple, under trees;
> Or walk the round with knights o' th' posts,
> About the cross-legged knights, their hosts;
> Or wait for customers between
> The pillar rows of Lincoln's Inn."

But the lawyers only come here now, when they do come, for worship, for the Temple Church is now a place of religious worship, belonging to the lawyers of the societies of the Inner and Middle Temple of London.

Half-way up the winding staircase that led to the Triforium, the large circular gallery surrounding the overarching dome, between the vaulting and roof, is the little penitentiary cell of the Temple, formed into the solid walls, and measuring only four feet and a half in length by two and a half in breadth, so that the unfortunate knight who had transgressed the rules of the order could not lie down within it, but, with a refinement of cruelty worthy the times, an aperture was left so that he could hear, see, and join in the devotional ceremonies of the church. It is positively known that Walter Le Bacheller, Grand Preceptor of the order, was confined and died in this cruel prison, and, could its cruel walls speak, we might know of others who have languished in their stony embrace.

Up in the Triforium, if any one has a taste in that direction, can be examined a host of monuments that were formerly scattered in and about the church. Here is that of Plowden the jurist, Howell, author of a once celebrated series of letters, and ancestor of Gibbon the historian, Lord Chancellor Thurloe, and other slabs, tablets, and sculptures chronicling the deeds, virtues, and characters of forgotten judges, long passed-away scholars, and an array of legal talent whose epitaphs are rich in Latin texts and quotations. It is indeed a museum of old monuments, and was well arranged, when, in 1842, seventy thousand pounds were laid out in restorations. A pleasant place, perhaps, for an antiquary, this garret full of tombstones, but one which the average tourist will not spend much time in.

Out into the old burial-ground about the building, we stop a moment at the monumental slab of Oliver Goldsmith, who is buried somewhere in the churchyard, but where, it is not positively known. It is but a step or two to the Temple Garden, a green island in a sea of brick and stone, surrounded by the hum and roar of the metropolis, that lashes its waves of busy life, its smoke, dust, and roar, to the very verge. Shorn, much as it is, of its former fair proportions, it is, from very contrast to its rude surroundings, a pleasant spot; once a delightful garden, sloping to the river side, where knights and squires, lawyers and judges, yes, and priests and monarchs, strolled.

But 'tis Shakspeare that has invested the place with its chief charm, for here he places the scene of the breaking out of that fatal and bloody feud of the houses of York and Lancaster, from which came the War of the Roses. Here Richard Plantagenet plucked his white rose and called upon his friends who thought he had pleaded truth, to pluck white roses too ; while young Somerset, equally confident, called on his friends to pull red roses for his cause. And then ensued that memorable dialogue, as natural to-day, when opponents detract with sneers each other's cause, as then.

But knights, princes, warriors, and all have passed away ; and so must our dream of old times, as we emerge once more into the crowded street, amid the roar of vehicles and the busy activity of the mass of humanity that surges and flows around us on every side.

And where shall we go next ? asks the new tourist. From Temple Bar scarce any direction can be taken but historic ground will be trodden, and be the wanderer's thoughts not on history but on city sights, he may, within a short distance, encounter the latter in every direction.

Down here amid the thunder of the city, one seems to get some idea of the vastness of London. After you cross over the huge viaduct at the foot of Holborn, you seem to feel the pulsations of its mighty heart ; the throngs coming and going, the inextricably entangled confusion of vehicles, and further on, the great bridges with railroad trains thundering over them almost every moment; or descending an iron staircase down into the bowels of the earth, you find iron veins stretching off in shining lines far into the distant darkness, with the trains ever coming and ever going, as the underground railway plies its never-ceasing business.

A walk towards the Thames, and that wonderful improvement, the Thames Embankment, bursts upon the view. Along what was once the shore, where in old times were mud and slime, rotting hulks, foul water, and old wharves, dilapidated old buildings of a forgotten age, old warehouses, ship and boat buildings, and all those unsightly objects of the river's bank that have been so graphically described by Harrison Ainsworth and Charles Dickens, now runs a magnificent road one hundred feet wide, its wall towards the river being of splendid hewn granite, and all along it a fine quay reclaimed from the river.

But at what a tremendous expense are city improvements made here, for this vast one had, in 1873, already cost over one million and six hundred thousand pounds sterling, or more than eight million dollars of our money; even this does not include the expense of widening and altering the streets that approach it; and it was not then completed. The money, to pay for this improvement, is raised by a tax of three pence to the pound on all ratable property in London, and from the coal and wine duties.

Of course London Bridge is the first one everybody visits. Only think of a bridge over which one hundred and ten thousand people and twenty thousand vehicles pass every twenty-four hours! The old London Bridge of the novelist is gone, and this present great nine hundred feet stretch of granite was finished in 1831, and cost over two million pounds sterling! There's a city item that gives an idea of the cost of city improvements in the modern Babylon. The great Waterloo Bridge, which is thirteen hundred and eighty feet long and forty-three wide, cost a million pounds, and, although charging but a halfpenny toll, takes about ten thousand pounds, or fifty thousand dollars, a year from foot-passengers alone; and the beautiful Westminster Bridge, eleven hundred and sixty feet long and eighty-five feet wide, is a spot from which there is a fine view of that wonderful piece of "gingerbread work," the Houses of Parliament. The view upon and from these bridges at night, when all the lamps are lighted, is one that should be seen, being a scene of singular and striking effect.

The American looks with astonishment at the cheap, and to him old-fashioned, looking buildings in Regent Street, fashionable street of shops; there are no marble palaces, extravagant buildings of outrageous architecture, as in Broadway, New York; but in the way of merchandise everything that money can buy is found in stock. A ride up to the West End or the fashionable part of the city, in the quiet old squares, looking at the exterior of the houses of sombre aspect, one hardly can realize the magnificence of the interiors, rich in upholstery, elegant furniture, paintings, statuary, and all that makes living luxurious. Servants answer at the door instanter, trained to the politest deference, even in tone of voice, and skilful in deferring to master's and mistress's wishes or whims. The service in an aristocratic English family, despite all the ridicule of servantgalism or of John Thomas, seems to me to be as near perfection as it possibly can be.

I have ridden through some streets in the more aristocratic part of the city, where were residences of the wealthy, where whole blocks, or terraces, as they were called, had an inclosed private roadway of forty or fifty feet in width between the house and the street, separated from the street by a wall, entrance being had for the private carriages of owners of the half dozen grand mansions of the block, only at each end of the inclosure. This inclosed place, or private street, was admirably kept, and the portion not actually occupied as a driveway beautifully laid out in flower-beds and shrubs, which often formed points for the carriages to drive around.

From these beautiful evidences of wealth, seen at their best in the height of the season, about the middle of June, it is but a brief journey first to the interminable streets of shops, thence down to that packed, wedged in, squeezed together part of the city below Temple Bar, or down Fleet Street, Lombard Street, St. Paul's Churchyard; or down the Poultry, beyond the Mansion House, where the stranger wonders how down here, and in this very rush and crush, so many tailors, furnishing stores, and stationery, boot and shoe, hats, caps, cutlery, and every species of retail establishment, can possibly flourish, jammed down among merchants, bankers, brokers, and all that sort of people, and no dwelling-houses anywhere to be seen.

But don't they utilize alleys down in the city? Step into a passage-way scarce a dozen feet wide, and you will find it packed with restaurant entrances. Some will be little narrow houses, with narrow staircases running from the first floor, which is occupied by beer and bar counter up to the two or three upper rooms, where Englishmen will pack in almost like herrings, to eat their noonday lunch of meat and beer, or sandwich and sherry.

Another unpretending entrance in an alley will usher you into a tremendous great restaurant lighted by an interior inclosed court-yard or skylights above. You encounter the clatter and noise of three or four hundred customers, and the rush of thirty or forty waiters. You pass by one great bar-counter, where in full view are specimens of the luxurious larder. Burly barons of beef delicately mixed with fat and lean, red and white, as though prepared by an artist purveyor; magnificent mutton chops, with broad, round masses of tender meat, and snowy, sweet fat that will brown so luxuriously; haunches of venison and great legs of Southdown mutton, that will make an epicure's mouth water; lobsters all alive, ho! great turbot, green turtles, sole, which none but an English cook can dress; ham and chicken, kidneys, pork chops, and an array of various kinds of cheeses, pickles, sauces, and appetizers, mild, pungent, or fiery, to smooth the delicate or spur the blunted taste.

There is a notable absence of the innumerable French dishes, "kickshaws," and side-dishes found in an American restaurant. The English restaurant runs more to substantials and solids, — beef, cabbage, and asparagus, chops and potatoes, a bit of plum-pudding perhaps, or gooseberry tart after the meat, but more frequently cheese and bread, washed down with wine or beer, constitute the city man's noontide lunch.

And here let me remark that the prodigious quantity of liquor drunk by the English astonishes the newly-arrived American. Maybe the high price at our own restaurants in a measure prevents it; if so, pray Heaven it may continue; but here, from poorest laborer to millionnaire, all seem to take something alcoholic. In the great restaurant I am speaking of, scarcely a man but drank his pale ale, bitter beer, claret, or sherry with his meal, but rarely anything stronger. Here and there some weather-beaten old campaigner, whose prim, square, solid cut, English costume, high stock, immaculate linen, carefully trimmed white whiskers, and shaven face mottled with good living, showed him to be a true Briton believing in good dinners, called for brandy-and-water; but these were the exception.

In other respects than those above mentioned, the restaurant was very much like an American one, except that you paid your bill to the waiter, with a few pence for himself, instead of paying at the counter as in America.

In these narrow passages down in the City, in the vicinity of the Bank and Exchange, restaurants swarm, and in them may also be found merchants, brokers, great importers, and often some of the heaviest firms in the metropolis, who, being known all over the world, and commanding by their great capital the attention of mercantile men, seem to glory in hiding themselves away in the most obscure nooks, in order, as it were, to enjoy the satisfaction of making other lesser capitalists take as much trouble as possible in getting at them. Down here in the City, as it is called, it teems with life from ten to four, and every street, alley, and passage seems to be rammed, jammed full of people, to such an extent that you wonder how there can be enough business to keep them all in occupation.

The poorer districts of London are an unpleasant picture to contemplate. Take any of those of our own great American cities, and multiply by ten or fifty, and you have it. Interminable streets of cheap shops below, and crowded tenements above; swarms of wretched, ragged, and almost naked children of all ages thick as flies, fighting, playing, sleeping, and screaming; idle, loafing men and blowzy women; reeking gutters and filthy odors; the most showy establishment the gin-shop, that flourishes boldly, brazenly, openly, and frequently.

CHAPTER IV.

But how, asks a friend, do the better class of English people live at home? To this I would answer, so far as I had an opportunity of observing, very much like well-educated, well-bred, wealthy American families; not at all like many American families who have wealth and little or none of the other mentioned characteristics. The more really aristocratic and wealthy the Englishman, the less, as a general thing, is his pretension or attempt at vulgar display. You may be as likely to encounter a lord, having a rent-roll of thousands a year, in a rough tweed suit and stout walking-shoes, among the Scotch hills, or sitting very quietly on top of the Brussels stage-coach beside you, in a plain travelling-suit, as you bowl over the road out to the field of Waterloo. There is no vulgar display of jewelry or costume about him, no supercilious air, no scattering of money or " damning the expense ; " in fact, it may be correctly said, there is none of this about any genuine gentleman of any nationality. Men who are sure of their position in society, and know that it requires no bolstering before the world, never boast of ancestry, riches, or superiority of intellect, and are quite ready to believe that there are others in the world not only their equals but even their superiors; that being settled in their own minds, they feel no necessity on their part to argue the point.

There is also in people of this class an absence of that effort to rise which is noticeable and evident in aspiring persons. I have known a wealthy Englishman to say he could not afford to pay ten pounds for an article which an American, whose entire property did not equal the former's annual rent-roll, bought without question. The first could "not afford" to squander money, to pay an extravagant or exorbitant price for a needless luxury, to which the latter, with his spendthrift liberality, never gave a thought, more than that it pleased him for the moment, and he had money enough on hand to buy it.

The dividing lines are distinctly marked, and the walls of society are high and strong in England; but, like the social barriers of the best society in our own country, hospitality is hearty, if they be creditably passed.

I have said that what I saw of life in an English gentleman's family is similar to that in many American ones. It may interest the untravelled reader to give a description of a single experience of it in detail.

I was once invited to a gentleman's country estate in England, a two-hours' ride from London. I was directed by letter of invitation how to reach the nearest station by rail, and informed that I would be met there on arrival. On alighting from the railway carriage at the end of my journey, I was at once accosted by a polite footman in livery, who, touching his hat, asked if myself and companion were the expected guests. On being answered in the affirmative, he escorted us to a carriage in waiting, upon the box of which sat the liveried coachman. The railway porters were directed to send our baggage — two trunks — after, in the cart in attendance, and the smart footman then, after seeing us safely bestowed, sprang to his place, and the carriage rattled away over the smooth English road, behind the well-groomed horses, at a smart trot. A three-mile drive brought us to the grounds, which were entered, and we were driven up by a winding avenue, beneath the spreading branches of tall trees, between which were long reaches of view of a well-kept park, with its close-cut, velvet lawn, till we arrived at the broad covered porch of the entrance of the mansion.

As we halted, the footman sprang down and opened the carriage-door, and another man-servant stepped from the porch to assist us to descend, which we did, meeting the host and his wife at the door, welcoming us in a hearty, cordial manner at the threshold. A step or two brought us into a large entrance-hall; the two servants took coats, wraps, hat, and umbrellas from us, and the host said that we must wish first to go to our rooms to prepare for lunch, which would be ready in half an hour. Two rooms, side by side, one for myself and the other for my wife, each commanding delightful views of the park, were assigned us.

A rosy-cheeked, white-aproned and white-capped chamber-maid attended madam, and a footman in a quiet livery, myself. The latter had my portmanteau brought to my room, unstrapped it, asked for the key, unlocked it, and asked if he should lay out any change of clothing for lunch. I designated a few articles, which he selected as if he had been my tailor for a lifetime, and then bestowed my other wearing apparel in wardrobe and bureau-drawers, with such slight comments as, —

"I will place the linen here."

"Coats, you will observe, please, are hung in this press."

"Brushes, combs, dressing-case, here."

He then laid dress-coat, clean linen, and dinner costume out for me, and indicating "hot water, sir; cold; writing materials," added, "Shall I assist you to dress? or would you please to order anything?"

"Nothing — thank you."

"Bell, please, if I'm wanted," said he, indicating the bell-rope; and, politely bowing, retired, closing the door noiselessly.

A comfortably furnished room, with blue-covered furniture, large, comfortable bed, with richly-wrought counterpane and pillow-cases, blue and lace curtains, and at foot of bed three deep windows, two commanding views of the beautiful grounds, and one of the distant country; and in the niche of the latter a little writing-desk, with paper, envelopes, paper-knife, stamps, bronze figure holding a little candlestick, sealing-wax, and all the paraphernalia for correspondence, either social or official. Floor carpeted with Brussels carpet.

Instead of the familiar water-fixtures of America, the wash-hand stand, with its outfit of rich English ware and supplementary hot-water pitcher; the walls adorned by a few proof copies of valuable engravings framed; two silver candlesticks before the glass upon the dressing-table; a vase with a fresh bouquet of flowers between them; and, in all respects, the room like that of any wealthy country gentleman in America.

A short time sufficed to remove the stains of travel, and we descended to meet our hospitable host. A servant, who started out somewhere from the staircase, — they seemed to start out from everywhere, like genii in a pantomime, to anticipate one's wants, — indicated the apartment to us in which our entertainers were, a room with wide windows reaching to the floor, and opening out upon the lawn which stretched its green carpet far away before us in gentle slopes, while at the side ran gravelled and flower-lined paths, and plots of various-colored blossoms, the perfume of which floated in at the windows.

Here, in this drawing-room, we were presented to our host's family of two children, — boys home for a few holidays, — his sister-in-law and son, and, with cordial greetings, were put at ease and made to feel at home at once, till the gentlemanly-looking butler quietly appeared, and announced that lunch was served. Giving his arm to my wife, mine host invited me to follow, which of course I did, escorting the hostess, and we proceeded to the dining-room, where stood the butler by the side-board, looking so much, in his dress-coat, white cravat, and gray hair, and general eminently respectable get-up, like a certain clergyman I knew at home, that I could hardly bring myself to think that he was there to turn out the claret for us.

Lunch consisted of substantial fare enough for a dinner, if one would make it so, — chops, broiled chicken, cold game pie, cold ham, and other meats, with pickles of various kinds, stewed plums, and various "goodies," or perhaps what might be termed English appetizers, — for the English lunch is the preparer for the later and more substantial dinner. The table was rich in damask, solid silver, exquisite glass, and shining cutlery; and the servants — a footman and maid, under the command of his highness the butler, at his post by the side-board — seemed to understand every move that should be made for the guests' convenience, and to exhibit the host's hospitality to the best advantage.

Ale, claret, and Rhine wines were served as beverages, a glass of the former seeming to be the English preference, and the serving of wine the only actual table-service which the grand butler performed. He even seemed a little wounded in his feelings that his master should presume to say, —

"Rollins, have some Bass ale served; perhaps it may be liked better than our home-brewed."

"Certainly, sir; I have ordered some."

And so he had, for the footman straightway made his appearance with it. The butler deftly uncorked the bottle; but the footman brought it to table and turned it out. As soon as the lunch was well along, this eminent personage, the butler, withdrew, leaving the service of actually waiting upon table to his subordinates, direction being no longer necessary.

After lunch, we had the rest of the day before us for amusement till half past six, when dinner would be served. The gardens were visited, with their gravelled walks, ornamental and fanciful flower-beds, and beautiful shrubbery; the hot-houses, with their grapes and wall-peaches and rarer plants; the kitchen-garden, with its turnips, radishes, lettuce, potatoes, and onion-beds. Then a little *détour* through a grove, and a rest on the greensward beneath the trees.

Returning, we gentlemen came through the stable-yard, paved with stone, well kept and clean, with its great stone water-trough in the centre, clock up over the door, and two or three of those corduroy-clad, straw-in-mouth sort of young fellows, the unmistakable English stable-boy, or, as we should call them in America, "hostlers." The appearance of the master, however, seemed to have an effect like that of the colonel of a regiment on a visit of barrack inspection. Each rose to his feet, caps came off, or were touched respectfully, when the wearers were spoken to.

In the well-kept stables we saw the tall carriage-horses, the ladies' saddle-horse, and the gentleman's blooded bay, good for a gallop across country, a serviceable horse-of-all-work for the brougham, another for anything needful, the groom's horse, and two clean-limbed steeds that I took to be hunters. There were also the stalls for working horses that were out upon the place, and for a "rough little cob," as the head groom styled him, that the boys were racing round with. The carriage-houses contained the stately landaulet, the more serviceable snug calling-carriage, a brougham, that heavy-timbered vehicle an English dog-cart, and a wagonette capable of carrying a party of six; so that, so far as transportation was concerned, our host was amply provided. Returned to the library, with its book-lined walls, deep windows, classic statuettes, and few costly oil-paintings, we chatted with our kind entertainers on the, to them, never-tiring theme — America and the Americans, till a bell rang which was the "preparation-bell" rung half an hour before dinner; and we all separated, to "dress for dinner."

Dining at an English gentleman's house is an important ceremony, and is done in proper form. One would no more think of presenting himself in a frock-coat or light-colored pantaloons at the dinner-table than he would in his shirt-sleeves or with his hat on. Dressing for dinner means full dress: the ladies in evening costume, and the gentlemen in *costume de rigueur* of black — dress-coat, low-cut vest, narrow black or white cravat, and spotless linen.

The dinner-hour varies from half past five to half past eight P. M. Many of the city men of my acquaintance left their business at about half past four, reaching their homes in the suburbs at about half past five, in time to dine at six or half past six, lunch having been taken in the city at about half past one.

On ascending to my room, I found the valet at my door, and my wife the little English maid, that had been detailed for her service, in like attendance. My guardian threw a critical eye over the interior of the apartment as I entered, glanced at the stock of towels on the rack, the two tall, lighted candles in the silver candlesticks before the dressing-glass, at the three others in a handsomely wrought candelabra upon a side-table, at my dress laid out upon two chairs and the bed, and desired to know if I would like "his assistance in dressing, or to dress my hair."

Being democratic enough to dress myself, I of course declined, and the well-drilled servant, indicating the bell-rope as before, with a desire "to please ring if he was wanted," once more noiselessly withdrew.

We all met in the drawing-room about ten minutes before the dinner-hour. The host begged the honor of escorting my wife, assigned me to the hostess, his sister-in-law to a clergyman who had ridden over to dine with him, another gentleman visitor to a lady acquaintance of the hostess; and when, a few moments after, the eminently respectable butler announced, "Dinner is served," we passed ceremoniously to the dining-room.

The sideboard flashed with the family plate; the damask table-linen, glittering cutlery, and cut-glass sparkled beneath the chandelier of wax lights; the butler stood at his post by the sideboard, just at the rear of the host's seat, in solemn state, a maid-servant behind madam's chair, and a footman at either side of the table. Immediately after we had seated ourselves, in obedience to a glance from the host, the clergyman, a bright, rattling fellow of twenty-eight or thirty, looking as though an officer's uniform would have become him better than the straight-cut clerical garments worn of the Church of England, suddenly checked himself in a galloping description of a flower show, — or I should say, sandwiched in between two sentences, *sotto voce*, "For what we rabout to receive metha Lord mekus truly thankful;" closing his eyes for a second only, and leaping back to worldliness with a speed that fairly took my breath away, and somewhat shocked my Puritan ideas of the solemnity due to an appeal to the Throne of Grace.

However, a blessing having been asked, dinner commenced by serving the soup, which was of the first course, as we observed on a *menu*, or little ornamental bill of fare, before each plate, — a convenient thing, at an English dinner, for regulating one's appetite, and the preventing of exhausting or throwing it away upon the wrong course. Fish followed the soup, and then came light wines, ordered by the butler, but served by the footmen. After the fish came boiled mutton, with delicious jelly and accompanying vegetables. Then salads and side-dishes. Claret wine was then served. Next beef and other roast meats; and now that the dinner was fairly inaugurated, the great butler himself served port and sherry, and assisted the ladies gracefully to champagne, filling to the brim without spilling a drop. Following the meats came a course of game, with the usual accompaniments of jellies and sauces. All this time a lively conversation was kept up, commenced at first and continued with your next neighbor till after the remove of fish, when either the wine or the effect of the generous dinner loosened the tongues of all in general, — hearty conversation across, around, and about the table.

Under the direction of the butler the removes were made with the regularity of machinery, and so timed that no hurry was noticeable, no noise or clatter of dishes heard, and at the finish of each course it seemed as though, just when you ceased, the next was being placed upon the board. The butler understood every expression of his master's and mistress's countenance; a quiver of the eyelid, and he dispatched his deputy to fill a half-emptied glass. The conversation turned on Madeira wine, and before the first sentence was half finished, I observed the butler dispatch a servant, who returned with a bottle in a twinkling; so that when his master said, "Rollins, I forgot to order some Madeira; perhaps our friends may like it," that worthy immediately responded, "We have some here;" and the squeak of the corkscrew mingled with his unctuous and respectful tones. A glance from the lady, his mistress, and this master of ceremonies proffered a choice bit, or had a change of plates, or proffer of side dishes, or vegetables, or service made with discernment that was wonderful. In fact, as manager of the dinner he was perfection.

After the different courses — which ended with tarts and a species of frozen pudding — had been served, then came the dessert of rich grapes, pineapples, hot-house peaches, and other fruits. These were in turn followed by figs, raisins, dried fruits, and nuts. With the fruits came in the host's boys, little fellows of eleven and thirteen. They had each a wine-glass of claret filled for them, and enjoyed themselves over a bunch of grapes, and such other fruit as they desired. They only spoke when spoken to, and left when the ladies rose to leave the gentlemen at their wine, as is the English custom. This occurred after the dried fruits, &c., had been discussed, when the hostess set the example by rising from her seat. She led the way to the door, which was opened by the butler, and was followed by the other ladies, the gentlemen standing as they passed out, and resuming their seats as the door closed behind them. The table, meantime, had been cleared of the remains of the dessert, a few fresh grapes, dishes of nuts, dry rusk and biscuit, alone remaining. The servants, with the exception of the butler, had retired. That worthy then personally placed fresh glasses where wanted, and set the decanters and bottles of wine before his master, then placed a handbell at his elbow, and in obedience to a nod softly vanished through a door.

There was at this dinner vastly more display than consumption of wine, as both host and guests were alike somewhat abstemious. I give, however, a faithful record of going through the form and fashion of an English dinner, that an idea may be had to what an extent the use of wines and liquors prevails in English families. After the ladies had retired, we sat and pleasantly chatted, the clergyman telling the merriest story of any of the party. Cigars were not introduced. "We'll go up into the billiard-room and smoke, if you like," said the host; but we declined the invitation, and continued our conversation.

At last our host turned out a glass of sherry, and drank from it, and passed the decanter to his right-hand neighbor, and thought, after it had gone round, "We had better join the ladies." I then ascertained that the English fashion — so mine host said, and said he knew not why it was so — was that the last glass of wine before leaving the table was one of sherry.

We found the ladies in the drawing-room, and immediately on our arrival coffee was brought in by a servant. After this we had music from the ladies, an inspection of a portfolio of rare engravings, and a collection of photographs of celebrated places on the continent, and conversation, the clergyman taking his leave about half past nine. At ten P. M., precisely, the butler came in and took a candelabra from one of the tables, and my host, turning to me, observed, "It is always our custom to have family prayer at morning and night. We shall be pleased to have you join us, if so inclined." Of course we were, and proceeding to the dining-hall, found the house-servants assembled there, who, after we were seated, also sat down.

The master of the house then read a chapter from the Bible, after which a prayer from the prayer-book, all kneeling during the latter. At the close, we returned to our drawing-room, and the servants retired. At half past ten we were summoned, ladies and all, to a side-room near the dining-hall, where upon a round table were laid out various compounds, which in England are thought to compose a good "nightcap," but which temperate people look upon as incentives to headaches, if not something worse.

Boiling water in a silver kettle over a spirit lamp was in readiness, to make negus from rare old brandy, or punch from transparent, mountain-dew whiskey, or hot rum punch from the fat-bellied bottles of red Jamaica, or gin toddies from the high-shouldered Dutch bottles of that compound, had we had taste or stomach for them. We were given to understand that we were not expected to retire to bed because of this *finale* to the feast, but that it was always at this hour this course was here served, and each followed out his taste and inclination of stepping in here at this hour, or before retiring, to suit their convenience.

On retiring, maid and man-servant were in attendance at our rooms as before, and we were informed that nine o'clock was the hour for family prayer and breakfast, but that the latter was served to guests in the house any time after that hour till twelve. We chose, however, to be ready at the first-mentioned hour next morning, when, as we entered the breakfast-room, we found the servants standing in line, awaiting us. Prayer was read, after which breakfast was served. By the side of each one's plate were any letters and papers that had come down for them by the early mail from London, and it was quite in order to open and read any letters while breakfast was being brought in, that meal being one at which no ceremony is required, our host appearing in a velvet shooting-jacket, and madam in a morning wrapper and plain collar. Everything at this meal was free and easy as possible, all ceremony dispensed with, a footman and maid performing the service, and those at the table reading aloud an occasional extract from the *Times* as they sipped their coffee, giving a bit of news from a letter, or making plans for amusement and employment during the day.

An English breakfast is a very different affair from the solid, bountiful repast of that name in America. The substantial sirloin or tenderloin steak you seldom see at an English breakfast-table; the nearest approach to it is "chops," and those are considered hearty for breakfast. Those dyspepsia-promoters, the American hot biscuit, are also missing. Neither are there oysters, or fried potatoes, or buckwheat cakes, and rarely a broiled chicken. Indeed, the art of chicken-cooking at all in England is inferior to that practised at our American first-class hotels. Neither is there hot brown bread, or Indian cake, or flapjacks.

Tomatoes, which are dressed and eaten in so many forms in America, and the various styles of serving oysters, seem to be but little known in England. A friend of mine, noticing that there were tomatoes exposed for sale at a green-grocer's, in a country town in England, near the hotel at which he was staying, ordered the landlord to provide some for his dinner, and, in answer to the question as to how he would have them served, replied, raw. Imagine his surprise at finding, when the succulent fruit was served, that the cook had scooped out the entire inside of it, leaving but a thin rind to be eaten!

A still more amusing story is told, of which it is averred that no less an important personage than the late George Peabody, the celebrated American banker, was the hero. It appears that Mr. Peabody had invited three Englishmen to meet two Americans at dinner, and on this occasion, having received as a gift ten ears of green corn, determined to renew the recollections of his youth, astonish his English and please his American guests by having it served up in the well-known American style.

Accordingly, at a proper time, plates of butter and salt were placed before each guest, and the banker, with something of an air of mystery, announced that he was now about to treat his guests to a well-known and delicious American dish of food, cooked in the American manner. It would be no novelty to his American guests, but the Englishmen must watch how it was disposed of by them, and follow their example and manner of disposing of it. Then, at a signal, enter a stately butler bearing a large covered dish, which he deposited solemnly before Mr. Peabody. In a moment more, in obedience to the banker's nod, he whisked off the cover, and there, before the astonished guests, was displayed a pile of *ten boiled corn cobs!*

The banker gazed for an instant in mute horror and dismay, and then found voice to demand an explanation, which was finally reached when the cook was summoned, — a fellow who had never before seen an ear of Indian corn in his life, — who replied that he had followed his master's directions to "strip off all the outside before boiling," which he had done most faithfully, not only husks, as was intended, but kernels also, so that the banker had only what is in America the mute evidence of the feast to indicate what were his good intentions to his guests.

The majority of heavy English diners make a very light breakfast; not but that my host had a profusion, but it was of the English style of breakfast: rashers of English bacon done to a turn; eggs dropped, fried, or boiled, the boiler placed before you on table, with minute-glass attached to regulate cooking to your taste, as no two persons like an egg boiled in the same manner; muffins, fresh, or split and toasted; broiled fish; a species of toasted or roasted herring; Finian haddock; cold meats, tongue, and pickled tongues, two kinds of cold meats, and cold game pies, at the sideboard, from which the servants helped you, or it was in order to rise and help yourself. Bread sweet, white, and close-grained, at least one day old; golden butter, and delicious honey to eat with it; tea or coffee from the silver service, at which madam presided, or a mug of beer from a silver tankard, if you preferred it.

Rising from the breakfast-table, we proceed to one of the drawing-rooms, with its open windows letting in the flower-perfumed breeze from the garden and lawn, and discuss how to amuse ourselves for the forenoon. Shall it be horseback-riding, croquet on the lawn, a jaunt over to the fish-pond and a row upon the water, or a ride in the carriage through the leafy lanes and the pleasant country? We chose the last; and carriages and horses were ordered, which soon appeared with their liveried drivers, and away we bowl over the smooth English road, my host's eldest boy scampering after or riding before us on his sturdy little pony.

Returned from the drive, some went to their rooms to write letters, the host to the library to see a neighbor who had called on some business matter relating to adjoining property, and others to stroll in the garden or beneath the great trees of the park, as inclination called. Lunch was a repetition of that of the day previous; but at dinner we had a larger company — three or four friends of the host, who had been invited to meet us, of which we were apprised at lunch, and also told something about them, their history or position, so that upon introduction in the drawing-room we were not compelled, as is sometimes the case on such occasions, to draw out from the person himself who he is, his profession or occupation, lest some awkward mistake may be made in expression or conversation.

When the carriages of the visitors were announced, at about ten in the evening, we, as guests, had received a kind invitation to spend "a few weeks, or at least a week," at the estates of each of our newly-made friends, which, however, time would not allow. The invitation, however, was none the less genuine and hearty, and, it was even insisted upon by the givers, should hold till we next visited Old England.

When the time came for leaving this elegant and hospitable home, the servants insisted upon packing, and did pack, our luggage, and more neatly than we could have done it; and when, informed that the carriage would be at the door in ten minutes, we went to our rooms, there were footman and maid with articles of wardrobe to be worn for the journey; and our trunks had been sent forward in a spring-cart. Of course footman and maid pocket the half guinea each, with bow and smile, that was slipped into their hands; and the eminent butler, who *accidentally* met me on the way down, and whose palm was similarly crossed, — for I had learned enough of English custom for that, — wished us a pleasant journey.

The footman held open the door of the landaulet, we stepped in, having first taken leave of our kind entertainers, when a servant appeared with salver and glasses for "a stirrup cup at parting," and then we rattled down the winding avenue, and away for the railway station. Arrived there, wraps, hand-luggage, &c., were carried to the waiting-room by the footman, our trunk pointed out, where it had been placed on arrival, tickets procured by the same active servitor, who gratefully received five shillings for himself and five for the coachman, and, touching his hat, wished us a pleasant ride to London, leaped to his place on the box, and was bowled away with the driver.

I have gone through somewhat in detail this account of a three-days' visit to the home of an English gentleman, in answer to numerous inquiries as to how the English gentlemen live at home, and the assertion that few except the novel-writer attempt any description, and that such description must necessarily be like the novel — not to be depended on as a truthful account.

It will be seen that, with some trifling differences, the life at an English gentleman's country-seat is very similar to that of our own men of wealth. To be sure, the American gentleman, as a general thing, would not permit his guests to fee his servants, and indeed many English gentlemen will not permit it. Whether my host was one of the latter class I never ascertained; but, it being a first experience, I determined that his servants should not have occasion to give Americans a bad name, and hence took the safe side. Feeing is so universal in England, and it seems to be so expected by any official who does you the smallest service, that your hand almost gets the habit of seeking your pocket whenever you ask a question that requires an answer conveying information.

The consumption of wines and liquors, as is well known, is enormous in England, and wine is used freely and liberally at the dinner-table, a well-stocked cellar being one of the first requisites of a well-ordered establishment.

One thing that charms American visitors, especially ladies from the northern states, who have been tormented almost out of their senses by the Irish peasants who pretend to serve them as servants at home, is the admirable service in these English families. All appears to move without a jar; the servants, to use an American expression, "run the house," and strive to anticipate a want and execute a wish before an order is given. Then, again, each one seems to know his position and to understand its duties thoroughly, and to take a pride in executing them properly. It seemed, while we were making the three-days' visit above described, that invisible servants watched us from behind concealed panels, and sprang out at the slightest possible provocation.

Did we leave our rooms but for fifteen minutes, everything misplaced was put in order again, a soiled towel replaced by a fresh one, or a garment dropped to the floor taken up, and everything set to rights.

It should of course be borne in mind that the servants in a family like this belong to it, as it were, and may be said to be part of the establishment, filling, perhaps, positions once occupied by their fathers or mothers, or other relatives, who may have served the father and mother of the present proprietor, and were, moreover, of the same nationality and religion as their employers. Then, comparatively few Americans are sufficiently wealthy, and others are too democratic, to support such a retinue of menials about them; or, as an American lady remarked, it is next to impossible to get, for any amount of money, eight or ten, or even four, servants in America that will live in any family a year in peace together.

CHAPTER V.

We often read in English stories or novels that one of the characters had "just time to catch the express train" for some place. This "catching a train," it should be understood by the American reader, is a very different affair from the catching of it in his own country, for it signifies that the individual had sufficient time to reach and enter the railway carriage just before the guard had closed the doors and given the signal to start. After that had been done, no matter who arrived, he was too late.

In America, however, if by dint of a smart run the belated passenger is enabled to reach the hand-rail of the last car of the rapidly receding train, as it is leaving the station, and is hauled on board minus his hat or a part of his coat, perhaps helped by railway baggage-masters to "catch the train," he is congratulated by the conductor on his skill in "jest savin' it," instead of being fined and reprimanded for thus risking his life. Indeed, the average American so thoroughly believes in taking the responsibility, that he resents the erection of gates, now being generally introduced in our great cities, separating the track from the withdrawing or waiting rooms, at railroad stations, or any interference with his getting on or off a train in motion, with the idea, perhaps, that no person in this land of liberty has any right to restrain him even from putting his life in jeopardy if he himself elects to do so.

The laws against getting on or off moving railway trains in England are very strict, and also in guarding the tracks at the stations and their vicinity, and are not to be infringed upon or broken with impunity, as an American friend of the author recently found to his sorrow.

He chanced to be on a train going to London, and had written to have his luggage from a certain point sent to meet him, to be put on board the train at an intermediate station. Arrived at the latter place, where the train stopped a few moments, he leaped from the railway carriage, leaving his wife and friends, while he sought for his luggage to place on the train; but in vain. Meanwhile the time for starting arrived, yet still he tarried, thinking to jump on at the last moment, American fashion, and started to do so, but was restrained by an official.

"But I must go on this train; my wife's aboard," said the anxious American.

"Can't help it, sir; train's in motion; against regulations."

"But *you* are going," said the traveller, as he marked the long train gradually moving, car after car, past them, and the official preparing to take his place.

"Certainly; I'm the guard — last man on. I take the van. Stand back!"

So saying, the guard, or, as we call him, the conductor, pushed back the American and leaped to his place on the step of the guard's van, or last carriage in the train.

Quick as he was, the American was equal to him, for with two or three bounds, despite the cries and rush of the porters, he leaped after the guard, clung to him on the step of the carriage, and both were whirled out of the station in that manner, after which they tumbled into the compartment of the guard together. That official was white with rage.

"I told you that you could not get upon the train when it was in motion."

"Ah! but you see I did."

"Do you know that we both narrowly missed being hit by that iron crane as the train went out of the station?"

"A miss, my good fellow, is as good as a mile."

"And you have broken the regulations, and made me and yourself liable to prosecution."

"O, fudge! The company won't take the trouble to prosecute, I guess," said the Yankee. But this time his national guess was incorrect.

The train was an express, and he rode in the guard's van more than fifty miles before another stop enabled him to rejoin his party in the other carriage and continue his journey to London, during which the matter passed from his mind.

Arrived at the station in London, our American secured a four-wheeler, selected his luggage, had it placed on the roof of the vehicle, bestowed wife and party inside, and was about following, when he was tapped on the shoulder by a quiet, plainly-dressed individual, who remarked,—

"Sorry to detain you, really; very unpleasant duty; but you are wanted on charge of assaulting the guard in the discharge of his duty as the train left Leamington."

Here the official displayed a paper and his credentials, leaving no doubt he was one of those "policemen in plain clothes" whom Dickens and the English story-tellers write about.

Here was a dilemma. A stranger in London, after dark, arrested! What should he do? He at once explained. He was an American tourist; was not aware of the law. His wife and he both strangers. "Hadn't even been to their hotel yet. Couldn't it be arranged in the morning?"

"O, certainly, if he would kindly give his card," the official would call at his hotel at eleven to-morrow.

No sooner said than done. The American whipped out his card-case, handed over the bit of pasteboard to the officer, who glanced at it, nodded to the cab-driver, who closed the door of the vehicle, and the party were soon rattling over the London pavements. As they whirled along, the first view of London by gaslight was forgotten in the explanation of the affair by the American to his wife. "But it is all over now, I guess," said he, "for, although I gave the fellow my name, I didn't give him my address, and he won't know where to come to-morrow, after all."

Here again was a mistaken guess, for a second thought might have informed him that the number of every cab admitted in the railway station was known; that he had given his direction to the driver before being accosted by the officer, and thereby the latter had obtained his address; and that, if the case had been of sufficient importance, the cab could easily have been followed by another, even if the driver had not been instructed to notify the officer where he left his fare.

However, our tourist, feeling somewhat uneasy, related the affair to an English friend, whom he met on arrival at the hotel, who did not relieve his anxiety by looking grave, shaking his head, and remarking they had best both go to the railway manager's office next morning. This they did, and, through the intervention of a personal friend of one of the directors, after apologies and explanations, the American departed, glad to have got rid, as he supposed, of this unpleasantness.

About five days after, having meantime changed his hotel, our American citizen had business down in the City, after transacting which he had agreed to meet his wife and a friend at Westminster Hall, to view that noted building. Standing near the entrance, and awaiting her coming, he was astonished to observe her to be accompanied by two gentlemen instead of one. The second was introduced as a person who had called at the hotel to see the American on private business. He was a respectable-looking individual of about fifty years of age, dressed in a pepper-and-salt suit, and, stepping aside, presented to the tourist his card, which bore the inscription, "Mr. John Lund, Chief of Police, Leamington."

He was very polite; was very sorry he had a disagreeable duty to perform; and he drew out a formidable-looking document, with a prodigious formula of English expression, and several staring seals, which cited the offence our traveller had committed upon one of her Majesty's servants, and summoned the offender to appear on the following Wednesday (it was then Saturday) at "the aforesaid" Leamington.

"I was coming up to London myself," said the official, apologetically, "and thought I would serve this, to make it as comfortable as possible."

It was useless for the American to state that the matter had all been settled by the railway manager; of this the polite chief of police knew nothing. The first arrest was probably at the instance of the officials of the railway company in London; but this was by the police authorities of Leamington, of which he was chief. The official would not be satisfied except by a visit of the American and responsible friend again to the manager's office at the London station, where it was arranged that the traveller would appear and answer on the following week, if the affair was not settled before; and the polite chief of the Leamington police took his departure.

However, the visit to Westminster Hall was given up for that day, and the American began to wish he never had jumped upon that railroad train. Supposing all right now, however, he forgot all about it again, until it was unpleasantly brought to mind on the following Sunday by a note sent him by private hand, from his friend, to a place where he was spending the day.

This note informed him that the affair had quite a serious look; that the general managers at Leamington had been mulcted for damages for an accident that occurred at that point a few months since; and that his jumping upon the train had been witnessed by two of the principal directors, as well as by one of the local police, and it was determined to punish any such criminal recklessness, hence the summons, &c. This the London railway official had by his personal influence succeeded in postponing for a few days, but an expense of three pounds ten shillings had been incurred, and perhaps it would be best to arrange that before Mr. John Lund or another official came up to London again.

Our American was now getting nervous and scared. He at once saw his English friend in London, and proceeded to "arrange" the matter as was suggested. Then, returning to his hotel, he ordered a cab to take himself and luggage to a railway station, bidding the landlord good-by as if going to Scotland. After being landed at the railway station, and after having discharged the cabman, he took another cab, and drove to a new hotel, in the hope that by this means Mr. John Lund might be dodged until he departed for Paris, which seems to have been successfully done; but the reason therefor was explained in the following letter sent to him by his friend, who had arranged matters, and who received it from the railway authorities.

"I think I have arranged matters for the withdrawal of the summons. The expenses incurred amount to three pounds ten shillings. If your American friend pays this, and at the same time wishes to benefit the Widow and Orphans' Fund Association of the railway line, a check for five pounds in full will be received."

It is almost unnecessary to state that the American's English friend did the needful instanter, and the American himself breathed freer accordingly, although it had cost him twenty-five dollars for jumping upon an English train in motion.

7

CHAPTER VI.

LONDON, according to the Registrar-General, covers an area of one hundred and twenty-two square miles, although it is described as thirty miles in circumference. To the newly-arrived American, London appears to be an aggregation of cities, a collection of interminable streets, with houses and public buildings rather dingy of aspect, and lacking that " smart," bright, and fresh appearance which characterizes American cities.

I might expend a volume of description and a year of time in prying about into curious old courts, streets celebrated in history, beginning with the old Watling Street of the Anglo-Saxons, and where in more modern Roman times was the centre of Roman Londinum; or into old mansions where kings, princes, and warriors have met, or scholars have studied; or on spots where fierce contests and bloody disputes have decided for the time the course of the rulers of the present foremost nation of the world. All about us in the old city are monuments of the past; even the commonest names upon the street signboards are indices to a page of history.

But "What is there new?" asked an American one morning, as we discussed our " chops and muffins." " Let us see the newest sights to-day;" and so it came to pass that we called a trim Hansom cab for a drive from the West End to the Bethnal Green Museum, or rather we should say to the Bethnal Green branch of the South Kensington Museum. Now this is a long ride, and a genuine Londoner would first have taken a 'bus on Oxford Street, ridden down to the Bank (fourpence), then another 'bus or the " underground," and another sixpence would have carried him to the desired point. But one of the best vehicles to see London in is a Hansom cab, and when two persons sight-seeing can engage such a vehicle, with a bright, well-posted driver, as we were able to, at one shilling and sixpence an hour, what American would hesitate? Accordingly, on our trip to Bethnal Green, or Bednal Green, celebrated in the old ballad of the Blind Beggar of Bednal Green, we determined to see as much as possible of London streets *en route.*

So away we dashed down through Oxford Street, with its shops and crowds of people, whirling carriages, and rattling omnibuses, till we debouched into Holborn, — " High Holborn," the Holborn Hill of old London; but scarce any one mentions it except as " Holborn," or " 'Oburn," now, for instead of the descent of the hill, a broad viaduct now gives a level grade for us to rattle over at a smart pace, and look downwards towards the old Fleetditch (was there ever such a place?) off towards Smithfield, or down at a terminus of that wonderful hole in the ground, the London Underground Railway.

Just before arriving at this great viaduct, we have passed the Holborn Bars, the position of which is marked by an inscription painted upon an old building, at which a toll is levied on " vehicles not belonging to freemen," entering the city. Only think of it, — " entering the city," — the country from which the strangers used to come, the great city has long since overflowed, and from these Holborn Bars you may now ride back into what was then the country for miles and miles, and not begin to be out of the city, or free from its endless succession of shops, streets, and houses.

Away we rattle and leave Holborn behind us; the throngs are denser, the vehicles innumerable, and the confusion greater, till we are down into the actual " City," as the Londoner calls it, in the very thick of London business. Cheapside and Poultry, near Newgate Street, and little narrow Paternoster Row, the place noted of the publishing-houses, past an end view of the great general post-office, amid the thunder and crush of all sorts of vehicles; past Milk Street, where Sir Thomas More was born, and little narrow Bread Street, opposite where the poet Milton first saw the light, and in which was the old tavern where Shakspeare, Raleigh, Beaumont, Fletcher, and Ben Jonson used to meet — the Mermaid.

There are historic events enough that are strung along Cheapside to make a catalogue of enumerations; and one thing you, as a stranger, like to hear in this vicinity, if you are near enough to Bow Church, as you have to be, owing to the noise, is the sound of Bow bells, and to see if by any effort of your modern imagination their chime can be converted into the ancient couplet they are said to have sung to Dick Whittington.

Here runs into the end of Cheapside, or the Poultry, as it is called from its hundreds-of-years ago poultry-market, "Old Jewry," of course once the quarters of the Jews, that the old Norman kings used to amuse themselves with hacking and burning, squeezing money from, and abusing, and all under the name of Religion. Many have been the attacks of popular fury directed upon this quarter, and the history of the Hebrews in London in past years, as elsewhere, is one of shameful wrong and persecution. There is very little of a Jewish character about the street now, except its name, and if you search history you will have to go back into the foggy, misty accounts of six hundred years ago to find when the Hebrews held possession of and gave the locality its name, when the first synagogue of the Jews stood there in 1264. If one wishes to see the Jews of to-day in London, let him take a walk through Holiwell Street, or Hounsditch.

But near the corner of old Jewry Street and Cheapside, or between it and a narrow lane called Ironmongers' Lane, stands a building called the Mercers' Company's Hall, and we halted to pay it a visit, for here is where stood the house of the father of Thomas à Becket, and is where that celebrated prelate is said to have been born.

These Mercers, and Fishmongers, Barber-surgeons, Grocers, Goldsmiths, &c., were the guilds or trades-unions of their time, and there used to be over a hundred of them, all with certain rights and privileges, and those which remain having halls, records, and histories preserved, are in themselves a rich mine of antiquarian lore. Some of these bear names of trades the very existence of which has passed away and is now forgotten, as, for instance, "bowyers," makers of bows, and "loriners," the latter name of which a *tailor* who served me had inscribed on his card with something of a flourish, showing that he was a member of that illustrious society. And loriner was the ancient name for harness and bridle-makers.

Thirty or forty of these city societies have halls; some are very rich, and the members in no way whatever connected with the trades which the name of the society represents. In fact, I think there is only one now, "The Stationers," that requires that its members shall be members of its trade. The members of others have the management of trust funds left for schools, hospitals, or homes for decayed members of the craft, which institutions are still in existence, and excellent charitable institutions.

In these old halls, several of which I visited, are many curious old records and relics which the custodian in charge, who is generally a garrulous old fellow, with the legends and stories of the society at his tongue's end, will, if it be set in motion by the magic of half a crown, rattle off curious old legends in the dim, dreamy, half-darkened halls to you, as he points to an age-blackened picture of some royal patron of the society, permits you to sit in the great, carved, uncomfortable arm-chair that has been the seat of a long line of departed presidents of the club, or lifts reverently from its case the silver loving-cup from which, for three centuries past, members have sipped their spiced potations. And it must be confessed that the present members of these city companies are much given to good eating and drinking at their quarterly or annual meetings, when they come together to give an account of the present management of the funds which the old founders left for the support of needy members, almshouses, or other charitable trusts above referred to.

This Mercers' Hall on Cheapside was one of the most celebrated of those of the city companies, and the society boasted sovereigns on its list of members — Richard II., who granted its first charter. Queen Elizabeth was an honorary member; also Sir Thomas Gresham, Caxton, and Whittington. A fine old picture of Gresham, a cup from which Whittington, perhaps, has sipped his punch, and specimens of fine old plate of the sixteenth century, are among the treasures of the Mercers.

And here it was, just back of this hall stood the house of Gilbert à Becket. Here it was, so the romantic story runs, that the Saracen maiden, an emir's daughter, whose heart he had won when a prisoner in the East during the crusades, found him after many wanderings. The faithfulness of her attachment is told in old English story and ballad, which describes her adventures in coming from her native land to England alone, and knowing but two words of the language, "London" and "Gilbert;" she sought her Christian lover, reached London, and at last, after tiresome wanderings from street to street, repeating the name of Gilbert, and winning all hearts by her beauty and modesty, had the satisfaction of finding him, and, what was better, finding him faithful and true; for he at once took her to his heart, presented her to his friends as his betrothed, and, after being baptized in the Christian faith, she became the bride of him she had so truly loved and faithfully sought.

Here is an extract from the ballad that the tourist may prime his imagination with when he halts at, as we did in the last chapter, or passes Becket's birthplace, near the corner of "Old Jewry," or bring to mind when he visits Canterbury Cathedral, and follows the course said to have been taken by the "turbulent priest" (as King Henry II. called him) when pursued by the avenging knights to the place where his brains spattered on the stone pavement beneath the fierce blow of Richard le Bret; the child of the English merchant and Saracen mother becoming one of the most celebrated martyrs in English history.

> " It was a merchant, a merchant of fame,
> And he sailed to the Holy Land;
> Gilbert à Becket was his name;
> And he went to trade with the Syrians rich,
> For velvets and satins and jewels, which
> He might sell on the western strand.
>
> " It was there he met with a Saracen maid,
> Of virtue and beauty rare;
> And behold, our merchant forgot his trade,
> His English habits aside he flung,
> And he learned to speak with a Saracen tongue,
> For the sake of that damsel fair.
>
> " They plighted their faith, and they vowed to wed,
> If Gilbert should e'er be free;
> How could she doubt a word he said?
> For her heart was trustful, pure, and mild,
> Like the heart of a young, unfearing child,
> And she loved him hopefully."

The merchant and fair Saracen planned an escape, but the latter was discovered, and the Englishman fled alone. The maiden escaped from her jailers, however, and some English sailors, pitying her beseeching tones of " London," which was the only word she uttered, gave her passage. When arrived at the strange city —

> " Through all that maze of square and street,
> With pleading looks she went;
> And still her weary voice was sweet,
> But now was " Gilbert " the name she cried;
> And the world of London is very wide,
> And they knew not whom she meant.
>
> " Now Gilbert à Becket was dwelling there,
> Like a merchant-prince was he;

> His gardens were wide and his halls were fair,
> His servants flattered, his minstrels played,
> He had almost forgotten his Saracen maid,
> And their parting beyond the sea."

But word was brought him, as he sat at the banquet board, of a beautiful Saracen, who wandered through square and street, murmuring "Gilbert" to all she met, and, as the ballad goes, "his conscience pricked him sore." He sought the wanderer out, found that it was indeed his Saracen maid —

> "And now there is nothing can part, save death,
> The bridegroom and the bride."

> "Their first-born son was a priest of power,
> Who ruled on English ground;
> His fame remaineth to this hour!
> God send to every valiant knight
> A lady as true, and a home as bright,
> As Gilbert, the merchant, found."

But the Hansom cannot stop here long in the rush of travel, so we rattle on amid the throng, on in between the Bank of England and the Royal Exchange into Threadneedle Street. Boys selling penny boxes of matches, uniformed shoeblacks at the corners, hawkers and street pedlers of everything, porters in a sort of uniform apron, and wearing a brass ticket or medal of office, cabs coming, going, halting, twisting and turning; omnibuses at this, the terminus of their route, discharging and reloading; snug broughams of rich old capitalists leaving or receiving their owners; hurrying clerks with pen behind ear and slip of paper in hand, policemen, letter-carriers in uniform with sacks over their shoulders, the important beadle at the entrance of the bank, stationery stores crammed with every article used in counting-house work, — all proclaim we are in the business centre of the great commercial capital of the world, directly opposite the entrance to the Bank of England, spreading its wings over eight acres of ground, keeping a thousand clerks at work, who have over six millions and a half dollars of the public and about one hundred and forty millions of private funds paid in every week, and who have to keep the accounts of over two hundred and forty thousand persons holding the national debt.

But we will not go over the old story of the Bank, so familiar to all, but let our driver, with his skill of twisting and turning, wind his Hansom in and out of the crowd till we are past Merchant Tailors' Hall, through narrow Threadneedle, and rolling along Bishopsgate Street, another old street, named from the old city gates, built in 680; "Bishopsgate within," and "Bishopsgate without," names used to this day, meaning that part of the city that was within the walls and without them. This used to be an aristocratic street about the year 1500, and there are some antiquated old piles here that look as if they belonged to about that period; but past them we rattle, past an endless, never-ceasing string of stores of every description, *en route* to Bethnal Green, where the "Blind Beggar" sat, whose fair daughter, as the ballad runs, was married to a knight, and at the betrothal, in a money-dropping match with some of the sneering gallants of the time, the apparent beggar surprising them by dropping a heap of gold pieces, double the size of that of his pretentious reviler, and finally declared and proved himself and daughter to be of noble birth, winding up the story in the usual approved style of a happy marriage.

We ride from Bishopsgate Street to Shoreditch, and are evidently in a cheap neighborhood, and one especially where bootmakers seem to congregate. Cheap John stores, greengrocers, fish-stalls, and a preponderance of small spirit stores, and children coming out from outlying alleys, are symptoms of a poor neighborhood; yet this, years ago, was a goodly city quarter, this east end of the town. Here, just before us, rises a church-steeple, St. Leonard's Church, in whose burial-ground sleep Burbage, the celebrated actor of Shakspeare's plays, and his associate, Will Somers, the noted jester of King Henry the Eighth, and Richard Tarleton, the clown of Shakspeare's plays in Queen Elizabeth's time, besides Cowley and William Sly, original actors in the great poet's plays.

The cab-driver, it seems, has heard of Will Somers, but the others are names unknown to him. "Never 'eard of 'em, sir; but Will Somers, you see, was a funny fellow who used, they say, to make the king laugh when he felt dull."

The Hansom turned into Church Street, and brought up opposite a fine open square, in which stood the object of our search. Bethnal Green Museum, at the East End of London, five miles from Charing Cross — a five-mile cab-ride — and still we were in a densely populated district. This Museum was placed here as a branch of the South Kensington Museum, which is in a more aristocratic quarter, in order that one of the poorest districts of London might have a means of free recreation, although I must confess, from the character of the collection, it seemed to me that the proper enjoyment of it must be far beyond the average comprehension of the poorer class, who would fail to see in many of the rare articles of virtu, antiquity, and bijouterie, anything but faded gilding or old trumpery. Let me not judge too harshly, however, for the open-mouthed wonder and the undisguised gaze of rapture of a rough group before Murillo's paintings and Landseer's almost living animals, proved their enjoyment of genuine art, and were mute evidence of the power of the artists.

This museum building is of dark-red brick, the front with three arches, and the sides two and a half stories high, looking like a very respectable railroad station. In the great open space of the grounds which surround it, and in front of the principal entrance, is an elegant fountain, made entirely of majolica ware, and consisting of vases, cups, and figures, from which the spouting streams of water rise in graceful jets, the whole being surmounted by the figure of St. George and the Dragon. The space in which this museum is built is one end of a great open plot that was bought as a gift to the poor in the reign of James the First, when this part of London, now a densely populated manufacturing district, was an open field.

This move to afford entertainment and instruction to the working classes, it should be understood, is supported and carried out by the government, although the collection on exhibition, when the author visited the building, was that of a private individual, Sir Richard Wallace, and occupied nearly the whole available space of the museum. It consisted of pictures and works of art of the rarest and most curious description.

The design of this museum, like its parent the South Kensington, is to afford instruction as well as entertainment, and that there should be exhibited an Animal Products Collection intended to illustrate the various applications of animal substances to industrial purposes; a food collection of the different kinds of grain from different countries, and all kinds of food such as could be exhibited, and methods of their preparation, — a most interesting part of the exhibition. Then there are woods and the different methods of working them, metals, &c., all of which will, when the design is carried out, form a grand trade museum, which here at the East End of the town cannot fail of being of great value to the mass of artisans who live in this vicinity.

On Mondays, Tuesdays, and Saturdays the museum is opened free from 10 A. M. to 10 P. M. Wednesdays, Thursdays, and Fridays are designated as students' days, and on those days sixpence admission is charged, although tickets are issued available both for this museum and for the South Kensington one at, weekly for sixpence, monthly one shilling sixpence, and quarterly three shillings. Yearly tickets for students' days are issued to any school at one pound, which will admit *all the pupils* of such school on all students' days for a year, — liberal arrangements enough to suit all who desire to go on other than the free days.

The site for this museum was purchased by money subscribed by noblemen and other wealthy people, and presented to the government in fee simple for the purpose of having a museum erected thereon, the government taking the whole matter then into its hands as a national affair. The committee making this offer submitted that the museum should be made educational in the widest sense of the word, and that convenient and comfortable refreshment rooms be added to the other attractions of the place.

The basement of the building, which contains several well-arranged, well-lighted rooms, has therefore a large space devoted to a restaurant, and the other rooms were used for library rooms, and for school-rooms, for instruction in drawing, engineering, designing, and other branches of science and art. The interior arrangement of this museum above the basement floor is simple and convenient for the purposes for which it was designed. It consists of a large hall, around which runs a double gallery; the first gallery is raised but a few feet above the main floor, and is about a dozen feet in height, and that above it, which is reached by staircases in the middle, is of much greater height, reaching to the light-arched roof, with its graceful iron frame; all the supports, balcony and railings inside the building are of iron; and light, admitted from the arched roof, and also at the sides of the galleries, is artistically managed. The galleries are very wide, sufficiently so for a row of large glass cases of six feet in width, or screens for pictures, and yet leave abundance of room for locomotion. The chief attraction, when the author visited this museum, was the magnificent collection known as the Hertford Collection of Art Objects, which filled the whole available space of the museum, except that portion of the lower galleries occupied by the food and animal product collections. It seems hardly possible that even the chance or thoughtless visitor can walk through this or the parent museum, and question the practical utility of such institutions with the people.

CHAPTER VII.

Two of the more modern wonders of London, and two of which too little has been said, and that travellers should not fail to visit, are but a short distance from the Kensington Museum, which I have recently referred to so frequently, — the Royal Albert Hall of Arts, and the Prince Consort Memorial or Monument. The Royal Albert Hall is a magnificent building, elegant in proportions, perfect for the purposes for which it was designed, and the noble proportions and conveniences of which cannot fail to excite the admiration of the visitor.

This great hall, which is designed for public meetings, musical entertainments, meetings of science and art, exhibitions, concerts, &c., is situated in Hyde Park, directly in front of the elegant Horticultural Gardens, and between the Cromwell and Kensington road. Directly opposite is the most magnificent modern monument in the world, — the Albert Memorial, — and near by the Kensington Palace and the Kensington Gardens, rich in their beautiful old trees and fine vista of view, making this one of the most pleasant and attractive spots in London. If Prince Albert had left nothing else by which he might be remembered, the design of this noble building, which he himself suggested, would be sufficient to perpetuate his name. Externally it presents the appearance of a vast circular building of brick, with high, narrow windows, above which was a broad band of colored mosaic work representing the peoples of all nations, other simple but effective ornamentations in the trimmings being properly placed.

The building really consists of two concentric circles or brick walls. Between these is a wide space in which are the staircases, lobbies, ante-rooms, elevators, &c., and in the lower portion of which, in 1873, was disposed a portion of the annual display of the International Exhibition, with the buildings of which the hall was easily connected by a covered passage and walk through the Horticultural Gardens. These corridors, or space between the walls, are admirably arranged, so that all noise or movement therein is entirely shut off from the audience within. But step within, and you have a view reminding you of what the form of Rome's Colosseum would be restored, only somewhat reduced, though by no means of insignificant proportions for these modern days.

A vast, perfect circus, with the seats rising one above the other, and the graceful curve of beauty greeting the eye at every turn, meets the view. The great arena seats a thousand persons easily and comfortably; an amphitheatre fifteen hundred. Midway rises a girdle of two tiers of boxes, which take in eleven hundred more, then circles round a graceful balcony, in which twenty-five hundred more may look upon the scene, and above circles a gallery where two thousand more may comfortably be accommodated. One hardly realizes the vastness of the building at first sight, so perfect are the curves, and so much is taken in at one sweep of the vision. At one end is situated the grand organ and the orchestra, in which space is afforded for two thousand performers; so that the seating capacity of this grand modern circus is fully eight thousand; and I have no doubt that nearly ten thousand could easily be accommodated within its walls. In fact, that is the number reported to have been present at the Masonic ceremonies which took place there, by which the Prince of Wales was created Grand Master of the order.

The dome of the building is entirely of glass, but a novel and pleasing effect is obtained by the suspension of a sort of tent beneath, — an idea borrowed perhaps from the *velarium* which shielded the audience in the Roman Colosseum, and which softens the glare of light, and imparts a certain air of grace and coolness to the space.

The dimensions given are: the greatest width, two hundred feet; length, one hundred and sixty feet; and height, from arena to dome, one hundred and forty feet. The dome is formed of huge iron ribs resting in an iron ring. The cost of this splendid building was over two hundred thousand pounds.

The *coup d'œil* from the front of the arena, when it is filled with spectators, is magnificent in the extreme; and the great organ, which some of the local guide-books aver to be the finest in the world, may be so, but it certainly was not played as well as that of Lucerne or Freyburg. The one thing that will strike the visitor who has opportunity to examine this building by daylight, as I did, is its many conveniences and improvements over ordinary exhibition-halls or concert-rooms. The chairs in the arena are roomy and comfortable, the boxes are commodious and well fitted, the spacious corridors I have before alluded to afford ample space for promenade; then there are refreshment-rooms, retiring-rooms, and in wings of the main building are a promenade-room, restaurant, and small concert-room, steam-engines which heat the building, run the elevator, blow the big organ, and keep ventilating-fans in motion that regulate the temperature of the hall. There are abundant doors for ingress and egress, and in fact the architects and builders seem to have been successful in remembering many minor points that are too frequently forgotten, but which conduce much to the comfort of a large audience.

The sumptuous and costly monument to Prince Albert, opposite the Albert Hall, would very naturally make one wonder what mighty warrior, great statesman, savior of his country, or public benefactor it was erected to commemorate, although perhaps it may be said no monument is too grand for a true and honest man. But when we consider what England and the whole civilized world owes to many of her sons who have scarcely memorial stone to mark their last resting-place, we look with some surprise at this *national* monument, erected to one not born on her soil, whose chief notoriety was that he was husband to the queen of England, and who, without being a man of any especial genius or great force of character, was noted chiefly for a blameless life, and as an upright man and exemplary husband.

The Prince also always had an ambition for forwarding all schemes which should tend to promote science and art, improve the condition of the humbler classes, and advance the cause of education. It was largely through his exertions that the South Kensington Museum, and similar free exhibitions and schools of art, were provided for the people. The English appreciated him as a true man, the queen loved him as a faithful and devoted husband, and it was her desire that this monument should be a national memento, as well as a work of great artistic beauty, to commemorate a blameless life, as worthy of imitation as great military deeds. And so here rises to-day the costliest and most elegant monumental structure of modern times, erected by the English people to a German prince.

The foundation for this splendid monument to rest upon is a lofty and square pyramid of handsomely chiselled granite steps, the length being nearly two hundred feet each side. The landings and platform of this grand staircase are paved with stone of various colors, taken from different quarries in England. After ascending this splendid flight of steps, the visitor arrives at the grand platform, laid in colored stone, as above described. His further progress is stopped by a massive and elegantly wrought bronzed or gilt railing, which surrounds other steps leading to the immediate base of the monument.

At the angles of the upper square, formed by the bronzed railing, as at the four corners of this pyramid of steps, are four remarkable and elegant groups of statuary, carved from that hard Italian marble known as "campanella," from the bell-like sound it emits when struck. Each of these groups is upon a huge pedestal, and weighs from twenty-five to thirty tons. They are colossal figures, allegorically representing the four quarters of the globe. That known as Europe is the work of Patrick McDowell, R. A., and consists of five female figures. Europe is represented by a female figure seated upon a bull; she wears a crown, and bears the sceptre in one hand and globe in the other. She is surrounded by four other female figures, in sitting postures. The figure of England is easily recognized, with the waves beating up against the base of the rock upon which she sits, bearing in her right hand a trident, and at her left the shield with the blended crosses of St. George and St. Andrew, her sculptured brow and features wearing an impress of conscious power and noble dignity. Italy sits on a broken column, with head slightly raised and hand uplifted, while the lyre and pallet at her feet are symbolical of music and painting,—a classical and beautiful figure. France is represented as a military power, a figure of determined mien, the right hand resting upon the hilt of a sword, while the left grasps the wreath of laurel. Germany is represented by an allegorical figure with studious and thoughtful brow, as she sits with open volume upon her knees.

Round this beautiful group of statuary in all its fair proportions I walked, and then turned to one of an entirely different character, but strikingly effective,—that of Asia, at another angle of the square. This is also typified by five human figures and an animal. Upon the back of an admirably sculptured kneeling elephant, apparently just about to rise, is seated an exceedingly beautiful semi-nude figure of an Asiatic woman, in the act of removing her veil. By the side of the elephant, with one hand resting upon him, stands a Persian, with calm, thoughtful brow, long beard, high, conical cap, graceful, drooping robe, and shawl-twined waist, the fringe and pattern all finely wrought by the artist's chisel, a pen in the fingers of one hand, and writing-case by his side. Then we have a sculptured representation of a seated Chinaman bearing in his arms a vase, while another specimen of that handiwork is by his side. Beyond him stands the Indian warrior, with his shield, cimeter, and barbaric weapons and costume, while near the Persian figure sits an Arab, true son of the desert, leaning against a camel-saddle as if just dismounted. The draperies in this group, which, as may be imagined, contribute largely to the effectiveness of the figures, have been admirably managed, especially in the female figure throwing aside the veil; and the costumes of the Arab merchant and Persian are very gracefully disposed. The sculptor, John Henry Foley, has achieved an ease and grace in grouping his work, and in the management of fine, continuous outline, that charm the eye of the spectator at almost any point from which the group is viewed.

Next comes Africa, wrought by William Theed. This also is a strikingly effective group, and executed with wonderful attention to details. A kneeling camel, fully caparisoned with barbaric harness,— a faithfully correct representation of the animal,— bears upon his back an Egyptian princess, with necklace, head-dress, and sceptre, Egyptian in fashion; her right hand rests upon a naked Nubian, who stands, staff in hand, by her side, and his hand resting upon a half sand-covered ancient monument. Upon the other side is seated an admirably sculptured figure of an old Moorish merchant of the Barbary States; his striped robe, bale of goods, wreathed turban, pipe, and the cimeter at his feet, all indicating the Moorish trader. To the rear stands, leaning upon his bow, a negro, with the shackles of slavery broken at his feet, listening to instruction from the genius of civilization.

Next comes the group typifying our own country, America. This is represented by what I consider to be the finest conception, if not the best executed, of the four groups, and have since learned this opinion was not entirely influenced by national pride, as it is also held by many well-informed English critics.

The group is exceedingly bold, vigorous, and full of life, aptly characterizing the progress, vigor, and power of our nation. The principal figure is that of a female representing the New World, seated upon the back of a buffalo rushing through the long grass of the prairie ; her brow is grand, her gaze forward ; in her right hand she bears a spear, and upon her left arm hangs a shield, upon which is emblazoned the eagle of America, the beaver of Canada, and other emblems. Upon one side of the buffalo, with hand outstretched as if directing his course, stands the female figure representing the United States. A starry baldric extends from right shoulder to waist, and an eagle's plume is thrust in the band about her brow, upon the front of which is a star, and another blazes at the point of her sceptre. Upon the other side stands, with face turned towards the United States, Canada, — a figure in furs and in a head-dress of leaves ; and at her feet are sculptured ears of wheat and a pair of snow-shoes, while at the feet of the United States is seen the almost emptied Indian quiver, and, disturbed by the tramp of the buffalo, the figure of a rattlesnake is stealing away through the long grass.

A seated figure with head-dress of feathers and carved staff, feather belt, and panther-skin robe, is designed to represent Mexico. South America is represented by an elegantly executed figure, a sort of cross between a ranchero and prairie hunter. His broad sombrero, carbine, lariat, and Mexican costume, however, show him to be designed by the artist for the half-breed Indian and Spaniard of farther South, still further indicated by the cattle-horn and South American lily at his feet.

All the figures in this group seem instinct with life, the **expression of the faces is superbly rendered, and the spec-**

tator feels that he is in the presence of a creation of real genius as he looks upon it.

After enjoying these wondrous groups of sculpture which have arrested our attention, we turn once more to the monument. Inside the ornamental rail, from the top of the pyramid of steps or grand platform to which we have ascended, rises a second or lesser flight, and upon this rests the podium of the monument, or sort of projecting base, eleven feet in height. The upper and lower edges of the podium are of granite, the intermediate portion of it being of marble; upon it, running round on all four sides, are sculptured, in alto-rilievo, a series of historical groups of the most eminent painters, sculptors, architects, and scholars of ancient and modern times. They are one hundred and sixty-nine in number, of life-size, and the four sides of the base are devoted severally to Painting, Sculpture, Architecture, Poetry and Music.

Here, for instance, on the eastern front, sits the figure of Raphael, gazing thoughtfully into a sketch-book; leaning upon one side of his chair is Michael Angelo; upon the other stands Leonardo da Vinci. Titian, in long robe, stands, palette in hand, near to Paul Veronese, who fondles a favorite greyhound; while the kneeling figures of Fra Angelico and others make up the group in that vicinity. Another contains the central figure of Rubens; around him are gathered Rembrandt, Holbein, Hogarth, Dürer, and others; and a third group shows Murillo, Poussin, David, Claude, &c.

The south front rilievos are beautiful. The central seated figure of blind, old Homer bows his head down to the lyre in his hands; at his feet on one side sits Dante, looking up as to its magic strains; on the other, Shakspeare, with hand to thoughtful brow, seems weaving pleasing fancies or wondrous thought. Milton stands by in musing attitude; and old Chaucer, father of English poetry, rests, chin on hand, in quiet attention. At the right and left stand Goethe, Handel, Virgil, Cervantes, and Molière. Besides this group on the south part are others, embracing Beethoven, Haydn, Mozart, Auber, Rossini, Mendelssohn, Weber, and others.

On the north front are the figures of the great architects of the world, the sculptors going as far back as 3090 B. C., and presenting Cheops, the builder of the largest of the Pyramids, at Gizeh, and Hiram of Tyre, and coming down gradually to the Grecian and Roman architects, and finally to Inigo Jones, Sir Christopher Wren, and Sir Charles Barry, the architect of the Houses of Parliament. The north side gives us the sculptors Phidias, Praxiteles, Cellini, Canova, Thorwaldsen, Flaxman, and many others of both ancient and modern renown.

Above, and rising from this richly ornamented podium, towers the lofty, gorgeously ornamented Gothic monument, to the height of one hundred and eighty feet from the ground. Upon the four angles of this podium I have been describing are four more groups of statuary in marble, representing the industrial arts of Manufacturing, Agriculture, Engineering, and Commerce.

These groups are also beautiful in conception, and I give a description in order that these details may convey, to the American reader, some idea of the splendor of this remarkable monument. Engineering is represented by a female figure with one hand resting upon a piece of machinery; in front of her is another figure, with compasses in hand, intent upon a plan; then, near by, kneels another, bearing a cogwheel in her hand, near whom is seated a sculptured representation of a navvy or English engineering laborer, while near about are scattered sculptured indications of the engineer's art.

In the group representing Agriculture we have the figure of Agriculture crowned with a wreath of maize, directing the farmer at his plough, while beside her sits a female with lap full of corn, representing the rich gifts of the earth to man, and near by stands the figure of a shepherd boy in his simple costume, with his sheep grouped about him.

Commerce is represented by a female holding a cornucopia, and extending her hand to a youth bearing the scales, a ledger, and purse, emblems of mercantile trade; two other seated figures, one representing an Eastern merchant with a box of Oriental jewels, and another with corn, the staff of life, complete this group.

The group representing Manufactures is another admirably executed one in all its details. The most prominent represents the genius of manufacture holding an hour-glass in one hand, while with the other she points to the beehive, emblem of industry. On one side of her stands a smith or machinist, and on the other a cloth-manufacturer or weaver, and a potter. These workmen are surrounded by articles of their manufacture, all faithfully wrought in marble by the sculptor.

We now come to the pedestal upon which the statue of Prince Albert is seated. This is beneath a magnificent Gothic canopy, or, as some readers will better understand it, in the open space of the monument proper, which reminds one of an immense and magnificent Gothic spire set upon a pedestal; the open space being what in a New England spire would be called the belfry. The roof or vault of this open space above the head of the statue is of elegant blue mosaic, on which is inlaid Prince Albert's coat-of-arms.

Notwithstanding the many bronze statues already mentioned, there are numerous others. This open part of the spire, or monument, is formed by four clusters of pillars, and at the angles of each of these columns, above the groups of statuary last described, are eight more bronze statues, four of them seven and a half feet, and four eight feet four in height, representing Astronomy, with head bound with a fillet of stars, and holding a globe; Philosophy, with finger pointing to her open book; Medicine, with cup in hand, and the emblematical serpent at her side; Chemistry, retort in hand; Rhetoric, with thoughtful brow, perusing a scroll; Geometry, with pair of compasses, and tablet covered with geometric figures; Physiology, with an infant on her left arm, while her right hand points to the microscope; and lastly, Geology, a figure with pick in hand, that has unearthed metallic ores and the remains of a pre-Adamite period.

And yet this is not all; for above the canopy in what might be termed the ornamental steeple of the spire, in niches, are eight other statues, each eight feet in height, viz.: Faith, with cross and chalice; Hope, with her anchor; Charity, bearing a burning heart; Humility, bearing a lighted taper; Fortitude, a warlike figure, with mace and shield; Temperance, bearing a bridle; Justice, with sword and scales; Prudence, with a serpent. Above these are eight figures of angels, also of gilt bronze, clustered round the base of the cross which crowns this most wonderful and elaborate monument.

The dedicatory inscription reads thus:

> QUEEN VICTORIA AND THE PEOPLE,
> TO THE MEMORY OF ALBERT, PRINCE CONSORT,
> AS A TRIBUTE OF GRATITUDE
> FOR A LIFE DEVOTED TO THE PUBLIC GOOD.

I should hardly be considered an American chronicler did I not finish this description with the cost of the work, which is stated to have been £120,000 sterling, of which £50,000 was contributed by Parliament, about an equal amount by private subscriptions, and the remainder by the Queen herself.

This somewhat minute description is made from notes of personal observation and inquiry, and because the monument was one of the newest and most attractive wonders of the great metropolis at the time of the author's last visit, and one that he had not previously seen described in detail.

CHAPTER VIII.

RETURNING home after a first visit over the ocean without having seen the Eternal City, is like the omission of the grandest chapter of a great book, a famous dish at a feast, the aroma of which reaches your nostrils just as you are leaving the board, the one more addition to his possessions which the capitalist covets to make him sleep secure, the one campaign which in results it seems would have overshadowed all the rest. You are enthusiastic to your friends about York Minster, but are silent when questioned of St. Peter's ; you have stood on the battlefield of Waterloo, but have not walked over the pathway trodden by Julius Cæsar and Pompey ; you have shuddered at the cruel dungeons contrived by the Council of Ten in Venice, but what are they to the pit in which Jugurtha was starved, and from which Peter was delivered by the angel. You may talk of the Cathedral of Milan, the glories of the Alps, the castles of the Rhine, but have you ever stood in the arena of the Colosseum, that one great monument which rises in the mind's eye and in imagination's vision whenever Rome is mentioned ?

Bright, enjoyable, and interesting as have been our interviews with history, face to face with the mementos of the past, if we have not seen old Rome, it seems to have been but the modern past and not that classic past which tinges our literature, was familiar to us in youth, and joins so closely upon mythological story as to possess an indescribable charm to the scholar, a world of romantic interest to the poet, and an inexhaustible field for the student.

And yet Rome itself to the hungry traveller must appear but modern, as he contemplates the Sphynx, the Egyptian pyramids, and those ancient monuments along the brown flood of the Nile, monuments that had fallen to decay

"Ere Romulus and Remus had been suckled."

But Rome! Rome — in our earliest days, it was common in school-boys' mouths. The speeches that had their birth in the Roman Forum were in our youth piped in shrill voices from the platform of the country school-house; the deeds of Roman generals recalled by modern captains, the commentaries of one of her greatest emperors conned with care by modern monarchs, and Gaul's greatest soldier, who shook all Europe with the thunder of his tread, proudly claimed himself to be the modern prototype of him who raised Rome to its highest pinnacle of military power and greatness, to be the acknowledged mistress of the world.

Rome! The field has been ploughed by every tourist; it has been turned, delved, and re-turned by every antiquary; it has been despoiled of its treasures by ancient vandals and modern virtuosos and curiosity hunters; poets and sentimentalists have made every foot of its soil familiar; painters and sculptors have produced and reproduced every wondrous picture or glorious creation of the sculptor's art till they greet us in the window of the cheapest print-shop, or claim our pity in vile plaster or the ornamentation of household utensils.

The most wondrous treasures of European museums are spoils from her very ruins. The "Sleeping Faun" at Munich, that was hurled down from the tomb of Hadrian; the "Dancing Faun" at Florence; the "Farnese Hercules," that stands leaning on his club and is a model of mighty strength, now in the museum at Naples; the "Venus de Medici," the exquisite symmetry and grace of which have made it the standard of excellence for the female form; statues, busts, marbles, vases, fragments of the temples, altars, and tombs, are but the splinters of the very bones of the once mighty queen city of the world.

Then the domestic life, the implements, manners and customs, amusements, games, and occupations of ancient Rome have been rendered familiar to us as those of our own ancestors, thanks to poets, historians, and artists, who never tire of going over the prolific field that still yields fruit, and which seems to possess equal interest to each new generation that comes upon the stage of life.

I had read much of the sensations of travellers on approaching Rome in their rides over the Campagna, the desolate and pestilential plain that surrounds it, the vast expanse out upon which the great city overflowed itself, and which was once the dwelling-place of senators and nobles, or was the site of old Etrurian towns that had risen to their prime, declined, and sunk into decay, ere Rome had risen to be an empire. I had read so much of the approach over this desolate plain, that I was getting myself prepared for it somewhat in the manner that visitors to Niagara Falls do who have read the romantic travellers' tales of the roar of the cataract being heard ten miles away, and who are continually putting their heads from the windows of the railway carriage to listen as they approach that locality, and have their faith in human veracity so rudely shaken by finding the very village of Niagara Falls, whose casements they expected to find rattling with a thunderous concussion, as quiet as a New England village of a Sunday morning.

Travellers have told how, when speeding over the Campagna at early morn, they have beheld through the then dissolving mist the great dome of St. Peter's suddenly lift its swelling proportions upon the line of the horizon, or gleaming in the ruddy rays of the setting sun like a huge balloon just ready to rise into the clouds; and that on the edge of the Campagna on one side rose the hills and ruins, all that is left of old Rome, and on the other the spires and churches of modern Rome; the great Capitol between an apt dividing line separating the papal church and the pagan palace, the home of the popes and the city of the Cæsars.

All this poetic approach through the desolate Campagna, with here and there the ruin of a crumbling and forgotten palace, or villa, and the event of the postilion stopping his horses and pointing towards the distant city with its sharp outlines against the clear Italian sky, as he shouted "*Ecco Roma*" to the wearied and expectant traveller, was lost upon me, who was whirled into a modern railway station amid smoke, noise, dust, and confusion, and packed off in a very modern-looking omnibus for the Hotel Constanzzi.

We rattle through what seems to be the outskirts of an Italian city, past what appears to be an abandoned burned district — old Roman ruins — into an Italian city, modern Rome, with tall, yellow-washed looking houses, with cobblers, green-grocers, and fruiterers, in little cavern-like holes of stores in the lower story, through a street with high walls that encircle gardens, turn in beneath an archway and into the grand courtyard of a modern Italian hotel, where we were greeted in tolerable English and better French, and found ourselves welcome to Rome.

However much of poetry or romance there may be in man's nature, it succumbs at once to the pleadings of hunger, and, next to the pleasure of appeasing that, is the comfort of a good bath, a luxury which the ancient Romans thoroughly understood, and to them we owe to-day the enjoyment of the purest and best water in Italy, a luxury indeed to us Americans, who have turned with disgust from the brackish beverage of Venice, or the lime-rock-charged purgative of Paris.

What sight shall we go to see first? We turn in the guide-book, first to churches. A most appalling list spreads out upon the pages of the volume; a friend tells us there are three hundred and sixty-five of them, one for every day of the year. We take up Murray's Guide-Book of Rome; it is a formidable volume of four hundred and eighty pages; and even condensed Baedeker gives Rome three hundred and seventy pages. The enthusiastic visitor who comes for a two or three weeks' visit to the Eternal City is in despair at the prospect before him, knowing that the bare impressions and mere taste that he shall get in that brief period will but provoke a fiercer appetite, which would require a three months' instead of a three weeks' visit to appease.

But, like all Americans who have too much to accomplish in too brief a period, we set about the best method of doing it, and call in an excellent and expert *valet de place*, who thoroughly knows old Rome, and who had historical knowledge, doubtless learned in his occupation as guide, at his tongue's end, and was correct, too, as we found by frequent tests. To Antonio Amadio, guide, we communicate our wishes, and he immediately plans or submits a plan, for he has had to do it a hundred times for American travellers, for sight-seeing for one, two, or twenty days, as we may please to order; and now whither shall we go first? To the Colosseum, St. Peter's, Palace of the Cæsars, Catacombs, Vatican? There is such an *embarras de richesses* that we are glad that the proposition is made to see a few sights well, and to commence with St. Peter's, which meets with general approbation.

Placed in our open barouche, we roll out of the courtyard of the hotel, and down past our first sight in Rome, which was a fountain on the Piazza Barberini. Four dolphins with upturned tails held a big sea-shell, in which was seated a Triton who was blowing upwards, from a horn-shaped shell, a slender stream of water. We wind through narrow streets, with tall buildings and cavernous shops, where fruit, tin, and copper ware, garlic, and cheap Italian merchandise are vended, and at the doors of some of which an unappetizing compound is being fried in hot grease; meet occasionally a sandalled friar, robed either in brown or black or gray, according to the uniform of the order with which he is connected; we pass students in uniform of cloak or colored gown or shovel hat, and now and then a pair of Italian soldiers, whom the monks call devil's children. We soon

TOMB OF HADRIAN. 125

whirl into more of an open space, and a great circular structure greets our gaze, which we at once welcome as an old acquaintance with whose counterfeit presentment we have long been familiar, — the Castle of St. Angelo, or, to speak more correctly, the Tomb of Hadrian.

Before us rises this great cylindrical monument surmounted with the bronze figure of the archangel Michael, with his flaming sword, in memory of one of those pretended miracles which the priests of the Church of Rome have worked so liberally, and have erected monuments and painted pictures of so plentifully all over Europe, that it seems as if the Church desired, as perhaps it did, to give the impression that miracles were an every-day affair with them, and no particular difficulty was to be encountered in performing them.

But we are about to cross the Tiber, and we do cross it over the bridge supported by the five arches raised by the Emperor Hadrian in the year 136 to connect his tomb with the then greater part of the city on the other side of the river. Ten great statues, eleven feet high, of angels, are on either side, and the entrance to it guarded by statues of Peter and Paul. But the castle or tomb itself is now simply a huge cylinder of travertine, (it is well you should know that travertine, which the guide-books mention so frequently, is a species of white concretionary limestone abundant in Italy, and which was freely used by the Romans for building purposes,) the travertine from which the splendid marble sheathing of Hadrian's time has been stripped. A huge cylinder, resting upon a square base or support — yes, huge, for this great square block upon which the big stone bandbox rested had a frontage of two hundred and forty-seven feet, and the circumference of this big mausoleum is nine hundred and eighty-seven feet. Think over these dimensions as they are now, and what a grand building is this, even in its despoiled condition, simply a round stone structure with an ornamental band like the architectural base of a coronet near its summit, from which rises a smaller structure fronting towards the bridge, bearing a clock, and in turn surmounted by the modern bronze statue of the angel before mentioned. The tomb of Hadrian undoubtedly owes its preservation to this day to its cylindrical form, rendering it more able to resist both the assaults of time and vandalism of men.

As it now is, it is but the mere suggestion of what it must have been in its prime as the magnificent tomb of the emperors, for it held the imperial dust of Hadrian, Antoninus, Marcus Aurelius, Commodus, Caracalla, and many others, and was, if we may judge from descriptions handed down to us, a mausoleum worthy of a line of monarchs. In its prime the rough travertine was sheathed in Parian marble, the great square base was intersected with the Doric marble pillars, between which were marble tablets for epitaphs; then came the great circular central tower, brilliant in white marble, and elegant with fluted Ionic columns. Above this rose another story, surrounded by Corinthian columns, between which were the choicest works of statuary from the sculptor's chisel; and on the roof were grand sculptures of men and horses. A magnificent prominent monument, which has doubtless successfully performed the office its projector had in view, — the handing of his name down to posterity.

But how vain man's efforts against the march of time! Three centuries swept past, and the tramp of the soldier, and thunder of the legions, and braying of the trumpet, shook the very dust of the old emperors in their funeral urns, as one of their more modern successors turned it into a fortress, and Goth, Greek, and Roman have held it; its splendid statues have been hurled down upon invading forces, its sheathing of rich marble torn away for new monuments or modern Christian churches; even the porphyry sarcophagus that held the ashes of a pagan emperor, removed by a modern Roman pontiff (Innocent II.) for his own tomb, and naught of that remains now but a mere fragment, which, after having served as tomb for another pontiff, Otho II., for seven centuries, is now the baptismal font at St. Peter's. A history indeed for the casket that was prepared for Hadrian's remains, and which has held pagan and pope through so many centuries, that its last remaining fragment should now be the receptacle of the element for Christian baptism! The sepulchral inscribed marbles were cut up to decorate a Christian church as late as the sixteenth century, and the great monument of kings and emperors has been reduced by sieges, spoliations, vandalism, and time to a mighty wreck of its former self, and, like many ruins of old Rome, grand even as a wreck.

We may stop at the entrance, where some of the soldiers who now occupy it as barracks are unpacking a wagon-load of round, black-looking bread, and, if we have a permit, look in and see what little is to be seen.

A great passage between the enormously thick walls winds round between them, and by gentle ascent carries you to the summit, or to the great chamber that Hadrian prepared for his last resting-place. This is in the centre of the building, and the niche occupied by his sepulchral urn and those of his successors is pointed out to you. You are surprised at the nicety of the stone work here, its exact fitting, and the unmistakable evidences, from the bolt-holes in the work, that the walls of these now gloomy passages were once sheathed with the richest marbles. The history of this castle or tomb would in itself fill a volume, and make a record of fiendish barbarities which even the most cruel African cannibal can hardly rival. Here will you look into Benvenuto Cellini's cell, who was confined here in 1537, when the fortress was a state prison of the papal government, and in endeavoring to escape from which he broke his leg.

Here it is the Cenci family were incarcerated, and the celebrated Beatrice Cenci, whose terrible tortures for a whole year, in the vain effort to make her confess to a lie, and whose murder by the papal authorities, is a story that even to this day, though nearly four centuries old, excites the liveliest indignation against those beings wearing human form, who acted more like cruel fiends from the lowest depths of Satan's kingdom. But here are the cells, niches quarried out of a mountain of rock; and here, out of a pleasant sort of library-room, or a great ornamental hall, which appears as a repository of archives, is another, where a cardinal was strangled by order of Pope Pius IV. We look into other cells midway up, and are shown great jars, which are said to have formerly held oil heated to throw down upon the heads of besiegers, but more probably held a store of that commodity and wine for the use of the besieged. But we tire of "man's inhumanity to man;" we mount to the top, and have a magnificent sight of St. Peter's and the surrounding country, an extended and transporting view spread out for miles on every side in the clear, beautiful Italian atmosphere.

We resume our carriages and ride on, and in a short time enter between the points of the great extended arms, as it were, of St. Peter's, — the central point, the church of the head of the Roman Church, the wonder of architecture upon which untold sums of gold and three centuries of labor have been lavished. A gigantic modern ecclesiastical monument, rich in works of modern sculpture and art, and beautified with those wrenched from old pagan temples that have rung with the tramp of Cæsar's legions, or from altars that have been wreathed in the smoke of pagan sacrifices to the gods.

We pause just inside the grand piazza, or great open space in front of the huge edifice, to try and get a proper idea of its vastness, which is almost impossible in a first visit. On each side of us extend from the church those well-known great semicircular porticos, or pavilions, so familiar to every one who has ever seen a picture of the building. These porticos, which join the front or façade of the church, converge as they extend from it, and are each in the form of an immense sickle, the handle part being next the church, and the two points the extremities, and between these two points we have just passed.

We descended from our carriages, and the longer we gazed upon the great work, the more its grandeur and beauty grew upon us. From the two points of the colonnades, or sickles, to the base of the broad steps that lead up to the church is a distance of about a thousand feet, a distance you can hardly conceive to be so great until you pace it, and one you will hardly care to test by pacing, if the day be warm and cloudless. But this deception is the first surprise which the vast size of everything about you causes, but which you soon become accustomed to.

The great porticos themselves, which at first seem a low row of pillars inclosing the area, you discover are supported by pillars sixty-four feet high and twenty feet apart, there being two hundred and eighty-four of these pillars, and each portico being fifty-five feet wide. The top of these grand pavilions is crowned with an army of saints, for one hundred and sixty-two figures, each twelve feet in height, look down upon the spectator, and the widest breadth between these two great encircling arms of the church is five hundred and eighty-seven feet. It is a grand inclosure to screen the approach to the church from any surrounding objects that might serve to distract the view; and the eye runs with delight over the graceful lines of beauty, the elegant pillars, the serried array of statues, the great façade of one of the grandest creations in architecture, and the most wonderful structure of modern times.

In the centre of the great inclosure, and relieving it from the otherwise naked appearance it might possess, rises the tall red granite obelisk that formerly stood in the circus of Nero, where it was placed by the emperor Caligula. It was the only obelisk in old Rome that was never thrown down, and which, after fifteen hundred years, was removed from the spot where pagan hands had reared it, now covered by a portion of St. Peter's Church, to its present position. Its removal was considered little else than a miracle, as the difficulties to be overcome by scientific and engineering skill in raising it from its old pedestal and conveying it without injury to this spot seemed almost insurmountable.

The great obelisk weighed about a million pounds; and Pope Sixtus V. required the architect Fontana to move it safely to this square, and place it upright upon the foundation that had been prepared for it. The story has oft been told to old and young; the anxiety of the architect in the great work which was to make or undo him quite; the prayers and blessings of the church for the work; and how nine hundred men, tugging at thirty-nine windlasses, at last raised from its foundations this monument of the bloodiest and most cruel of tyrants, till it swung clear of obstructions and in the air, and was afterwards slowly lowered down upon great rollers prepared for it, and by their means rolled to this spot, to be raised to the foundation prepared for it. Here, forty-six windlasses, eight hundred men, and one hundred and fifty horses tugged at the ropes, and raised the huge mass into position; and here it was that, as the story is told, just as the great obelisk was to have been placed upon its pedestal, the ropes, stretching by its great weight, prevented the accomplishment of the architect's plans, who had not calculated upon this, and the vast pillar remained in the air, while he knew not what to do to shorten the ropes, till a sailor in the crowd cried out, despite the edict that silence should be preserved and none should speak aloud, "Wet the ropes! Wet the ropes!" which was done, and the shrinking caused by their drenching enabled him to carry out his calculations successfully.

But there it stands, a graceful granite needle, rising one hundred and thirty-two feet in height, and surrounded at its base by a double circle of granite posts. On either side the two handsome fountains, forty-three feet in height, throw their sparkling water-jets up thirty or forty feet into the air, to tumble back, in broad sheets, into granite basins; and one is reminded of the plan, on a lesser scale, of the obelisk and fountains at the Place de la Concorde in Paris. It is something to think of that you look, as you gaze upon this obelisk, upon a shaft brought from Heliopolis by Caligula, in a ship described by Pliny as "nearly as long as the left side of the port of Ostia."

But let us turn our attention to St. Peter's. Like most visitors who have advanced thus far into the square, I was disappointed by having the noble proportions of the huge dome cut off by the great façade of the building, which is three hundred and fifty-seven feet long and one hundred and forty-four feet in height. Above this is a balustrade with statues of Christ and the Apostles, apparently of life-size, but which are actually eighteen feet in height. After ascending the broad flight of marble steps, we find ourselves in the vestibule, which is really a grand structure in itself, being four hundred and sixty-eight feet long, sixty-six feet high, and fifty feet wide. A fine view or vista is had by standing in its centre and looking either side of you, the view being terminated on one side by an equestrian statue of Constantine, and on the other by one of Charlemagne, neither of which struck me as remarkable pieces of sculpture.

But there, in the walls, between the doors, among other inscriptions, is the Latin epitaph on Adrian I., who was pope from 772 to 795, by Charlemagne, in blank verse, the first few words of which, translated, read:

> THE FATHER OF THE CHURCH, THE ORNAMENT OF ROME, THE FAMOUS WRITER, THE BLESSED POPE, RESTS IN PEACE. GOD WAS HIS LIFE, LOVE WAS HIS LAW, CHRIST WAS HIS GLORY, &c.

But we hardly pause to examine the great bronze central door, which belonged to the old church of 1431, with its bas-reliefs of saints and martyrdoms, or the holy door that is opened but four times each hundred years, for the great loaded heavy leathern curtain is all that is between us and the interior of this majestic temple. This great leather-bound curtain, which hangs before the ever open door of the great cathedrals of Europe, is not always an agreeable obstruction to pass, loaded as its edges often are with accumulated dirt from its contact with thousands of greasy hands that have thrust it aside, and it is not, therefore, pleasant or agreeable to have it flap heavily back into your face, as it is likely to do if one follows too closely those who precede him.

But we push the heavy screen aside, not without a quickened beat of the heart, and step within the wondrous temple that it conceals, into an atmosphere that is ever its own, and into the midst of a wilderness of wondrous architecture that is fairly bewildering.

From a glance at the polished marble pavement under foot, the eye at once glides away along the great central nave, a surpassingly grand vista, eighty-nine feet broad, and more than five hundred feet in length, and one hundred and fifty-two feet high. On each side, massive Corinthian pillars rise, pilasters crowned with elegant capitals, arches leading into lofty side-chapels, over which are recumbent angels, the great, vaulted semicircular roof, enriched with sunken panels, ornaments, sculptures, bas-reliefs, and mosaics — a prodigality of decoration in every direction.

But then, the vastness of the interior is what astonishes the visitor. Distant people appear dwarfed to the size of children. You go up to the fluting of a pillar, and find it to be a niche big enough for a life-size statue. You approach the infantile cherubs that support the shell of holy water near the entrance, and find them to be children six feet in height, and begin then to educate the eye to the vastness of the scene before you, beautiful in all its harmonious proportions. Glancing down at the pavement, we find marked the comparative length of St. Peter's with other noted Christian churches. Thus, St. Peter's is six hundred and thirteen feet; St. Paul's, London, five hundred and twenty; Milan Cathedral, four hundred and forty-three; St. Sophia, three hundred and sixty. Another interesting record in the marble floor is a round slab of porphyry, where emperors stood when crowned by the Pope.

Almost the first walk one takes, after the surprise and wonderment of his first eye-sweep of the nave is over, is down towards a row of faintly glittering lamps, that the visitor sees before him upon a circular balcony of marble, and which appear in the distance like a large wreath of yellow roses. These lamps are in clusters of three, are one hundred and twelve in number, and are kept constantly burning. They surround the sanctum sanctorum of the great church — the tomb of St. Peter. The visitor finds on reaching them that the balustrade that holds them is placed above two flights of marble steps that lead down to the door of the sepulchre, in which you are required to believe repose the mortal remains of the apostle, and before which, in papal robes and in the attitude of prayer, is a wonderfully executed marble statue of Pius VI.

Beneath the great dome, you look up, and almost forget that it is a creation of man's art, or that there should be any desire to look up, any more than to bend one's gaze upon the sky which we know is ever above. Feet and inches seem to convey but a faint idea of the proportions of this grand pile. The height from the pavement on which I stood to the top of the gorgeously decorated dome, or base of the lantern or little cupola that surmounted the dome, was nearly twice as high as Bunker Hill Monument. The four great pillars that, you observe, support it are over two hundred and fifty feet in circumference, and the interior of this magnificent globe is one hundred and thirty-nine feet in circumference on the inside; and we afterwards find that there is another entire cupola outside, as we ascend it, and that there are commodious stairways and rooms between the two domes.

So while we stand, and calculate that four or five domes like Boston State-House might be put in here; that two buildings like the Capitol at Washington could be piled one on top of the other between where we stand and the top of this great temple, we begin to appreciate its vastness. In the niches of the supporting pillars of the dome stand statues — life-size they look on approaching, but the guide-book records them as sixteen feet high. As the eye soars up again into this magnificent vault, with its recesses, arches, spandrels, and decorations, the gaze is arrested by the four medallions of the Evangelists, with their emblems, that appear from where you stand like smoothly executed paintings, but which, when you climb to them, are mosaics of pieces of colored stone big as your thumb, and the figures great staring giants. St. Luke, with a hand that would answer for a dinner-table, grasps a pen seven feet in length, and each letter of the mosaic inscription that runs round the base of the dome — fair-sized letters as seen from below — is in reality six feet high. These figures give a faint idea of the vastness of the proportions of St. Peter's; but its architectural management is such that all appears to harmonize, and the great distance reduces the coarseness of these huge dimensions into proper proportions.

Another object by which the visitor educates his eye is the *baldachino*, or canopy, that stands near the opening or descent to St. Peter's tomb. This canopy to the grand altar, which is directly over the tomb itself, appears but an ordinary pavilion under the centre of the great dome; but it is nearly a hundred feet high; and, with all your admiration at the wonders of St. Peter's, you cannot repress the wish that Urban VIII. had shown himself less a vandal and left the great plates of ancient bronze where they belonged, in the Pantheon, instead of stripping them off to melt down for the ornamental screen to this modern altar; for he took nearly nine thousand pounds of the Roman bronze for this purpose from that pagan temple. In fact, go where you will in Rome, one will find that the finest of the old pagan temples, erected to Jupiter or Mars, or other heathen deities, have been laid under contribution for modern Christian churches. The Colosseum appears to have been a quarry for modern palaces, and the Pantheon and Caracalla's Baths a mine of marble and sculpture for various popes whose brains have burned with desire of architectural improvement and decoration.

After lingering round this wondrous *point d'appui* beneath the dome, my gaze was attracted by another one of those world-renowned objects whose acquaintance we make in early youth in the story-books, and continually renew in travellers' letters, novelists' descriptions, and pictured representation, — the seated bronze figure of St. Peter, whose metal toe receives so many labial salutes as to require no chiropodist, but, rather, a protector against the constant attrition which wears away even the solid bronze. This is a seated life-size bronze figure in a chair of white marble; a stiff and ungraceful statue, with one hand grasping the pontifical key, and the other upraised in the attitude of bestowing a papal blessing, first two fingers extended, and thumb and last two closed. The bronze toe of the seated figure projects a few inches beyond the pedestal, and an examination of it revealed a smoothly-worn depression caused by contact of innumerable lips of the faithful.

While I was standing here, two or three gathered near, apparently waiting their turn after I should have finished what they might have considered my devotions. I therefore stood aside, when first approached a woman leading a little child. She kissed the bronze toe, pressed her forehead against it a moment, and then held up the infant to apply its little lips. Then came a ragged, greasy-looking fellow, with red vest and what had once been a velveteen coat with metal buttons, but was now a dust-colored remnant. His coarse, wooden-soled shoes were stained with the dust of the Campagna, and his complexion tanned by the sun to the hue of darkened Russia leather. He clasped the foot with both hands, kissed reverently, fumbled at a pocket, and took out an old rosary, and went to a side-chapel and knelt silently before an altar where a number of candles were burning. Then came a workman, apparently, who brushed the bronze toe with his sleeve before kissing; and, finally, a gentlemanly-looking individual, clad in Parisian garments of latest style, approached, and, after wiping the point of the extended foot with great care with his perfumed linen handkerchief, he too bent his lips to respectfully salute it. Thus I witnessed the customary salute from the different grades of visitors who make their pilgrimages thither.

An attempt to describe St. Peter's in detail will hardly be expected from any traveller or writer of ordinary experience. The great side-chapels which we visit are large enough for ordinary churches. On every side the eye encounters rich decorations, marbles, carvings, frescoing, and gilding. The monuments in St. Peter's are not of remarkable historical interest, being chiefly tributes to the popes, and none of them earlier than the sixteenth century.

The Tribune, as it is called, at the extreme end of the nave beyond the dome, and beyond what is known as the choir in cathedrals, is as a whole a florid and incongruous piece of architecture. At the base is a grand altar; at each side, upon two great ornamental pedestals, stand two mitred figures, one with extended hand, the other reading from a book; behind these are two others, whose extended right and left hands, apparently, hold or point to a large ornamental casket between and above their heads, in which you are told is inclosed the identical chair in which St. Peter and many of his successors sat, when officiating as head of the church. Above this, two cherubs support the inevitable tiara and keys, and above them is a glory of numerous angels and rays of golden light, the dove forming the centre and the surroundings being rich in gilding and frescoing.

Speaking of relics, of which every Romish cathedral, even the humblest, has some, it will be remembered that the four great relics at St. Peter's are the lance which is said to have been that with which the soldier pierced our Saviour's side; the napkin pressed to his face when he was staggering under the weight of the cross, and which is said to have ever since retained the impression of his features; a fragment of the true cross, and the head of St. Andrew. These relics are exhibited on Holy Thursday, Good Friday, and Easter Day, but from a balcony so high in the air that they cannot be distinguished.

The papal monuments are to a certain extent of the same general character — rich and elegant in sculpture and execution, but all representing the deceased pontiff, standing, reclining, or kneeling in his robes of the church, the inevitable tiara and keys, the representations of angels, cherubs, or the virtues of Truth and Fortitude, allegorically treated, being prominent in all.

In the first chapel we were interested (as all are who travel in Italy, and hear Michael Angelo's name mentioned so frequently in every church, convent, and public building) in the marble group of the Virgin with the body of the dead Saviour on her knees, as being one of his first works, executed when he was but twenty-four years of age.

The monument to Clement XIII. by Canova, in the right transept, is one that will hold the visitor's attention — the figure of the Pope in marble; kneeling, and on either side of him, a figure of Religion bearing a torch, and Death, with reversed torch, all beautifully executed. At the base of the monument, guarding the door of the vault, are two noble figures of lions, magnificent representations of the animal in marble, with strength and savage majesty faithfully delineated in every line and feature. Another interesting monument is that of Innocent VIII., who was pope from 1484 to 1492. He is represented in marble, in a recumbent position upon his sarcophagus, and again above it in a sitting posture, bestowing the papal blessing, while one hand holds the sacred lance above alluded to, which pierced the side of our Saviour. This tomb and that of Sixtus IV. are the only two that were replaced in the church after the destruction of the old one, its predecessor.

The tomb of Benedict XIV. is a fine one, showing his statue supported by statues of Science and Charity; and the chapel of the Holy Sacrament contains a superb tabernacle of lapis-lazuli and bronze, and the tomb of Sixtus IV., in bronze, elegantly ornamented with bas-reliefs. Here in this chapel, with nothing to mark his resting-place but a slab in the pavement, rest the ashes of Julius II., who, it will be found on consulting history, deserves the largest share of the credit of raising this magnificent edifice.

The attention of American as well as English visitors is alike attracted to the monument to the last three members of the Stuart family, James the Third, Charles the Third, and Henry the Ninth. It is the work of Canova, and represents a marble obelisk, with a marble mausoleum at its base, guarded by winged figures of genii, which the guide-book tells us received their stucco breeches in the time of Leo XII., because their nakedness was an offence to his ideas of modesty. Near here, in the chapel of the Baptistery, is what remains of the red porphyry vase which formed the cover or upturned bed of the tomb of the Emperor Otho II. It is twelve feet long, and, as before stated, was formerly the receptacle of Hadrian's ashes, but is now a baptismal font.

My note-book has points of admiration for various other sculptures and wonders, made in my hours of wandering, all too brief, amid the marble miracles of this mighty temple — pictures, statues, bas-reliefs, mosaics, sculptures, and marbles innumerable, that I have not space to mention, and could hardly do so intelligibly without giving a detailed description of the building. An expert *valet de place* will point out rich yellow marble wainscotings from some of the old pagan temples of Jupiter, or Venus, or Mars, columns of beauty said to have come from the Temple of Jerusalem, and other wonders, as you pass from point to point.

In St. Peter's are confessionals, it is said, for every known language; and there are in the church forty-six altars, two hundred and ninety windows, three hundred and ninety statues, and seven hundred and forty-eight columns. And this great church, we are told, stands over the vaults containing the mortal remains of "eight apostles, eleven fathers of the church, eleven founders of orders, and thirty-five canonized popes," while the very bronze columns which support the canopy of the great altar are filled with the bones of martyrs, which were exhumed from the Vatican catacombs when they were swept aside to make a foundation for the present great church of St. Peter's.

St. Peter's should not be visited hurriedly, or with a large party, who will rudely disturb with the clatter of tongues the hushed reverence which its grandeur and beauty impose upon you as you stand beneath its marvellous dome, feel dwarfed by the side of its huge pillars, and note the comparative silence which seems to pervade the interior, no matter how many be present. One hasty visit, and you bring away a confused recollection of a lofty dome, fretted ceiling, long nave, a confusion of statues, pillars, and "apotheosis of popedom," as Frederika Bremer calls it. A quiet, leisurely saunter, with time to spare, and a revisiting again and again, is necessary to enable the mind fully to grasp and properly appreciate its grandeur as a great architectural wonder.

The cost of the main building of St. Peter's, which was dedicated November 18, 1626, but may not be said to have been completed until Pius VI. built the sacristy in 1780, was over *ten million pounds sterling;* and the annual expense now of keeping it in repair is about six thousand five hundred pounds, or over thirty-two thousand dollars — a bagatelle, when it is considered what some of our modern

American politicians expend in furnishing and keeping city-halls and custom-houses in repair.

The floor or lower part of this great Christian temple having been "done" by the tourist, an ascent to the dome is the next wonder that awaits him. The ascent is not by means of stairs, but by a broad, paved, gently ascending, zigzag walk, up which a horse or mule might easily travel.

On the walls on the side of the staircase are inscriptions recording the ascent of various monarchs and distinguished personages, the most recent being that of the Prince of Wales, who went up into the ball February 10, 1859. On our way up we stepped out upon the roof of the façade, where stand the statues of our Saviour and the Apostles, which we find to be marble giants eighteen feet high. We look over the huge, breast-high balustrade down into the beautiful piazza that is spread out one hundred and forty-four feet below us, with its obelisk, fountain, and moving groups of visitors dwarfed by the distance; we gaze around and observe the two cupolas, of one hundred feet in height, which are on either side of the great dome which soars in its swelling majesty far, far above them three hundred feet further into the blue air; and here also are five smaller domes which are above the great chapels; then there are huts or habitations for custodians who have the care of the roof upon which you walk about in different passages, like, as it were, a series of streets in the air, and begin to get still newer ideas of the hugeness of St. Peter's as you step in and resume the ascent of the dome that towers above.

Up, up, still up, till at last a gallery is reached which you step out into and look downwards, instinctively clutching the iron railing that protects, and look away down to the pavement as from the basket of a balloon. The people on the floor have lessened to Liliputians, the great, hundred-feet-high baldachino has shrunken to the size of a four-posted bedstead; atop and behind the huge pillars is a wide alley-way in which workmen are walking. One is hung down, seated in a loop of rope, fastening a series of decorations to points at the head of the flutings of the great pillars, and he makes progress from one to the other by giving a vigorous push with his foot and swinging out, like a spider on his thread, ten or a dozen feet into the open space, and coming back in the next fluting. It fairly makes you giddy to look at him.

But when you get up to the upper gallery, close to the swell of the dome, where the mosaic work, that appeared so smooth and elegant from below, is now as coarse and rough as ill-executed scene-painting, and can hardly read the letters that surround the rim, they are so big, and the look down calls for so steady a head that, though the strong iron rail comes up full breast-high, but the coolest of the party will make its circuit, — then we realize the magnitude and wonder of this work of human hands. It requires a steady head to walk around this railed passage-way, and the very steadiest of the steady to stand close to the rail and look down from this height to the pavement, four hundred feet beneath. But the glories of the dome and lantern, their elegant decorations, ornamentations, and coloring, are around and about the astonished visitor, and, gaze which way he will, new wonders greet him.

Back to the passage between outer and inner dome, and up we mount, and step out upon a little gallery, not visible from below, which we find is at the base of the ball, and from which a view of the surrounding country is had, as from a private-box seat in the top of a high mountain. Then comes an ascent into the ball, made by an almost perpendicular stair, and through a space that can be passed by but one person at a time. Although I had the privilege of a five minutes' visit inside this great hollow globe, with thirteen other visitors, who, like myself, desired probably to say they had stood in the ball of St. Peter's, I am not prepared to say the experience was an agreeable one, and was glad to get down to the outer gallery, and enjoy the extended view and pure atmosphere, before descending to *terra firma* again.

CHAPTER IX.

HAVING seen the most magnificent of modern Christian temples, I next bent my way to the most splendid of the pagan temples of *old* Rome — the Pantheon, that model of ancient architectural beauty which even now, with its perfect interior, its simple grandeur and proportions, notwithstanding the vandal additions of various popes, who seemed to vie with each other in plundering pagan temples, or rendering the beautiful structures, which they could not rival or approach, hideous by their additions or alterations, — even with the mangling that the Pantheon has received, it rises in my recollection as a thing of beauty that is a joy forever.

The impression of its faultless beauty came over me as I stood in the centre of the perfect circle of this great temple to all the gods, — a rotunda one hundred and forty-two feet in diameter and one hundred and forty-three feet high. There are no windows, but a perfectly circular aperture in the top, of twenty-eight feet in diameter, admits a light that lights the whole, and through which the blue Italian sky and fleecy clouds are seen. Around on all sides are now Christian altars, and the great niches are vacant that once held marble figures of heathen deities; the magnificent bronze plates that sheathed the most perfect dome in the world are stripped away; nay, even some of the stone and marble work is whitewashed or otherwise disfigured; and yet you cannot stand upon the floor of this magnificent old temple to the gods, built twenty-seven years before Christ, without involuntary expressions of admiration at its perfect beauty of proportion.

What must it have been in its prime, with its magnificent front, not as now sunken as modern Rome, or as successive modern Romes have heaped their soil up over the old city, till now you step *down* into the Pantheon; what must it have been eighteen centuries ago, when its magnificent portico, with its grand front of over one hundred feet, supported by sixteen Corinthian pillars thirty-six feet high, (which still remain,) was *above* the level of the street, and was approached by a flight of six marble steps, and the vestibule a beautiful vista of white marble pilasters, the pediment above was ornamented with glorious bas-reliefs, (you may see the holes in which the bolts holding them were placed, to this day,) and the roof, sheathed with bronze, which Pope Urban VIII. not only was vandal enough to strip off and melt down for bronze columns and cannon, but perpetuated the act, that there should be no mistake as to who the despoiler was, by recording it in a Latin inscription over one of the doorways? Then he increased the outrage by adding two ugly bell-towers to the dome, — "asses' ears," they are very justly called; — and another pope, Benedict XIV., who was pope from 1740 to 1758, tore away beautiful marbles from the upper part of it to adorn buildings he was erecting.

But despite all this, the grand and perfect beauty of the temple could not be destroyed, and we can imagine, standing here upon what was once the elegant pavement of porphyry and marble, how grandly the pagan altar reared its height beneath the then perfect vault of bronze, and the smoke of ascending sacrifice rose through the great opening direct to the nostrils of mythical Jove himself, and in these now empty niches, fifty feet above the pavement, there stood looking down upon priests and people the colossal sculptured figures of Jupiter, warlike Mars, and majestic Minerva, Apollo with bent bow, or with lyre in hand, and Vulcan pausing over his thunderbolts. The sides of the vast circle glittered with polished marbles and elegant carving; the attic or roof gleamed with sculptured silver and bronze, and was upheld by caryatides of Syracusan bronze. Statues to Rome's emperors and senators peopled niches at the entrance and in the porticos, and Marcus Agrippa's superb temple to the gods was one of the glories of old Rome.

The ancient bronze doors remain, and the Corinthian pillars, of red granite, with marble capitals, roughened and blackened with the breath of eighteen centuries, will continue to command attention, exact admiration, and remind the student of the architecture of classical times; but all around the interior in the different recesses he will find the modern altars of the Roman Catholic church, with their florid and tawdry ornaments, tinsel and frippery, which illy accord with the ancient surroundings. The building is said to be a species of brick work, and was coated or veneered with marble, but the exterior coating was stripped off by the spoilers of modern times. So also was plundered the sculptured silver on the interior of the roof by successive vandals.

Rome built and raised her most costly and beautiful edifices from the spoil of plundered cities, and by the captives brought by emperors " home to Rome, whose ransoms did the general coffers fill;" and the law of compensation, or of retribution, was at last wrought upon herself, and by some of the very people from whom she had wrenched fathers, husbands, and brothers, treasures and spoils; base barbarians, whom proud Rome once despised, ran riot through her streets, plundered and despoiled her temples, and only consented to leave Rome's supplicating ambassadors their lives on condition of their surrendering everything else.

The approach to some of these splendid relics of ancient Rome takes the romance and poetry most thoroughly out of the tourist; and that to the Pantheon, through dirty streets, beggars, and hucksters, who follow and pester one to the very door of the temple, but illy prepares you for an admiration of its beauties, and too often, on departing, rudely destroys the sentiments which a contemplation of its interior has aroused.

Where next?

To the Capitol! The Hill of Kings, the very sanctum sanctorum of the Roman state, the scene of the birth of the most important events of Rome's history. There where her senators assembled and their laws were made, where, winding up the hill, after his triumph through the city, came the victorious Roman general to receive the senate's thanks and conqueror's laurel wreath; the site of Rome's fortress that our boyhood's story told us was saved from an invading foe by the cackling of scared geese, the place where the Tarpeian rock reared its precipitous height, and the scene of Brutus's oration to the people after the murder of Julius Cæsar.

What a grand place is the Capitoline Hill in our imagination, and what a magnificently big place we always thought it must be from its history, and the temples that were said to have stood upon it, and the scenes enacted there! Away back to the time of Romulus they tell us the gate of the fortress on the hill was opened by Tarpeia, and I went and stood on the spot a little above where the ruined arch of Severus is, as the place where the besieging soldiers, in obedience to the promise of the traitress, threw off for her, as a reward for her treason, as they had promised, "that which they wore on their left arms;" not the coveted golden bracelet, but the heavy bronze and iron shield; and, crushed beneath the weight of metal, she received fit reward for her perfidy.

It must be confessed a powerful amount of imagination is required to rehabilitate this hill as antiquarian and historical authorities describe it. How they found room for so many buildings there puzzled me on looking at it, for either the ancient edifices must have been of circumscribed dimensions, or else the grand hill of the Capitol, the head of the empire, state, and republic, must be now sadly shorn of its ancient dimensions.

Here it was, away back in the time of Tarquinius Superbus, B. C. 535, so the legend runs, that the splendid temple of Jupiter Capitolinus was built on the rocky platform. It was two hundred Roman feet square, with pavement of mosaic, and gates of gilt bronze, and underneath it was kept that old bundle of palm-leaves known in the story as the Sibylline books. Tarquin's building is said to have stood two hundred years, and then came a more splendid one after its destruction, B. C. 83. This went down A. D. 69, and of course another was erected; and on this hill Titus and Vespasian celebrated the fall of Jerusalem. But like all other of Rome's rich temples, that on the Capitoline Hill attracted the cupidity of vandals, who stripped it of its splendors A. D. 455. On arriving at the disappointing little Capitoline Hill, it seemed to me there was so little space that I "overhauled my note-book," as Cap'n Cuttle would say, wondering how, besides the temple to Jupiter Capitolinus, there could have stood here, or on the adjacent height, so many points of interest as set down in history, namely, old Numa's Temple of Faith, Temple of Jupiter Tonans, Juno Moneta, Temple of Honor, temples of Mars and Venus; and it was up here somewhere (I could not place the locality) where once was the fortress from which, during a siege, the Romans threw loaves of bread, so the story runs, down into the enemy's camp to cheat them into the belief that they were abundantly supplied with provisions, while in reality they were perishing with hunger.

All these old legends come up fresh in your mind, or a group of tourists talking with each other of what they have read and studied of old Rome, will recall them when visiting these historic spots.

But our carriage stops at the foot of a broad flight of stairs known as "La Cordonnata," put here in 1536, but taken from the Temple of the Sun on the Quirinal. They mark, however, the sight of the ancient staircase that led to the Temple of Jupiter Capitolinus, and at the foot of which, marked by the spot where the end of these stairs touches at the left, Rienzi the tribune was killed. Near this staircase, through a little garden, we were shown two or three underground arches, which are said to be part of the lower portions of the celebrated temple to Capitoline Jove, to whom we have made such frequent reference.

Two great carved lions are at the foot of the broad staircase, and at its summit we discover two ugly colossal marble figures, Castor and Pollux, standing by the side of their steeds. These two are transfers, having been brought here from the Ghetto and placed in this position, and at the top, along the edge of the platform, are other statues, which probably the guide-books tell of; I remember examining some carved armorial trophies called the trophies of Marius, and looking with some interest at a genuine old Roman mile-stone brought from the Appian Way. I then turned about and stood in the square of the Capitol of Rome, one of the historical spots in the world that every student longs to visit.

Here it was, and a disappointment at last, looking like a very modern square; the flight of steps on one side, and three somewhat modern and by no means remarkable-looking buildings on the other three. In the centre, however, stood the majestic and grand equestrian statue of Marcus Aurelius, with outstretched hand, in attitude of command, the most perfect statue of antiquity that has come down to us, being one of twenty-two bronze equestrian statues that existed in Rome in the fifth century. It formerly stood near the Arch of Severus, was removed in 1187 by Pope Clement III. to the front of the Lateran Church, and placed in this square by order of Paul III. in 1187. In the year 966 a prefect of Rome who rebelled against Pope John XIII. was hung by his hair from this horse; so the steed has a story if not a pedigree. The pedestal on which it stands was cut by Michael Angelo from a solid piece of cornice found in the Forum. It was also here, in this open space, that Brutus spoke to the people after Cæsar's murder; here over this ground great Cæsar walked.

We crossed the square back to a corner near the right hand of the head of the staircase after ascending, and looked over what we were told was the Tarpeian Rock, an eminence looking down into a dirty alley, and giving one the impression that the rock must have been razeed, or the surface below have changed its character and been filled up since Manlius was hurled down there by the patricians, who envied his popularity as the friend of the people. All these statues, staircase, and buildings, being comparatively modern, leave but little else than the hill itself to recall anything that was really as ancient Rome stood, and even the hill must have been shorn in size and changed in form since then.

Upon the three sides of the square stand the Church of Ara Cœli, the Palace of the Senator, and the Palace of the Conservatori, containing a collection of some of the most interesting objects in Rome. Here we saw magnificent specimens of ancient Roman statuary, a group of a lion attacking a horse, found in the bed of the river Almo; and what is said to be the only authentic statue of Julius Cæsar.

Here, also, is the famous bronze Wolf of the Capitol, a rough-looking representation, but it is interesting to look upon the figure referred to by Cicero. And that familiar statue, familiar from the thousands of copies that have been made of it, of a boy extracting a thorn from his foot is here, an act simple enough in itself, but represented in this statue with such wonderful fidelity as to command admiration even from the casual spectator.

The Capitoline Museum, opposite to the Palace of the Conservatori, is rich in antique sculpture, Roman remains, and antiquities. Here is the famous mosaic, found in Hadrian's Villa at Tivoli, which has been copied so often into ladies' mosaic breastpins, "Pliny's Doves," on which some doves are represented sitting upon the edge of a vase drinking and pluming themselves. This mosaic is composed of quite minute bits of stone, one hundred and sixty different pieces having been counted to the square inch.

In the same hall with this wonderful mosaic were some most interesting specimens of ancient sarcophagi, elegant in rich allegorical carving, a feast for the art-student. That known as the Prometheus Sarcophagus is thickly covered with carving, and is chiefly interesting as telling in sculpture the whole fable of Prometheus which may be readily traced out upon it. Prometheus is seen seated with the vessel of clay by his side from which he has formed his model of man, and around him are the different deities bestowing upon his creation their different gifts, while at one side are the representations of the four elements necessary for the formation and support of man, namely, Fire, represented by a group round the forge of Vulcan; Water, by a water god reclining on a sea-monster; Earth, by a female figure with cornucopia of fruits; and Air, by Æolus and flying chariots. Here, also, are the beautiful statues known as the Venus of the Capitol, Leda and the Swan, and Cupid and Psyche.

The Venus of the Capitol, so called, is a very perfect and beautiful statue, and said to have been found walled up in a niche where it had evidently been hidden for protection; it was placed in this museum by Pope Benedict in 1752, and is a Greek work ranking third in merit as a statue of the goddess, — those of Milo and Medicis being first and second, though this is a point of dispute, as many art critics consider this superior to the Medicean statue. To any lover of art, however, it is a wonderfully beautiful creation, and quite perfect, the only restorations that have been necessary being a part of a finger on the right, and the first finger of the left hand.

One of the most interesting portrait galleries in the world is the hall here known as the Hall of the Emperors, containing nearly one hundred splendid busts of Roman emperors and their wives.

This Hall of the Emperors is a curious study, as affording the student some idea of how near his imagination has approached reality with regard to the personal appearance of the various tyrants, brutes, gluttons, voluptuaries, and coarse conquerors who have in succession ruled Rome in the past; for the faithfulness of very many of these busts has been verified and their authenticity proved by various circumstances, such as their comparison with coins and medals, inscriptions, and the positions where they were discovered, and other proofs which leave but little doubt that a majority of them were portrait busts sculptured during the life of the persons they were designed to represent.

In this hall of busts, or, in fact, in any one of the museums of Rome, he who is at all interested in Roman history, in art or antiquity, and who for the first time finds himself surrounded with all these voiceless though speaking relics of the past, pointing out, corroborating, and emphasizing the history that he has studied and read, and who desires to tell what he sees to others who, less fortunate than himself, have not looked upon them, finds himself embarrassed beyond measure. Where to begin? What is the most worthy of note? To be sure and examine the great and noted works, — familiar as household words from frequent description, and not to omit the enjoyment of other records of Roman art and history that surround him, and that carry one back to the time of the Cæsars, or the exciting scenes of the Roman Forum. Again, in the bare enumeration and comment upon what one sees here, we run the risk of appearing to reproduce a guide-book. The author, therefore, mentions a few of the historic objects that more especially attracted his attention, and they are described simply as specimens of this priceless collection of ancient art.

The seated statue of Agrippina, daughter of Agrippa, and grandmother of Nero, in the middle of this hall, is sure to attract the attention from its beautiful simplicity of pose, its sad but majestic expression of countenance, and its natural attitude, while the sad record of the ill-fated but noble-spirited lady gives additional interest to this marble representation, which those who have read of her can readily imagine to be a faithful portrait by the sculptor.

A fine head is that of Poppea Sabina, second wife of Nero, and killed by that brute by a kick, in a fit of passion; the head and neck are beautifully formed of white marble, and the plaits of hair are carried round the head; and you are shown the remains of bronze pins which probably once held a bronze wreath or head-dress.

Quite a curious figure was that of Lucilla, daughter of Marcus Aurelius, as showing the skill used in the management of different-colored marbles; the drapery is so arranged as to appear like a striped robe of two different colors; the face and neck of the figure are of white marble, but the hair, which is made to take off, of black.

Here we see the bust of Septimius Severus, he to whom the arch was erected, who built the great wall between England and Scotland, and died at York, A. D. 211. Next comes Caracalla, son of Septimius, who made his name celebrated by the magnificent public baths that he commenced, that bear his name, and the ruins of which are to this day one of the wonders of Rome. Near by is a bust of Caracalla's murderer, Macrinus, who held his ill-gotten power but a year, when he in turn was deposed and executed by Heliogabalus.

We must not forget in the inspection of the marble portraits of these emperors of bloody succession, that of their predecessor, Augustus, the first Roman emperor who was acknowledged the undisputed monarch of Rome by the victory of Actium, B. C. 30. Then here is Domitian, the last of the twelve Cæsars, a cruel brute, who reigned eleven years, and was murdered in the Palace of the Cæsars, A. D. 96; a fine bust of Trajan, whose name with the general reader is inseparably connected with the most elegant and tasteful of all historic columns — Trajan's Column, erected in his honor by the senate and the Roman people in 114; and Hadrian, noted, as we know, for his architecture, circus, great mausoleum (Castle of St Angelo), and magnificent villa near Tivoli.

Nero's bust! It is unnecessary to recall the bloody deeds that will invest this bust with interest. The story of his brutal murder of his own mother, his licentiousness and cruelties, and the destruction of a great portion of Rome by fire under his bloody rule, are familiar to every schoolboy; and though his senseless dust has forever mingled with the elements, it is perhaps a somewhat retributive justice that nearly every visitor pauses before the imperishable stone to trace out in the sculptured representation of the features those characteristics that placed him in the catalogue of the most cruel tyrants and bloodiest of men. Among others of the most noted busts are those of Titus, who conquered Jerusalem, Vespasian, Marcus Aurelius, and Diocletian.

Besides the Prometheus Sarcophagus before referred to, there are several others equally interesting, some of which I can hardly pass without notice. One is known as that of the Vigna Amendola, found on the Via Appia. This has carved upon its front a fine representation of a battle between the Romans and the Gauls, with the general of the latter thrown from his horse, and in the act of stabbing himself, probably committing suicide at the mortification of defeat. Throughout the whole scene the representation is of a fierce fight between Gauls and Romans, and the story, as told by the sculptor, is that the victory which was won by the Romans was one dearly bought, for representations of slain Romans, as well as their enemies, are depicted; and, in the rush and throng of intermingling hosts, Gaul and Roman vie with each other in deeds of valor; but Gallic prisoners in fetters, women and children in tears, and other indications, are of Roman conquest. It is thought to represent a battle before Pisa, B. C. 225, where a Gallic chief killed himself as above described, and a Roman consul fell in the fight, which latter act is also depicted among the figures of the group.

A still more celebrated sarcophagus is that which was discovered underground by some farm laborers, and in which, on being opened, was found the celebrated Portland Vase now in the British Museum. The fine bas-reliefs upon this are illustrative of scenes in the history of Achilles. On one of the ends he is shown as discovered by Ulysses among the daughters of Lycomedes of Sycros, where he has revealed his sex by choosing the sword out of all the other ornaments offered by Ulysses, which were for female use. Upon another side we find Ulysses again, and in the act of rousing Achilles to avenge the death of Patrocles; upon another, his departure; and on the third, Priam at the feet of the great warrior entreating of him the dead body of Hector, and bringing a carload of gifts as ransom therefor. The ashes which were found in this sarcophagus were supposed to be those of Alexander Severus, who was killed, A. D. 235, and his mother, Julia Mammea.

The Endymion Sarcophagus, which is in the Hall of the Faun, is another one of these remarkable monuments upon which mythological fable is depicted; this was found under the high altar of the church of St. Eustace, in the time of Pope Clement XI., between 1700 and 1711. The front part of this is illustrated with the story of Endymion, who is represented rapt in slumber, and Diana, who is stepping from her chariot, is gazing admiringly upon him; above is an allegorical figure, representing Sleep. At the left, Diana has re-entered her chariot, and the horses are springing forward at the start; a female figure, half shrouded by a cloud of night, looks upward at the departing goddess, and between the two groups is Mount Latmos, with sheep and goats, and an altar to the god Pan depicted upon it. The cover has five sections of sculpture representing the life of husband and wife, the death of the latter, and her entrance into the Elysian Fields.

That which is known as the Amazon Sarcophagus is remarkable for the great beauty and rare excellence of its alto and basso relievos; inside it, besides the ashes of the deceased, there were discovered petrified balsam, a gold ring with an emerald stone set therein, and a round garnet. The bas-reliefs represent battles of the Amazons, depicted in spirited style, the battles being between Amazons and Athenians, one of the most commanding figures clad in cuirass and helmet being designated as Theseus, the slayer of that half bull, half man, mythological creation, Minotaur. Upon the cover the carved figures of captive Amazons are excellently represented; and this sarcophagus is considered important archæological authority, inasmuch as the arms represented upon it as used by the combatants are a perfect illustration of those described by Plutarch as used by the Amazons.

The last of these interesting sepulchral monuments that I shall occupy the reader's attention with is one that had but quite recently been placed in the museum, and which stood at the time of the author's visit in the centre of the Hall of Bronzes. It was discovered in 1870. This monument is one which was erected about A. D. 96 to a youthful prodigy named Quintus Sulpicius Maximus, so the inscription informs us, who died at the early age of eleven years and five months, but who was possessed of such extraordinary talent that he gained the prize for Greek verses over fifty-two other competitors.

One of the honors of this victory consisted in the successful competitor being crowned by the emperor with an oak-leaf crown, fastened with strings of gold, at the Capitol, in presence of the people. This tomb, which is a sort of architectural structure, has a statuette of the youth in a kind of niche; he stands holding a roll of manuscript in one hand, while the other is raised in the attitude of speaking. The pilasters on each side of the statuette are covered with Greek verses, which are understood to be those of the poem for which the youth received the prize; the subject being, "The arguments of Jove in reproving the Sun for intrusting his chariot to Phaëton." Poor boy! he evidently, like many of the present day, cultivated his mental at the sacrifice of his physical strength, and gained intellectual fame at the expense of life itself.

But there is yet a wealth of other sculpture to see besides the portrait-busts of Roman emperors: the stories of mythology in marble, the magnificent sarcophagi and vases, and the full-length, graceful statues of gods, goddesses, nymphs, fauns, and athletes, that once enriched the glorious old city, and contributed to make it indeed the wonder of the world.

Dug up from old temples, delved from among shattered columns, or dredged from the river's bed, where they have been hurled by the invading host of Goths and Vandals, or the destructive hand of the spoiler, come these often exquisite works of the ancient sculptor's chisel, which those of modern times strive in vain to rival.

If our indignation is sometimes aroused at the ruthless manner in which some of the old popes destroyed the magnificent temples of ancient Rome to decorate or build up their own modern structures, and perpetuate their own names at the expense of those interesting monuments of antiquity, it is somewhat appeased by the efforts which their successors of a more modern date appear to have put forth for the preservation of the fine specimens of ancient art that remain, are discovered, or dug out from the ruins over which modern Rome is built. This Capitoline Museum, which was begun by Pope Clement XII. in 1730, and augmented by his immediate successors down to Leo XII., and with occasional additions and improvements to the present time, is an indication of this desire to rescue and preserve to the modern world and art student these priceless relics of antiquity.

One almost wants a condensed history of Rome for a

hand-book, as "Murray" and the other guide-books give but the mere names of statues and sculptures in the museums, taking it for granted, I suppose, that all who visit Rome are sufficiently well read not to require explanation, or perhaps, what is the more correct reason, that fuller explanation would require too much space. I have endeavored, therefore, in my own notes to give those historic associations which invested certain objects of antiquity with additional interest to myself. Doubtless the facts may be well known to many readers, but, even if so, it will do no harm to strengthen memory by repetition.

The Hall of the Centaurs is so called from two magnificently carved figures of Centaurs in dark marble which were found among the ruins of Hadrian's villa. The marble appears to be of extraordinary hardness, and susceptible of a beautiful polish; and the faces of the Centaurs, and the sculpture of the hair of their heads, and in fact all the minor details, prove that their sculptors were masters of their art. Close inspection shows that each of these figures has been cleverly joined together, and the hand-books tell us they were broken in fragments when first discovered among the ruins. They are among the most interesting specimens of sculpture in the museum, as regards the skill in which they are wrought in every detail, and are full of life and expression. The marks upon their backs show that they were originally ridden by Cupids, and a copy of one of them in white marble, found near the Church of St. Stefano, Rome, which is now in the Museum of the Louvre at Paris, has the Cupid which is preserved, still upon its back. The youngest of these Centaurs has the skin of an animal he has slain swung over his arm, a crooked club upon his shoulder, and, with one hand upraised as he trots gayly along, is one of the most spirited statues I ever looked upon, and one the admirable execution and finish of which draws you to it again and again to view and admire.

Next, in the Hall of Philosophers, as in that of the

Emperors, the enthusiast may look upon portraits of those thinkers of antiquity whose words they have read, studied, and perhaps groaned over in student life. Here are Socrates, Aristides, whom the voter could not bear to hear called "the Just," and old Diogenes of tub and lantern notoriety, and mechanical Archimedes, Demosthenes the orator, Sophocles, Euripides the celebrated Greek tragic poet, and Thucydides the Athenian historian; also a bust of Julian the Apostate (Flavius Claudius Julianus), so called, as will be remembered, because, although a nephew of Constantine, he returned to the worship of the pagan gods, and endeavored to restore the old religion.

I will not tire the reader with descriptions of beautiful bas-reliefs of mythological story, according to Ovid, in this hall, or those of Perseus and Andromeda, and the Rape of Hylas in the next; but hurry on to that marvellous work of art, one of the great sculptures of antiquity, that is one of the magnets of Rome and one of the art gems of the world, — "The Dying Gladiator."

I am not going to quote Byron's celebrated stanzas, although, if the sculptor had desired to have had the story he has told in marble reproduced in poetry, it could not have been more perfectly done. Neither am I going to repeat the explanation respecting the figure being that of a dying Gaul, and not a gladiator. It was always a gladiator to me, and I have so pictured his fight in Rome's great circus, —

"Face to face
With death and with the Roman populace," —

the desperate struggle which he must have made for life and victory, and the thoughts of far-off home, wife, and children, as he leans upon his hand, while "the arena swims around him" as he grows giddy from the loss of the life-blood that ebbs from his heart, — I have cherished this version of the story of the statue so long, that it will be ever the Dying Gladiator to me. How I enjoyed this perfect piece of sculpture, that not only enlists but absorbs the attention, possessing that marvellously attractive power owing to its dramatic character and its story, which it tells so distinctly in attitude and expression, that you insensibly wait with bated breath to see the arm which supports the dying man, as he droops his head in agony, relax, and his dead body fall prostrate upon the shield beneath him!

How marvellously correct in anatomical detail, how simple and grand in conception and execution! How patiently must the sculptor of this wondrous work have studied the effect of the gradual approach of death upon the human frame, to have delineated it in this figure so perfectly that one feels as if he stood in the very presence of the dread destroyer!

Fortunate indeed for us who came after him was it the poet wrote those grand stanzas that make us appreciate, take in, and enjoy the subject with a pleasure that fills the soul with a grander appreciation of it as we link immortal verse to glorious sculpture.

But one wonder follows on another's heels, and I stand opposite another great work of art, but of different character, in this same hall. It is the statue known as the "Faun of Praxiteles,"—the marble faun that Hawthorne wrote of. Ah, how much do we owe to these poets and authors! This figure, so decided a contrast to the one we have just been looking upon, none the less beautiful in its character, is that of a youthfully delicate young man of exquisite mould, standing in easy attitude, leaning against a tree, his left hand resting carelessly upon his hip, the right holding a flute, while over his right shoulder is thrown the lion-skin with head and claws on.

The easy attitude of this figure is perfection itself; the grace of the pose, as well as its naturalness, is wonderful, as is the expression of countenance; the features, marble though they are, seem just on the point of breaking into a pleasant smile, — so much so that you can scarcely help smiling yourself at the roguish, handsome young man, who seems to have paused for a moment in his sylvan ramble to gaze pleasantly at you with an easy *nonchalance* that makes one all but forget the wondrous skill, and careful, patient labor that must have been required to produce from senseless stone anything so like a living figure.

Another faun is the one in a room known as the Hall of the Faun, — a figure found in Hadrian's villa, which appears to have been prolific in good things, if we may judge from the number that have been discovered there by modern antiquarian searchers.

This beautiful statue is of red marble, and represents one of those mythical beings, a faun, holding aloft a bunch of grapes with its right hand, the skin of an animal being thrown over the left arm; the graceful pose, easy, natural attitude, and wonderful execution of details in the work, like that of its fellow-statues, marking it as the creation of a master-hand, and conveying an impression of lightness, ease, and grace that one can hardly associate with a marble statue. The pedestal used for this figure is a votive altar to Jupiter found in 1745 on the Via Appia, and is handsomely sculptured with representations of sacrificial ceremonies and emblematical figures.

We leave the Capitoline Hill, descend a flight of steps, pass along till we come to a point that commands a view of a ruin of three beautiful Corinthian columns, one of Rome's ruined triumphal arches, and further on ruined pillars upholding a temple's lofty façade. I descended into a large, open space that was below the street-level; above me rose the Capitol I had just quitted, the stronghold of Romulus, the temple of Tarquin the Proud, and glory of the emperors, the birthplace of an empire that existed for nearly nineteen hundred years. And this spot that I now stand upon, which has been overwhelmed by an additional crust of earth and ruins, like all the rest of old Rome, — why, this must be classic ground. These graceful pillars I recognize as the originals of bronze reproductions, pictures, and photographs, — the columns of the Temple of Vespasian; and near at hand the eight Ionic columns uphold what is left of the portico of the Temple of Saturn, the ancient god of the Capitol. Let us recall that here, before this very temple, once sat Pompey and listened to the orations of Cicero.

Cicero! The Roman Forum! We must be in that birthplace of Roman law, celebrated for the wisdom of great statesmen, and the eloquence of great orators. To be sure, the hand of time has gradually heaped the soil each succeeding century, till now it is twenty-four feet above that of old Rome. It has overthrown temples, arches, rostra, and columns, till but a few crumbling relics remain, — enough to excite curiosity, and evoke contests between antiquaries. An illustrious spot indeed is the Roman Forum, and every foot of the ground about us teems with associations of historic interest.

"Who," — writes George S. Hillard, the well-known classic scholar, in his "Six Months in Italy," — "who that has the least sense of what the present owes to the past, can approach such a spot without reverence and enthusiasm? Especially, what member of the legal profession, unless his heart be dry as parchment, and worn as the steps of a court-house, can fail to do homage to the genius of a place where jurisprudence was reared into a perfect system, while Druids were yet cutting the mistletoe on the site of Westminster Hall?"

And why is it not a sacred place to a scholar, a student, a schoolboy, a reader even, — one of the most remarkable spots upon the earth, crammed with events, with actions that had their birth here, and that for fifteen centuries had so marked an influence upon the whole civilized world? In fact it was here, when the power of Rome was at its height, that the destinies of the world were discussed. Like the hill of the Capitol, the names of successive structures that have come down to us in history as having occupied this space — which was about four acres, the Forum being one hundred and eighty yards long by seventy broad — are so numerous that antiquaries are sadly at a loss where to place many of them.

The supposition of those not familiar with Roman history is, that the Forum was simply a place of orators, instead of what it really was, a court of justice, public exchange, house of representatives, public square, market-place, and political hall of assembly, all rolled into one. Here the popular representatives of the plebeians, the people, assembled and discussed political matters, and here the great orators harangued them. Here Cato, Cicero, Cæsar, and Marc Antony have spoken; indeed, this spot, from the time of Romulus down to Augustus, was the very heart of the Roman empire, the pulsations of which were felt throughout the whole world.

I stood looking up at the modern Capitol, resting upon its great structure of broad blocks of stone called the *tabularium*, one of the earliest architectural relics of Rome, and then passing over near to it, stood on the site of the tribune, the pulpit, or rostrum from which the orators spoke to the people, now a sort of semicircular wall faced with marble. Here is where Cicero with his magic eloquence swayed the Roman people at will, — a glorious speaker, a philosopher, and man of culture. Here was where he spoke to hushed crowds of the populace, and pronounced his stinging speeches against Antony. And here is where, in spirit of mean, dastardly revenge, Antony placed his head and hands after his inhuman murder; and Fulvia, the widow of Clodius, revenged herself against the bitter, unpalatable truths that had been uttered by the bold, fearless tongue, by piercing it with a pin she wore in her hair, and spitting in the dead face, the gaze of which, when living, had looked into the bloody deeds of such as she, and exposed them to public gaze. Here also the head of Octavius was placed by Marius, and perhaps it was in imitation of the old Romans that the more modern English put condemned heads on the spikes of Temple Bar.

We may go on a short distance beyond the Arch of Septimius Severus to the site of the Temple of Concord, and there recite the orations of Cicero against Catiline before the senate upon the very spot where they were delivered; and it was here in the Forum, not far from the rostrum, that the survivor of the Horatii was condemned to death but saved by the overwhelming voice of the people, who refused to part with their brave champion. I walk a little further and find a sort of square platform of rock, the remains of the lower fragment of some temple-wall, apparently, but really the site of the Altar of Vulcan, near which sat Brutus when he saw with stern justice his own sons led to execution.

Moving out towards the middle of the Forum, we make our way over debris and by a devious path to the foot of a tall column, a handsome Corinthian pillar, the excavation of which knocked over the theories of antiquaries and scholars completely, — the column of Phocas. Nobody thought of Phocas, or of a column to him. Byron called it

"The nameless column with a buried base;"

but when the "buried base" was brought to light, lo and behold, the inscription showed it to be, not, as was supposed, part of a building, Temple of Vulcan, or Bridge of Caligula, but a column erected in 608, with its base resting on the actual pavement of the Forum.

A superb spectacle the Roman Forum must have presented, with its beautiful temples, statues, and triumphal arches, when in its prime, as one may easily imagine from these veriest fragments that the destroying hand of time has left us. The Via Sacra, or sacred way itself, upon one side of the space, with its magnificent marble arches at each end of the line, was where the grand triumphal processions of Rome's emperors and generals came after their bloody raids (for they were little else) upon distant nations; here, chained barbarians, as they passed along, gazed upon the evidences of the wealth and power of their scarcely less barbarous, certainly none the less cruel conquerors.

These triumphal arches are magnificent relics of Rome's luxury, power, and art, and the visitor cannot help realizing it as he stands before that most beautiful one, the Arch of Titus, commemorating the destruction of Jerusalem, and being, therefore, interesting from its connection with Scripture history, and its bas-reliefs, which have furnished designs for many illustrations for modern editions of the Bible and Scripture history.

For upon its white marble piers are elaborate representations of the costly spoils of the sacred city of the Jews, which the conqueror brought home to Rome, — the familiar seven-branched candlestick, golden table of shew-bread, trumpets of the jubilee, &c.; and we find that the description of old Josephus, read in boyhood, is correct, and that the woodcut illustration of the great holy candlestick, which is represented in the old pictorial editions of the book, is the exact counterpart of that sculptured upon this arch, which the slaves and soldiers are bearing upon their shoulders in the triumphal procession.

Upon this arch is also represented the conquering emperor returning from Jerusalem in his chariot surrounded by his troops, holding his sceptre in one hand and a palm branch in the other, while a figure of Victory is in the act of placing the laurel wreath upon his brow. The face of the figure of Titus is almost completely destroyed; mutilated, it is said, by stones cast at it by the Jews whose defeat and subjugation this arch commemorates. Indeed, to this day it is averred that no Jew will pass beneath this memento of the Roman conqueror's victory, either in their walks or business, but go around it; for it perpetuates the memory of their wrongs and the name of their oppressor. And farther beyond is the great Colosseum, where he pressed them with such severity that the Hebrew laborers went down by thousands beneath the taskmaster's whip, and the more wealthy were squeezed a few years after by Domitian, his brother, until the last coin that persecution could wring from them was obtained.

The arch is a page of marble history, — verified history, unlike many other Roman ruins, — seventeen hundred years old; and, though many may prefer the construction of the Arch of Constantine to the more simple and solid style of this, they can hardly examine the sculptured decorations with so much interest.

This arch, when in its prime, and with the beautiful white marble of which it is constructed shining in the sunlight, must have presented a splendid appearance. It is exactly as high as it is long, being fifty feet in height and fifty feet long. The width of the passage, or single arched opening, is nineteen feet, and the thickness or breadth of the arch sixteen and one-half feet. This arch and the Colosseum, which Titus completed and opened, remind us that we used to read that he was an industrious emperor, and that it was he who said, after a day of leisure, "I have lost a day."

The three best preserved and most interesting arches in Rome are those I have referred to in the immediate vicinity of the Forum and by the side of the way over which the victorious triumphs passed, namely: that of Titus just described, and those of Constantine and Septimius Severus.

The last-named arch is smallest of the three, and its base rests on what was the ancient level of the Forum, giving the visitor who descends to it an idea of the change that has occurred in grade since the days of old Rome. This arch was erected to commemorate the victories of Severus over the Parthians, Arabs, and various Eastern tribes, A. D. 203. It has one grand central passage, and two side or lesser ones. It was of pure white marble, and when in its perfect state had a group of sculpture upon the top, consisting of a triumphal car drawn by six horses. In the car, says one authority, stood statues of the emperor and his sons, Caracalla and Geta, though the guide-books say it was a bronze chariot with a figure of Severus being crowned by Victory. I am of the opinion of the historian, however; who puts the two brothers in the chariot, as they erected the arch, and would hardly let this opportunity of gratifying their Roman vanity pass. Geta was murdered by Caracalla when he succeeded to the imperial purple, and in the inscription on the structure Geta's name was erased by his brother.

This arch has also four elegant columns on each side of its fronts. The sculptures upon it appear to delineate the wars of Severus, and groups of warriors in battles, sieges, councils, and marches, figure conspicuously. One scene represents the siege of a city in which the battering-ram is being worked most effectively upon the walls of the enemy. However, the guide-books pretend to tell and enumerate all the scenes in the life of the emperor which these sculptures represent. The arch to his honor perpetuates his name, which is also recognized as that of one of the most cruel persecutors of the Christians; still, he was a tolerable emperor for Rome, as emperors went in those days, and had eighteen years of power. The reason why he caused comparatively less blood to flow in Rome than some of his predecessors may have been from the fact that his active employment in Britain, and with other powers that he was continually combating, kept him too busily employed.

The Arch of Constantine, which every visitor to Rome will remember as standing near the Colosseum, seems to be the best preserved and finest of the three; but many of its sculptures and bas-reliefs are known to have been those which were carved to honor an emperor who flourished two centuries before Constantine, — Trajan, — as they were taken from an arch formerly existing, erected to that emperor and placed upon this, which is now one of the best preserved and most interesting monuments in Rome, apart from its antiquity, — having been dedicated to the first Christian sovereign.

The inscription sets forth that the senate and Roman people have dedicated this triumphal arch to the emperor, because he, with the greatness of his mind and with his just arms, at the same time revenged the state on the tyrant and on his (the tyrant's) political party. The sculptures, however, represent Trajan (not Constantine) entering Rome; offering sacrifices to the gods, (which a Christian emperor of course did not do;) Trajan's triumph over the king of Armenia, &c.

This arch has one central and two side arches, and had four elegant Corinthian columns on each front. The fine sculptures are on the attic above the great arch, in two medallions over each of the smaller arches; and there are flying figures with trophies immediately over the great arch, besides friezes and bas-reliefs on the sides by the smaller arches, and carved allegorical figures at the base of each Corinthian pillar. The lower bas-reliefs on the arch are of the deeds of Constantine, but are far inferior in execution to those above, which were plundered from the Trajan arch, the ruins of which existed down to 1430, according to historical accounts; thus it appears that even in Constantine's time the example of appropriating the monuments of their predecessors for their own glorification was set, which modern popes of Rome have in many instances faithfully followed. Clement VIII. appropriated one of the eight Corinthian columns of this arch, and carried it away to finish a chapel with.

It may be well here to remind the reader that the Arc de Triomphe du Carrousel, situated in front of the principal entrance to the Palace of the Tuileries, in Paris, erected by Napoleon I. in 1806, is an imitation of the Arch of Severus.

We could not leave the Capitoline Hill and Roman Forum without a visit to that hole of horrors, the Marmetine Prison, an historic dungeon with which are connected so many associations that one does not like to miss it among the list of sights to be seen. There is but little doubt expressed by the antiquaries that it was here, after being dragged in chains behind the triumphal chariot of Caius Marius, where Jugurtha was shut up and starved to death. The prison now, or the upper part of it, is made into a little church or oratory, with religious emblems and votive offerings hung about; and what most strikes one, as he sits down and waits for the dirty brown-frocked monk to prepare the greasy tallow candles for descent into the lower or real dungeon, are the massive blocks of stone of which the structure is composed — strength enough to confine a Titan. In ancient times there was no staircase, but prisoners were let down through a trap door or hole in the roof. Now, however, a monk (for a gratuity, of course) shows you down a flight of stone steps into the dungeon described by Livy and Sallust. The latter describes it as "a place about ten feet deep surrounded by walls, with a vaulted roof of stone above it." The dungeon is hemispherical in shape, and about twenty feet in diameter, although it seemed of smaller dimensions to me in the brief time I stayed, and the whole appearance of the place was as fearful and dungeon-like as the most vivid imagination could desire. Its damp, cold, pitiless stones have been witness to the most terrible scenes of torture and suffering, for the visitor here stands within the inclosure which, built four or five centuries before the Cæsars, was the prison where Appius Claudius, the emperor who endeavored to obtain possession of the daughter of Virginius, slew himself to escape the vengeance of the people; and here was the brave Manlius Capitolinus immured, despite his services to his countrymen, which weighed as nothing against the power of the nobles. Here, as the triumphs turned aside after their grand march through the city and Forum, were captive kings and chiefs plunged after having been exhibited as a spectacle to the populace. The alleged accomplices of Catiline were strangled in this gloomy vault by order of Cicero, who came forth himself bearing the news of their death to the people in the Forum, exclaiming, in answer to their clamorous inquiries, "*Vixerunt*" (they *have* lived).

A cruel cavern it is indeed, for within it Julius Cæsar basely thrust the king of the Gauls who surrendered himself voluntarily to save his people, and, after keeping him six years captive, murdered him here. Sejanus, the favorite of Tiberius, met his just fate within these walls; and Simon of Goria, the last brave defender of Jerusalem, after being dragged and scourged at the chariot-wheels of Titus, in his triumphal entry into Rome, also yielded up his life upon the floor that for twenty-three centuries has been soaked with the blood of chieftains, senators, kings, and emperors.

Yet it is not these events that render it so interesting a spot to the Christian visitor, for it was here that Peter and Paul are said to have been confined for nine months during their imprisonment in Rome; and I confess, as the monk who was acting as our cicerone pointed out what he averred to be the very pillar to which these apostles were chained during their captivity, that, although I did not reverently kiss it, as did a Roman Catholic of the party, I could not leave without laying my hands upon the spot upon which might perhaps have rested the hands of those who had pressed the blessed palm of Christ within their own. The little fountain or well in the floor, the Romish Church must, of course, ascribe a miraculous origin to: they say it sprang up at the bidding of the two apostles for them to baptize their jailers whom they had converted. As we came up the staircase, our guide also called attention to a depression or indentation in the stone, which is said to have been the impression made by the head of St. Peter, who was rudely thrust against it by his jailer. It is thus the Church of Rome, by the demand for such credulity as this, and appeals to the most ignorant, really tends to shake historical belief in other characteristics of ruins, relics, or localities, that have a certain amount of authenticity.

Chief in my memory of this horrid prison, however, was that it had been the dungeon of Jugurtha, and of Peter and Paul, and it was one of the things to be seen in visiting Rome in my mind years before this experience. Having accomplished the visit, we made all haste to leave its gloomy recesses and damp atmosphere which Jugurtha even in his day compared to "a cold bath," and emerged into the upper chamber, and thence once more into the more genial atmosphere and under the cloudless blue sky of Italy, all the more beautiful in contrast with the gloomy cavern we had quitted, and the terrible scenes which a visit to it recalls.

The soil of modern Rome seems to be an earth shroud over the remains of the ancient city; and to get at the entrance to temples, the sites of forums, and the courtyards of palaces, one must dig down through the dust of centuries. The wave of earth wells up over the steps of the Pantheon, and has surged its billow around the base of the Colosseum, so that excavations give it the appearance of being surrounded by an earth work thrown up from just without its outer barrier. The once proud Palace of the Cæsars, until a few years past, slumbered beneath a flourishing vineyard; and you may now, curiously enough, see the different strata of Rome's history, as it were, indicated in the structures that each rise above the other's ruins, — the Wall of Romulus, the structures of Tarquin, the Palace of Nero, — literally one atop of the other.

As I came, one day, to an excavated square, with serried rows of the broken lower parts of columns that were evidently the fragments of some ancient temple, I knew, as I sat down upon one huge shaft that seemed long since to have been raised from the excavated area below, and laid in the more modern street alongside the rail that guarded the brink, that I was looking down into Trajan's Forum. I knew it by the tall, graceful column that stood there to the memory of the great emperor. Familiar as an old acquaintance, it reared its tall height, wreathed with the chronological story of his victories, and brought to mind its counterfeit presentment in the Place Vendôme at Paris (erected by a great emperor of modern times, ambitious to be remembered as a modern Cæsar), and by monuments of a similar description.

Paris did not have to wait for Goths and Vandals, as did Rome, to destroy its historical monuments that in recording the deeds of their great emperor preserved alike the chronicle of the bravery and victories of their own forefathers. No! Paris had its own barbarians always within its walls, who were ready to wrench from its foundations the monument of cannon conquered from the enemy's battlefield, and prostrate it ignominiously in the filth of the street. The ascendency of men over madmen, however, has replaced the modern French monument; and the old Roman one to Trajan, from which it was copied, has always remained firm upon its pedestal since raised by the senate and the Roman people, A. D. 114, and is to-day one of the most beautiful monuments remaining of the Eternal City. It is one hundred and thirty feet in height, and composed of successive blocks of marble, "thirty-four in number," so the guide-books tell us, piled one upon the other. These are covered by a spiral band of carvings or bas-reliefs from the base of the pillar to the top, the carvings ingeniously and gradually increased in size from two feet in height to double that size as they near the top, so that harmonious proportions are preserved to the eye of the spectator from below.

The figure of Trajan holding a globe in his hand formerly crowned the summit; the globe is now in the Hall of Bronzes at the Capitoline Museum, and Trajan's figure is replaced by a statue of St. Peter upon the column. This ought to be removed and the emperor's statue restored, that it might be a less incongruous specimen of antiquity; for the apostolic statue is out of place upon the column of the pagan emperor.

The Forum of Trajan, which is here buried under modern Rome, was one of the most splendid in the ancient city; and here stood his arch, from which were plundered the elegant bas-reliefs alluded to as taken to decorate the Arch of Constantine two hundred years after, and the splendid equestrian statue of the emperor, — a statue which, as the story runs, excited the envy of Constantine, who wished "that he had such a horse," and was told "that he must first make for him such a stable." Here were also glorious temples and splendid statues in bronze and marble; but the breath of time has withered them into dust, all but this one great marble finger-post pointing to the past.

An excavation around this column was made in the sixteenth century, and further work of excavating done by the French in 1812. Indeed, when the tourist sees how much of this work of excavating was done more recently at the Palace of the Cæsars by Louis Napoleon, when he was emperor, while the French army were in Rome propping up papal power with their friendly bayonets, he is half inclined to be selfish enough to wish that Italian liberty might have been postponed till there had been laid bare a few more secrets of the buried past. The great pedestal, seventeen feet high, is covered with sculptures of Roman warlike weapons and armor; winged figures support the tablet bearing the inscription; and why is it the guide-books take it for granted that all travellers are expert Latin scholars, and never in any instance translate these most difficult of Latin sentences, with their abbreviated words, for the benefit of those whom they puzzle?

The inscription upon this column, which no guide-book pretends to translate, and which but few give in the original, states that "the Senate and the Roman people dedicate this to the Emperor Cæsar, Divus Nerva Flavius, Nerva Trajan, Augustus Pontifex Maximus, in his 17th tribunate, 6th consulate, and 6th emperor, in order to proclaim what greatness was his. The mountain has been removed that there may be place for so great a work."

This last sentence alludes, probably, to the fact that excavations were made and part of a hill removed for the completion of the Forum and column of the great emperor.

The lower part of the shaft itself, which is about thirteen feet in diameter, springs out of an immense wreath. The sculptures that run around it are very well preserved, and must be a most interesting study to the antiquary and student. The column is of pure Carrara marble, and its workmanship inside as well as outside something quite remarkable, as within, the thirty-four blocks have been cut into a spiral staircase. When we consider the careful matching of the hollowed blocks that the chronological sculpture should be a perfect, continuous spiral, the staircase be exactly matched, and the whole structure architecturally perfect, we are again impressed with the skill of the builders of old Rome, and the point of excellence to which mechanics as well as the arts had been carried in those days. Trajan's Column is an illustrated pillar of history. Its sculptures are said to display nearly two thousand five hundred human figures, besides horses, bridges, fortresses, rivers, and warlike weapons; but it is the sculptured scroll of actors whose names and deeds are forgotten save that they lived and were conquered. The ashes of Trajan are reported to be buried underneath the base of this magnificent pillar, a worthy monument of an emperor, " who," says Gibbon, " made war only to secure peace, and left the Roman empire greater and more prosperous than he received it from the hands of his predecessors."

Another column in Rome, modelled after that of Trajan, although not equal to it in artistic execution, is that of Marcus Aurelius, which stands in a square known as the Piazza Colonna. This was also erected by " the senate and the Roman people," A. D. 174, to the emperor, in honor of his victories over the Marcomanni. It is of the same general design as the Column of Trajan, the shaft being, like that, surrounded by a spiral band of bas-reliefs or carvings running from base to summit, representing battles and military scenes in the emperor's life. As a whole, the sculptures are inferior in design and execution to those upon the shaft of Trajan.

This column is built of twenty-eight blocks of white marble, and is eleven feet and six inches in diameter at its base, and its height, including the pedestal, one hundred and twenty-two feet and eight inches. Inside there is a spiral staircase composed of one hundred and ninety steps, and on the summit stands a statue of St. Paul, ten feet in height, of course as incongruous an addition as that to Trajan's Column. The blunder of denominating this column that of Antoninus Pius is told in the guide-books, and the tourist will do well to bear it in mind, — as it is even now frequently denominated the Antonine Column, — for Marcus Aurelius's name was Marcus Antoninus. The reader will recall the author's description of the ancient bronze equestrian statue of this, one of the best of Roman emperors, in front of the Capitol. The glories of old Rome were rapidly decaying when he assumed the imperial purple, but his energy, justice, philosophy, and purity of mind stand out in marked contrast with the characteristics of the many bloody tyrants who had preceded him.

A few steps from this square and we are in that of Monte Citorio, where we may look upon another column, in comparison with which the one we have left is but of modern date; for this, an Egyptian obelisk erected to an Egyptian king more than six hundred years before Christ, was brought to Rome from Heliopolis by Augustus, and was set up in the Campus Martius as a sun-dial. Old as it is, the hieroglyphics upon the ancient red granite shaft are clear and distinct, and doubtless record the Egyptian monarch's deeds as faithfully as the spiral-twined shafts do those of the more modern rulers of Rome. Pope Pius VI. joined the five fragments of this fine obelisk together, and raised it from where it had fallen to this position, where it now stands surmounted by a bronze globe, which it rears one hundred and thirty-four feet into the air.

The old popes did a good thing when they preserved and set up those splendid monuments of antiquity, the Egyptian obelisks which the emperors brought home as spoils to Rome, as they are among the interesting objects that to-day attract the tourist's attention. That in front of St. Peter's has already been referred to, and there are several others, chief among which, however, is that known as the obelisk of the Lateran in the Piazza di San Giovanni. Here, indeed, I felt I was in the presence of antiquity, standing before this tallest obelisk in Rome, a shaft one hundred and fifty feet high, cut in honor of the Pharaoh Thothmes IV., seventeen hundred and forty years before Christ!

Daily on my sight-seeing excursions did I drive down from the Hotel Constanzi, — so named after its landlord, formerly an expert courier, and at the time I was in Rome a very good hotel-keeper, — daily did I drive down through Barberini Square, or Piazza Barberini, I perhaps should say, and past the Triton fountain, where the great Triton seems to have exhausted his lungs to but little purpose, inasmuch as he sends a stream of water through the shell at his lips ridiculously small in comparison to his apparent size and strength, — drive past an opening into another square, and on to the old or more modern city.

"What square is that, Antonio?"

"Piazza Cappuccini, Monsieur. Would Monsieur like to visit the Convent?"

"Convent of the Capuchins! Why, that is the place where the monks' skeletons are used as decorations for funeral chambers, is it not?"

"Yes, Monsieur, they use the bones for decoration of the burial-place."

One of the very places I had a curiosity to see. According to travellers' stories, both written and verbal, I had pictured to myself a long series of vaulted passages, hundreds of feet in length, whose gloomy extensions were like the Catacombs of Paris, of mortuary architecture, pillars of skulls, architraves of ribs, and podium of thigh-bones, with curiously fashioned cells, each holding the dried or mummied specimen of the pious brotherhood, ghastly reminders to those who were to come after of how frail a thing is mortality. So now I addressed myself to the task of visiting this famous burial-place.

We descended from our carriage at the church of the Convent, founded in 1624 by Cardinal Barberini, a brother of Pope Urban VIII., who, while his whole family were building splendid palaces, only built and endowed this convent and church, and appears to have been a man of very moderate ambition and real humility. The Barberini Square is called for his family.

A brown-frocked, not over-clean specimen of the brotherhood admitted us into the church, which in itself has but few attractions, and does not appear to be very well cared for. It is chiefly remarkable for several very fine pictures, the principal one of which is a magnificent one by Guido, representing the archangel Michael trampling down Satan. The figure of Michael is magnificent, with his pure, angelic brow, and sweet yet noble expression, as, poised just above his adversary, he brandishes aloft the sword with which he drives the rebellious angel down, never to rise again.

A picture of the "Death of St. Francis," by Domenichino, and one of "Ananias and Saul," by Cortona, attracted our attention most, and near the high altar our monkish guide pointed out the tomb of Alexander Sobieski, the son of the king of Poland. In front of the altar Cardinal Barberini is buried, and his epitaph, which the monk called attention to as typical of the humility of the holy man, reads, —

HIC JACET PULVIS, CINIS, ET NIHIL.
("Here lies naught but dust and ashes.")

With a somewhat quizzical smile, the brown-robed brother

withdrew two of the more eager members of our party, — ladies who, after making the detour of the church, were about passing through an entrance into the monastery, — and, plucking them by the sleeve, intimated that none but those of the masculine gender could pass through its sacred precincts. Hence that portion of the party composed of the gentler sex, who desired to visit the cemetery of the Capuchins, which was our aim, was compelled to make a detour outside the building, while we passed through the monastery. A shabby old convent it appeared to be, and looked as though the presence of a dozen or twenty good scrubbing-women would have done essential service.

There were, we were informed, about two hundred monks here, although we saw scarcely a dozen. Their cells were simple, narrow apartments, with three-legged stool, wretched bed, crucifix, and little wooden table bearing a black prayer-book or rosary, and lighted by a narrow, prison-like slit of a window. The refectory was an immense room, with long tables set, at which the monks took their meals. A dingy, cheerless-looking place enough it was, and in the halls, save occasional little fonts of holy water at certain points or passages as we passed through, there were no decorations or ornament; and this dull old hole of retirement for monkish beggars was uninteresting enough, — at least the portion of it we were permitted to see.

Our cowled guide soon reached a door, which he unlocked, and we descended into the celebrated burial-place of the brotherhood, where we found the ladies, who had been admitted by another entrance, awaiting us.

I was wretchedly disappointed in the place, and found that the long-bow had been drawn to its fullest extent by ingenious writers. It was a long, narrow apartment, not beneath the level of the ground, but lighted by grated windows that appeared to look out upon a dilapidated old garden and stable-yard. The cemetery is an apartment about fifty feet long perhaps, and twenty or thirty wide. About two-thirds of the width, and the whole length, were occupied by four or five compartments or divisions, like potato bins, which are filled with earth brought from Jerusalem, and in which each monk, as he dies, is placed in his robe and rosary to mingle with its sacred dust. From the length of time this earth has been used for this purpose, and the number of cowled brothers who have slept their last sleep in it, I fancy that an analyzation would reveal seventy-five per cent. Capuchin to twenty-five of honest earth by this time. The earth, or place, or dry atmosphere, or all, seems to have the property of drying away, not rotting, the flesh from the bones of those buried, for there was not the slightest offensive odor in the place.

As the burial-place is far too small for the convent, whenever a brother dies they dig up the one who was buried the longest, and inter the last deceased in his place. The bones of the disinterred are used for decorating and fitting up the four burial-bins or sacred compartments into grim and horrible mortuary chapels. Chandeliers of skulls and thigh-bones, ornamental frescos of the small bones of toes and fingers, altars of leg and arm bones, and twining designs of bits of vertebra, — every part of the human skeleton put into this grim and horrible architecture and decoration.

Not only is this lavish display made of the last remnants of mortality, but in a niche in each of the divisions above mentioned is the skeleton, or dried mummy, of some worthy brother, who perhaps was thought to have been too good in the flesh to be broken up and mingled indiscriminately with his fellows. And there they sit in their mouldering cowls, the shining bones peeping out here and there through the rents in their tattered robes, and their eyeless sockets and grinning jaws seeming to express a hideous laugh; or with a bunch of withered flowers, as one had in its bony grasp, and in its half fallen-over position, and head pushed at one side, having a sort of terrible expression, as though it had perished in the act of plucking the flowers that it held. Quite the contrary was another, whose expression and attitude gave it the appearance of a convivial brother; or, if one could imagine such a thing, a drunken skeleton, — a sight at once horrible and laughable.

The place, to those not used to such sights, was a veritable hall of horrors, such as might be imagined or told in a ghostly romance, — a grave-digger's museum, a charnel-house drawing-room, — a lesson for ambition, and a hint from the King of Terrors; something which makes those of weak nerves shudder, and hope they shall not dream about it at night.

Our monkish guide, who pointed out all the striking features of the place, and even knew some of the skulls by name, and had known one of the dried-up brothers in the more plump flesh of life, spoke with great *sang froid* of being interred there himself, as the others had been, when his time should come.

In this wish, however, he may be disappointed, for, since the author's visit, King Victor Emmanuel, who is doing a work of civilization in abolishing many of these collections of legalized beggars in Rome, has taken this convent in hand, and on the 5th of August, 1875, the building was confiscated by the Italian government. The monks, who were all men past forty years of age, to the number of two hundred, were summoned to the refectory, where the king's proclamation was read, setting them free, and granting them a sixty-dollar pension. Many of them — having never done a stroke of work in their lives, fat from laziness, and dirty from not having put forth exertion enough to keep themselves clean, awkward and unused to the ways of men — will undoubtedly seek some other convent not yet suppressed, where they will live a like secluded, idle, and lazy life to the end of their days. But the convent, or a portion of it at least, is to be utilized for a warehouse, and the cemetery, with its grisly architecture and decoration, will cease to be one of the sights for tourists to see and writers to describe, as all these dismal relics of mortality will be decently buried.

CHAPTER X.

I have seen the Vatican, that is to say, I have visited it, several times, and when collecting together, after my last visit, a pile of memoranda, guide-books with annotations and marginal references, note-book with jottings and diagrams, and sundry photographic views, and setting them aside, I sat down and attempted to recall what I had seen into something like regular order, it seemed like endeavoring to record a dream a week old.

Three or four consecutive visits to these interminable galleries — wondrous as a fairy dream, magnificent as an Eastern fable, and bewildering in their never ending succession of art, novelty, antiquity, beauty, ingenuity, and history, — put mind and imagination into such a whirl and confusion that it seems almost impossible to give a clear idea of anything you have seen in this marvellous and unexcelled collection.

It is the grandest museum in the world; it has had old Rome's imperial ruins, buried sculptures, marbles, and statues to draw from for centuries, and successive popes have rivalled each other in building splendid additions for rich, rare, and priceless collections which each added to it, decorating them by the pencils of great artists, till walls, and even ceilings, became artistic wonders, and the halls and galleries caskets worthy of the gems they contain. He who attempts to write of the Vatican is at a loss where to begin or what to describe, the collection is so vast, the beauty is so inimitable.

He who is a lover of museums of art, taste, or antiquity is like a beggar set down in a room full of gold and told it is his own — the prospect is so boundless, the vista of delight so never-ending, that it fairly intoxicates, and one must pause, get sobered and steadied, in order to collect his ideas that he may utilize any portion of the vast wealth that is thus placed within his grasp.

It is absurd to suppose that one can see or properly appreciate a tithe of this priceless collection in the time ordinarily devoted by tourists in Rome; indeed, it seems that three or four visits do little else than confuse one and impress him with the idea that to give it a thorough study and inspection he would have to remain in the Holy City an ordinary lifetime.

I cannot pretend, and shall not attempt, to do more than give the reader a few sips of the cup to arouse taste for the enchanting draught at this fountain of art when he himself shall visit it. Indeed, I feel that the few visits I have made to it, though careful as far as they extend, have given me but comparatively small insight into its prodigality of art, amazing richness of antiquities, and wondrous treasures of sculpture, literature, and historic relics. In fine, the Vatican overshadows all other museums in the world in size of collection and in wonders of painting, frescos, and statuary. Its wealth is the result of hundreds of years of labor, ambition, and bequests of genius to posterity. Here the student may study ancient and modern art, sculpture, and painting from the most perfect models in existence.

As a pile of buildings the exterior of the Vatican is not striking, impressive, or attractive; it is simply an assemblage of different edifices, of no uniformity of architecture, as they were built at different periods by different architects, and have since been altered from time to time by different popes, or connected together by various methods to suit their convenience. But within, there are numerous superb architectural displays and magnificent effects in the construction of its vast halls, colonnades, and staircases. The Vatican is said to contain eight grand staircases, two hundred smaller ones, twenty courts, and about five thousand chambers of various sizes, although one authority (Baedeker) gives it "eleven thousand halls, chapels, saloons, and private apartments." Most tourists, however, like the author, will not probably take the trouble to verify either of these statements by actual count, but will find themselves, after repeated visits, passing many objects that need not be viewed a second time, and also pass by very many which they will not have time or inclination to view at all, till they find their circle of observation gradually narrowing down to those great wonders of art that are of world-wide celebrity, the beauty of which is attested by each succeeding generation.

The papal custodians are not over-obliging to visitors, and the arrangements, at the time of the author's visit, were anything but conducive to convenience. The visitor, after seeing the Sistine Chapel and picture gallery, instead of being permitted to pass through a portion of the building to the sculpture galleries, as formerly, was compelled to descend to the entrance-door, take carriage, and make a considerable detour to the other side of the building to reach them by an entirely different entrance. This involves considerable time, which one does not like to sacrifice, especially as the longest time permitted to visitors was between the hours of nine and three, and this is shortened nearly half an hour by the custodians, who commence at about half past two to clear the apartments most distant from the entrance, so that the gates may be promptly closed at the hour. But it is of no use complaining, for it is the Pope's palace and museum, and, in view of Victor Emmanuel's reforms, he probably does not feel very anxious about inconveniencing his officials, or they themselves, more than is absolutely necessary.

But for all the inconveniences, real or imaginary, that the visitor experiences, the conviction forces itself upon him that the world owes much gratitude to the pontiffs whose liberality and skill brought together these wonderful examples of art.

Before passing the gates and ascending the magnificent flight of stairs which we saw before us, I paused to view the fine perspective, and to inspect the extraordinary uniform of a group of the Pope's guard that was standing at this point. These men are evidently selected, as were the French *cent gardes*, and Frederick the Great's grenadiers, for their height. Their uniform is more gaudy and theatrical than the "beef-eaters'" of the Tower of London. That of the privates or halberdiers is of alternate stripes of red, black, and yellow. The breeches are large and baggy, reaching just below the knees, and the legs are inclosed in black and yellow striped stockings. The coat or jacket reached a little below the hips, and was, like the rest of the dress, of broad, red, black, and yellow stripes. A white, round ruff about the neck, and a cavalry helmet almost shrouded in the white feathers, completed this extraordinary and strikingly conspicuous uniform. The privates carried a staff about eight feet in length, the end being a spear and axe, the whole very like an ancient halberd.

The dress of the officers is similar to that of the men, except that their helmets are crowned with red instead of white feathers; and the one that I saw had on a regular metallic cuirass, or breastplate, like that worn by the French cuirassiers in the time of Napoleon I. — a terribly uncomfortable costume for guard duty in a warm climate, however pretty it might look in pictures or pageants. These absurdly dressed guards of him who claims to be the vicar of Christ and the successor of St. Peter, are but one of the curious costumes, religious and military, that are continually greeting our sight in the Holy City.

There are, of course, the different orders of monks, distinguished by their gray, or black, or brown cowls, including the Capuchins before alluded to, who sleep in their dresses and change them only once in three years, and those friars who go about begging with a sort of fire-bucket looking pail for cold victuals, cash, or anything they can get; and the cardinals' servants or attendants, in curious, old-fashioned liveries which always have an appearance of being two or three sizes too big for them. Then there are the different orders of students for the priesthood, distinguished by the color of their long robes or outer cloaks, or great shovel hats; and the white-bonneted sisters of charity. In fact, the frequent meeting and constant presence of these different religious uniforms remind the visitor that he is at the chosen home of the Papal Church. Besides these, there are still the oddly-costumed, brigandish-looking peasants and families that come in for artists' models or to beg of such strangers in the travelling season as halt to look at the high, peaked hats and ribbons, and swathed legs and gay jackets of the men, and gaudy aprons, big hairpins, and scarfs of the women. But I am keeping the reader all this time at the foot of the staircase leading in to the Vatican; and a glorious staircase it is, fit for popes and emperors to ascend. The Scala Regia, or great staircase, with its beautiful perspective, lofty arches, and grand colonnade of pillars, is a sight to be remembered.

I had heard so much of the Sistine Chapel, and its marvellous ceiling painted by Michael Angelo, that I was disappointed at the general effect on first sight of it, especially from its contrast with newer and brighter frescos seen on staircases and halls before entering this wonderfully decorated room. To me it seemed that Angelo's work was much in need of a good cleaning. I chanced to be with but a small party, with a guide who knew the custodian, and who therefore let us have our own way and time for examining the works of the great master. A long table covered with green baize, which had been left in the chapel, afforded an opportunity for examining these celebrated frescos without that back-breaking process and the fatigue usually incurred by gazing upward for even a cursory inspection.

Stretched upon my back at full length upon the convenient table, did I, opera-glass in hand, run over the productions of the great artist's twenty-two months' labor. The "Creation," "Fall," and "Deluge;" in the centre the prophets and sibyls, "Mockery of Noah," "Israelites in the Wilderness," "David and Goliath," angels, cherubs, &c., they have all been described again and again; but notwithstanding this, and their dingy appearance, as one looks upon this wonderful ceiling, the impression forces itself upon the spectator that it is the grand work of a master-hand, especially in contemplating the noble figures of the sibyls and prophets, and he can but regret that the whole work should be in a place so ill contrived for admitting sufficient light to see the artist's work, so grand in conception and wonderful in execution.

That wonderful picture, "The Last Judgment," the reproduction of which all are so familiar with, was another disappointment, for it is faded, blackened, and blurred by lamp-smoke, age, and neglect; and my preparation for the original having been obtained from well-executed steel engravings, — good, clean, pictorial impressions of the great work, — naturally enough led me to think that if it was so grand and beautiful in reproduction by the engraver's art, the original in colors must be a marvel. It was grand, but a disappointment as regards freshness and vividness; and now the question forced itself continually upon my mind of how glorious the work must have been when fresh from the artist's pencil, and untarnished by smoke and age.

This great picture extends from floor to ceiling, at the upper end of the chapel. In the centre sits the figure representing our Saviour judging the world; and below, the seven angels, sounding their trumpets summoning the dead, who are breaking from their graves and shrouds; and at the right, the well-remembered group of Charon with his crowded boat-load of the damned, whom he is driving overboard, and into the clutches of expectant demons, by a vigorous application of his paddle. Above, I noted the well-known figures of the saints about to receive their glorious reward: St. Catherine and her wheel, St. Bartholomew and his skin, St. Andrew and his cross, St. Lawrence and his gridiron, &c.; while saints and the righteous with cherubs and angels are floating upwards amid clouds to the home of the blessed.

Dimmed, faded, and its effect destroyed by lack of light and the grand altar, the great picture only conveys the impression to the spectator of what a wonderful collection of nude figures, in every possible attitude, and with every variety of expression, it must have been in its prime. And, with the knowledge that here in this chapel is a great artistic work that one ought to get up more enthusiasm over, I could only feel a sense of gratification that I had an opportunity of looking upon this, the most perfect result of the great artist's long and active life, and celebrated as one of the wonders of art in the world, and wishing that it was in perfect condition enough to command enthusiastic admiration.

But Michael Angelo was indeed a wonderful man, painter, sculptor, architect, commander, — industrious as well as wonderful; and it is not surprising his name is so continually quoted in connection with art in Italy when it is considered how conspicuous a place he occupied during his life in its advancement, the monuments that he has left behind him, the results of great genius united to incessant application and unflagging industry. Let the visitor, as he stands before this great picture, grand even in its decay, remember that the artist commenced it in his sixtieth year, and toiled over it for seven years before it was completed. It is a picture that is now more of a subject for artistic study than for the admiration of amateurs.

In order to reach the Museum of Statues I passed through a splendid corridor, known as the Corridor of Inscriptions, a great gallery twenty-one hundred and thirty-one feet in length, the sides lined with early Pagan and Christian epitaphs from sarcophagi. There are hundreds, I believe thousands, of these epitaphs of persons in all degrees of life, from slave to nobleman, and many of them very curious as describing the trade or business of the deceased, which it appears in ancient Rome were much the same as we have to-day; and some of the lines to butcher, baker, or captain, are in as bad taste as those that disfigure tombstones and monuments in our own land to-day.

A grand hall of sculptures is that called Braccio Nuovo (the "New Arm"), built by Pius II. in 1817, two hundred and fifty feet in length, lighted with twelve great skylights, and filled with gems of sculpture. This anywhere but in Rome would be a museum in itself, and simply as a grand hall constructed for a museum is a splendid specimen of architectural taste and elegance. It is divided into numerous niches, so that statues are set in a series of arches, twenty-eight in number, and then, before the pilasters which separate them, are as many busts on pedestals of red granite; other busts on consoles are at the intersections of the arches; and bas-reliefs are placed between the frieze and keys of the arches. The floor is elegant mosaic, and the light from above is equally and pleasantly distributed. In fact, the whole effect is that the objects of sculpture furnish the gallery, so perfect is the harmony the one with the other, an example to be studied by our modern projectors of museums and art collections.

Now the visitor begins to encounter old acquaintances, or, I should say, those that he is familiar with from reproductions that have found their way to every part of the civilized world. Here stands Silenus, adorned with vine-leaves and grapes, leaning against a tree, and smilingly regarding the infant Bacchus, whom he holds in his arms; the magnificent statue of the Emperor Augustus, found in 1863, of heroic size, and interesting as having his cuirass sculptured all over with small bas-reliefs relating to his achievements. The armor and drapery are wonders of sculpture. Here is the graceful statue of Ganymede pouring into the cup the libation for the gods. Then we have an exquisitely beautiful figure marked in the catalogue as "Diana contemplating Endymion." The sleeping youth, however, is wanting, but the graceful and exquisitely modelled form of the goddess, in the gentle, bending attitude that she has assumed, shows plainly enough that he should be beneath her loving gaze to complete the group. Here stands Euripides, with his broad, intellectual forehead, holding his poetic scroll; and the orator Demosthenes, declaiming against the fickleness of Athenians in refusing to listen to him, with indignation and force expressed in every line of his face.

Ah! there, at the head of the hall, rises one of those figures that are such splendid specimens of refinement, of form, and grace of attitude: the athlete standing in the act of cleansing his left arm from perspiration and dust with the strigil, a bronze sort of scraper used by the gladiators for that purpose. The slender but compact and athletic frame, graceful attitude, youthfully beautiful head, flowing hair, and the elasticity that seems to pervade the gracefully rounded limbs, hold the spectator like a spell. No wonder that Tiberius, in response to popular clamor, had to replace the original in bronze, taken by him to adorn his palace, at the baths of the people, where it had been set up by Agrippa, who, as Pliny tells us, brought it from Greece, for it is a figure of grace and beauty that commanded their admiration as it does ours to-day.

An exquisite figure of Venus rising from the sea, in the act of arranging her hair, the lower part of the figure beautifully draped, deserves more attention in the guide-books than it gets; indeed, the visitor must not depend entirely upon guide-books or guides to tell him the best objects of art, or he may lose many exquisite productions.

The colossal group representing the river Nile consists of a huge reclining figure of a man leaning against the Sphynx. Sixteen children are clambering over him, while one of his hands holds the cornucopia, from which the waters have flown, and one little cupid, with folded arms, is bubbling out of it. The base, or pedestal, is sculptured all over with pigmies combating crocodiles and hippopotami, and figures of the ibis and lotus flower. This curious group was found in the time of Pope Leo X., between the years 1513 and 1522.

One of the most conspicuous objects in this museum is a grand, full-length statue of Minerva, found among the ruins of a temple on the Esquiline Hill. It is in excellent preservation, and is cut from Parian marble. The goddess is crowned with the familiar helmet. Her right hand holds her spear, near the butt of which a serpent, emblem of vigilance and health, is coiled. A cuirass is seen at the right shoulder, beneath the graceful drapery which falls to the feet, and the whole figure is inexpressibly grand and dignified, as the goddess of wisdom should be.

I must leave many, many beautiful creations of the sculptor's chisel without a word of comment, as many and many abler writers have done before me, for there is a grand army of statuary in the other halls awaiting our review: so we bestow only a passing glance upon such notable figures as a colossal head of a Dacian from Trajan's Forum; a magnificent colossal vase in the Etruscan style; the central ornament of the gallery, cut from black Egyptian basalt, adorned with leaves, wreaths, grapes, and birds, a splendid piece of work which was found on the Quirinal Hill; a finely sculptured bust of Marcus Antoninus the Roman triumvir, and the enemy of Cicero; and that of Æmilius Lepidus, his colleague, both found in a grotto near the Porta Maggiore; a fine figure of Mercury and others; for, under the guidance of an expert *valet de place*, we find ourselves in the gallery known as the Chiaramonti Corridor, receiving its name from

Pius VII., that being his family name. The gallery was built by another pope, but owes its modern embellishments to the latter. Here we are staggered by the intelligence that there are more than seven hundred sculptures for us to inspect, collected from other collections found among ruins and purchased by the Pope, the whole arranged by Canova in two long rows, and subdivided into thirty sections, each lighted by a large window.

In the Chiaramonti Corridor, and in the midst of the Chiaramonti collection, the visitor feels that he is surrounded by priceless art wealth; he has about him portraits of the old Roman emperors, orators, and poets, cut from living models; the columns, statues, and sculptures that decorated the niches of pagan temples and the halls and habitations of the rich; the very sacrificial altars upon which offerings were made to the gods, with the sculptured story of their mythological deeds told in bas-relief upon their base or sides; statues of the gods themselves, such masterpieces of art as to invoke art worship in these modern days; the superb sarcophagi with sculptured stories and rich adornments upon them, last resting-places for the ashes of the rich, the production of any one of which would require a sum that would be a small fortune to many a man to-day. Bas-reliefs; poetic, emblematic, and historic epitaphs and inscriptions, that bring us face to face with the times of the Cæsars; and so many wonders in artistic sculpture, that we think if these are but the fragments, splinters, and remains of the ancient city, what a glorious spectacle it must have presented, with triumphal arches, statues, temples, and columns, when in its prime.

Here in this corridor I paused to look at two beautiful recumbent figures representing Autumn and Winter. The former was surrounded with the sculptured attributes of the season, flowers, grapes, fruits, &c., and was found on the Cassian Way. The latter is a recumbent draped figure with various sculptured symbols about it. A statue of

Urania, and a beautiful one of Clio in a sitting posture, with scrolls of history at her side, and near by was a statue of a priestess found in Hadrian's Villa. The visitor will come to the conclusion, from the number of statues, columns, and vases found in Hadrian's Villa and at Caracalla's Baths, that they were luxurious emperors, and liberal patrons of the arts, or, to say the least, were very liberal in the art decoration of buildings and villas. One can hardly realize how beautiful a fragment of sculpture even may be, until he sees some of the wonderful *torsos* here in Rome.

A headless and armless statue — said by some to be a portion of the figure of Diana, by others Ariadne, but enumerated in the catalogue as one of the daughters of Niobe — will claim attention in this gallery, and its graceful drapery especially be recognized as truly artistic. The colossal and helmeted bust of Pallas is magnificent, and is by some said to be Rome personified in this figure. We pass by with a glance at Bacchus with his everlasting grapes and vine-leaves; altars, busts of Jupiter; Juno and Child, found in the Quirinal Gardens; Hercules resting after his labors; Gladiator killing a lion; Wrestlers wearing the *cestus*; two superb statues of Tiberius: one sits holding the sceptre and sword in his hand, his breast partly covered with a tunic, and his head crowned with a wreath of oak-leaves; the other is also in a sitting position, — a majestic figure, clothed in the Roman toga. The papal government paid twelve hundred dollars for the purchase of the latter, — not a very great price for a grand statue.

It was in the reign of Tiberius, however, it will be remembered, that Christ was crucified at Jerusalem, and, cruel as this Roman emperor was, he did not molest the Christians, although he suffered persecution of the Jews to be carried on without stint. Although this emperor is styled the execrated successor of Augustus, it is of interest to look upon these well-preserved and portrait statues of the sovereign to whom Pontius Pilate wrote his letters respecting our Saviour.

One of the very best imperial busts known is that in this gallery. It is distinguished for its good preservation, the whiteness of the marble, and moreover its noble beauty. It represents the Emperor Octavius Augustus in his youth, probably soon after he came into public life as the avenger of his uncle, Julius Cæsar. It is a fine head, although the original lives in history as a little lame boy, with weak eyes and snuffling speech; but his craftiness and skill carried him through many trying situations successfully to the age of seventy-five years, and, contrary to the manner of many of his successors, he died a natural death in bed, and was not murdered.

A beautiful little statue is that of Cupid in the act of bending his bow, called one of the best copies of the original by Praxiteles. This figure was found in fragments, and has been most skilfully put together.

One of the best heads that has come down to us is that on the bust of Venus, which is here beside that of Ariadne. It is a most elegant and graceful representation of the ideal beauty in excellent preservation, and the graceful arrangement of the hair might be commended to ladies of to-day. It was excavated from in front of the Baths of Diocletian, in 1804. A beautiful specimen of Greek workmanship, found in the year 1791, and supposed to belong to a rich Roman in the time of Nero, is the statue of Silenus, that stands in the attitude of presenting with one hand a cup of wine towards a panther that is gazing at him, while with the other he holds over the animal his crook or staff. The Gardens of the Quirinal yielded up a superb colossal bust of Isis, which we see here with its ample veil, and neck adorned with necklaces made of acorns. It is sculptured from Pentelic marble.

But we will leave behind "Hercules with Ajax in his Arms;" altars to Apollo, Diana, Mars, and Mercury; Hermes and Bacchus, squeezing grapes in a cup; the bust of Cicero, with its penetrating and caustic expression; a little statue of Ulysses with the Phrygian cap on his head ; Æsculapius ; Hercules strangling the serpents ; and other subjects equally interesting, as the reader will readily judge these are, from their very names ; for, like the object of Macbeth's ambition, "the greatest is behind." New wonders are to come, so we ascend elegant marble steps, and find ourselves in that important part of the Vatican known as the Pio Clementino Museum. This large building, erected by the Popes Julius II., Innocent VIII., Paul III., and Leo X., and enlarged by Clement XIV. and Pius VI. by the addition of various galleries, is affirmed to be the most magnificent gallery of ancient sculpture in existence. It is indebted to the munificence of Pius VI., according to Murray, for more than two thousand specimens.

The square vestibule is called the Vestibule of the Belvedere, from the beautiful view it commands of Rome, and in the middle of the vestibule is that splendid relic of antiquity known as the Torso Belvedere. This is a colossal fragment, a mutilated statue in Greek marble, of herculean proportions. The head, upper part of the breast, both arms to the shoulders, and both the legs below the knees, are gone, and yet such is the correctness of representation in every anatomical detail of this mere trunk of man, so wonderfully is it finished, that it may well be called, as by the poet Rogers, a "mass of breathing stone."

That it is a wonderful work of sculpture has been attested by so many masters of the art, that those who see in it nothing but a mutilated fragment must remember that the skilled and practised eye of the sculptor sees the beauties of his art even in this fragment of work. And when one comes to give it a close and critical examination, he will find that the curves, roundings, wrinkles, and depressions of actual flesh are so wonderfully and perfectly moulded, that it appears as if the artist must have shaped it like clay in plastic form, rather than with the more laborious chisel which he had to employ on the brittle marble. The actual flesh-like appearance of belly, lower breast, and hips, in fact all that part of the trunk remaining, is so striking, that I looked on this old fragment from the chisel of Apollonius, son of Nestor of Athens, found near Pompey's Theatre, with increased interest, as I recalled the grand proportions of some of Michael Angelo's nude figures; for I remembered the great sculptor and painter declared that to it he was indebted for his instruction in representing the human figure. And in his old age the great artist used to be led up to it, that he might pass his hands over it and enjoy, in the sense of touching, the fine proportions and lines of beauty that were denied his sight.

To be sure, the "reading up" of some of these great works of art in the world surrounds them with a halo of poetical interest; otherwise I might perhaps have looked upon this as did a companion, — a quite well-informed person in many things, — who begged I would "come along, and not waste so much time over an old smashed statue, when there were so many perfect ones to be looked at."

Speaking of reading, almost every schoolboy who has read of Rome has read the story of Scipio Africanus and his battles with Hannibal. It was he, it will be remembered, who "carried the war into Africa," two hundred years before Christ. It is therefore interesting to those who have an antiquarian turn of mind, to look upon the sarcophagus that once held the mortal remains of the great-grandfather of this celebrated Roman general, who was consul under the republic, B. C. 298, and, as the inscription upon his stone coffin tells, a noble general himself, showing that Scipio came of good stock. This inscription, which is of the most ancient Latin handed down to us, and which the guide-books give in the original, they, as usual, all neglect to give an English translation of for the benefit of the unlettered. Here is a translation: —

"Cornelius Scipio Barbatus, born of a brave father; a courageous and prudent man, whose prudence equalled his beauty. He has been among you consul, censor, ædile; he took Taurasia, Cisanna, and Samnium; having subjugated all Lucania, he brought away from it hostages."

When the sarcophagus of this gallant old general was opened in 1781, two thousand years after his death, his skeleton was found entire, and upon one of his bony fingers a ring, which is still in existence, in the collection of antiques of an English nobleman. The sarcophagus is a great, square, ash-colored, stone structure of albano stone, cut in Doric style, and familiar from the many reproductions and pictorial representations of it that have been made. It is one of the most interesting authenticated relics of Republican Rome. The tomb of the Scipio family, from which this sarcophagus was taken, was discovered near the Appian Way in 1780, and, besides this, the coffins of the grandfather and son of Scipio Africanus. The latter was buried at Liternum, where he died, causing to be inscribed on his tomb, "Ungrateful country, thou shalt not have my bones."

This Clementino Museum, the vestibule of which we have just entered, contains some of the most splendid apartments in the Vatican. Among them are the Hall of Animals, the Hall of the Biga or Chariot, the Gallery of the Muses, the Circular Hall, the Hall of the Greek Cross, the Grand Staircase, and the Cortile of the Belvedere. The last-mentioned is a large space in form of an octagon, surrounded by an ornamental open portico. In the centre of the space is a fountain, and round about it are various curious sarcophagi and vases, which we pass for the grander works in the four cabinets inside the portico.

The first that commands attention is the cabinet of Canova, containing the two striking (no pun intended) statues by Canova of the Syracusan boxers, Creugas and Damoxenus, two life-like figures opposed to each other in combat, and, as any member of "the fancy" would say, in anything but a scientific attitude. One stands with his right arm raised, leaving his side wholly unprotected, at which his antagonist, who has brute force and violence expressed in every line of his countenance, appears to be aiming a blow with the ends of the fingers of his open, extended hand, — a straightforward thrust.

"A foul, foolish way of striking for the one, and a stupid oversight of the other to leave his side unguarded," said an American near me, who was regarding the group. "I wonder if that was the style of the old Roman boxers?"

Probably not; for, as the story runs, the one who raised his arm agreed to present his side unguarded for a blow from his adversary, who, disregarding the laws prescribed in the games, struck forth with his fingers, piercing between his adversary's ribs, and killing him on the spot.

The two figures are admirably executed in all anatomical details, but have that expression of the coarse, brutal force of a pugilist, rather than that of a noble-minded athlete, as seen in the older statues.

Near these stands Perseus with the head of Medusa, an exquisite piece of Canova's work. The figure holds the sword in one hand and the Medusa head in the other, and the mantle falls down in such graceful and natural folds from the shoulders to the feet, as to almost cheat the spectator into the belief that it is really folds of linen thrown upon the statue.

That beautiful statue called the Mercury of the Belvedere, or the Belvedere Antinous, is an image of blooming youth that is absolutely faultless in its execution. The longer you gaze the more its exquisite proportions grow upon you, and it seems as handsome as a blooming, youthful male figure can possibly be without being a woman. Perfectly symmetrical in all its proportions, with calm, thoughtful features, yet those of youth and beauty, with round and apparently elastic limbs, well-balanced head, and drapery thrown over the left shoulder, the figure stands the perfection of the sculptor's art. It was discovered near the Baths of

Titus, on the Esquiline Hill, in the year 1779, and is sculptured in Parian marble.

We now come to the cabinet containing that wonderful group, the Laocoön, — a group so familiar to all the world from its representation in every picture-book of Rome, child's histories, and plaster reproductions in art galleries, and even paintings. A group so well known to you as this can hardly excite much enthusiasm, you think. But wait till you see this, the original, and you will find, like all the great wonders of ancient statuary, the originals are really inimitable, — they cannot be successfully copied. You seem to see the beauties, the grandeur, the story, in marble, the poetry of the sculptor that you have heard, read, and studied, and tried to appreciate when looking at copies, now for the first time, as you gaze upon the great original.

And an enjoyment it is to gaze upon the very statue described by Pliny as standing in the palace of the Emperor Titus, sculptured from a single block of marble. Yes, here was a group of statuary described by an historian not half a century after the death of the Saviour, which was taken from the ruins fourteen hundred and fifty years afterwards at the very place in which he had located it; for it was dug out of the ruins of the palace of the conqueror of Jerusalem in 1506. This grand group must of course have been a perfectly ideal one, for the sculptors could have had no model representing men in the folds of enormous snakes, nor the convulsions of their bodies while in the agony of those terrible coils; and yet the highest authorities of each succeeding generation pronounce them perfect in all anatomical details, and the agony of expression all that the most careful study of features, aided by powerful imagination on the part of the artist, could accomplish. The artists had in their mind the perpetuation of a great event in the, to them, divine history of the gods, — the punishment of a priest of Apollo and his sons at the very altar by the god's messengers of wrath, the serpents.

Laocoön, as the story goes, was engaged in offering a sacrifice to Neptune, when Apollo sent two enormous serpents from the island of Tenedos, to destroy him. Hastening through the sea, they seized upon the priest and his sons upon the very steps of the altar, and destroyed them, and by their death decided the fate of Troy; for it was Laocoön, it will be remembered, who warned the Trojans against the great wooden horse left behind by the Greeks after their apparent retreat, and, his death being considered divine judgment, his advice was unheeded, a breach made in the wall for the admission of the Grecian image, and the result was Troy's ruin.

I need not describe the group, — the magnificent figure of the father falling back upon the altar, his superb head and the features upon which the excess of agony is visible, the thorough anatomical study that is visible in every detail in the whole group, the contrast of action of the elder to that of the more youthful figures, the management of the serpents, whose coils, although they inclose the whole group, are so arranged by the sculptor that they shall in no way mar the proportions of the figures or conceal any of their beauties.

It is a story in marble that you may study for hours; it is a conception the ingenuity of which you may wonder at; it is a work, the laborious care and skill of execution of which may well fill you with wonder and astonishment, and one respecting which many have agreed with Michael Angelo, who at the time of its discovery pronounced it to be a miracle of art. . A more modern critic, George S. Hillard, an American classical scholar and author, very truly says, "It stands upon the very line by which the art of sculpture is divided from poetry and painting," and "is one of those productions that would have been pronounced impossible had they never been executed."

One wonder follows on another's heels, and too fast they follow, too, for real enjoyment in these four chapels of art, for the art lover who for the first time pays his devotions in each. If he does it, as nearly all do, at one visit, he must indeed feed to very gluttony on art; for either one of these, it seems to me, ought to be enjoyed by separate visits; but it is these great wonders of art, like many other European sights, must be enjoyed as we have opportunity. So we must thrust aside for the time being all our thoughts and contemplations of the Laocoön for that noblest embodiment of a god in marble — the Apollo Belvedere.

There he stands in the well-known and graceful attitude, his face one of noble and god-like beauty, the pose of the graceful head with its luxurious and flowing ringlets indeed like that of a god, the lofty brow noble and intellectual, and the graceful drapery over the left arm just sufficient to relieve the slender but beautifully rounded figure, radiant with youthful beauty. It is a statue that is simple, grand, and fascinating; its grace, lightness, and animation go to every heart; and this statue is also one that we find we have hardly had a correct idea of until now gazing upon the original, for the reason that, on looking at the original, the inferiority of copies is appreciated.

There seems to be a controversy among antiquaries and critics respecting the Apollo Belvedere statue. The generally accepted theory was, and still is with many, that the god is represented as just having discharged a shaft from his "unerring bow" at the serpent Python, with fatal effect. Byron, in "Childe Harold," calls him "Lord of the unerring bow," and says:

> "The shaft has just been shot . . .
> With an immortal's vengeance."

Another poet, Henry Hart Milman, adopts the same explanation in his perfect description of this elegant statue in the following lines:

> "Bright kindling with a conqueror's stern delight,
> His keen eye tracks the arrow's fateful flight;

> Burns his indignant cheek with vengeful fire,
> And his lip quivers with insulting ire;
> Firm fixed his tread, yet light as when on high
> He walked the impalpable and pathless sky;
> The rich luxuriance of his hair, confined
> In graceful ringlets, wantons in the wind
> That lifts in sport his mantle's drooping fold,
> Proud to display that form of faultless mould."

The restorations of the right forearm and left hand were made in accordance with this theory of the statue representing the god standing in the position as just having discharged the arrow at Python; but it seems that the discovery of a statuette in all points similar to that of the Apollo Belvedere, and evidently copied from the same original, shows that the original did not hold the bow in his hand, but the ægis or shield of Jupiter, made for him by Vulcan, bearing upon its front the head of Medusa, and used for putting to flight a fatal enemy. The ægis bearing Medusa's head was symbol of storm and tempest, and was lent to Apollo, according to Homer's Iliad, and with it he drove back the hosts of the Achaians. Hence it is decided by some authorities that the extended left arm (restored) bore the terrifying shield, and that by the same reason the left hand, also a restoration, is not in correct position.

It is unpleasant to have all our early dreams and the idols of our imagination thus rudely shattered, and, notwithstanding the antiquarian research which places a shield upon the arm instead of a bow in the hand, I still hold that as "lord of the unerring bow" the statue better fills out one's idea of the true representation of the god. This grand work of art, supposed to have been executed in the time of Nero, was discovered near Antium in 1503, and was among the earliest specimens of ancient sculpture placed in the Vatican, forming, in fact, a nucleus around which a large portion of the present collection of the gallery of statues has gathered.

Around, in the vicinity of this court of the Belvedere, are

several magnificent specimens of huge bathing-tubs cut from elegant red porphyry, red granite, or porphyry and black basalt. These great tubs are huge in size, but elegantly sculptured, susceptible of, and have a polish on them like glass, and were found at the Baths of Caracalla; and, with their sculptured lions' heads, rings cut from the solid stone, and excellent workmanship, are as striking specimens of the luxury of their time and evidence of the abundance of skilled labor in those days as can be produced; for the labor upon them must have been enormous, and the skill required to produce the artistic effect, displayed even in these comparatively common objects, is of no common order, as can easily be seen by the visitor.

In the hall, in the immediate vicinity of the Apollo Belvedere, stands a statue larger than life of Hygieia, with the symbolic serpent about her arm, and cup in hand. This figure will strike every person who has ever seen the Zenobia of the American sculptor, Miss Hosmer, by its many points of resemblance, and suggests the thought that the artist of the latter figure may have used this as a study.

From these art chapels, where we have been paying our homage to the grand art models of the world, we pass on to what might perhaps be denominated a menagerie in marble, which is known as the Hall of Animals, and is the rarest and finest collection of animals in Greek and Roman sculpture in existence. Having passed two colossal dogs that guard the entrance, we find an inlaid pavement, black and white pilasters of Egyptian granite, and rich and beautiful marbles and mosaics attracting the gaze.

Of what is before us we can take but a passing glance. The two greyhounds playing together, a graceful group; the Hercules dragging away the Nemæan lion; a fine statue of Commodus on horseback; a beautiful group, well preserved, of a shepherd sleeping, with his goats grazing about him; beautiful group of a stag attacked by a dog. But I shall only be re-enumerating a catalogue to go on; suffice it to say that there is sufficient of the curious as well as the artistic work of the sculptor's chisel to make one long to give more time than the author could devote to it. I remember among other objects an admirably sculptured goose in a perfectly natural attitude, showing that the sculptor had studied the habits of the bird of the Capitol; a toad in antique red marble, and a lobster in green, looking very like a real one; magnificent lions, a panther in striped marble, and a superb tiger in Egyptian granite; a huge lion in gray marble, the very king of beasts himself; and to my astonishment a cow, sculptured from brown marble, an admirably executed figure, too; and a sow surrounded by twelve pigs.

You are astonished at the fidelity of execution and the life and grace that seem to be put into the stony representations of animals who would seem to be out of the pale of art, be it rhinoceros' or camel's heads, baboon, or even a hedgehog, rats and crabs, for they are all here.

The Hall of Statues, so called, is a magnificent gallery richly decorated, and the pavement inlaid with beautiful marbles of different colors. Great marble pilasters with Ionic capitals of white marble support grand arches and superbly decorated vaults and ceiling. The hall is a long gallery with walls of marble, a wondrous decoration above, and a double line of great masterpieces of art on either side for the visitor to inspect, and directly in the middle of the hall a superb bath of Oriental alabaster.

In this hall stands the statue of Clodius Albinus, the colleague, but afterwards the opponent of Septimius Severus. The armor of this figure is sculptured with dancing figures, and the statue itself stands upon a pedestal upon which is inscribed that it marked where Caius Cæsar's remains were burned. A sitting figure of Paris, larger than life, I halted to examine, because the names of the artisans of the imperial mint, who in the time of **Trajan** dedicated it to Hercules, are sculptured upon one side of the pedestal, to the number of more than sixty in all.

Here you will see a specimen of the supposed original work of Praxiteles, which is therefore, I suppose, denominated in the guide-books as the Genius of the Vatican. It is the half figure of a Cupid in Parian marble, the wings gone, but the place at the shoulders where they were fastened distinctly visible. The statue was brought from Greece by Caligula, and is spoken of by Pliny as having been admired in the portico of Octavia. It was discovered by Gavin Hamilton, a Scotch painter, in the Via Labicana. It is a figure of most exquisite expression, and the head especially a marvellously beautiful piece of sculpture.

If the visitor undertakes to examine and study all the sculptures in this gallery carefully, he will find that he has no light task before him; nor can the author undertake to enumerate even the most distinguished.

The celebrated statue of Ariadne, daughter of Minos, lying upon the rock on the sea-shore of Naxos, after being abandoned by her unfaithful lover, is another story in marble. The countenance displays grief and despondency even in sleep; the head resting upon one arm, and the other thrown above it, the graceful folds of drapery over the lower limbs, and the tunic that has partly dropped from the left shoulder revealing the beautiful bosom, — are details wrought out in the marble with such faithfulness and exquisite skill that I cannot resist referring to this beautiful statue.

Nor can I pass unmentioned a sitting figure of Nero as Apollo (heaven save the mark!) He is represented as crowned with laurel and playing on the lyre, and the statue is one of the few that escaped the destruction ordered by the senate and the outraged Roman people.

This Gallery of Statues and the Hall of Busts are, as it were, all one collection, and divided only by an archway, the latter being a continuation of the former. On each side of this archway sat two grand figures in easy attitudes, as if resting themselves in their senatorial chairs after having delivered an oration. Supposing they must have been great orators or emperors, I consulted my catalogue to find that they were Posidippus and Menander, two Greek poets, or rather masters of Greek comedy, *supposed to be* the original works of Cephisodotus, son of Praxiteles. They are both in excellent preservation, and fine specimens of portrait statues.

A specimen of the oldest and best style of Greek sculpture is a colossal sitting statue of Jupiter, represented holding his thunderbolts and sceptre, and with the eagle at his feet. This was one of the first sculptures placed in the Hall of Busts, and is one of the best in it. Portrait busts in abundance we must pass with a glance, such as that of Hadrian, found at Tivoli; the best known bust of Caracalla; a beautiful head of Isis crowned with diadem and lotus flower; a beautiful helmeted head called Menelaus, the helmet adorned with sculptured representations of the combats of Hercules and the Centaurs. This portion of the Gallery of Statues, known as the Hall of Busts, although a small part of the museum, is rich in likenesses, and is really quite an important and interesting one in an historical or mythological point of view.

Out from the Hall of Animals I strolled into another, — *Sala delle Muse*, Hall of the Muse, — an octagonal hall enriched by sixteen Corinthian columns of gray Carrara marble brought from Hadrian's Villa, and paved with rich arabesques and mosaics. What a beautiful room this seemed, the very chosen home of art, — the softened light streaming down from above, its large dome decorated with elegant frescos appropriate for the place, such as paintings of Homer singing his poem and Minerva listening in the clouds above, Apollo and the Muses; Tasso, Virgil, and other poets.

Besides myself, there chanced to be but two other visitors whom I could see, and they were standing motionless in mute admiration of the noble and graceful figure of Melpomene, one of the best of the statues of the Muses, from which this chamber takes its name.

Standing, poniard and mask in hand, with her loose hair intermingled with grapes, a grave expression of countenance, and beautifully sculptured drapery, the figure was one with so many lines of beauty visible, that it is worth more study than we could give it, for here were her sisters, also, to claim our notice: Thalia, seated with her sandalled feet peeping from beneath her robe, and her head crowned with ivy; Terpsichore, with her ivy crown and musical lyre; Calliope, which some consider the finest of the whole, seated in meditative attitude upon a rock with tablets in hand, and drapery so perfect as to make that portion of the sculptor's work absolutely faultless — artistic perfection; Clio, crowned with laurel, with scroll of papyrus across her knees; Urania, globe and stylus in hand; Polyhymnia, with head wreathed with roses, and the rich folds of her mantle falling to her feet; Erato, with tortoise-shell lyre; — all these beautiful figures sculptured elegantly in marble, and, with the exception of Urania and Erato, I think, were discovered at the rustic villa of Cassius, in Tivoli, in 1774.

Here is a fine statue of Silenus clothed in a tiger-skin, and squeezing a bunch of grapes into a cup, a sort of primitive wine-making that has been improved upon. Then there was a bust with such a Silenus cast of countenance that one might well take it for a head of the foster-father of Bacchus, had not the Greek sculptor taken care to have cut the name of Socrates upon it. We are reminded, however, that although Socrates was the greatest philosopher of his age, he was one of the ugliest-looking men of his time. This may be comforting to those remarkably plain-looking people of our own day, who are generally most enthusiastic in praising the beauties of the mind.

Then there was old Diogenes, like many people nowadays, whose rude manners were endured on account of his smart sayings. While I was looking at the statue of Lycurgus, the Spartan legislator, who stands pointing to his eye destroyed by a passionate youth in one of the tumults which his reforms excited, and remembering that I had studied the story that this bearded old law-maker had abolished gold and silver currency, and substituted iron in its stead, I remembered that we did not erect statues in America to those who compelled us to use substitutes for gold and silver, but were more inclined to immortalize those who should restore to us the metallic circulating medium.

These meditations were interrupted, however, by the official whose duty it was to warn us that the time had arrived to move on, as the museum was to close, and who seemed to have an Italian suspicion that the pencilled notes grasped in my hand were some species of illegal memoranda that laid me open to suspicion; whereupon a sharp discussion ensued between that functionary and my *valet de place*, which was ended satisfactorily, as I had "taken no drawings," and gratefully on the part of the custodian, who was now getting better acquainted with us, as he pocketed a franc *pour boire*.

Are we never to get through with this museum of statues, this wilderness of marble? Verily, I thought so myself, as I sauntered among them day after day, hour after hour, and almost guiltily felt that I had passed by many serried rows without even a glance, in order to see those which none could afford to miss. So, when I stood in the rotunda, or circular hall of the Vatican, "Sala Rotonda" they call it, I found that this was one of those halls that should on no account be omitted.

The architect who built this beautiful hall took his idea for its form from the dome of the Parthenon, and it seems as if built especially to receive its grand central ornament, a magnificent cup of red porphyry, forty-six feet in circumference, found in the Baths of Diocletian. This cup or vase, which looks like a great card-receiver, is so beautifully polished as to seem partly filled with water. One can but reflect what an enormous amount of time and labor, to say nothing of skill, must have been expended on this vase, since, even if it could be reproduced to-day, it would not pay to do it, the expense would be so great. It stands upon the largest and most beautiful mosaic known, which was found at Otricoli in 1780. It is a series of concentric bands, representing combats of centaurs, water-nymphs, tritons, and sea-monsters, and beautiful wreaths of flowers, with a grand head of Medusa in the centre. The outside border of the passage around the hall is in black-and-white ancient mosaic, representing scenes in the life of Ulysses, Neptune and his sea-horses, and other mythological monsters.

The cupola of this beautiful hall is upheld by ten fluted pilasters of Carrara marble, between each two of which are niches to hold the large statues; and before each pilaster are red marble brackets for the busts, which, with the elegant gilding and ornamental wall-painting, combine to render this an appropriate and rich casket for the gems it contains.

The principal attraction is the colossal bronze statue of Hercules, twelve feet in height, which was discovered in 1864, hidden in a marble case, while digging to repair the foundation of a palace that now stands where once stood the Theatre of Pompey. The statue represents Hercules leaning upon his club, with a lion's skin thrown over his left arm. In one hand he holds the Hesperidian fruit, and the whole form exhibits the strength which the demigod was said to possess.

Another colossal statue of note is that of Antinous, with ringlets flowing down over neck and shoulders, and head crowned with flowers. Then there is the colossal head of Hadrian, found in his mausoleum, now the Castle of St. Angelo (which has already been described), and supposed to have belonged to a colossal statue of the emperor. The Juno Barberini, which stands in another of the ten arches of this rotunda, is a superb colossal statue, and said to be one of the most perfect specimens of antique sculpture in existence. Of course it is "said to be," or "supposed to be," a fine copy of a similar work by Praxiteles. He and Phidias were probably quoted by the Roman and Grecian critics of sculpture, as Garrick and Cooke are to-day by our modern theatrical scribblers. The noble expression of the face of this statue is that of a goddess, its finish admirable, its arrangement of drapery and whole execution grand, and all artists recognize in it a masterpiece in marble.

I cannot leave the rotunda without, a word respecting the beautiful colossal sitting statue of the first good Roman emperor, Nerva, who had no claim for that rank but a good character and correct life, something rare in those who aspired to be emperors in his day. This statue is one of the real treasures of antiquity preserved in the Vatican, and represents Nerva with majestic countenance, characterized by force and dignity. The upper part of the body is bare and the head crowned with a bronze wreath of oak-leaves. Merivale, in his " History of the Romans under the Empire," says this statue embodies " the highest ideal of the Roman magnate, the finished warrior, statesman, and gentleman of an age of varied training and wide practical experience ; " and " if we really contemplate his likeness in the noble figure in the Vatican, we may fairly say of the prince, as the historian affirms of the general, ' You might easily deem him good, you would willingly believe him great.' "

As the hall of the rotunda was specially designed for its contents, so in a measure was that known as the Hall of the Greek Cross, so called from its shape, it being divided into four compartments. It was constructed more especially for the two enormous sarcophagi of red Egyptian porphyry placed respectively in the right and left arms or compartments of the cross. This porphyry, so hard to cut, is susceptible of a high polish, and the sarcophagus of it here, which was taken from a mausoleum of the daughter of Constantine the Great, gleams like a purplish-red carnelian, and is indeed a colossal gem. It is ornamented with bas-reliefs of Cupids gathering and pressing grapes, and figures of sheep, birds, festoons, and arabesques. This costly coffin once held the remains of the daughter of Constantine, who died A. D. 354.

The other sarcophagus, opposite, is still larger, and is said to have occupied the constant labor of twenty-five sculptors for nine years, who worked diligently by orders of the Emperor Constantine to make a costly casket, worthy as a receptacle for the remains of his mother. It is sculptured with her portrait bust, and with equestrian figures and representations of the triumphs of the emperor; and, besides being a monument to her whose ashes it held, is one of patient industry and enormous labor, and, like some of the great porphyry vases, when the present money value of labor, even in those countries where it is cheapest, is taken into consideration, the result to be obtained now upon such a work would not warrant its being undertaken.

In the middle of this Hall of the Greek Cross is a magnificent specimen of mosaic pavement, in circular form, and inclosed by a railing to protect it from the profane tread of the moderns. It was discovered in the Villa of Cicero in 1741. It is a set of circles, festoons, and symbolic figures, and among others is a beautiful representation of a bust of Minerva, with the head of Medusa on the breast, helmet, and shield. On a portion of one of the rings of mosaic were various phases of the moon represented, also planets, tragic and comic masks, &c., all in beautiful and quite fresh colors. In this hall is the half-draped statue of Augustus, which is remarkable for the likeness it bears to the first Napoleon, and perhaps may have led him to think he really bore resemblance to some of the Cæsars in look as well as military achievements.

In this hall I was halted by the guide to view what was called the Venus of Cnidos, a statue somewhat larger than life, and said to be the most perfect copy known of the Cnidian Venus of Praxiteles, which was lost in a fire at Byzantium at the close of the fourth century. It is really a majestic and lovely figure, but is marred, in my opinion, by a bronze drapery which covers the lower limbs.

We leave this hall and its wonders behind as we ascend to the *Sala della Biga*, or Hall of the Chariot, a splendid hall, octagonal in form; dome modelled after style of the Pantheon, and supported by eight fluted columns with Corinthian capitals. The pavement of this hall is elegantly inlaid with different specimens of rich marble, in which appear the family arms of Pius VI., who erected it especially to receive the ancient Biga, or two-wheeled chariot, from which it takes its name. The original of this beautiful restoration in marble — for it is mainly a restoration of an ancient Grecian chariot and horses — once stood in some temple dedicated to the sun, and it is really a magnificent work of art. Only the body of the chariot and a portion of one of the horses are ancient, but its skilful restoration gives us doubtless a correct idea of the antique Grecian and Roman chariot.

The body of the chariot was used for a long time as an episcopal throne in the Church of St. Mark in Rome. It is beautifully carved with foliage, arabesques, and scroll work. So is the pole, which terminates in a ram's head, and the wheels, of which lions' heads form the hubs; the horses are in spirited action, poised upon their hind legs; and all that is wanted is the Roman charioteer, leaning forward, reins in hand, and standing beside him, with shield advanced on left arm, and javelin raised on high for deadly cast, the helmet-crowned soldier of the Roman legion.

Notwithstanding the romance thrown around the war-chariots by the old poets and painters, and beautiful as they look in sculpture, they must have been terribly inconvenient and uncomfortable vehicles in reality, the body resting as it did directly upon the heavy axle without the intervention of springs, with a stiff, immovable, and clumsy pole. They must also have been exceedingly dangerous to have ridden in, in battle, from their liability to upset, and the effort necessary on the part of the occupants to keep upright during their terrible jolting. It is probable that chariots in battle may have existed more in the active imaginations of poets and historians than in reality, for it would certainly seem safer for a soldier to fight on foot than in one of these clumsily contrived vehicles.

The visitor may study charioteer as well as chariot here, for not far distant stands a beautiful statue of a Roman charioteer of the circus, dressed in costume, his body adorned with corselet and bands, his left hand grasping the reins, and his right bearing the palm-branch of victory won in the race. Upon a sarcophagus here is represented a chariot-race in bas-relief — that of Pelops and King Onomaus, described in the tragedies of Sophocles and Euripides.

Ah! Here is an old familiar friend, — familiar from the many times we have seen him, interesting as an illustrator of the athletic games of the Greeks and Romans, — Discobolus, or the quoit-thrower, in the act of hurling the discus or quoit; giving us in his attitude the manner in which the quoit was held, and one of the positions taken by the players in throwing it. This figure, so full of life and action, was discovered in 1781, and is so well known as not to require description; as is also its companion, the Discobolus in Repose, which is a far more beautiful statue, as it stands in its simple, natural attitude, with the right foot thrown forward, the left hand holding the discus carelessly at the side, the right hand slightly extended, ready to receive the disc that he shall soon transfer to it, and as though half pointing to or indicating a position to be taken by the player, who appears to be thoughtfully regarding the ground before him. This beautiful statue, the reproductions of which are so frequently seen in our public galleries, or the halls and libraries of private dwellings, is in excellent preservation, and one of that exquisite beauty of style which insensibly claims your admiration to such a degree that you linger long before it and hesitate to leave for other attractions.

But go we must, and hardly pause even to look at a noble statue of that old Athenian general and philosopher, Phocion, with helmeted head and simple and beautifully executed drapery. Go we must, for we were desirous of change, a rest from statues and sculpture.

It must not be supposed, however, that these descriptions are the result of consecutive visits to the Vatican, for, should the tourist or visitor commence such an undertaking with the determination of seeing the whole contents thoroughly, he would not only soon find pleasure become labor, and labor exhaustion and satiety, but would despair of carrying out any such idea. Description is given in these pages, of the Vatican collection as a whole, for convenience' sake, though repeated visits to it, made at intervals, the intervals being occupied by excursions to other sights of entirely different character, enable the visitor the better to enjoy and appreciate what he sees of it. I say what he sees of it, for it appeared to me that no one, unless he lived a dozen years in Rome, and devoted himself entirely to that object, could accomplish it. Looking, gazing, walking, wandering through galleries, is terribly fatiguing work, and after a while your critical examination, noting in note-book or storing away in memory, becomes so much like a regular task, that you are wont to ask yourself, And is this travelling for pleasure? Is this leisure, or is it severe labor? Your aching limbs and tired brain at night are apt to incline you often to the latter opinion. But it is after one's return home that much of the real enjoyment comes in the recollection of what has been seen, refreshed by notes, photographs, and other mementos of the journey. Then history becomes doubly interesting, and the art treasures of the old world are invested with a charm not known before.

I confess to looking forward to the Etruscan Museum, or Collection of Etruscan Antiquities, with pleasurable anticipation, but feared exhaustion from other sight-seeing before I might be able to reach it. Much as we may be interested in the ancient Roman antiquities, it is something still more interesting to pass from galleries in which they are preserved, into others containing those of a nation that was in existence anterior to the foundation of Rome, a country which embraced almost the whole of Italy, before Romulus and Remus had fixed the site for their city.

Dionysius wrote, "The Etruscans do not resemble any people in language or manners." But one thing is certain, from what little is known of them, that they exerted an immense influence on Roman, and even European civilization.

The seventh and earlier part of the sixth century before Christ was probably the most flourishing Etruscan epoch, and the nation had then been in existence for half a thousand years. Historians place its decline as standing in an inverted ratio to the rise of Rome.

The Etruscans possessed a high degree of civilization and art long before Rome was heard of; in fact, the Romans borrowed from and imitated them in utensils, works of art, buildings, — for the Romans sent to Etruria for architects for some of their most famous buildings, and their vases, caskets, and jewelry were sent into Rome, or imitated by Roman workmen. And it is this beautiful workmanship of jewelry and ornamental work of the ancient Etruscans that you see in this museum, that causes you to be astonished that so little improvement should have been made in so many hundreds of years. These people appear to have been the inventors of those beautiful patterns of Etruscan jewelry which are produced to-day exactly after the ancient model, with scarcely a variation, and indeed but very little superior in style of workmanship.

The Etruscan Collection, founded by Gregory XVI. in 1836, is composed of relics excavated from 1828 to 1836, and also many recent discoveries, and is contained in twelve rooms. In these rooms we find beautiful vases, jewelry, domestic implements, and warlike weapons of this people, who flourished a thousand years before Christ. I can only glance at a few of the most notable wonders of the collection.

In one room, an elegant bronze statue in full armor, with helmet on and doublet beneath his cuirass, gives you a realistic, or I may say the real, figure of which you so often see the counterfeit presentment in Flaxman's spirited illustrations of Hector, Ajax, or Achilles, and the workmanship and details of the figure are wonderful in their finish. Hung upon the wall here are helmets, shields, handsomely wrought mirrors, with wrought and engraved designs about their rims, upon their handles of fanciful figure, or on their backs. Here are braziers, with fire apparatus that is as beautiful in design as can be made at the present day: the tongs are on wheels, and are wrought out so as to terminate in serpents' heads; the handle of the shovel is a swan's neck, and the fire-rake is wrought into the shape of a human hand.

I could hardly bring myself to believe that the elegant collection of Etruscan jewelry that was exposed in a glass case was worn by a lady three thousand years ago, for our jewellers to-day scarcely excel it in workmanship, and certainly not in design. Here rests a superb wreath of oak-leaves, which to-day would form an elegant crown for a lady's head, and not be considered rude or antique in workmanship; beside it rest the ear-rings, heavy and massy, in solid gold, which were worn by the same wearer, and her seal rings and beautiful bracelets, also in rich wrought gold. These, we are told, were taken from the tomb of an Etruscan princess, over whom was inscribed in Etruscan characters, "ME, LARTHIA," signifying, "I, the Great Lady." She was a great lady three thousand years ago, and they presumed her name to be so great that it would endure forever, which was probably the reason they neglected to record it; so that, when the tomb-riflers of our day came to find what time had spared of this grand dame, all that was known of her was, that she had lived and wore right regal ornaments; and here they are.

That her "greatness" was honored by her descendants was evinced by the fact that it was several hundred years before any other Etrurian of sufficient greatness was found fit to occupy the remaining half or compartment of the tomb in which she rested, her compartment being walled up with spices separating it from the other. Finally a high-priest of Etruria died, and, like the Great Lady, was buried with all his ornaments in the other half of the tomb. And the study of these is a most interesting one to the antiquary. Here are his armlets, the fillets to bind the plate of gold upon his head; and this, and the plate of gold for the forehead, which is here also, are considered by some to have been similar to the head-dress of Aaron — an impression heightened by his priestly breastplate, reminding us of the Urim and Thummim breastplate of the Jewish priests, containing, as Milton says, —

> "Those oraculous gems
> On Aaron's breast."

In this room is the bronze couch upon which this dignitary was found lying, or rather where the ornaments were found beside and about his heap of mouldering dust, and the great incense-burner that was found by his side. And the incense was so strong that, notwithstanding it had been undisturbed for thirty centuries, its aromatic perfume, when set on fire by the finders, was so powerful as to drive them all from the room.

The beautiful articles of jewelry that are displayed here really seemed more like an exhibition of modern novelties than of ancient art. There were different styles of ear-rings, some wrought into the shape of a ram's head, some into that of a bird; chains, necklaces as fine and delicate as that filigree work the Genoese turn out to-day, and which is so familiar to tourists; elastic gold armlets in the shape of serpents; gold myrtle and olive wreaths, rings, and a warrior's breastplate, magnificently embossed.

Of the warlike and other bronze implements are very many which, by their elegant workmanship, surprise you as much as does the gold jewelry. Splendid candelabra, the patterns of which to-day are those that ornament our drawing-rooms; elegant circular shields, some of them three feet in diameter, one with its wooden lining and the leather straps through which passed the warrior's arm still perfect, though it may have failed to shield him faithfully, for it is pierced with a lance-thrust; battle-axes, cuirasses, greaves, and helmets identical in character to those represented upon the ancient marble statuary we have been examining; spears, or javelins; a long, curved trumpet, like those we so frequently see in bas-reliefs of carving on monuments and arches; the strigil, or bronze flesh-scraper used in the baths, — the instrument that the statue of the athlete in the Braccio Nuovo holds in its hand; jugs, weights, and household implements, all showing the perfection of civilization in their workmanship.

Among the other rooms in this collection one of the most interesting is that containing a splendid array of vases, excavated from the ruins or sites of Etruscan cities. These are the original patterns from which copies are made to-day, their designs and workmanship being equal to the best of modern production. Black vases with red figures upon them, light yellow vases, deep red with black figures, and various in party-colored hues. The designs upon these elegant vases and urns form also a splendid collection of designs of mythological story, interesting to the classical student, and such correct representations of the poetic old fables that one has but little difficulty in recognizing them. There are Achilles and Ajax, Apollo attended by the Muses, Hercules at his Labors, the Death of Hector, the Rape of Proserpine, and scenes from the Trojan war — a bewildering collection. The other rooms contain sarcophagi, architectural fragments, bas-reliefs, frescos, and mosaics.

In the Egyptian Museum, the few antiquities that I had opportunity to examine made Rome's antiquities to seem modern. Mummies there were of course, for no Egyptian collection is complete without them; and it is a curious experience to be looking at the preserved corpse of a priest of Ammon of the city of Thebes, who flourished about eighteen hundred and thirty years before Christ, or at a time corresponding with that in which the patriarch Jacob lived; and you wonder if the black marble statue of a woman you stand before can really be, as they say it is, that of the mother of Rameses II., called by the Greeks Sesostris, and whose son, Menephtah, we find, by overhauling history, was overwhelmed by the Red Sea when pursuing the Israelites.

One of the most ancient and curious objects here is a scarabæus in jasper, with an inscription, in eleven lines, celebrating the marriage of Amenoph III., bearing a date ascertained to be no less than 1680 years B. C. Then comes an ancient necklace engraved with the name of Renoubka, an ancient king who flourished in the time of the patriarch Abraham. Two lions in black granite, each side of the colossal statue of Sesostris above mentioned, were found near the Pantheon in 1448, in the ruins of the Baths of Agrippa, and the hieroglyphics upon their base, it is said, tell that they date from the time of King Nectanebus I., one of the builders of the Temple of Philæ, on its granite rock in the middle of the Nile, 357 B. C.

Shall we ever get through with the Vatican? So thought I, as with aching limbs, a crowded brain, fatigued with ever succeeding, never ending novelties and wonders, bothered by custodians who sometimes were so fussy as to wish to inspect and even forbid my making notes in my notebook, and absolutely forbidding — which in my case was perfectly unnecessary — that I should make any drawings. The tourist on his first visit to Rome, no matter how thoroughly he resolves to see this great collection, will come away leaving portions of it absolutely unvisited, and others walked through as hurriedly as if on the way to a railroad station. A description of its contents would fill a volume, yes, a dozen, if fairly written out.

Now, when one is told that the Vatican Library contains over fifty thousand books and twenty-five thousand manuscripts; that it is the oldest and most celebrated library in Europe; that it contains, notwithstanding its comparatively small number of books, some of the most priceless of literary treasures in the world, such as a manuscript of Virgil of the date of the fourth or fifth century; a manuscript of Dante in the handwriting of Boccaccio, with marginal notes by Petrarch; a manuscript of Tasso; Henry VIII.'s love-letters to Anne Boleyn; the Roman manuscript of Terence in the ninth century; the Bible of St. Gregory, &c.; let him not anticipate that he is going to enjoy the same freedom and courtesy that he has experienced in the Bodleian or British Museum, or that he can personally inspect all these literary treasures. He is fortunate if he gets inside the rooms and sees the rich caskets in which they are inclosed; for it is but between nine and twelve o'clock that visitors are admitted, and then only when it is not some red-letter day of the church; consequently they are closed to visitors for over two hundred days of the year.

If you are fortunate enough to obtain admission, you see no serried rows of books marshalled upon their shelves, and but small array of curious manuscripts to enlist your wonder and study. You enter by a small, modest door, and are fairly dazzled by the grand hall that spreads out before you, two hundred and twenty feet long, twenty feet wide, and thirty feet high, lined with frescos. Beautiful pillars, the friezes and vaults covered with magnificent pictures in fresco, decoration, carving and gilding, an elegant marble pavement, gifts from sovereigns to popes, great malachite vases, crosses, fonts of Sèvres and Berlin porcelain, bronzes, and rare articles of *virtu* — you are bewildered with a plethora of most gorgeous decoration and splendor which seems to you but a gilded dream when you recall it afterwards.

Library! Books! Why, we forgot all that part of it. Why didn't we call for books or manuscripts? Well, the amount of red tape, blanks to be filled out, writings to be sent, and orders to be obtained from high officials, before such privilege can be obtained, is such that few attempt it. Then, again, you rarely — if you are fortunate enough to get inside — have more than opportunity to look at the rooms and decoration ere you are obliged to leave.

To be sure, you are told that the books and manuscripts are in the carved and gilded presses and cases that we passed in our whirl of wonderment; but, as far as the rich collection of literature being of any advantage to the world, — it is a miser's treasure in the earth, a light under a bushel, in the way it is now managed, with every possible obstacle placed in the way of the scholar, student, or visitor.

Wey, in speaking of the manuscripts of the Vatican Library, says: "There are eighteen Slave manuscripts, ten from China, twenty-two from India, thirteen from Armenia, two from the old land of the Iberians, eighty in Coptic, and one from Samaria, seventy-one from Ethiopia, five hundred and ninety of Hebrew origin, and four hundred and fifty-nine of Syrian, sixty-four from Turkey, seven hundred and eighty-seven from Arabia, and sixty-five from Persia, illustrated with fine miniatures."

The whole collection of Greek, Latin, and Oriental manuscripts is twenty-three thousand five hundred and eighty — the finest in the world; but these fusty, musty old parchments, many of them, are only intelligible to scholars of great erudition, and only accessible through a labyrinth of circumlocution.

No visitor thinks of leaving the Vatican without having visited the Gallery of Pictures, or of visiting that gallery without having seen Raphael's great masterpiece, The

Transfiguration, finished immediately before his death, and beneath which his body lay in state before his funeral. The subject is so familiar as not to require description; it has been criticised and described till even those who have never seen it almost know it by heart. Our Saviour, rising in the midst of a glorious transparent light, with the figures of Moses and Elijah on either side of him; the three disciples fallen terror-stricken upon the ground; and below, in the lower part of the picture, the group of figures in which the three principal ones — the kneeling woman, and the epileptic boy in the arms of his father — are all grand pieces of composition, and the heads and expressions of the surrounding groups all studies of great artistic beauty. The whole painting is distinguished by its grace of grouping, and, if the expression may be allowed, its dramatic points and the forcible tableau-like position into which the groups seem to have been thrown, in order, seemingly, to make the greatest possible impression upon the spectator. Raphael is said to have received a sum equivalent to three hundred and twenty pounds for painting this picture, — none too much, as all will agree who look upon it. Whether it is the "greatest painting in the world" or not, I will not venture an opinion, but that it is a wonderful creation of art, even the inexperienced will admit in looking upon the beautiful grouping and coloring, the life-like expression of the figures, and the general harmony of the whole grand tableau that is so vividly displayed, and your average tourist who does Rome and the Vatican must put it down in his note-book as one of the sights not to be missed.

From this grand creation the visitor turns to others, such as Domenichino's Communion of St. Jerome, a picture which has a story, which is this: The monks of the monastery of Ara Cœli employed the artist to paint it, but on its completion had a quarrel with him, and only paid him about fifty Roman *scudi* — a little more than fifty dollars of our money — for the picture, and even then locked it up in some dark, out-of-the-way closet, and refused to place it on their walls.

They afterwards called in Poussin to paint an altar-piece for their church. Upon his asking for canvas, the holy brothers brought out this picture, and desired him to paint over that. Poussin, astonished, refused to destroy so beautiful a painting, gave up his commission, and making known to the proper authorities the existence of the picture, it was afterwards placed in another church, and finally removed to this place, where it is one of the principal attractions.

The old saint is represented as having been brought, half naked, emaciated, and dying, to the magnificent gate of a monastery, where two priests in superb ecclesiastical costume — in striking contrast to his miserable condition — are about administering to him the sacrament. The attenuated and emaciated figure of the saint, as he lies feebly upon the monastery step, is wonderfully well done, — so true to life as to be a perfect counterfeit; the noble, dignified figure of the priest, the rich folds of his robe, and the head of one of the figures bending over the saint, — all excite admiration from the most casual observer.

When you leave the Hall of the Chariot, already described, you come to a long corridor, three hundred feet in length, known as the Gallery of Vases and Candelabra. It is divided into six sections by beautiful Doric marble columns of different colors, and each of the sections contains specimens of ancient vases, sarcophagi, cups, mosaics, and statues.

The great candelabra in this hall are wonders of antique art. They are of white marble, beautifully sculptured, and upon their bases are wrought spirited bas-reliefs of mythological story. One, found near the Gardens of Sallust, has a representation of Hercules carrying off the tripod of Delphi, Apollo and an attendant, &c. Another has a representation on its base of Apollo flaying Marsyas; and another that of Silenus and Bacchante, dancing fauns, &c.

These great candelabra, eight in number, dug out from the ruins of the temples of old Rome, have blazed with the flame at sacrifice, feast, and game, when the smoke went up from heathen altars to the gods; and yet, despite this, and even despite the pagan emblems that still adorn them, some of them, since their discovery, have done duty in Christian churches.

We can only glance at a few of the most notable treasures of this section of the great world of wonders we have been so long traversing. Near the entrance of the first division of the gallery are two trunks of trees in white marble, and upon the branches of one a nest containing as nestlings five little sculptured cupids. In this hall we saw a statue of the celebrated Diana of Ephesus, larger than life, in the costume in which she was said to have been worshipped in the temple of Diana of Ephesus. This costume is a sort of tight-fitting swathing, ornamented with figures of sphinxes, lions, bulls, and stags' heads. Her breasts, sixteen in number, are said to typify the sixteen cubits of the Nile's rising, and a necklace of acorns and mystic signs adorns the neck of this remarkable figure, which was found at Hadrian's Villa.

I have lingered about and around so many specimens of sarcophagi in the different halls of the Vatican that I almost hesitate to attempt descriptions of any in this hall, where I was surprised to find several very beautiful ones not at all referred to in my guide-book. These ancient sarcophagi give you the old mythological stories in bas-reliefs upon their sides and lids, which it is often very interesting to trace out. A splendid one in this gallery bears upon its sides the sculptured representation of Apollo and Diana destroying with their deadly arrows the family of Niobe. The central figures of the group are an old man and woman vainly trying to save the children from the fatal shafts, while the various attitudes of the figures, in fear, supplication, and agony, are finely represented by the ancient sculptor.

The lid of this great casket has on its border, very appropriately, a representation of dead bodies. Upon the top of this sarcophagus stood two exquisite vases of rose-colored alabaster, and another of translucent marble or alabaster, beautifully marked with concentric rings. The life-size figure of the Lacedæmonian virgin racer, with bared bosom and legs and short dress for the race, is a fine piece of work, as is also the sarcophagus representing the carrying off of the two daughters of King Leucippus by Castor and Pollux, and the huge bowl or crater with the bas-reliefs representing the vintage by fauns, cupids, and old Silenus; and gems of vases in marble, jasper, polished porphyry, red granite, or black basalt, standing on antique altars, bearing inscriptions no doubt of interest to the scholar or archæologist, but which we had not the time to stop and trace out or translate.

The visitor who has enjoyed by frequent visits the wealth of art and beauty already described, will perhaps pass through what is known as the great Gallery of Maps somewhat hastily, although it is another one of those gorgeously decorated halls with a beautiful perspective. The Gallery of Maps is an immense hall, nearly five hundred feet in length, lighted by thirty-four windows, those on one side looking into the Court of Belvedere, and the other into the Vatican Gardens; and all the view we had of the gardens was from the windows, for we were obliged in this instance, for lack of time, to give Nature the go-by for Art. In the spaces between the windows on either side are enormous maps of the provinces, possessions, and cities of Italy in 1581, and they are curious specimens of the geographical knowledge of those times. Between the windows are also marble benches and a row of seventy-two Hermes, or ancient busts of orators, poets, fauns, &c., upon high pedestals.

The vault of this grand apartment is an arch of splendor in its rich decoration of statuettes, carving, gilding, coffer and panel work, and fresco painting. The picture in the middle vault represents our Saviour intrusting the keys and the flock to St. Peter. The walls around the windows and maps are beautifully decorated with festoons, wreaths, arabesques, and grotesque allegorical ornamentation. The contents of the gallery, however, are of course much less interesting than those of others, and tourists whose time is limited seldom give it more than a mere cursory examination, or none at all.

We must now enter the Gallery of the Arazzi or Tapestries, called so from the fact that these wondrous hangings were made at Arras, in Flanders. Shakspeare, it will be remembered, calls tapestry hangings *arras* in two familiar plays: in "Hamlet," where Polonius is described as concealing himself behind the "arras"; and in "King John," where Hubert says to the attendants who are with him to assist in putting out young Arthur's eyes, "Heat me these irons hot; and look thou stand within the arras," &c.

The tapestries have a singular history, which is told at length in the guide-books, of their being stolen in 1527, restored in 1554, carried away again in 1798, and recovered again in 1808. They were skilfully wrought in wool, silk, and gold, and contain so much of the latter that on one occasion when they were recovered, the Hebrew purchasers were just commencing to burn them for the purpose of melting out the gold contained in the embroidery. The paintings from which they were copied, as is well known, were the celebrated and familiar cartoons of Raphael. The tapestries were woven in 1516 to decorate the walls of the Sistine Chapel on festival days, and are divided into two parts: those of the old school, or first series, being those from the hand of Raphael himself; and the second series, or new school, executed after his death by his Italian and Flemish pupils. There are twenty-two in all; those of Raphael, such as The Lame Man Healed by Peter and John, Miraculous Draught of Fishes, &c., are too familiar to require description, while the others represent such scenes as The Stoning of Stephen, Slaughter of the Innocents, and Adoration of the Shepherds. Some that have been restored are quite fresh and beautiful in their colors and tints, and others are sadly faded by time and rough usage.

All too short was our stay in those beautiful galleries that run around three sides of an open space, and are called the *Loggie* and *Stanze* of Raphael, with their superbly decorated ceilings that gave me the back-ache from continued looking upwards for an hour or two, for the thirteen sections of the vaulting contain forty-eight beautiful representations of scenes from the Old Testament and four from the New. No wonder this superb pictorial display is called "Raphael's Bible," for you may read, in these illustrations, parts of the Old Testament by the graphic and gracefully presented pictorial representations of its most familiar scenes: commencing with the creation of light, separation of light from darkness; then the creation of the sun and moon, creation of Eve; Deluge, Lot's flight, Joseph sold by his brethren; and continuing with Biblical history till we come to the Israelites crossing Jordan, building of Solomon's Temple, &c. The four scenes from the New Testament are the Adoration, the Wise Men of the East, Baptism of Christ, and Last Supper.

The "Stanze" of Raphael also are not only richly decorated on the ceilings, but upon the sides of the different rooms — especially in those known as the *Stanza della Segnatura* and the *Stanza d'Eliodoro*, which were painted by Raphael himself unaided — are numerous beautiful fresco pictures of allegorical figures, Bible history, and mythological subjects.

Among the most remarkable of these is the one familiar from its reproduction in engravings, The School of Athens, with its fifty-two figures representing ancient philosophers and scholars, such as Plato, Aristotle, Socrates, and Pythagoras, all the figures being most gracefully and naturally posed and placed without the least appearance of crowding. The Expulsion of Heliodorus from the Temple of Jerusalem is another wondrous work of art that fairly stirs the blood like a martial poem as you look upon it. Its beautiful coloring, vigor of expression, and dramatic grouping are perfect, and it may justly be said to be one of the artist's greatest triumphs.

We pass by the Mass of Bolsena, Attila kept back from Rome, to halt at another painting of great beauty, and in which the different effects of light have been marvellously well managed — The Deliverance of Peter from his Prison by the Angel. The angel is depicted as arousing Peter, and the effulgent light which surrounds him seems to make the metal armor of the sleeping soldiers fairly glitter in its beams, while from the other side of a grated window comes the light from the red glare of torches, which shines upon another group of soldiers, with singularly natural effect; and still another effect of light is introduced in a representation of that from the moon, which is seen shining in the distance, — the whole forming one of the most admirably effective and wonderfully artistic managements of light in pictorial effect that I have ever looked upon.

The Oath of Leo III., Coronation of Charlemagne, and on one long wall a spirited and vigorous battle-scene of Constantine against Maxentius, with men and horses, banners and weapons intermingled in furious conflict, are among the other attractions in this series of halls. This latter picture is said to be the largest historical subject ever painted. It was designed by Raphael and painted by Giulio Romano, and its representation is distinguished for vigorous action and warlike energy.

The reader will be spared a description of that part of the Vatican appropriated as the papal residence, or of an audience with Pius IX., as his Holiness was suffering from indisposition during most of the time occupied by the author's visit, and he was, therefore, obliged to leave Rome without having seen the Pope, — a circumstance which, although somewhat to be regretted, there is some compensation for in the reflection that it gave other tourists who had been there, whom he afterwards met, so much satisfaction to know that they had enjoyed that privilege " when *they* were in Rome ; " and " O," they " wouldn't have missed it for anything ; " and " You ought to have seen him if you had not seen anything else there ; " and " You missed one of the greatest things in Europe." This may be all true, but aching limbs and a fatigued brain indicated to me too well the hopeless endeavor to put what ought to occupy months of sight-seeing into a few weeks, as does the effort to write even the results of it in the comparatively few pages necessary to leave space for other scenes and experiences, and avoid the risk of becoming tedious.

As one hardly knows how or where to begin to inspect the treasures of the Vatican, so when one gets fairly within its walls, unless he has abundance of time at command, he is puzzled as to what portion to race through or what to leave unvisited. But, even with sufficient time for frequent visits, comfortable and careful examination, or the enjoyment one would desire, is abridged by the manner in which time is apportioned for the admission of visitors to different portions of the collection.

Thus the visitor, who may perhaps have seen all but what will require an hour's inspection in a certain gallery, comes next day to find that portion is closed for that day, and only open once or twice a week ; or, having arrived at the end of a large hall after a wearisome tramp, instead of being permitted to pass across a vestibule into the next succeeding museum, finds his further progress stopped by an inexorable iron gate or grating, and is forced to retrace his steps, descend and go around the building to another entrance, thereby losing from half to three-quarters of an hour in reaching it, only to find that he has but an hour left of the time allotted for the gallery to be open, and that will be abridged by the attendants at least one quarter, many of whom seem determined that intrusive foreigners shall stay not a moment longer in these sacred precincts than regulations allow.

Previous preparation adds so much to the enjoyment of a visit to this wonderful museum, that too much cannot be said in its favor; and the American intending to visit Rome, who has not, as he may think, had the advantages of such education, to enable him to enjoy it to its fullest extent, should by no means neglect even the briefest opportunities of preparation in the way of historical reading. The leisure hours of a single season devoted to Roman history and mythology will be found to add immensely to one's enjoyment; indeed, the very stories of our youth become of service to us in a visit to old Rome, and the smallest bits of information respecting its history, or legends that have been laid away in the storehouse of memory, are found to be of service.

A thoroughly ignorant man visiting such a collection as that of the Vatican in Rome, is like a deaf person at a concert of music; he sees the motions of the performers, and, although his friends may communicate to him the purpose for which the motions are made, he can have no perfect idea of their effect, and certainly but little enjoyment or appreciation of the real merits of the music.

The collection at the Vatican is so vast and so varied that one must be dull indeed, and have improved but few of the natural advantages possessed by all men, not to find some department and many objects that will arouse his interest, or enlist his attention. The time devoted to it by tourists only allows a passing glance at a few of the most prominent objects in the principal apartments. And not only is it the historical antiquities and wondrous works of ancient art which the visitor encounters that excite his interest, but the architectural beauties and superb decorations of the halls themselves, wherein the old popes have sought to perpetuate their names as patrons of the arts, and where successive artists have contended with each other for supremacy in conception, design, and execution.

CHAPTER XI.

The Colosseum! That one great central figure in all imaginations of ancient Rome, and, in fact, one that always rose in fancy's pictures when we wondered if we should ever visit the old city. That sturdy enduring monument of the past, that has witnessed the triumphs and excesses of successive tyrants, echoed to the shouts of Rome's populace in her palmiest days; whose arena has been soaked with the blood of barbarian gladiators and Christian martyrs; whose walls have withstood the assaults of vandal conquerors, the inexorable tooth of time, and, more than all these, the vandal-like assaults of modern Romans themselves!

The Colosseum! I actually felt a nervous thrill when we started off to visit this mute link between to-day and distant centuries. It was a pilgrimage to tell off one of the great beads strung on time's rosary, and fitting it was that we should again stroll, on our way to it, through the Roman Forum, where all around, above, each side, and under foot, were the remains and the very dust of the mighty power that made such an indelible impression upon the history of the world as to be felt for centuries after it had ceased to exist.

The successive destructions by fire and invasion that threw down hut, palace, and temple, and the architectural monuments which each ambitious emperor erected to perpetuate the glory of his name, some upon the very ruins of those of his predecessor, give us a Rome of to-day eighteen feet or more above the Rome of the Cæsars, and we walk over a soil in which it is impossible to dig in any direction to the depth of a few feet without striking relics of the past which lie in regular historic strata, one above the other.

In the Roman Forum, and on the way to the Colosseum ! the very Forum that knew Cato and Julius Cæsar, and rung with Cicero's orations ; where Virginius slew his daughter, and where Scipio discomfited his accuser on the anniversary of the day he had overcome Hannibal ; where the Roman populace had so often been swayed by the winning promises and the largesses of emperors, stirred and aroused by the magic of eloquence, or with ungrateful or avenging daggers struck at their best friends or bloodiest tyrants ; and through which they had thronged in eager crowds to the great white marble circus, with its rings of arches crowned with a purple canopy, to witness gladiatorial or wild-beast combats !

And what do we see as we pass along the route through this brief and narrow space, so crammed with historic events ? The two great shattered arches, furrowed, seamed, and crumbling as beneath the veritable gigantic teeth of Chronos ; here and there a group of pillars, graceful in their loneliness, beautiful even in their ruin, fragments left, as it were, by the destroyer to show how grand and beautiful was that he had overcome. As we approach the Arch of Constantine, the grand oval with its shattered side bursts upon the view, with its series of arches and its grand circular sweep of pillars, column, and cornice, recognized at once as an old familiar friend ; the brown travertine, the shattered and crumbling edges of the topmost walls, and the waving weeds and flowers here and there high up among the crumbling masonry that writers and poets tell of, — all were there.

We descended one of the roadways which are on each side, for it will be remembered that this great amphitheatre was built in a hollow on the site of the great lake in the gardens of Nero's "Golden House ; " and it is said by some authorities that when the Emperor Vespasian drained the lake for a site for his amphitheatre, he at the same time pulled down Nero's Palace. We pass the ruins of the Palaces of the Cæsars, as they are called, above which, until the excavations made by Louis Napoleon, bloomed a flourishing vineyard. The appearance of the earth and stone and fragments here is as if the roadway and surroundings were of ground-up, burned bread ; a dried sponge — scoria — exhausted earth that had been palace-wall and peasant's hut and street pavement, crushed, smashed, burned, buried, excavated, time-worn, till the very life of the very stone was sucked out and only the husk left behind.

But we are close upon the Colosseum, well named by the venerable Bede, for it is a colossus among the other ruins ; and even now, after having been degraded to be fortress, factory, and stone quarry, and plundered by ancient vandals who wrenched off its marble sheathing for the metal bolts in the wall, and by modern desecrators who carried away its solid blocks of stone to build four palaces, — despite all the injury wrought by ancient spoiler and modern plunderer, it is still impressive from the symmetry and grandeur of its proportions ; while the interior arrangements, which can plainly be traced, for the accommodation of more than eighty thousand spectators, were so perfect as to elicit to-day the admiration of modern architects.

The Colosseum was one of those sights that looked, as we approached it, just as I had fancied in my imagination it would. There were the rings or open arcades of regular arches, one above the other, with the pillars between, — three orders of architecture being seen in its four stories. There before it was the brown hillock or cone, all that remained of the great fountain that in the days of Rome's splendor sent its sparkling waters into the air to fall back into the great marble basin round which the gladiators gathered after the combat or games to wash and receive congratulations from patrons, master, or friends. The rich and warm brown tint of the great ruin beneath the blue of the Italian sky, and surrounded by the verdure in the neighborhood, is all in perfect harmony of coloring, making a picture grateful to the eye.

The shape of the Colosseum, a grand ellipse resting on arches, is familiar to all readers. There were eighty of these open arches in the three lower stories in the whole circumference of the building, each arch being fourteen feet and six inches in width, except at the extremities of the diameters of the ellipse, where they are two feet wider. Between all the arches are columns, or *were* columns, throughout the whole circumference, and each successive ring or tier of arches and columns was of a different order of architecture: the lowest plain Doric, the next above Ionic, and the third Corinthian. Above these, if the reader will look at pictures of the Colosseum, he will observe was another circular tier, consisting of a wall without open arches, but decorated with Corinthian pilasters, and pierced with windows for light and ventilation. Above this was a great entablature in which are the holes which held the masts supporting the great awning or curtain that shaded the audience from the sun, known as the *velarium*.

We may get some idea of the magnitude of the structure from the fact that all that now remains in any degree entire is only three-eighths of the whole circumference. The whole structure covered about six acres of ground. The total height was one hundred and fifty-seven feet, the different stories of arches being respectively thirty, thirty-eight, thirty-eight, and forty-four feet high, which, added to the entablature, makes the height above mentioned, although some authorities place the total height at one hundred and ninety feet. A few more figures of dimensions may be suggestive: for instance, that you must walk one third of a mile to accomplish its circumference, and the space occupied by the arena is two hundred and seventy-eight feet long by one hundred and seventy-seven in width.

We descended towards this great monument of the past, and halted at its lower arches to look up at the huge blocks of travertine, of which it was built, some of them five feet high and eight or ten feet long; and the holes where many were held together by iron clamps, or where the marble sheathing was fastened to them, are still visible. There are also discoverable upon these blocks the builders' signs and marks, indications of their having been hewn, squared, and numbered before being raised to their position. This perfectly quarried stone was too great a temptation for the Roman princes of the fifteenth century, who saw in it a mine of wealth for the construction of their palaces, and whom we of these more modern times have to anathematize for doing more than even the scythe of Time would have done towards its destruction; for the Farnese, San Marco, and Barberini palaces were built of stone plundered from its walls; and that one of the spoilers at least was conscious of the outrage he was committing is evidenced by the manner in which he is described to have set about it.

This was the Cardinal Farnese, who, after long importunity to his uncle, Paul III., who was Pope 1534–50, and a setting forth of his need of a little of the useless stone that he represented was falling to ruin and decay, at length extorted a reluctant consent from the old pontiff that he might take as much stone as he could remove in twelve hours. He improved this permission by setting four thousand workmen at the task for that length of time, and, as may be reasonably inferred, obtained a very respectable amount of building material for his new palace.

The structure is guarded jealously enough now, however, for in my walk through it I chanced to see a two-inch marble chip amid a heap of debris, and had scarcely transferred it to my pocket as a memento of the visit, ere one of the military guardians of the place was at my side to inform me that "*il est defendu, Monsieur,*" (it is forbidden); and I was forced to throw down the bit of stone again. A little further on, however, when a friendly arch interfered between the soldier and his commanding officer, he communicated to me that he had some very fine specimens of fragments of marble and antique carving found here, to sell, which he would be glad to bring to my lodgings if desired.

We owe to the French the clearing of the accumulated rubbish of centuries from the arena of the Colosseum, and to Pope Pius VII. the building of the wall that supports the shattered part or end of the gap. I halted at the lower arches, which, as I arrived at them, began to give me a new idea of the magnitude of the structure. Above many of them I could plainly trace the Roman numerals, such as XXV, XL, XXXI, which, as they were all used as places of ingress and egress for the vast multitude who attended the games, were doubtless numbered that each might know the proper entrance to reach his place without trouble or confusion. We walked round this vast outer corridor of entrances, halted at one wider than the rest, above which were no figures, and which is said to have been the imperial entrance, the passage by which the emperor passed to reach his place to grace the games by his imperial presence.

And over this road to the spectacle may have passed Vespasian or Trajan, Hadrian, Domitian, or Titus the conqueror of Jerusalem; the last-named reminding us that this great monument to Rome's glory, this relic and reminder of her savage cruelty and lust for blood, which was dedicated by the Roman conqueror of the Holy City, is said to have had twelve thousand captive Jews employed upon the labor of its erection, its very stones cemented with the groans and tears of a captive people beneath the taskmaster's whip, as were those of the Pyramids of Egypt, where the Hebrews were also captives and the Egyptians the tyrants. Round under this great lower tier of arches, this huge lobby to the amphitheatre, passed the incoming and outgoing crowds on the days of the games and gladiatorial combats.

We reached the gate of entrance, guarded by a custodian, and passed in from the outer circle of entrance arches to the next series; and here we had opportunity of marking the wondrous skill with which the architect or architects, whoever they may have been, planned this vast theatre for the accommodation of the one hundred thousand spectators it was designed to contain, so that there should be no confusion attending their entrance or exit, and that the different classes should be able to reach the positions designed for them without coming in contact with each other after entering.

The name of the designer of the Colosseum has not come down to us, though it is well known that the structure was commenced by Vespasian A. D. 72, and dedicated eight years afterwards by Titus, after his return from the conquest of Jerusalem. But, whoever the designer was, his plans for the convenience and accommodation of so vast an audience seem as well-nigh perfect as they possibly could be.

I had now got within the second corridor, which, like the outer one above referred to, ran entirely around the building, and within this was another; eighty walls, corresponding with the number of entrance arches, radiated inwards from the second corridor, and supported the structure; and between these walls were the staircases leading to a third corridor, which also ran around the building. Then came the eighty division walls again, with spaces for the staircases and passages leading to the inner or fourth corridor, divided from the arena by a huge wall, upon the top of which was the lower range of seats for spectators of the highest rank, who sat fifteen feet above the level of the arena, and were still further protected, when wild-beast combats took place, by a metal network or trellis.

But I am not going to describe the Colosseum as it was, although, to every visitor of an imaginative turn who comes here, its ancient magnificence may be filled out in his own mind's eye. I interested myself first by climbing to the great square, ruined blocks, which are said to have been where the emperor sat to witness the games, and thinking that here had Vespasian and Titus and Domitian, Caracalla and Hadrian sat, as the group of gladiators paused beneath, before engaging in mortal combat, to salute them with uplifted arms with, *Ave Cæsar, Imperator, Morituri te salutant.* ("Hail, Imperial Cæsar! Those who are about to die salute thee.") To which the imperial tyrant, with nod of approval, replied, *Avete vos.* ("Health to you.")

Shattered like the great empire that was raised with blood, strengthened by conquest, and made splendid with the spoil of nations, is the proud throne from which the emperors looked down upon the bloody circus, — a few jagged rocks with no semblance of seat or dais; the circle of the podium, or lower ring, just outlined here and there by the line of ruins that runs around in jagged deformity. It requires a pretty strong stretch of imagination to reproduce it as the high marble wall, decorated with bas-reliefs and statuary, and peopled with prætors, consuls, ædiles, and vestal virgins, who sat here to witness some of the most terrible dramas ever enacted in ancient Rome, — who looked upon men cut down by thousands, or saw them torn by ravenous beasts without a shudder, and whose exultant *habet!* as the weapon of the more skilful gladiator crushed the life out of his panting adversary, applauded "the wretch who won."

But I climbed down from my perch from the emperor's seat, and then we explored the stairways and passages, and some of us ascended away up to the highest point where it was safe to go, and looked down, as did the Roman people a thousand years ago, upon the bloody ring beneath; and I could not but notice that at whatever point we paused, the whole of the arena was visible, it evidently having been so contrived that the spectacle should be in uninterrupted view of the whole of the vast assemblage.

It is a grand view, this sight of the whole vast theatre, or all that remains of it, below you, and the great stone circle, huge even seen from this height, stretching out its vast ring on either side. It was a realization to me of youthful dreams, a fruition of hope, to stand here upon the top of the amphitheatre of imperial Rome, and look down upon its tier on tier of arches, brown, crumbling ruins, fringed with flowers and grass or waving weeds, great yawning black chasms here and there, where the masonry had fallen in, and opposite me the ridgy, ragged edges of the partition walls, standing sharply out in the shade, like crayon-lines or the ribs of the great skeleton from which the flesh had mouldered and fallen.

Turning, I looked upon the Forum, the triumphal arches, and the landscape, and Rome's hills beneath the blue bending azure of an Italian sky, and found that an Italian sun was all too fervid to dream or sentimentalize under; and so, having climbed about from point to point of the different circles of the great amphitheatre, wherever the guardian who followed us would permit, (and to some places he would not permit,) I prepared to descend and visit the different points of interest in and about the arena. And here I may observe that clambering about upon some of the upper portions of the structure is extremely dangerous, owing to the deceptive appearance caused by grasses or vegetation near the edge, which the incautious explorer may approach too near, and be precipitated down a ruined archway, or from one platform to that beneath, if he undertakes to elude the custodians of the place, or explore portions which have been shut off from visitors or over which they are forbidden to pass.

Descending, I found myself behind the podium, or lower wall, that directly inclosed the arena; and here we were shown various interesting remains: one a long passage recently opened, which led from the arena floor to the Palace of Titus, and another which led to the menagerie. There is a long covered passage, which has been opened, that ran completely around the arena, just back of the inner wall, and which, our cicerone informed us, was used as a passage for the slaves and those who did the work of the arena to pass from point to point to perform their duties while the combats were going on, so as not to cross the open space or interrupt the proceedings.

Then we went into two great dens, recently cleared out, where the wild beasts were confined, close to the arena, so they could be easily freed and sent out to take their part in the scene before the populace. In another passage running around the arena are smaller dens, with holes above, through which the occupants could be fed. The various chambers, galleries, dens, and great arched cell-looking apartments behind the podium must have been those that held gladiators, beasts, horses, chariots, and slaves. It is really the "behind the scenes," as it were, and where hungry wild beasts were imprisoned; where fierce gladiators, armed and impatient, waited their turn to distinguish themselves in mortal combat beneath the imperial eye; where trembling martyrs heard the fierce cry of the assembled thousands that crowded the circus hungry for their blood, and demanding them to be brought forth. And here is one of the entrances through which the gladiators stepped forth into the arena beneath the excited gaze of a hundred thousand spectators. And I walked forth through it on a bright, beautiful spring day, paced across the arena, and stood in the centre of the Roman Colosseum, beneath and before the emperor's seat upon the podium.

No one who is at all familiar with the bloody scenes enacted on this spot and in this great ellipse, so famous in the world's history, can stand here for the first time without a thrill of emotion. Imagination at once recreates the vast circle; and tier on tier of galleries rise above the visitor; great swelling waves of spectators, all with their terrible eyes of eager anticipation centred upon one object: and you feel that he who stood there was the focus of that observation. You can almost imagine you hear the hum and murmur of the vast throng in the marble balconies that ring in the bloody battle-ground, — the muffled growls of the wild beasts behind their iron gratings in the lower wall of the arena, becoming more distinct in the hush of expectation that succeeds, as the spectators lean forward in breathless interest when the gladiators cautiously approach each other to cross weapons in deadly combat.

Here stretches the great elliptical arena, strewn with its colored sand or sawdust, to afford firm footing for the combatants and absorb the blood of the slain; around it the first wall, the podium, fifteen feet in height, sheathed with smooth marble, its top lined with the gilded netting, — protection against the spring of some lithe leopard or frantic tiger; at intervals, pierced with openings for the entrance of gladiators or wild beasts, the latter apertures guarded by bronze portcullis gratings, which can be hoisted from above when the animals, hungered from long fast, are to be set at liberty.

Upon the podium we see the elevated chair of the emperor surrounded by his friends, magistrates in their curule chairs, persons of rank, prætors and consuls. All around this wall rise sculptures, statues, and decorations; and as the eye sweeps over its circuit, it encounters the Priests of Jupiter and the Vestal Virgins, admitted to this favored position by virtue of their office. Two grand principal entrances divide the circle of the podium, affording points of admittance for processions of gladiators, chariots for chariot-racing, or displays of pageantry.

Above the podium rise the three great tiers or circles of seats, each separated from the others by a broad promenade or platform. In the first tier are fourteen rows of marble benches for senators and Roman knights. Then, above this, sixteen serried rings of the plebeian populace; then another division terrace or landing place, above which ten circles of the soldiery and *pullati,* the lowest orders of the common people, looked down; and away up above all is the open gallery, where the men work the ropes that manage the huge canopy that shields the spectators from the sun. The occupant of the arena looked up at tier on tier of faces rising one above the other, far up, as it were, to the sky, holding him down below as the central point or focus of their fixed gaze.

Here, within the very space we stand upon, has the blood of the early Christians poured out its precious libation, and, while lying bound within their cells beneath the podium, they have heard the terrible cry that ran all around the vast area of, " The Christians to the lions! the Christians to the lions!" until pushed forth into the bloody circle at one side; the bronze portcullis at the same time was hoisted opposite, and the starved and ferocious beasts were let loose upon them, or they fell beneath the arrow-shots of the soldiery. Here the Emperor Commodus himself essayed the hand-to-hand combat. Of course, he was victorious and slew his adversary, — for woe be to him who shed imperial blood; and his adversary's poor weapon, bent and shattered beneath the tempered steel of the heavy imperial sword, as it crushed down into the bloody dust the poor slave, cloven to the teeth; and the royal conqueror strutted round in lion-skin mantle, imagining himself Hercules, amid the servile shouts of the spectators.

Let not the reader unfamiliar with Roman history imagine that only two or three gladiators or half a dozen wild beasts were let loose at once in the amphitheatre. Had this been all, a far smaller space would have sufficed. This vast area was the result of a bloody appetite that grew upon what it fed, and a thousand savage beasts a day have fallen within its dreadful circle; gladiators by hundreds at a time have closed in deadly contest with each other, and piled the ground with scores of slaughtered combatants.

Here Titus, at the dedication of the building, and on his

return from the conquest of Jerusalem, slaughtered five thousand wild beasts; elephants fought with lions, tigers with bears, bulls with leopards; and ostriches, stags, boars, giraffes, and even cranes and pigmies, were brought into the arena. Here Hadrian celebrated his birthday by the slaughter of a hundred lions and as many lionesses, besides eight hundred other wild beasts; and the arena was so arranged, as has been recorded and since been proved by recent excavations, that it could be flooded with water and the spectators treated to a representation of a sea-fight, the combatants being gladiators in galleys that met upon the water and engaged in deadly contest.

Invention seems to have been racked to present novelties to the people, as is evidenced by the varieties of combatants, the descriptions of which have come down to us.

The Roman emperors, from Titus down to Honorius, A. D. 403, for nearly four centuries, sat in this great theatre to view the terrible scenes enacted upon the inclosed space we were now pacing over. Titus, conqueror of Jerusalem, took delight in these gladiatorial contests. Domitian, his cruel brother, who delighted to see men killed for sport, and who spiked flies on a pin to amuse himself, sat upon the podium, and was in all his glory here in the gratification of his cruel and sensual spirit. Gladiatorial battles, fierce and bloody sea-fights, and women as gladiators, were features of his entertainments. Trajan, after his triumph over the Dacians, looked down here upon tremendous struggles, in which thousands of combatants were engaged. Other frequenters of the Colosseum were Hadrian, his successor, already referred to, under whom the Christian Bishop of Illyria yielded up his life on this spot; the bloody Commodus, who came so near meeting his merited death by the hands of the assassin in the narrow passage leading to his seat in this very amphitheatre, — a passage which some guides try to point out to you; Caracalla, the parricide; Philip, who, about A. D. 248, celebrated the one thousandth anniversary of the foundation of Rome here with gladiatorial combats, games, and chariot-racing; Claudius, conqueror of the Goths; Æmilian and Aurelian, in whose reigns men were exposed to wild beasts, and those not devoured hewn down by gladiators.

But amid these bloody recollections of the place, as we follow the line of emperors down, comes to us a record of another character, — that of a practical joke that is recorded to have been perpetrated by the Emperor Gallienus, son of Valerian. The story runs that the emperor's wife, having been cheated in the purchase of some jewelry, fell into a violent rage with the jeweller, and demanded a terrible punishment upon him, and one that should be a warning to all jewellers in future of the danger of cheating an empress. Gallienus assented; the fellow was arrested, and sentenced to be thrown to the wild beasts in the arena. He was dragged there, half dead with fright, when the next games took place, and at the appointed time, when his part of the performance was to occur, was thrust forth into the ring, where, half fainting with terror, he sank down upon the red sand as the bronze portcullis of the wild beasts' den was hoisted, when, instead of a hungry lion springing upon him, or a terrible tiger leaping forth, out walked an old hen!

In reply to the indignant demand for an explanation by the empress, her imperial consort declared that to be very simple; for as the man had, according to her account, terribly cheated her, so he had been terribly cheated in return.

The Emperor Probus had, about A. D. 280, a grand wild-beast slaughter here, and at another time he had in the ring six hundred gladiators and seven hundred wild beasts. At length Constantine, in 330, made a law prohibiting gladiatorial combats, but the people were too fond of the bloody spectacle to yield it.

Seventy years after, however, when Christianity was nearly four centuries old, and the brutal gladiatorial combat was in full progress, a Christian monk leaped from the podium into the arena, and, rushing amid the combatants, entreated them with prayers to separate. Enraged at the interruption, the Prætor Alybius bade the gladiators kill the intruder, and the monk Telemachus paid the penalty of his life for his noble endeavor; but it was a successful one, for the Emperor Honorius abolished gladiatorial combats from that time; and Telemachus, who was hewn down by gladiators, marked with his death the day of the last gladiatorial combat in the Flavian Amphitheatre.

The reader, who has followed the author in his visits to St. Peter's, the Capitol, the Forum, the Pantheon, the triumphal arches and columns, the Vatican, and Flavian Amphitheatre, will perhaps think he has seen a large portion of old Rome. While it may be admitted that the sights above enumerated have, to use the tourist's expression, been "done" systematically and pretty thoroughly, it will be found, if the visitor has any enthusiasm as a tourist, antiquary, or student, that he has but taken the introductory steps towards making himself acquainted with the old city; and, let the appetite grow as it will upon what it feeds, the material that is still presented for fresh repasts is rich and almost inexhaustible: so that the traveller with tastes that are gratified by visits to the historic spots and ruins in this city of youthful study and later dreams, finds, as did the author, the brief space of time that can be devoted to it from an ordinary European tour insufficient to do justice to scarcely half that which it seemed should not be omitted.

There must necessarily be much in foreign cities that will be hastily visited, or entirely omitted, by both tourists and authors, as each devotes the larger portion of his time to that branch of sight-seeing most in accordance with his tastes and desires. Hence, we read many descriptions to obtain complete accounts.

The splendid marbles, vases, and other decorations that are seen in the museums of Rome, as having been found at Caracalla's Baths, naturally excite a desire to visit the ruins of those celebrated structures, — that is, with most people; for there are exceptions, as in the case of one tourist, who told us he was "tired enough of old ruins without going to look at what was left of an old bath-house!"

And this expression brings us to the consideration that there are many that read, as well as many that travel, who have an incorrect idea of Roman baths; deriving their impressions, probably, from baths of modern times, and supposing the ancient ones to be like the modern, except that the former were more luxurious and perfect in fittings and appointments.

To obtain an idea of the extent of this Roman luxury, the tourist should by all means visit these interesting ruins; and he will be astonished to find himself in the midst of arched passages, a long extent of ruined walls, great halls with lofty, shattered ceilings, and elegant mosaic floors with beautiful colored designs wrought in the pavement, — a collection of ruins which requires the walk of an English mile to encompass them. The buildings must have been in the form of a large parallelogram, exterior or outer buildings of forty-two hundred feet, inclosing an inner or great court, which was cut up into various divisions. In this great inner court was a grand building on arches, which was seven hundred feet long by four hundred and fifty broad. These great buildings now present to the spectator only a series of roofless ruins, with great fragments of arches and walls; and you may pass through what were once large and elegant halls and apartments, well defined by lines of masonry, from which the decorations and rich marbles have been stripped, as is plainly evident by fragments that here and there remain, or a patch of what was once one great sheet of mosaic pavement.

The numerous halls and apartments of this extensive ruin will indicate to the visitor how complete must have been this grand establishment for the comfort and luxurious enjoyment of the people. First, for the purposes of bathing, there was every possible auxiliary and convenience that could be devised, — the Apodyterium, or disrobing room; the Sudatorium, or vapor bath; Tepidarium, or tepid bath; Caldarium, or hot bath; Frigidarium, or cold bath; and the Unctuarium, or perfuming and anointing room, where the bather was perfumed and anointed with oil. The remains of these, in various stages of ruin, are traced out, and also the vaults beneath, by which the water was heated by means of furnaces or stoves. Then there was one large, open swimming-bath, open to the sky above, in which, we were told, a thousand could bathe at once; and indeed the space, as it looks now, appears as if very nearly that number might have done so. The Caldarium, or hot bath room here, was a circular, Pantheon-like building, lighted from above.

But it was not alone for bathing and swimming that the people resorted here; for there were, besides the baths of different temperature, gardens and fountains, libraries, rooms for discussions, theatres for athletic games, shady and pleasant walks, an arena for running and wrestling, refreshment shops, perfume and fancy bazaars, and halls for poets to recite their verses, lecture-rooms and theatres for comedy performances, with seats for spectators; all of which made the Baths a place of resort, not only for the cleansing and refreshment of ablution, but a great place of amusement, entertainment, and luxurious enjoyment of the Roman people. These baths were said by ancient authority to be capable of accommodating sixteen hundred people; and the price of a bath was a *quadrans*, the smallest piece of money, from Cicero down.

Beautiful statues, rich frescos and mosaics, magnificent vases, great porphyry tubs for private bathing-rooms, some of which are now to be seen in the Vatican Museum, and elegant carvings and bas-reliefs, were among the splendors lavished upon the Baths, which were, as will be seen, a place of gathering for intellectual and physical recreation. All around and through these ruins are heaps of marble or alabaster, or porphyry and granite chips, and the temptation to bring away fragments of the colored mosaic pavements that have recently been uncovered is such that tourists are constantly followed by a soldier or custodian to see that not a fragment is stolen. It would have been well had the surveillance commenced a little earlier, before the magnificent columns of granite were taken away by the popes and the Farnese family, causing the great vaulted roofs of the outer surrounding porticos to fall in and become a mass of shapeless ruins. The princes of the Farnese family were great ruin-plunderers, their palace being built of stones taken from the Colosseum, its two great fountains dropping their jets into granite basins seventeen feet in length and four feet deep, taken from the Baths of Caracalla, and a sarcophagus from the tomb of Cæcilia Metella adorning (?) one of its porticos.

The ruins known as the Palace of the Cæsars are surrounded with such a halo of the old legendary Roman story, and present so many interesting specimens of Rome's early grandeur, remains of which were brought to light and exposed to modern gaze by the learned scholar, Pietro Rosa, under the direction of Louis Napoleon while emperor of France, that one shrinks from attempting any description on account of the temptation to recapitulate the events of Rome's earliest history, commencing with the somewhat mythical Romulus and Remus legends. It is sufficient to say, in the brief allusion that we shall make to these ruins, known as the Palace of the Cæsars, and the recent excavations made, that they are of the most interesting character to the student from the fact of their being upon the Palatine Hill, which was the very foundation and site of the city of Romulus; and that you are shown here, excavated far down below imperial Rome's ruins, buried under the buildings and palaces at the time of the Cæsars, the massive wall of the four-sided Rome described by Tacitus, — enormous blocks of masonry. Here they show us the walls of Romulus, built of a sort of lava rock, found precisely where the oldest chroniclers of Rome have located them.

Indeed, these excavations have tended to verify much that had been for many years received as little else than mythical legends of early Rome. We can as tourists, however, but bestow a passing glance upon this compressed mass of historic ground, so to speak, which, although but a trapezium with two sides three hundred yards in length, and the other two four hundred, has, like the Forum, historic ruin enough heaped up in it, and is the scene of historic events enough to keep historians and antiquaries busy for centuries to come, as it has for centuries past.

The house of the Emperor Augustus was here, but Domitian was the first one to build a palace, and, rambling among what appear to be mere jagged remnants of ruin, you are told they are the authenticated remains of his imperial edifice, and others are of the Palace of Tiberius; or you walk along what was once the street **Via Nova**, described by Ovid; or are shown where was once a gate mentioned by Virgil in his Æneid. Here was Cicero's house, and here Mark Antony and Cæsar lived, — for it was for centuries an aristocratic quarter of Rome; and here we see the substructure of the temple of Jupiter Victor, which was in all its magnificence two thousand years ago. Here is where Caligula walked, and Nero dwelt and enlarged his luxurious palace, his golden house, in the direction of the Colosseum.

But the most interesting portions of the whole mass of ruins are the rooms of Roman dwelling-houses of the time of Augustus, that have been excavated; and the apartments in the house of Livia, who was the divorced wife of the Emperor Augustus, which gives us back the patrician Roman house of eighteen hundred years ago. There is the vestibule, opening on to the *atrium*, or grand entrance hall; then we are introduced into the chambers of honor, private living-rooms, and baths. Upon the walls of several of these apartments still remain beautiful decorative paintings, which prove to us that that art has not advanced materially even in our day; for the superb coloring and beautiful patterns of the frescos which still remain would be ornamental and elegant in the decoration of any house of the present time. Galatea, upon the waves, with Nereids beside her, is represented in one painting; Io and Argus are represented in another; and the decorative borders of scroll-work and small designs are elegant and artistic, and look quite bright and fresh, though they are preserved, so it is stated, by a varnish which is made up after an old receipt described by Pliny, which is applied soon after their exhumation. The designs in delicacy of coloring are said to be superior to any of the Pompeiian discoveries.

The House of Livia, on the Palatine, is the best preserved of any of those excavated, the shape of the apartments being easily marked out by their remaining walls and lines of masonry. We inspected one, evidently a library, or students' recitation room, according to the old inscription upon the wall, which stated that "here an oration was to be spoken once a month." There were other rooms in which still remained strips of the elegant marble veneering in various colors, that once formed the dado work or "mop-board." Fragments of elegant pillars that had upheld lofty halls, and lines of strips of marble that once were the base of palaces, were scattered about, all that remains of the latter being great brick walls from which the costly marbles have been stripped; and I went away, around, and below at the base of the hill, imagining that it was here, perhaps, that Romulus traced the *pomœrium* of his city; and here I looked upon the ancient arches of Tarquin's time, far below the ruins that I had just walked over, and above which, layer upon layer, rose the monuments of the pride of successive generations of Roman aristocracy, who for so many years, rather than leave this favored spot, reared their palaces over the crumbling ruins of the dwellings of their predecessors.

The first ride that one takes out of Rome is over that great historic road which rises first in his mind, built three centuries before the birth of our Saviour, but over which the Apostle Paul journeyed, on his way to Rome, as described in the Bible, in the twenty-eighth chapter of Acts, — the Appian Way.

"And so we went to Rome. And from thence, when the brethren heard of us, they came to meet us as far as the Appii Forum and the Three Taverns; whom when Paul saw he thanked God and took courage."

It is a broad, straight road, paved with blocks of volcanic stone, and lined with shattered fragments of the splendid mausoleums and tombs of those who were once great, noble, and rich, but whose wealth and fame and history have perished like the crumbling monuments raised to commemorate them.

A thorough inspection or description of the hundreds or perhaps thousands of remnants of tombs that line both sides of this great historical avenue into the Eternal City would be interesting to the antiquary, but tedious to the ordinary reader. In fact, the tourist who has inspected forums, amphitheatres, and museums, and examined tolerably well-authenticated relics and sculptures of antiquity, which are, by association or otherwise, connected with great historic names, will hardly feel, on the Via Appia, like spending much time over what was once the handsome tomb of a Roman tax-gatherer, or that of Plinius Eytychius, erected by Plinius Zosimus, a freedman of Pliny the younger.

But we were interested, as we were just starting out, to be told, at a certain point, that here stood the Porta Capena, where the survivor of the Horatii met his sister on his return from the memorable combat, and slew her with a blow of his sword on seeing her express grief for one of the Curatii who had fallen beneath his victorious blade; and it was at this gate that Cicero was received by the Roman people and senate on his return from banishment, B. C. 57.

We halted to view the Tomb of the Scipios, from which the sarcophagus in the Vatican, already described in these pages, was taken. It is simply a series of narrow passages, like the tombs of any distinguished family, dark and to be explored with candles, and containing little now but the apertures where the sarcophagi were placed, the more pretentious monuments being, of course, elsewhere, these being but the catacombs for the reception of the mortal remains.

The old Arch of Drusus, which is a heavy, plain structure, with a great mass of masonry on top of it (part of an aqueduct it was utilized to support), was erected in honor of Drusus, who was the father of the Emperor Claudius, and who died B. C. 9. We look up at it as we pass, as being the same structure beneath which the Apostle Paul passed on his entrance into Rome. About one hundred and fifty yards beyond this, on the right, was discovered the first Roman mile-stone of the Appian Way, which I had inspected with much interest in the square of the Capitol, not far from the head of the flight of steps leading up to it.

The great, round, fortress-like tower that meets our gaze after a two-mile ride, is a familiar one — the Tomb of Cæcilia Metella, wife of Crassus. This grand monument is one of the best preserved in Rome, and has defied time for two thousand years. It is seventy feet in diameter, sits upon a huge square foundation, and is built of large blocks of hewn stone; it has a white marble frieze, decorated with bas-reliefs of the skulls of oxen and wreaths of flowers, and above it rise the battlements of a fortress, which were added when it was turned into a stronghold, in the thirteenth century. The marble coating, as usual, of this tomb was stripped off by Pope Urban VIII., and used to build and decorate the Fountain of Trevi in the city; and the sarcophagus within, as has before been mentioned, was taken by the Farnese family. The inscription records that the monument is to the daughter of Metellus Creticus, wife of the triumvir Crassus. A magnificent tomb it was for the wealthiest Roman's wife, who, with all the money he expended for the preservation of her precious dust, left us only the knowledge that she died his wife, and that this was a monument of his love and pride.

A rusty-looking, mahogany-visaged custodian, with the remnants of what might have once been a bandit-peaked hat, but which was now badly crushed out of shape, and boasted of but one dirty green band, was anxious to show us some of the interior, and pointed to a narrow door in the wall; but we were in no mood to explore the interior, which contains now but little of interest, and so left the would-be cicerone with his old hat in one hand and a silver lira in the other, grateful and gratified.

After leaving the tomb of Cæcilia Metella behind us, the other tombs and monuments became more numerous and more distinctly defined, several appearing to have been somewhat restored and we began to be more fairly out on the Roman Campagna, and also to enjoy "the prospect beyond the tomb." This we find in the broad Campagna, with its distant Sabine and Alban Hills, which have that beautiful violet blue tint so peculiar to distant mountains beneath this atmosphere. Then across the great silent plains you can mark the long, sinuous line of ruined arches that mark the aqueducts which once stretched from the cool fountains of the Sabine Hills to the city, and conveyed their water thither, giving Rome pure drinking fluid, and supplying, doubtless, its great baths.

These great aqueducts are other monuments of the wealth and wonders of the ancient city; for here is one, the Aqua Marcia, constructed B. C. 146, which stretched its arches of masonry away out to the Sabine Mountains, a distance of fifty-six miles; while the Aqua Claudia, put up by the Emperor Claudius A. D. 50, was over fifty-eight miles in length. The water to-day in Rome is esteemed by tourists "the best in Europe," can be drank freely, and except, of course, in very hot weather, with safety. Down in the city proper the

Trevi water is esteemed the best. At the Hotel Constanzi, being on higher ground, we were furnished with Marcia water, from the same source that the old Romans were served. For six or eight miles, stretched over the Campagna, do the ruined arches mark the course of these great public works of the Roman emperors; and that the water supply was an all-important one is seen in the fact that good authorities state that, when all the aqueducts were in operation in Rome (in the imperial epoch), the supply must have been fifty million cubic feet in twenty-four hours, or ten times the actual supply of London for the same time. Rome is to-day a city of fountains; you find them at every turn and in every square, and there are said to be in modern Rome over six hundred, while ancient Rome boasted of thirteen thousand.

We sat and looked out at the picturesque ruins of the aqueducts, which are so romantic in the real landscape as seen against the Italian sky and brown hue of the Campagna, with the hills behind them, and generally so hard and artificial in the attempts to represent them in pictures; and realized, as we did so, why so many artists attempt the difficult task of rendering a counterfeit presentment of the beautiful proportions of their arcades upon the canvas.

We pass many monumental remains, and halt near one which has a bas-relief upon it, which is said to be near the spot where Seneca was put to death, according to Tacitus, "near the fourth mile-stone," by Nero's orders; here is another to Lollius Dionysius, who, it seems, was a banker in the Esquiline quarter, a wealthy man, and could afford to be buried upon the Appian, and have a good monument; then there is another to the Rabinius family, with three sculptured heads upon it; Quintius, tribune of the 16th legion; Demetrius, a wine merchant, and so one succeeds the other, some mere masses of masonry, which time has smoothed, melted, and squeezed into an irregular slab of stone, with a few indistinguishable characters upon it, and others mere slabs of conglomerate, mixtures of lime, pebbles, and brick, which were once probably sheathed with rich marbles, long since plundered to build the temples and palaces of those who came upon the stage of life so long after as to have no feeling of honor for the unknown sleepers whom the monuments were raised above. Enough remains, however, to show us that these mausoleums must have been grand in proportion and magnificent in design, some as fit for palaces for the living as sepulchres for the dead, for at the sixth mile-stone are the remains of a huge tomb called the "Round Castle," and which was said to be the tomb of Messala Corvinus, a poet, and friend of Horace. This tomb, which is larger even than that of Cæcilia Metella, was also transformed into a fortress in the fifteenth century, and is now in ruins.

The Church of "St. Paul Extra Muros," as it is called, a building of modern date, inasmuch as it was completed in 1854, stands on the foundation of the magnificent basilica which was built to commemorate the martyrdom of the apostle, and which is said to mark the site of the place where he suffered and was buried. It is upon the edge of the Campagna, and in a part much affected by the malaria, except in the winter months; hence, although but early in June, the author did not feel like devoting too much time in and about its interesting precincts. The first sight on entering the vast interior is one which excites an involuntary exclamation of admiration. Entering by one side of the transept, you look down the vast nave, which is three hundred and six feet long and two hundred and twenty-two feet wide, with four great ranges of granite pillars, eighty in number, surmounted by mosaic pictures of the Popes, a most striking and magnificent view. An enormous amount of wealth is piled up here in this building, the result of contributions levied on all Roman Catholic countries; but, being modern, it contains but very few historic remains. As a superb interior, however, the effect is grand and imposing.

A great arch (a regular triumphal arch — in a church —) separates the nave from the transept. It is a relic of the old church, and was built by the Emperor Honorius in 440, has elegant mosaics of our Saviour and the apostles above its lofty curve, on each side. Right under this arch stands the baldachino, which is a sort of ornamental cupola, supported by four elegant alabaster pillars, which were presented by Mehemet Ali, Pasha of Egypt, — so it will be seen the Romish Church does not hesitate to incorporate the gift of the infidel Saracen into its holy edifices any more than the marble plundered from the ancient pagan. Under the baldachino rose the altar, and beneath is said to repose the great apostle.

Although but little of ancient historic interest is to be found here to claim the visitor's attention, he cannot but be struck with the amazing richness of the building, and the vast amount of costly workmanship that surrounds him. The elegant malachite altars, presented by the emperor of Russia; beautiful chapels; colossal statues of saints; elegant frescos; the five great aisles; magnificent colonnades, and the floor of elegant jointed and polished marble; the elegantly wrought capitals of the pillars; the richly veined marbles of various colors with which the walls are sheathed, — all show that modern Romish Christendom poured out its millions with a lavish hand to replace the church founded by Constantine, rebuilt in 392, and which had stood for fifteen centuries a monument to the great apostle until its destruction by fire in 1823. It is fresh, dazzling, and elegant, a modern temple, seeking to vie with those of more ancient times, and as such, one of the most interesting monuments in Rome.

The real mother church of Rome, that of which the Pope is pastor, is not, as many suppose, St. Peter's, but the Church of St. John Lateran; which has so much of a history, and the title it now bears, perpetuating as it does the name of an illustrious Christian and a celebrated pagan, gives it such an interest, that we cannot leave it out.

This was the first cathedral of Constantine, and it was near Trajan's Pillar that the emperor came forth, abjured his belief in the heathen gods, and declared himself a believer in the religion of Christ. Here, in the year 312, the power of Polytheism was finally broken, the religious belief that had built superb temples to the gods, had lived for centuries, that had made old Rome rich in architectural wonders, whose emblems are to us to-day creations of beauty that we vainly seek to rival, — here its power was broken; and that of the Prince of Peace that had, despite persecutions, and trials, and oppressions, flourished and increased, received at last imperial recognition. The emperor not only declared that the priests of the Church of Christ should receive the same privileges as other priests, but his intention of building a Christian church in his Lateran palace estate, east of the Cœlian Hill. His example of freedom of conscience and toleration was forgotten a few centuries after, when popes came to reign in place of emperors.

Constantine's palace estate was on what was once the property of an old Roman family called Lateranus. Lateranus had been expelled from the senate, exiled from Rome, but afterwards recalled, and finally put to death by Nero, who seized his property; and the name of this estate, unjustly acquired, was by popular voice thus perpetuated.

So much for historical facts; and we now walk up to the entrance of the present edifice, of course by no means that of the old emperor. His church, in which he is said to have labored with his own hands, and which was consecrated in 324, stood nearly six centuries, but it was thrown down by an earthquake in 896; rebuilt again in 911, when it was dedicated to St. John the Baptist, and was described by Dante the poet as a glorious building; but, four hundred years after, in 1308, it was almost entirely destroyed by fire. It was soon after rebuilt, but burned down again in 1360; then the great Petrarch sang of its departed glories. Pope Urban V. was determined the memorable Christian temple should live, and it rose under his hand to completion again in 1370; and the present church, with a mere remnant of the one rebuilt in 911, and various additions and alterations by different modern popes, is all they have remaining of Constantine's creation, after a thousand years' struggle with time. In fact, all that really remains is probably the site of the first church, though I doubt not that some accommodating cicerone, if it were made worth his while, would discover for the curious visitor the foundation-stones of Constantine's cathedral: a task I was not disposed to undertake. Its history, it will be seen, is like other Roman monuments of antiquity; the work of men's labor, ambition, and pride is levelled by time or vandalism, reared again to fall once more upon the original ruin, till, one above another, we have historic strata of masonry and architecture.

We entered the church by a portico, passing a bad statue of Henry IV., and found ourselves in the transept, rich in its many-colored and beautiful marbles and great frescos above, representing scenes in the life of Constantine. The church is three hundred and eighty-four feet in length, and the nave, which is grand in its size and design, has five aisles; but the magnificent ancient columns have been covered with plaster and stucco work, and huge statues of the twelve apostles are in front of them in niches.

Right in centre of the transept rises a very beautiful baldachino, or, as the guide-books call it, canopy, — they appear to be about the same thing. It is a sort of Gothic design, supported by four pillars and statues at the corners, very nicely executed. Below this, we were told were preserved the skulls of St. Peter and St. Paul, and inside the great altar they pretend to have a table at which St. Peter celebrated mass!

In this transept we also saw the fine Altar of the Sacrament, and its four fluted bronze columns, which were, according to historical documents of the thirteenth century, brought from Jerusalem by the Emperor Titus after his destruction of that city. This church is rich in beautiful chapels opening out of it, which belong to various noble and wealthy Italian families. Each has its altar, and is fitted up and decorated according to the taste and wealth of the owners. The Corsini chapel is one of the most richly fitted, being elegantly built in form of a Greek cross, and beautiful in its marble decorations and sculpture. The elegant altarpiece is in mosaic work, the walls are superbly inlaid, and a bronze statue of Pope Clement XII., of this family, guards a porphyry sarcophagus which he took from the pagan Pantheon for his Christian coffin. The sarcophagi of the other members of the Corsini family are in a vault beneath this chapel. Another beautiful chapel is that of the Torlonia family, rich in marble, gilding, and frescos, containing a fine statue of Piety; and over its magnificent altar hangs a fine picture of a Descent from the Cross.

In and out of these rich and ostentatious displays of human pride the visitor passes till he is surfeited with the parade of marbles, altar-pieces, crucifixions, and monuments. A two hours' visit is double what most tourists give it, and unless you have recourse to notes and memoranda, you will be likely to carry away the usual confused recollection a tourist does after following a cicerone speaking none too perfect English, and rattling off his explanations in parrot-like style, while you vainly seek in your guide-book for particulars which ought to be there.

I preserve two extremely pleasant experiences of our visit to the Lateran distinctly in memory. One is the beautiful view from one of its porticos, at one end of which is Constantine's statue, colossal in size, said to have been discovered at his Baths, and the only authentic likeness of him. This view from the portico takes in the Alban Hills on one side and the Sabine Mountains on the other, and between, on the level campagna, you see the picturesque and ruined arches of the aqueducts in the distance; nearer, Rome, ancient and modern, is below us, — all forming a most interesting picture.

The other experience is the fine old Cloister of the Monastery, into which the custodian takes you by a side-door — a beautiful, antique-looking inclosure, surrounded by ancient arches that are supported by twisted or fluted columns, surmounted by a frieze of fine old colored marbles. This cloister was built in the twelfth century, and from beneath its shadowy arches you look out upon the courtyard it incloses, which is rich with wild roses and fragrant flowers, and among them was a curious circular well, adorned with crosses and carvings, a production of the sixth or eighth century. This quiet old sanctuary had the very odor of religious meditation about it in all its harmonious lines of graceful architecture.

"And what is this?" asked we one day, as our carriage, which at last we allowed to be driven from point to point by our guide at his own will on a sight-seeing excursion, halted, and we entered a building and found ourselves upon a marble floor from which ascended a central and two side flights of stairs. But a second glance told us at once, if the guide had not promptly answered, "The *Santa Scala*, — the Holy Staircase, Messieurs."

An antiquity indeed is this celebrated flight of steps, if not an authenticity, and I was glad to look upon the twin relic, if it may be so expressed, of the bronze statue of St. Peter, for they were always associated together in my mind from the wearing out they received from the touch of the faithful, — the great bronze toe of the statue from constant kissing, and this holy staircase, deeply worn by the knees of devout pilgrims.

For fifteen hundred years these steps have been piously reverenced by the Papal Church as being those which our Saviour ascended from the house of Pilate in Jerusalem after trial; they were brought to Rome by Helena, mother of the Emperor Constantine, in the year 326.

The entrance hall, or portico, whence these steps ascend, has three lofty arches. On each side of the principal one, beneath which is the holy staircase, are two fine marble groups, one representing Judas betraying his Master with a kiss, and the other said to be "Ecce Homo," although the inscription upon the pedestal gives no indication to that effect. The steps themselves are twenty-eight in number, and are never profaned by footstep, being ascended only upon the knees by the devotees, who receive certain indulgences from the church after having performed the act, and paid for it; which latter act I saw one poor exhausted-looking woman do with a whole handful of copper coin, which she threw in through a grating, after reaching the top of the staircase; rising with difficulty to her feet from the tiresome knee journey.

The way the pilgrimage is performed is as follows: The penitents, taking a rosary in their hands, kneel upon the first of two marble steps, say a prayer at each, and then come to a broad landing-place, on each side of which are fonts of holy water, from which, having moistened their fingers, they make the sign of the cross, and then proceed, rosary in hand, to the lower one of the holy steps. These are marble, covered with wood, with the exception of small apertures, rimmed with brass, through which a spot of the step may be touched by the lips; and it is averred that the covering has to be renewed yearly. Up these steps, one by one, upon the knees, the worshipper ascends, kissing each step through the aperture as he comes upon it, and saying a prayer over his rosary before leaving it for the next. About three-quarters of an hour is consumed in getting to the top in the prescribed manner, and I noticed that the wood covering was well worn by the knees of the worshippers, and the brass rims of the apertures had been polished to glittering brightness by the frequent contact of their lips.

Martin Luther once began the ascent of this staircase, step after step, in the usual manner, painfully, upon his knees; but when half-way up, he suddenly seemed to hear the whisper of a divine voice say, "The just shall live by faith," and he rose to his feet, descended, and left the place.

The dark, vaulted ceiling above the staircase is covered with frescos, and at the top is an altar, above which rises the scene of the crucifixion. On either side of the holy staircase are others, which we ascended in the usual manner without ceremony, and from the top of which we were permitted to look through a grating into the *Sanctum Sanctorum*, — so holy a place that none less than the Pope can officiate at its altar.

It is a picturesque old interior, with Gothic arches, twisted columns, and ornamented ceiling, and contains an altar upheld by porphyry columns, above which is a silver casket containing relics.

We descended, and gratified a round, jolly-looking monk so much by buying some of his card photographs of the place, that when he smiled and bade us adieu, he seemed more like an English Boniface in a dark cowl than a ghostly brother of the adjoining convent.

I knew the little temple of Vesta the moment we halted by it, and had seen it so often reproduced in miniature in the fancy-goods stores at home, that here in reality it seemed like an exaggerated inkstand. It is a beautiful little circular building of the time of Trajan, consisting of a sort of inner core, only twenty-six feet in circumference, surrounded by an outer perfect circle of beautiful Corinthian columns, each thirty-two feet in height, the outer circle being one hundred and fifty-six feet in circumference.

One of the pillars is broken off near the base, and the ancient roof of this temple, long since gone, is replaced by an incongruous one of red tiles; while our idol, as to its being a temple of Vesta, is thrown down by the antiquaries, who declare it to be nothing of the sort, but more likely that of Hercules.

Not far from here are many interesting points. Our guide took us to all that now remains of the old Palatine

Bridge, now called *Ponte Rotto*. A modern suspension bridge connects with what remains of the arches of an ancient bridge which was carried away by an inundation; but it is interesting to know, when you get over as near the centre of this bridge as you can, that you stand over the site of the bridge begun by Æmilius Lepidus B. C. 180, and finished by Scipio Africanus forty years after; and from here the guide will point out fragments that look like rocks above the water, which is all that remains of the oldest bridge in Rome, — the structure built by Ancus Martius, B. C. 639, and one interesting to every schoolboy who has read or declaimed Macaulay's ballad of ancient Rome, "Horatius;" for this is all what remains of the bridge which Horatius Cocles and his two brave companions defended against the whole Etruscan army under Lars Porsena. Horatius, in the ballad, says to his consul:

> "Hew down the bridge, Sir Consul,
> With all the speed ye may;
> I, with two more to help me,
> Will hold the foe in play.
> In yon strait path a thousand
> May well be stopped by three."

And the three defended the passage and "kept the bridge" till it was hewn down beneath them, leaving the sweeping Tiber a barrier between Rome and the advancing foe.

Not far from this point we went down near the river's bank to see that wonderful work of ancient Rome, the *Cloaca Maxima* (Largest Sewer). It speaks well for the sewer-builders of ancient Rome that their work, after twenty-four hundred years, should still be performing the functions for which it was originally intended. There is little to be seen at the point we visited except three concentric courses of stone in the form of an arch, like what any one would suppose the outlet of a large drain to resemble. This great sewer extended from the Forum to the

Tiber, and was written of by Pliny as "an immense work," and he states that against earthquakes and the assaults of time "the work of Tarquin remains impregnable." And now, more than a thousand years after Pliny, still the Cloaca "remains impregnable."

Rome's palaces are rich in art, and two which no tourist omits are the Barberini and the Rospigliosi. The chief attraction of the latter is the great picture, Guido's Aurora, a poetically treated subject familiar to all. Apollo in his car, surrounded by the twelve hours hand in hand, and preceded by a cherub bearing the torch of day, starts across the heavens to begin the day. This picture is on the ceiling of a small pavilion, or *casino*, as it is called, which we approached through a beautiful garden over a walk bordered by lemon-trees laden with the yellow fruit.

In the beautiful tints of the clouds with the hues of the approaching light, the spirited action of the horses of the car of Phœbus, as they start off upon their aërial journey, the graceful poses of the figures that surround the car, and that of Apollo himself, as he bends forward against the morning breeze that blows back his flowing drapery, the exquisite and harmonious blending of colors is so smooth and perfect that, as you continue to gaze upward at the picture, you can almost imagine you are looking at the clouds, and that the glorious car will whirl away on its mission to open day to the world below, while you are looking at it.

It is somewhat tiresome to the lover of art who may wish to study a painting like this for any length of time, to be compelled to gaze directly upward, unless, perhaps, he may be able to do so from a couch. An arrangement of small mirrors upon a table below enables the spectator to view the reflection of this grand tableau without the fatigue which a lengthened upward gaze inflicts, and copies by different artists were placed about the room for sale, there being generally one or two engaged in copying the picture, it being one that is both populár and salable.

The reader is happily spared any description of the immense Barberini Palace, for the author, save the picture gallery, saw comparatively little of it. Such world-renowned pictures, however, as Guido's Beatrice Cenci and Raphael's Fornarina, are creations which, once seen, one remembers a lifetime, and whose wonderful effects are such as to render description tame, and the effort to convey them powerless.

That simple, sad, but beautiful face of Beatrice, upon which deep sorrow and exquisite loveliness are united; the large, lustrous brown eyes; the light hair falling from the head drapery; the sad expression and history written in every lineament, are indescribable and strikingly impressive. The legend that Guido painted it in prison the night before her execution, and her sad story and tragic fate, lend additional interest to the picture.

The Fornarina, by Raphael, is the figure of a beautiful woman uncovered to the waist. She has large, dark, and lustrous eyes, rich, dark hair, around which a shawl is twisted, a beautiful neck and bust, and is in all respects an elegant figure in the full bloom of womanhood, and is said to be a beautiful woman of low birth who was beloved by the artist. The picture is certainly the representation of a beautiful woman, and calculated to remove some of the sad reflections excited by a perhaps too lengthened gaze at the picture of Beatrice Cenci.

CHAPTER XII.

DIFFICULT indeed is the task to finish Rome, hard indeed the necessity to leave the city of one's longings, with its wonders half explored, its lessons half studied, and its monuments with but brief acquaintance. But, labor as the ordinary tourist may in the brief space of the few weeks generally allowed, if he be anything of an antiquarian, a lover of art, a student of history, or he who delights in reminiscences of the past, each day of his experience will prove to him how inexhaustible is the field before him.

We return from our farewell rides to the Pincian, whence we have looked down upon more modern Rome, and met the modern carriages of to-day, with their gay occupants in Parisian costume chatting and laughing gayly, and the promenading crowds with their odd mixture of students in cloaks of gray or sombre colors, with a sprinkling of monks and beggars. The Pincian Hill, with its beautiful garden, with cypresses and pines, elegant plants and flowering shrubs, and pleasant walks, whence we looked upon the city, and beyond it the broad campagna, — the Pincian, where are the ornamental bas-reliefs, pretty columns, fountains in cosy nooks; and where Rome's modern aristocracy disports itself of an afternoon, — the Pincian, that was the site of the famous villa of Lucullus, who won fame and wealth in his campaigns in Asia, and entertained Cicero and Pompey here most royally and extravagantly, and from the terrace of which we took a new view of St. Peter's and the castle of St. Angelo.

Then we part with regret from the old Palatine, with its freshly uncovered ruins, itself the very foundation of Rome, a concrete mass of historic rock and soil, every foot of which we walk over identified with Rome's story; and at every point, gaze where we will, rise shattered fragments and remnants of Rome's history and glory. We must take a farewell gaze at the Colosseum, enduring monument of luxury, cruelty, and power, the Forum, the very heart of old Rome, and stand once more upon the hill of the Capitol, look over the Tarpeian Rock and at the ruined columns, the great triumphal arches slowly yielding to the tooth of time in the great city of the past, where art, power, and greatness existed, that left their impress upon the world which is felt even to this day.

You feel that the task is but half accomplished, nay, but scarce begun, there are so many more ruins to be explored, monuments to be studied, churches to be visited, sites of historic events to be sought out, erroneous impressions to be corrected, antiquities to be seen, and curious researches to be made. But these are the emotions that press upon the mind of all who become interested in Rome, and who leave it as a mine half opened, a banquet scarce tasted, or a grand volume with but a glance at its pages. Rome is the museum of the world, the focal point of interest to student, artist, and antiquary. He who loves what is beautiful, and looks with admiration upon that which is great, will enter the portals of the City of cities eagerly, linger there long and lovingly, and depart reluctantly.

I had but brief time for shopping in Rome, and, as a general thing, found shopkeepers there like other Italians, ready always to charge a foreigner — especially an American — nearly double the price they intended to take. The gay-colored Roman scarfs, cameo cuttings, bronze designs of Roman ruins, Etruscan jewelry, mosaics, and stone cameos, are the articles that tourists buy as the portable novelties of the city. The wax or composition beads known as Roman pearls are another; but there are two kinds of these, a genuine and a counterfeit. The latter, although pretty to look at, have an unpleasant way of half melting upon a lady's neck by the heat, and inclosing her in a necklace of paste. The sculptors' and painters' studios claim the attention of many Americans visiting Rome ; and while some excellent works of art and beautiful copies are obtained, it is also true that some atrocious caricatures, especially of the painter's art, are shipped from Rome to the United States, that are not worth the expense of transportation.

It is rather a sudden descent from a flight of the imagination, after you have passed by temples and beneath triumphal arches, and when you are tramping over a dusty road, thinking that this ground once shook beneath the tread of Cæsar's buskined legions, to have your meditations rudely disturbed by a voice from one side of the causeway, " Blag yer boots, sir ? "

You start as waking from a dream. Is it not a dream, and did you hear aright ? By the side of the street kneels a swarthy Italian boy: his jet-black eyes sparkle beneath his ragged cap, as he holds out a veritable shoe-brush in one hand and points to just such a shoe-box as you have seen the shoeblacks of London and New York use, and again says, " Blag yer boots ? " The fellow's limited stock of English was successful, and I shook off the last dust of Rome from my feet under the manipulations of a Roman bootblack.

Rome is left behind, far behind ; and from the portal of the railroad station, as we emerge in Venice, we see the group of gondolas — water-omnibuses to the hotels — crowded round the landing, and get the fresh breeze of the Adriatic, grateful and cool after a long and somewhat fatiguing ride.

Again, on the luxurious cushions of our little water-carriage, the lusty arms of the gondoliers are sending us forward upon the Grand Canal, beneath the tall palaces that lift their lofty walls from its bosom.

" Hotel Danieli, Monsieur ? " inquires the gondolier.

" No," (forewarned, forearmed.) The Danieli has a broad piazza, or expanse of stone, a promenade directly in front of it, the resort of fruit-sellers, gondoliers, loungers, and promenaders, who laugh, talk, sing, chatter and patter, far past midnight, and begin very early the next morning: so that, during the season of open windows, one may easily fancy himself sleeping in the street, or rather trying to; for, unless accustomed to slumber upon the Exchange, or in the midst of a town-meeting, the enjoyment of such refreshment will be found impossible.

"Grand Hotel," — an hotel altered from two palaces (they are all altered from palaces in Venice), on the Grand Canal, opposite the Church of the Santa Maria della Saluta. The waters of the canal plash up to the marble steps of this house, and we sit in the deep windows of our *salon* beneath the shelter of Venetian awnings, and look down upon boats passing and repassing on the tide beneath us. From the rear of the house, through narrow streets and tortuous alleys, breaking out every now and then into open squares, the pedestrian may reach the Rialto, the Piazza San Marco, or other points of interest. Curious indeed is the experience of going from point to point on foot in Venice, which one may do if he will make the necessary detours. You pass through streets scarce ten feet in width, with high buildings on either side, — effectual protection against the rays of the sun. Every now and then the street is crossed by a canal, over which will be thrown a light iron or arched stone bridge; and, as you halt upon it in crossing, you may look between the tall buildings, up and down the watery highway, that has none of the poetry of the "Blue Adriatic" about it, but reminds one, in its sombre shade, of a stream of ink rather than water.

Here, on these side canals, one sees some of the domestic and every-day life of the Venetians, — that is, such of it as is out of doors. Water-boats are pumping drinking-water into somebody's residence, replenishing the great tank kept to contain it; a garbage-boat is receiving its unsavory contents at back doors; another rusty old boat has brought home to a house a day's marketing, which seems to consist chiefly of onions and vegetables; and another, laden with stone and bricks, is being laboriously sculled along by a single grayheaded old oarsman. Over a bridge, and your narrow street goes on a score of feet, and then may end at a blank wall, if you have neglected to swerve to the opening that came into it at right or left, but which appeared to lead, as it sometimes does for a short distance, in an opposite direction to that in which you desire to go; or you follow on, having, as you supposed, left the Grand Canal behind you, and come out, after various windings and bridge-crossings, upon its shore again, some fifty or sixty rods above or below where you started from. Some of these narrow streets are far from being agreeable, either to the eye or to the olfactories.

Filthy wine and beer shops, reeking with fumes of vile tobacco; cheap cook-shops, where dirt and garlic reign triumphant, in neighborhoods where tinkers' shops, dirty meat, and vegetable stores stand side by side with old-clothes shops, out of which peer the sparkling black eyes and unmistakable nasal organ of the Hebrew, are crossed by canals that are narrow and odoriferous, and upon which garbage and straw are floating about. In the doorways are old people and ragged children, who gaze wonderingly at you as you hasten along, till the alley strikes into an open square down which the garish sun is pouring, and in the middle of which is a well, with half a dozen women waiting about it, with copper buckets or kettles for a supply of water.

On first arrival in Venice, the tourist from the interior, upon entering his apartments, the windows of which, if they look out upon the Grand Canal, are sure to be thrown wide open, is more than likely to inquire, "What is this smell?" somewhat dank or musty, not dreaming it is but the scent of sea-water to his unaccustomed olfactories, which he very soon ceases to notice. But as, on landing from my first sea-voyage, I inhaled with pleasure the fragrance of green turf and the welcome earthy perfume of the land, so was there a similar sensation on visiting the Public Garden of Venice, a spot a short distance above the Arsenal, where the novel sight of green turf and trees, and the scent of grass, flowers, and herbage, are grateful to the senses, after long experience of gazing upon marble and masonry, and inhaling the saline breeze that comes up the canal.

I had seen nearly all the sights of Venice which tourists visit, and enjoyed in reality the pictures of imagination, and was dreamily floating down the canal with a friend in his private gondola, manned by two stalwart gondoliers. A fanciful, fresh-water, sailor uniform of blue breeches reaching to their knees; white shirt, with broad, blue-edged collar, and Leghorn hat, with broad, blue ribbons with floating ends; black shoes, and spotless white stockings reaching to the bottoms of the pantaloons, which were loosely fastened just below the knee with three little silver buttons; sailor-knotted neckerchiefs loose about the broad, ample collar; two lightly-touched olive complexions; deep, dark eyes, wavy hair, and pencilled moustaches, — and you have a picture of my friend's gondoliers: fellows whose muscular arms, by an imperceptible turn of the oar, would write an elegant calligraphic flourish in the water, which would flow swiftly past you in wreaths, foam, bubbles, and water-lines, as graceful as smoke in the summer atmosphere. The regular rise and fall of their dripping oars was as rhythmic in cadence as perfect poesy, when they shot their graceful craft down the Grand Canal, or wound in and out the aqueous highways that thread the ancient city; their warning shouts, ere rounding the angle of a palace wall, as musical as the notes of an operatic tenor.

There is no better place, no more fitting time, for dreamy, poetic imagination, for luxurious laziness, for misty musing, sentimental castle-building, for realization of youthful romance on a moonlight evening, than in one of these easy water-cradles, like the one in which we were reclining, with its perfumed morocco cushions, its pretty awning with silken hangings and lattices, in place of the black, ugly-looking sort of cabs of the ordinary gondola; while the soft matting of colored wools beneath our feet, the padded and cushioned sides of that part of the boat in which we sat, rendered it a cosy nest in which one could recline at ease in almost any position he chose to assume.

We had watched a procession of gondolas with colored lanterns float down from the Piazza, headed by one with guitars that were tinkling a melody that sounded like musical water-drops amid the swish of oars, and had sent off with a dozen copper pieces the two beggars who row round in a gondola playing a hand-organ, and were watching the reflection of the tall palaces in the glassy mirror beneath the kindly shadow which rendered decay picturesque and the hue of age and green rime of neglect invisible; and the silver atmosphere seemed to softly descend from the most lovely blue that ever colored the vault of heaven.

The tall, elaborately ornamented façades of the palaces of old Venetian families whose very names are forgotten, rose like ghosts of the past: here and there lights sparkled in the deep windows; and at one, more brilliant than the rest, was a gay group on the marble steps, bidding adieus beside the two tall vases at either side, ere stepping into the fairy craft that awaited them, — not lords and ladies of the Venetian court, with purple and velvet and silks, swords and *stilettos*, but, alas for imagination in these degenerate days! only a party of tourists, with tourist-pouches slung across their shoulders, and parasols and fans in hand, leaving their hotel, once a palace, to be sure, but now reduced to baser uses.

We glide down close to the stone steps that are at the foot of the platform, upon which stands the fanciful and superb Church of Santa Maria della Saluta, whose huge arches and majestic dome rise like a marble mountain above the canal, and our gondoliers rest on their oars just beyond it for a few moments; for a gondolier load of students halts at the hotel opposite to sing to the foreign guests, and we to listen to the sweet music of their Italian voices.

It always seems as if there was a liquid music in the Italian voice — at least in that of singers — which is not possessed by those of other nationalities. "*Viva Italia, viva el Rey!*" is the patriotic song that brings out sweet tenor and vigorous bass in harmonious unison at the close of each stanza; and then, after a brief pause, they drop into the delicious song of "Santa Lucia," in which their voices blend together like the strains of a huge music-box, as the chorus comes floating across the water to us. There is a momentary hush as the last chord ceases; then vociferous English and American applause and clapping of hands from the hotel piazza and windows, and, we are sure, a plentiful shower of franc-pieces. A nod to our boatmen, and the gondola shoots away in obedience to the graceful and noiseless thrusts of their skilfully wielded oar-blades.

And now come in view the Columns of St. Theodore and the Winged Lion, standing out black and upright in the moonlight, with the figures upon their summits sharply cut against the blue moonlit sky, as we lie gazing at them from our luxurious couch.

We look through the little square of the Piazzetta that leads to the great Square of St. Mark beyond, — on one side the Doge's Palace, with its short, thick columns and pointed arches, upholding another row more light and graceful, crowned with quatrefoils; on the other, beneath the colonnades, sparkle lights from the *cafés*, and beyond the square is alive with them beneath the porticos; and the shadows falling from the buildings sharply define one side of the broad pavement in the bright moonlight, as though shaded by crayon. Gondolas are arriving and departing; groups landing for a half hour's lounge in the Piazza, to sip coffee and smoke cigarettes, or eat ices, in front of the *cafés* in the square, while the luxurious melody of Strauss waltzes from the band fills the old historic inclosure with delicious strains.

The scenes of power, cruelty, and greatness that have been enacted here, between the two tall columns that stand, sentinel-like, upon the shore, are in themselves a history; for here once rose the fearful scaffold upon which the masked executioner swung his broad blade, in obedience to the decrees of the fearful Council. Here Cooper, in his "Bravo of Venice," locates the final scene of his story: — "Between the lofty pedestals of St. Theodore and the Winged Lion lay the block, the axe, the basket, and the sawdust, — the usual accompaniments of justice in that day. By their side stood the executioner."

A little black mass of gondoliers and loungers now occupied the very spot, forming a circle round a fellow who stood upon a stool haranguing them, and offering some cheap article for sale. The music from the band suddenly ceased, the chatter of many voices in the Square and the patter of many feet upon the pavement became audible, and the deep boom of the bell came from the great clock-tower, as the bronze giants upon its summit struck with their hammers the sonorous metal. Our conversation naturally turned upon the former greatness of the Bride of the Adriatic, her commercial power, wealth, and pride, — from the climax of her power and splendor at the end of the sixteenth century till, in the seventeenth and eighteenth, she lost Cyprus, Candia, and the Peloponnesus, and her commercial prosperity gradually diminished. Then came Bonaparte as conqueror, wrencher open of inquisitorial prison-cells, and breaker of tyrannical fetters in 1797; then the revolution of 1848, the hated Austrian yoke in 1849, under which she chafed for sixteen years; and finally free Italy, under Victor Emmanuel, in 1866.

The scenes that had been enacted here in and about this great Square, this heart of the old Republic, have been the theme of poet, novelist, and historian; it is one of those spots in the world that you seem to be well acquainted with when you first set foot in it, and find each familiar monument marking the spot of historic pictures that are familiar to all, though they have long since taken their place in the dim gallery of the past.

It was here we talked over the stories of old Venice, as told by poet and historian, while our gondoliers slowly urged our light craft along close to shore, and again the great bell boomed beneath the giants' stroke — two !

"Not two o'clock ?"

"No," replied my companion; "that is the chime for the second quarter, the half hour; and do you know that there was a time when I thought that great bell would be the last one I should ever hear, and that it would tell off the last hours of my existence ?"

"Indeed," said I; "then you must have had an attack of fever in Venice, and lodged in the Hotel Belle Vue, next the Clock Tower."

"No," said my companion, lighting a fresh cigarette, "I lodged in no hotel, but in one of the strongest prison-cells of the 'Council of Ten.'"

"One of the prison-cells ? Ah! for amusement, I presume ?"

"Not in the least; it was anything but amusement, I assure you, for I was imprisoned against my will there but a few years since, and in one of the cells in which state prisoners were confined three hundred years ago."

"You surprise me," said I. "Pray tell me how it chanced, the cause of your imprisonment, and how you were released: by the consul, I suppose ?"

"No," said my friend, smiling as he sent the little smoke wreaths into the air through the open lattice; "you will never guess it. But, singular as it may appear, I was imprisoned without legal proceedings of any kind, and for no crime, debt, or offence; and I believe, for a time at least, I had some idea of what must have been the sufferings of political offenders in those terrible cells in which they were incarcerated by their cruel judges."

I was more than ever surprised at this modern exercise of ancient Venetian tyranny, and of course urged my friend to give me the particulars, which he at once proceeded to do.

CHAPTER XIII.

"You remember," said my friend, "that when I first came to Venice, I remained here for quite a length of time, indeed until the waning season warned me to take my departure. Like all young, enthusiastic, and romantic tourists, Venice was a city of romance and a fairy land to me. I re-peopled every old palace with the senators or nobles who formerly dwelt in it, and whose deeds and history I was familiar with long before I had stepped within their ancient habitations. St. Mark's, the Piazza, the Ducal Palace, and the Rialto, I visited again and again, and in the great hall of the palace imagined how I should have carried myself as one of the powerful Doges; or I sat in the little chamber of the terrible Council of Three, till the shadows deepened, dreaming over the scenes that had been there enacted, till warned by the custodian that the time for visitors to depart had arrived.

"By frequent visits I became quite well acquainted with the principal custodian of the ducal-palace apartments that are shown to visitors, an acquaintance which became positive friendship on his part after his palm had been crossed by a silver franc two or three times, instead of the paper lira which was the Italian currency.

"I used to enjoy the opportunity afforded to study at leisure the beautiful pictures of Paul Veronese in the Hall of the Council of Ten, and lounge backward upon a wooden bench and gaze upwards at Zelotti's beautiful frieze and the rich ceiling, with its exquisite paintings; or halted in the little ante-room, — now they call it a guard-room, — and, hoisting the window curtains, let the afternoon sun pour its light in upon the rich coloring of the picture of the Rape of Europa, in which the maiden was being seated on the snow-white bull by attendants, while flowers and garlands were falling from the hands of cupids in the air above, and foliage, trees, and figures were all blended into one beautiful combination of the painter's art.

"In the Hall of the Council of Ten, on a dais at one end of the chamber, were the three chairs upon which the Inquisitors sat when they interrogated their trembling victims; and when the noisy groups of tourists scurrying through the room with open mouths and guide-books, as the *valet de place* led them rapidly from point to point, and adapted his explanations to suit the position he might be occupying or to meet the desire of the inquirer, had gone, and the old hall was cool and quiet, I would sit in the principal inquisitor's chair, and dream of the dark scenes with which the place was haunted, and start from my reverie to hear the cry of the gondolier come faintly, mellowed by distance, through one of the high windows. It required but little effort of the imagination to repeople this old hall with the ghosts of the past, or imagine the tribunal in the lesser one known as the *Sala dei Capi*, that of 'The Fearful Three,' where more private investigations were made.

"There they sat, three dark figures, with black robes reaching from head to foot, scarcely revealing a line of the form; the cowl-covered heads, the black masks through which the glitter of dark eyes came like shafts of death, as they fastened their gaze upon you. Their table, black, with a white cross emblazoned upon the side of its covering towards the prisoner; and below, in front of them, at another table, a monkish-habited clerk took down the prisoner's replies, the audible scratching of his pen, as it travelled over the paper, breaking the silence of the terrible chamber.

The lamps, suspended overhead by chains, cast an uncertain glare upon the scene, seeming to throw the inquisitorial Three into a deep shadow, or serving, as their rays sparkled upon the steel weapons of a couple of masked halberdiers on either side of the prisoner, to remind him, even were he not in chains, of the hopelessness of escape.

"How often was the trial a mere farce, the examination a mere pretext, and the introduction of the paraphernalia of religion, or the semblance of justice, a mere mockery. Placed before the terrible Three, the prisoner must have felt that his imprisonment or death was but a foregone conclusion, and turned with sinking heart to follow his guard over the Bridge of Sighs to the gloomy dungeon below the waters of the canal, or up into the terrible fastnesses of the *Sotto Piombi.*

"So thought I, as I stood musing, with folded arms, on the spot which I conjured up in my imagination must have been in the days of the Republic occupied by the prisoner. The afternoon shadows were lengthening, and the triple boom of the great bell from the clock-tower sounded like the bell tolling for a prisoner's execution. I was tapped upon the shoulder, and, with a thrill, turned, almost expecting to see the masked halberdier beckoning me with his steel-gloved hand to follow, but only encountered the smiling old custodian, who, with an expressive rattle of his bunch of keys, informed me that he was about to close the apartments, and had very nearly forgotten I was there.

"The old fellow, who was accustomed to permit me to wander about these rooms at will, had on various occasions pointed out many a curious memento of the past, among others the cells or rooms in the *Sotto Piombi,* or 'under the leads,' which were said to be cold and cheerless in winter, and hot as an oven beneath the rays of the Italian sun in summer. They were constructed of massive timbers, the doors heavily and securely iron-bound, swinging easily to the touch into place, and closing with such nicety that no aperture in the wall could be discovered.

"In one of these cruel dungeons, now turned into a storeroom for old lumber, we deciphered, cut into the almost ironlike beams, a sentence in Italian invoking a curse on the Republic; and in another place, a spot where the light from the little grated window fell, was scratched a rude representation of a wreath inclosing the names — Lucia, Giovanni, — scratched doubtless with hours of patient labor by the prisoner during his captivity. American tourists as a rule, especially such as had read Cooper's novel 'The Bravo of Venice,' were always desirous of visiting these cells, most of which were turned into old lumber-rooms, and somewhat difficult of access from their position beneath the roof, and the approach through a corridor plentifully decorated with dust and cobwebs.

"In order to gratify curiosity, two or three of those in the best state of preservation were shown to visitors, especially one which was kept in quite good order and condition, and which has especial interest in this story. It was a square, solid box of beams of wood, which, by the seasoning of age, seemed to be as hard as iron. Its thickness was shown in the door, which was itself a section of the cell more than two feet in thickness, yet so nicely poised that it swung to its position by a mere touch of the finger, fitting snugly into place. There was a sort of broad wooden bench, strongly suggestive of a funeral bier, said to have been the prisoner's couch by night and seat by day.

"This cell was lighted by a window eighteen inches square, grated by strong iron bars let into the stone work outside the inner wooden casing. Through the grating close at hand you could catch a view of part of the Campanile Tower, and far out at the left, in the distance beyond the leads, which obstructed the view immediately beneath, you could see the dome of San Giorgio, and beyond that the blue waves of the Adriatic."

"You seem to remember the place well," said I, as my friend paused in his narrative.

"Indeed I do; every part of it is vividly impressed upon my memory, and I have good reason to remember it, as you will see by my story.

"I had been in the Piombi but twice: the first time with a party of tourists in the usual style, and once with the old custodian upon the occasion when the ancient carvings I have mentioned were pointed out to me.

"One afternoon, as usual, after a lounge through some of the rooms of the old palace, and a new look at the beautiful pictures of Paul Veronese, Tintoretto, and Titian, and an inspection of the curious map of the world, which the patient old monk, Father Mauro, wrought out in 1457, showing all that was known of the world at that time, I bade the old custodian, who chanced to pass me, good afternoon, and was about to stroll out again, when the thought came over me to visit the cell under the roof, and take a more thorough look at it, as I might not again come here.

"I followed in the direction in which the custodian had gone with his keys, but he seemed to have taken some turn that carried him out of sight, for I was not able to overtake him, and I found myself in the familiar ante-room of the Council of Ten. Passing out, I came to the little door of modern wooden gratings at the foot of the flight of stairs that led to the cells up under the roof.

"What need of a guide or permission? I have time and can go by myself. But, as I felt for my watch, I was vexed to find that in making a change of dress I had left it upon the dressing-table of my lodgings. I tried the door. Pshaw! it was fastened. A small, cheap-looking lock enough, to be sure, but sufficient to keep out curiosity hunters who had not paid toll to the custodian. Wait! We will test its efficacy. In a moment a bunch of the half dozen keys, which nearly every man carries in his pocket, were out. I tried one, — two, — three. The fourth, the key of a cheap trunk, fitted the lock. It yielded easily, and the light latticed door opened before me, and swung to after I had entered, with a sharp snap, — one of those cheap little cupboard spring-locks, made to keep a door closed, rather than for protection.

"I scrambled up the stairs till the light grew dim, and finally was in the imperfectly lighted passage at the top. A dozen paces or so, and I was at the door of the cell, which was open, and I entered it, going up to the little window which in the gloom framed a bit of bright sky, like a blue patch surrounded by dark crayon.

"A cool, fresh breeze blew from the water; and the draught was delicious as I leaned my chin upon the iron cross-bar, and looked out upon the distant water, upon which were three or four white-winged craft skimming along before the breeze, and the black forms of one or two gondolas slowly cutting the waves.

"I wondered how many prisoners had whiled away the dreary hours of captivity by looking out, as I was doing, at the liberty that was far beyond their reach, and longing to be in one of the swift-sailing craft, that it might bear them away to freedom.

"I turned about, and, with eyes unaccustomed to the darkness, could scarce make out anything within; but there was little to make out besides what I have already described, except a dilapidated old chair with a ruined cushion, that had been probably placed here as useless lumber.

"There was the prisoner's bench and couch. Was it long enough for a couch? I had a fancy to try it, and, taking the old chair-cushion for a pillow for head and shoulders, stretched myself upon it beneath the window.

"'If the weather was as comfortable as this,' mused I, as I lay watching the shadows of the iron bars in the sunlight on the opposite wall, while the gentle draught of air blew over me from the little grating to the door, 'the prisoner did not suffer much in that respect.'

"How long I thus reclined, thinking of the former occupants of the prison, I know not, but was suddenly conscious that I was not alone. A tall figure, robed apparently in a long cloak that fell from shoulders to heels, completely enveloping his person, and with a dark cap, which served to conceal his face, stood before me. Seeing that I observed him, he made a beckoning gesture, and pointed to the door. Actuated by an unaccountable impulse, I obeyed, and found myself passing through a vaulted passage that I certainly had never seen before, and, preceded by another figure, robed like the first, in black, but carrying a torch in one hand, while the other held a huge bunch of keys.

"What could this mean? I turned about, but the first figure that had beckoned me was scarce six paces behind; and I now noted his features were concealed by a black mask, through which the glitter of his eyes sparkled in the rays of the torchlight; and I also observed, as he raised his arm with impatient gesture for me to proceed, the flash of steel in the girdle at his waist. With a heart thumping against my ribs, as I recollected I carried neither of the traditional American weapons (bowie-knife or revolver), I turned again, and proceeded after the torch-bearer, at whose waist I also noted both belt and weapon.

"On we went, through a low, arched passage of solid masonry, till an entrance was reached in which swung, half open, a low, Gothic-shaped door, studded with heavy iron bolts: through it passed the torch-bearer, myself after him; and after entering a few paces, I turned, and found he who followed me had done the same; and immediately after he had entered, the heavy door swung gently together, the sharp click of a spring-lock, as it did so driving the blood back to my heart with a thrill at the thought I had allowed myself to be kidnapped into a secret unknown dungeon by strangers, without even the semblance of a struggle for my liberty.

"Turning about, I found myself in a sort of round, or, I may say, octagonal chamber. In addition to the door behind me, by which I had entered, were two others at the right and left, but closed and guarded, each by a motionless figure standing beside them. Opposite where I stood sat two figures behind a table, upon a slightly raised platform, dressed like him who had accompanied me to the place: between them was a vacant seat, which he immediately took; and I at once perceived, by the deference paid to him, that he was of the most distinction of the three.

"Just below this table was another, at which sat a cowled figure, masked, but whose shaved head, as he bent over the paper upon which he was writing, revealed him as a monkish clerk. All this I noted in a gaze swiftly thrown around the apartment, without discovering any other opening save the three doors. The stone ceiling above was blackened by torch-smoke, and the air close and oppressive.

"But why was I brought here? Why this hideous masquerade, which, despite all I could do, inspired me with secret horror?

"The silence was broken by a voice from one of the three at the table:

"'Prisoner, your name.'

"'Prisoner!' said I, starting at the word; 'by what right am I arrested, and for what offence.'

"'That you will learn presently,' was the reply; 'give to the court your name.'

"I gave it.

"'Age, occupation, and profession."

"Half mechanically, I responded.

"'State to the court your actual purpose in visiting Venice.'

"'The court? By what court am I examined, and who are you that demand to know of my affairs?'

"'The Inquisitorial Court of Venice holds you before it for examination. Best be direct, and answer promptly,' responded my interrogator.

"The Inquisitorial Court! Could it be that I was in the power of the terrible Inquisition, and that institution was still in existence?

"'Best answer quietly, my son,' came in a low tone from the lips of the monkish clerk, as he raised his head, revealing a long, white beard that fell from beneath his mask, through the eyeholes of which that same devilish glitter that characterized the judges seemed to flash.

"'I am a citizen of the United States,' said I, 'and demand instant release; I appeal to the American consul; I deny the right of any such secret arrest or examination as this. Who are you that dare treat a free American citizen in this manner?'

"A low laugh, in the silence that followed my furious outburst, came to my ears, as the inquisitor replied:

"'Listen, prisoner! You are in the presence of a court founded and in operation before your country was known by the civilized world to be in existence. You are here to reply, and we to question. We are prepared for all emergencies, as this court has been for centuries.'

"While these words were being uttered, I endeavored to collect my scattered senses, and consider the best method to proceed. Shut in on every side, there was no chance for a dash for liberty. But my soul rebelled at the mocking sneer with which my appeals had been met, and the feeling of dread gave way to the fierce desire to wreak a just vengeance upon the heads of this infamous council. But how?

"At one side of the monk's table stood a headsman's axe and block; at the other a stake, to which were attached a large iron ring, chains, and fetters,—emblems, doubtless, to strike terror to the hearts of prisoners, or a refinement of cruelty, in reminding them of the block or stake to which they would be condemned. The torch-rays fell upon the gleaming blade of the axe, scarce six paces from where I was standing. With that weapon in my hand, some of the tyrants that dared tamper with a freeman's liberty should feel the weight of his arm.

"'Prisoner,' again said the inquisitor, 'will you answer the questions of the court?'

"'No! I defy you!' shouted I, making a spring forward towards the headsman's blade. But I was instantly seized on either side by a grasp so powerful that I failed to advance a foot from my position. Two stalwart guards, who stood but a pace behind me, had seized each of my arms in their iron gripe, and I remained pinioned and immovable as if in a vise.

"Neither judges nor clerk had even started at my sudden movement, but remained calm and immovable as though nothing had occurred, but the low mocking and sarcastic laugh of the inquisitor, that came to my ears as I stood panting with exertion, caused every feeling of fear to give way to that of rage and indignation.

"Again the silence of the place, which for some seconds seemed interrupted only by my heavy breathing, was broken by the calm tones of the inquisitor:

"'Prisoner, do you still refuse to answer the questions of the court?'

"'I do,' panted I, 'and deny your right to question me, a free citizen, before a secret tribunal; and no power on earth shall make me answer to it.'

"'Have a care, prisoner, lest the court proceed to use means to force you to reply.'

"'Force! Have a care yourself,' retorted I, 'how you use force, lest you suffer the consequences.'

"Again the mocking laugh, as the inquisitor said:

"'We have arranged all that. Do you reflect that all that may in future be known of you is that a man has disappeared in Venice, — fallen into the canal, perhaps; the probability, a possibility, if we choose to have the body found floating there a few days after it is so suggested?'

"A cold sweat burst forth from every pore. I felt this was too true; no friend or relative was in the city with me; indeed, no inquiry could be made, except by my landlord, for weeks, as to my disappearance. I was ignorant where I was, except that it was in a stone dungeon, and inaccessible to any from the outside world except such as my kidnappers chose to admit.

"I stood silent for a moment, and my breath came thick and fast as I realized my terrible position.

"'Prisoner, are you prepared to answer?' came again the cold, determined tone of the inquisitor.

"'I will answer nothing,' said I defiantly; 'do your worst.'

"'Perhaps the prisoner will recall his refusal when he finds what means we have at hand to enforce compliance,' said the judge, as he made a signal to the guard at one of the side doors.

"The door slowly swung open, revealing a small arched apartment in the solid stone work, lighted by a single lamp depending by a chain from the ceiling. Its light revealed to me a horrid sight, that sent the blood back to my heart, and caused an involuntary shudder. In the middle of the apartment, extending nearly from one end to the other, was a huge oblong frame, consisting of four wooden beams raised a little from the floor, and at each end were cords, levers, wheels, and pulleys.

"I recognized it only too readily. It was the terrible rack, upon which prisoners were placed to extort from them confessions when the ordinary means failed.

"I was still in the iron grip of the two guards. What could this mean? Was I indeed actually in the power of a secret tribunal in a Venetian dungeon, and would they dare inflict torture upon me, or was this a masquerade of friends at my expense. The latter thought gave me new hope, and I turned again; but it was a horrid reality, and I met only the stern gaze looking through the eyeholes of the masked judges, the arched stone cell, and heard the pitiless voice, which was one entirely unknown to me, ask:

"'Does the prisoner refuse to answer?'

"A fierce effort for release, which seemed scarcely to cause an effort on the part of the iron muscles of my captors to restrain, was my only reply.

"The inquisitor nodded, and I was borne to the terrible engine of torture, and bent down backwards by main force towards the hard beams. It was a fearful moment, despair lent me strength, and as my captors strove to bind the cords that were to pinion my limbs to the cruel machinery, summoning all my energy, and with a mighty and tremendous effort that seemed to swell my veins to bursting, I broke from them, sprang to my feet, dealing the foremost guard a tremendous blow that felled him with a heavy shock to the floor, when lights, inquisitors, rack, and prison seemed to vanish like a vision, as they were, and I found myself prostrate and panting upon the hard floor — awake.

"Awake! But where? The great drops were upon my brow, my heart was knocking like a trip-hammer at my ribs, and, although dungeon and inquisitors had disappeared, all was dark as Erebus. My hand was bruised and aching from the blow struck, and it seemed that the shock of my enemy's fall was yet ringing in my ears. I lay still panting and listening, but all was silent as the grave. My nostrils were filled with a cloud of dust, which it appeared that my struggle or fall had caused, and which set me to coughing and sneezing. Was it a dream, or had the lights been merely extinguished to prevent my escaping? No; I was certainly awake, but the atmosphere was close, the impenetrable darkness oppressive, and the silence awful; but all at once it was broken by the melodious boom of the bell from the great clock-tower.

"One! two! three! Either three o'clock or three quarters past the hour. And then came faintly to my ear the cry of a distant gondolier; and as I turned slightly from the position in which I lay, my eyes caught a patch of light on the opposite wall. It was the moonlight shining through the grated window; and as my heart began to beat less rapidly, and I to collect my scattered senses, the whole truth burst upon me. A load was lifted like a mountain from my mind. I had fallen asleep on the prisoner's couch in the cell under the leads, sprung off it in my struggle on the rack in my dream, and fallen upon the floor. I must have slept here till long after dark, but how long?

"Let us see. I leaped to my feet and advanced rapidly to the grated window, but had taken scarce three steps ere I was felled almost prostrate and bleeding by a sudden blow upon the forehead.

"Ah! It is not all a dream after all, and there *is* some one here. But as I lay prostrate and listened, I heard not the faintest rustle of garment or movement or sound betraying another's presence. For full five minutes, quietly where I had fallen, did I strain every sense to catch a movement, and held my own breath in vain hope to catch the respiration of my opponent, but all was silent as the grave.

"The thought of being here in this gloomy cell at night with an unknown adversary was terrible. The nervousness of the fearful dream returned tenfold. I felt carefully in my pockets for a weapon, knowing all the while I had nothing but a contemptible little one-bladed penknife; but this I took out and opened, and after a while, rising to my knees, made a sweep with it in my right hand as far as I could reach, but met no obstacle.

"I began to recall the story of duels in dark rooms that I had read when a lad, and how long two opponents had waited with cocked pistols or bared weapons, with strained senses, to discover their enemy's whereabouts, till at last a faint respiration betrayed it, and the weapon discharged in that direction by its flash exposed him who discharged it to his enemy. How I longed for a pistol, and how I strained the sense of hearing to catch some indication of my adversary's presence; but in vain.

"Grown weary of remaining in a kneeling posture upon the hard floor, I resolved to rise to my feet at all hazards, and slowly and cautiously rose to an upright position, and had nearly attained it when my head encountered some obstacle. Putting up my hand, I found it to be the sloping beams of that part of the apartment, and it at once flashed upon me that no human hand had inflicted the blow I had received, but that it was the result of hastily moving in the darkness in that direction, which was really the fact.

"Again I felt as if a weight was lifted from my mind, and with a deep inspiration of relief, and extended hands to guard against further accident, I groped my way almost fainting to the little window, which I reached, and, resting my chin upon its sill, eagerly drank in large draughts of the pure air and looked out upon the blue moonlit sky which never appeared to me so beautiful, and the distant waves that sparkled in the beam more lovely than ever before. The reaction was so great, and the feeling so grateful as of having escaped some terrible peril, that I can hardly express what a sense of gratitude and happiness I experienced at standing there and knowing I was safe, and had only had a terrible dream, and was not shut out from the pure air of heaven or from beneath the lovely blue sky, — was free and not confined in a dreary dungeon.

"But as my thoughts began to get into their usual channel once more, and my nerves steadied again, the question of my real position began to present itself to me. Here I was at night, up under the leads in a cell in the Ducal Palace. The apartments must of course be closed for the night. I was indeed a prisoner till morning, but how long was it till morning? I remembered, when felled to the floor by the blow from the beam, to have heard the bell from the clock-tower strike. Was it one o'clock, or would the next peal be the quarter past some other hour?

"I must wait patiently and endeavor to ascertain. It came at last, one solitary boom, the same as first heard, and again I was tortured with doubt, until the next stroke came — two. It was half past something, certainly, and so I waited, and never did moments move on more leaden wings, till at last the three-quarters were pealed out, and then the welcome stroke which was to tell me the hour would come in fifteen minutes more.

"I never moved from the window. I felt I could not look enough upon the blue waves now dancing in the beams of the descending moon. I think that I uttered a prayer of thanks that the vision of the Inquisition had not been a reality, but it seemed as if the hour would never arrive. I even began to imagine it might have struck and I not heard it, and then I laughed to myself at the idea, and began counting off seconds and checking every sixty with one of my fingers, and had got to the eighth when the bronze hammers began their work on the sonorous metal, and I counted aloud. One, two, three, four, five, six, seven, eight, nine, ten, eleven, twelve!

"Twelve o'clock! Midnight! And I must wait from midnight till at least seven or eight o'clock in the morning before the custodian would come. However, I felt quite cheerful about what I considered this brief imprisonment, and had busied myself stanching the blood from the cut on my forehead, and thinking of the surprise I should occasion the custodian in the morning, and the story I should have to tell of my vivid dream of Venetian tyranny, when it occurred to me that I might as well occupy the time by passing out of this close and uncomfortable cell, and groping my way to the more spacious apartments below stairs. Accordingly, moving slowly with outstretched arms through the dense gloom, I sought the door. 'It was but a short distance from one side of the cell to the other, and, groping forward through the darkness, my outstretched hands soon encountered the opposite wall, but I felt vainly for the opening.

"I could not be mistaken. If I recollected correctly, it was directly opposite the little grated window up to which I had walked on first entering; and, turning about, I observed the light of the now sinking moon shining through that, directly opposite where I stood. Again I sought the open door, moving my hands slowly along the smooth old oaken beams till I reached the angle forming the corner. I had missed the opening in some unaccountable manner, probably passed to the left of it.

"Starting from my new position, I carefully felt my way back to where I supposed the door must be, but still continued to meet an unbroken surface, till my further progress was stopped by the angle of the wall at the extreme right. What was the meaning of this? There *was* a door upon that side certainly, or had I got turned about in my sleep, as people do sometimes when waking from sound repose at midnight, and are compelled to get up, or to take hold of the footboard of the bed, to convince themselves that their position has not been reversed since retiring.

"Again I carefully felt my way the whole length of the partition. To my touch it was smooth and unbroken as a single block. Reaching the angle, I followed the wall along, came to the opposite side, and reached the window, from which I saw the moon was now nearly out of sight, rendering the darkness of my prison still more pitchy. I continued my course, passed the window, feeling every inch of the way with hand, and trying with pressure of foot and knee as I progressed; but the space appeared unbroken by opening, aperture, or hinge, and at last, having completed the entire circuit of the cell, I again stood grasping the bars of the little grated window with a beating heart.

"It was plain I was shut in, but for what purpose and by whom? And again my nervous imagination suggested that this might be another portion of a dream. So I whistled, sang a stave of a song, shouted, and otherwise thoroughly convinced myself that I was completely awake, and then began to rack my brain as to how it was I became shut in, and why it was I was unable to find the door of my prison.

"Just then the great bell struck.

"One!

"Only one o'clock. But one hour had passed, and I had at least three more to wait until daylight.

"I cannot recall all the thoughts that ran through my mind during that terrible night, but it seemed as though every story of imprisonment from Baron Trenck to Jack Sheppard, and every romance, novel, and history, in which I had ever read of a prison-cell, came back vividly to my recollection, and the successive booms of the great bell on the clock-tower as they told off the quarters of the hour, — I imagined how they must have sounded all too quickly to the wretch who had but a single night to live, and heard it thus checked off by the bronze giants with all too ready hammers, though to me they were laggards in their work.

"The moon had now gone down, and all was darkness, but this did not prevent me from again making a careful circuit of the apartment, and even for a third time, so confident was I of having mistaken the opening; but now each effort was attended with the same result, and after the circuit I reached the little grated window whence I had started.

"Anxious and fatigued, I again stretched myself upon the wooden bench upon which still remained the old chair-cushion that had served me as a pillow, and turned my face towards the window with a feeling of despair to wait patiently for the morning's light to aid in effecting deliverance. As I did so, I saw, in the dark blue of the sky without, a single sparkling star that seemed to be twinkling in between the iron bars like an emblem of hope; and as I lay gazing at it, and thinking what a companion one of God's beautiful lights like this must have been to the solitary prisoner who enjoyed the privilege of this outlook, so rare in the ducal prisons, tired nature succumbed, and I was again in the land of dreams.

"This time I was spared so fearful a nightmare as before, and my worst experience was in imagining that I was lying at the foot of a deep, dark shaft of a mine, looking up at the opening that twinkled far above me like a single star upon a black sky. Again, I was a wretch bound and prostrate upon the hard boards of a rough cart, being dragged to execution, the rough inequalities of the road, as we jostled over it, bruising every aching joint, and the great bell tolling the knell of death as we neared the scaffold, when I awoke again with a start.

"My limbs indeed ached with the hardness of my wooden couch, and the final strokes of the bell of the clock-tower outside accounted for another portion of the dream; but welcome daylight had arrived and already partially illuminated the gloom of my prison. Rising to my feet, I straightened up my aching limbs, and once more went to the little grated window, my source of light and air, and looked out. It was broad daylight now, sure enough; the morning sunbeams sparkled on the distant waves; I could hear far off shouts of gondoliers, and see the distant water-craft again, and ere long heard the stroke of the hour, — seven.

"Now for a thorough look for the door of this terrible dungeon, to find it and go forth. By the dim light, to which my eyes had become accustomed, I discovered the main features of the cell, with which I was already tolerably familiar: a four-sided room of heavy oaken beams, as before described, the roof of the side in which the grated window was set being sloping, and not sufficiently high for me to occupy an upright position. In the middle of the apartment was the prisoner's wooden bench, or couch, upon which I had passed my few hours of troubled slumber, looking more bier-like than ever.

"But where was the door?

"I walked directly to the spot where I felt confident it ought to be, but, closely as I examined, I could discover only what seemed to be an unbroken wall to the apartment.

"It was no nightmare now, but a fearful reality; a riddle, the solution of which I must bring my keenest senses to bear upon, and I felt it. My sight had now become so accustomed to the imperfect light that I could examine my prison with a tolerable degree of distinctness, and indeed the morning was so far advanced that the rays of daylight coming through the barred window made portions of the cell easily discernible.

"It was perfectly evident to me that the door must have been shut during my first slumber the night previous, but how, by whom, or for what purpose, I could not imagine. On calm reflection I came to the conclusion that the custodian or some friend, having discovered me sleeping, had thought it would be a pleasant practical joke to thus incarcerate me for the night, and that they would promptly liberate me in the morning.

"But it was now morning, and the clock-tower bell had struck eight as I sat on the bench moodily turning over these thoughts and reflections.

"The Ducal Palace was open for visitors, I remembered, from nine to four; the apartments generally all cleared at five P. M., which was about the time I had ascended, led by my prying curiosity to this accursed prison. It could now be but an hour before the custodian and his officials were on duty. At or before that time he or whoever had perpetrated this wretched joke, if joke it was, would come and release me.

"Slowly the moments rolled along, but not the sound of any approach broke the silence till at length, after the last stroke of nine had sounded, I could endure waiting no longer. I went to the wall where the door ought to have been, examined it closely, held my face down to discover any current of air, and tried with finger-nails to detect the crack. There were cracks enough, horizontal and longitudinal, for that matter, and through one of the latter I felt, or fancied I felt, to my great joy, a current of air; the door must be here, and I threw myself with all my force against the spot and each side and about it, but without any more perceptible effect than against a solid wall of masonry. The ancient Venetian builder had succeeded all too well with his devilish contrivance of security against outbreak, and, panting with exertion, and with perspiration streaming from every pore, notwithstanding coat and vest had been thrown off for the effort, I staggered back again to the oaken bench as the clock struck ten.

"What effort should I make next? I felt faint and sick, and now for the first time realized the want of nourishment, and that, since a light lunch nearly twenty-four hours previous, nothing had passed my lips. From the hour of waking, throat and lips were parched with thirst, both from the excitement and the exertion I had made, and now the longing for water was intolerable. Tongue, lips, and throat seemed dry unto bursting, and my heart beat quicker at the thought of dying of thirst and hunger in this terrible place, as I cursed the thoughtlessness that led me to wander up here alone and unnoticed.

"I had not tried shouting for help, and why should I not? But it seemed as if my parched tongue refused its office, and my efforts only resulted in a hoarse sort of shriek for help, which certainly could not be heard through the thick walls of my prison; and I soon found this effort becoming little more than a hoarse whisper, and so tottered to the window once again to inhale the reviving air and look forth, while yet I might, upon the blue sky, the beautiful distant waves, and listen to what faint sounds of free life without might float up to me from the busy city far below.

"The hammers of the bronze giants were again busy, and the great bell of the clock-tower began to toll off the hour of noon. Twelve o'clock, and yet no signs of my liberation.

"There was a rush as of many wings; a flock of pigeons passed in sight of my prison-window — the pigeons of St. Mark, that always come into the square at the stroke of two to be fed with their governmental ration of grain. They were gathering in anticipation of the approaching hour of their daily feast. A dozen alighted upon the leads below, not twenty feet from my window. Could I not in some way make these to be carrier-pigeons, giving intelligence of my fate. But I had no means of entrapping or enticing them any nearer to me.

"A thorough search of my pocket revealed nothing but a penknife, a bunch of keys, my purse, a few letters, and my note-book.

"My note-book! I would turn this to account, at least while I had the strength to do so. I wrote severally in English, French, and as well as I was able in Italian, which I then knew but imperfectly, these words:

"'Help! A visitor who has been accidentally shut in a cell in *Sotto Piombi* in the Ducal Palace, and is dying, writes these lines. In God's name, help at once!'

"These I folded and indorsed, 'Look Within,' and then threw them out through the grated bars of my prison, hoping they would flutter into the square below and be there found. They dropped upon the leads, and one fluttered in between two little projections and was wedged firmly, and the others did not come in sight from under the great overhanging sill that projected beneath my window. So, with trembling hands, I wrote and rewrote half a dozen more, folding them and throwing them out as far as I possibly could, and was tortured to see some of these little white missives lying upon the leads in plain sight, with not a breath of air to waft them to those who might set me free.

"Again the great clock struck. Two!

"Great heavens! will relief never come? I sought the bench in the middle of the room again. Could I wrench up a portion of this to pry my way out in some unthought of manner? But no; it was as firmly rooted as St. Theodore's pillar, and I sank down panting and exhausted, dropped my now fevered brow into the palms of my hands, and tears of nervous grief and excitement trickled through my fingers. I was weak, faint, and exhausted from want of nourishment, and from the air, which was hot, close, and oppressive; besides which, the exertions I had made to free myself from the place, the excitement attending upon the terrible dream, all acting upon a somewhat nervous temperament, were beginning to have their effect.

"I sat, I know not how long, in a half dreaming state of stupor. The pictures of my youth all ran before me like a vivid panorama, — school, school-fellows, play-ground, beautiful green fields, woods, delicious brooks whose waters never looked before so sweet and cool, orchards with broad boughs laden with tempting fruit. Then again the scene changed, and the tables of a grand feast were before me, in an empty banquet-hall; the smoking viands made the mouth to water with delightful anticipations, and red wine sparkled in crystal glasses. I started forward, an unbidden guest, to the board, but was held back by an invisible power, while a voice said:

"'What would you? There are no guests here?'

"'There is no one here.' I seemed to hear the words with startling distinctness.

"'No one here!' 'There is! Good God! Here is a man shut up in this fearful place!'

"There was no mistaking this sound; I was dreaming or insane. Raising my head from my hands, and leaping to my feet, my eyes were almost dazzled by the light that poured in from the open door of the cell, in which stood a party of visitors, two ladies and two gentlemen, and beside them the old custodian.

"A start back, a faint shriek from one of the ladies, and an exclamation of surprise from one of the men, evinced their surprise at my unlooked for apparition.

"'For God's sake, save me — you speak English — shut up here — accident — save me!' cried I in a hoarse whisper, and fell forward in a dead faint at their very feet.

"When I recovered I was reclining upon a great settee or sofa in the Chamber of the Council of Ten; a gentle sort of perfumed breeze seemed to be playing upon my brow, which I discovered came from the fan of one of my liberators; the great window above me was opened, and an abundance of glorious sunlight poured in with the air through the casement. The old custodian came breaking through the group with a bottle of wine that he had run to one of the restaurants in the square for, and never was nectar more delicious than the first glass of that *vin ordinaire*.

"In a quarter of an hour I was sufficiently recovered to tell a portion of my story, but I shook as with an ague fit from nervous agitation; and as Dr. Richetti, who had been hastily summoned, arrived, placed his cool hand upon my brow, and felt the rapid leaping of my pulse, he quietly commanded a postponement of further particulars, and I was half carried, half led across the Piazzetta to his waiting gondola, which was swiftly rowed to my hotel.

"Ah! the luxury of the cool couch, the pleasant subdued light through the Venetian awnings, and the happy sense of liberty that I experienced. But it was many months ere I could get that terrible night out of my dreams, and, though more than six years have elapsed, yet now and then it occasionally comes before me in dreamland. And it is not surprising that the boom of the great bell of the clock-tower should always be associated in my mind with that fearful twenty-four hours' imprisonment."

My friend drew a long breath, and with an involuntary shudder, as the bronze bellman beat out the hour of twelve, he wiped the drops of perspiration from his brow, and, as our gondolier halted at the steps of my hotel, bade good night with the promise of a sequel and explanation of the strange adventure, over our coffee and cigarettes, on the morrow, when we should sit in the Piazza, in front of Florian's.

The *granita di limone* was cool and refreshing as we sat in our chairs well out into the square in front of the restaurant the next evening, and the two strolling musicians with mandolin and guitar had sung a pretty Italian melody and been well rewarded with copper coins, and we were both looking up at the deep, glorious blue of the Italian moonlit sky, as the old bell-tower sentinels beat out the hour of nine, and recalled to mind the story of the preceding night, and I reminded the narrator of his promised explanation.

"It is simple enough," said he. "If you will believe it, that terrible night's experience had such an effect upon my nervous organization that for nearly a week I feared to sleep, it so perpetually recurred in my dreams, and for the first three nights the doctor furnished me with a watcher, and I was kept quiet until the nervous excitement was allayed, and in little more than a week's time sat here as we are now, telling the leading particulars of my incarceration to Dr. Richetti one afternoon, and accounting for various incidents in the affair.

"My previous meditations below stairs upon old Venetian tyranny, the snap to of the little spring-latched wicket door, the doctor remarked, had put the current of thought in proper direction for the dream of dungeon, inquisitors, and rack. In starting from the dream I had struck my hand against the half-opened but easily swinging door of the cell, and thereby closed it. This was the blow at the guard in the dream, and the door opened inwardly. There chanced to be no visitors who cared to see the place until late, hence the delay in my liberation; and, had not this group of Americans desired to make the exploration, I might have remained there another night, or until the place had chanced to be visited.

"As the doctor and myself were then chatting, a young Italian gentleman came towards where we were sitting, and, bowing to the doctor, who was an acquaintance, begged pardon in the Italian tongue for the interruption, and said that he wished the physician, as he understood English, to translate for him a little billet-doux in that language that had fluttered to his feet, he knew not from where, as he came from his gondola through the Piazetta. He handed what appeared to be a small bit of gilt-edged paper to the doctor.

"The latter unfolded it, read it, laughed, and looked towards myself as his interrogator stood, cigarette in hand, awaiting an answer with some anxiety.

"'Listen,' said the doctor; 'this is the translation,' and he read in Italian one of the messages I had pencilled a week before, and thrown out of the dungeon-window. 'But there is no need of any help now,' said he to his astonished friend; 'permit me to present you to the prisoner who has been rescued.' This was the third of my aërial billets-doux which had been picked up since my release; one in French, had gone to the police, who, before its finding, having heard of my adventure, had directed the custodian to put a stronger lock on the lower staircase lattice-door, and never to leave the building without visiting the cells; and the other in bad Italian was discussed by a group at one of the *café* tables as a clever attempt of some Englishman to play a practical joke."

"But, the lady in the group, she that fanned you after rescue, by all the rules of romance you should have been married to her," said I.

"Bah!" said my companion; "never saw her but once after, and then only by a singular circumstance recognized her. The carriage of a party of which I was one took us to visit the Capuchin church vaults in Vienna, and halted at the church entrance. As we descended, another party that had but just been below, guided by the old friar with his candle, came out.

"'Ugh! a gloomy place: seems like being released from a prison to get into the sunlight again,' said one of the sight-seers, as they were taking their places in their carriage.

"'Yes, indeed,' said a lady's voice; 'but did you ever hear how Kate and I released a gentleman from a dungeon in the Ducal Palace at Venice?'

"'No, indeed; how was it?'

"I turned sharply round at this, but the door of the

carriage clapped to at that moment. I merely caught the words, 'Why, you see —,' and I only saw a carriage load of ladies and gentlemen roll away with the blue ribbons of the speaker's Paris hat fluttering like farewell streamers in the breeze."

CHAPTER XIV.

I COULD not leave Venice without visiting the Arsenal, a place all-important in her history of maritime greatness, and which was for a long time the most celebrated and extensive navy-yard in the world. It is formed by a number of small islands, which are connected together by bridges, and surrounded by a wall of two miles in circumference.

In the somewhat brief visit we made to this noted place, one could not help noticing what evidences this great work still displayed of the former naval strength and commercial power of the great maritime republic. The spot seems to have been admirably chosen for the purposes designed, and of course the natural advantages must have been much improved since its foundation in 1320. The great basins, dry and wet docks for vessels, and vast warehouses, workshops, massive piers, besides constructions for ancient work now useless, astonish the visitor. The rope-walk here, with one exception, that of Toulon in France, is said to be the largest in Europe, and is 1038 feet in length, the building being upheld by ninety-two pillars of Doric architecture.

We were rowed down to the landing as near as practicable to this grand remnant of Venetian power, and, after landing, approached the principal entrance, pausing to look at the battlemented walls, the great square castle-like clock-tower on one side, the marble lions in front, and the marble statues of Neptune, Mars, and four or five other figures surmounting the ornamental pillars before the great archway above, upon which is the figure of the inevitable winged lion, with the golden book between his paws, and upon the summit of the pillars before and behind him two large balls, or globes. This gateway, as an inscription on one of the pillars tells us, was made in 1460. Before going in we pause to look at the stone lions that guard the entrance, not from any beauty they possess, for they are clumsy effigies, but because they were brought from the Peloponnesus in 1685, and because one, which has inscriptions cut upon it that are untranslatable, is said to be a memorial of the battle of Marathon.

We pass in at the entrance, present our permit, and, after inscribing our names upon the book of registration, are given in charge of one of the guards, who, courteous, polite, and patient, allows us to stroll pretty much at will and spend as much time in examination and sight-seeing as we desire; a proceeding somewhat unusual on the part of such officials, but in this case, I presume, a matter of semblance of military authority to see that visitors conduct themselves properly, pry into no forbidden places, and do not steal or carry off any relics.

It is said the French destroyed many important portions of the works of the Venetian Arsenal, and carried away many of its treasures and antiquities, but enough remains, even at this late day, to indicate what an enormous work must have been carried on here at the height of Venetian commercial supremacy, when there were employed nearly sixteen thousand laborers, besides women, to cut and sew sails. In the earlier period here was where the great Venetian war galleys were built and repaired, some of them over two hundred feet in length, and capable of accommodating a thousand men. These vessels, it will be remembered, were propelled by rowers, sailors, and galley slaves, some by double banks of oars; and a naval engagement in the days of those craft was a very different affair from that of modern times; for then they ranged their ships alongside the enemy, and the battle became a hand-to-hand fight, requiring more exercise of brute courage than seamanship. The commanders selected were also those noted as bold and successful soldiers: indeed, a sole dependence on maritime tactics would have been disastrous in the extreme.

I find, by consulting authorities, that at one period Venice had the carrying trade between Europe and the East, and in the thirteenth century she had more than three thousand vessels sailing under her flag. In the palmy days of the republic, during time of peace, there were thirty of the national vessels chartered by private individuals, each of which transported cargoes of the value of sixty thousand pounds sterling. It was in this arsenal, or navy-yard, that the practice of building or repairing vessels under cover was first introduced; and there still remain nearly a hundred of these dry docks, although the two or three that I visited, unlike the ship-houses in the American navy-yards, contained no rotting, unfinished hulls of past administrations. It appears, however, when the French took possession, they found vessels unfinished that had been on the stocks seventy-five years, construction having stopped owing to lack of material and the decadence of the state. Some of the great ship-houses appear to have been turned into warehouses, and others are doubtless pulled down. There may still remain ancient fragments in some; but if so, I did not push my investigations far enough to find them, for the sun was hot, and, after ascertaining that besides these dry, there were eight wet docks, I made for the more interesting part of the place, which is the Armory.

This contains a large collection of ancient and curious weapons of war and military trophies. Among these is the suit of armor of Henry IV. of France, given by him to the republic in 1603. All sorts of helmets, cuirasses, swords, magnificent Toledo blades, and others of marvellous workmanship, with inlaid Damascene blades and hilts; carved cimeters captured from the Turks, and great boarding-pikes that might be used in thrusting at the enemy as the galleys ranged alongside. Specimens of the steel crossbow and bolts, and even the ordinary bow and skin quivers, with arrows still in them, hung upon the walls with maces, curious battle-axes, and wondrous armor.

In the centre of the hall was a mounted figure; man and horse sheathed in mail of elegant workmanship of Milanese steel, and the armor of Doge Żiani, who flourished in 1176. Among the trophies displayed on the walls, one which is especially noteworthy is the great flag of the Turkish admiral, taken at the celebrated battle of Lepanto, gained by the Venetian and Spanish fleets over the Turks, October 7, 1571, and in which fight Cervantes, author of "Don Quixote," was wounded. Displayed near it is the armor of Sebastian Veniez, captain-general at Lepanto, also that of Augustus Barberigo, and a Tunisian banner and a Turkish flag taken at Friuli in 1472.

Here again we are reminded that the American revolving pistol is no modern invention, for among the collection of fire-arms is a revolving pistol said to have been invented in the fifteenth century. Talk about revolvers and metrailleuses! Why, here we saw a five-barrelled cannon of the sixteenth century, and another of the same time, which, as far as exterior examination went, was a well-made and effective weapon, that was a sixteen-barreller. The collection of cannon in this armory is said to have been very fine, but, like many other portions of the collection, it was taken away or nearly broken up by the French when they came into possession under Napoleon, as above noted.

There are still a few specimens of elegant and curious antique workmanship. One is a gun, made apparently of steel, and elegantly ornamented with inwrought gold leaves, vines, and other ornaments. The muzzle is a griffin's head, from the open mouth of which poured forth the deadly fire of destruction upon the foe. Near the vent arranged for purposes of a sight was a miniature figure of a cavalier, with drawn sword, astride the back of a dragon. Other specimens of fire-arms, rude in invention and beautiful in workmanship, weapons such as swords, pistols, and battle-axes, that had belonged to Italian captains who had won honor in the service of the republic, were displayed on the walls or in cases; and the theatrical-looking seat used by the Doge when visiting the Arsenal was among the curiosities displayed.

Another interesting department is the model room, which contains models of all kinds of water-craft from the ancient galley down to the modern frigate. Here are displayed fragments of old galleys that have served in action, their beaks or prows; fragments of galleys captured from the Turks; a fragment of the last Bucentaur, or state galley, in which the Doge was wont to go in great pomp and state for the ceremony of marrying the Adriatic. The last Venetian Bucentaur perished in 1797. It was a gorgeous state barge, and must have almost rivalled Cleopatra's in magnificence, for the gilding alone cost more than forty thousand dollars. The model of it preserved in this museum shows it to have been a gorgeous affair, elegantly carved, decorated, and gilded in every possible part visible to the eye. Two hundred rowers propelled it, and upon its different lofty decks were grand saloons, place for a full band of musicians, servants, sailors, soldiers, and noblemen. This grand vessel was not rowed by ordinary sailors or galley slaves, but by a picked body of men who were proud of the service, and who enjoyed peculiar privileges from the state for this and other guard and maritime duty performed by them at the Arsenal, and in behalf of various state dignitaries. The plans, sectional drawings and curious models of antique naval architecture that are displayed here, must be a most interesting study to those who are familiar in the least with ship-building. The relics of old battles and mementos of the warlike prowess of the Venetians in many cases were unfamiliar to myself, and the guide-books give only a meagre explanation, or none at all, of who many great captains, whose names ended with an *i*, were, and so we pass numbers of these trophies with but a glance.

But the glories of Venice are a story of the past, and this great arsenal, with its docks and piers, like the Colosseum in Rome, serves to show, by its very immensity, as a skeleton of other days, what must have been the power that called it into being and once clothed it with life and activity.

Verona! the very aroma of Shakspeare's plays seemed to be in the atmosphere as we rolled in a rattling old vehicle through its streets, and remembered Valentine and Proteus, the two gentlemen of Verona, and looked with interest at a ragged, unkempt cur, wondering if he was a descendant of Launce's dog, as our carriage whirled past the broad entrance to a great church into which a straggling crowd of worshippers were going to some vesper service, for the air was as filled with the clangor of bells as an American city on the morning of the celebration of Independence day. Close by the church was a gateway: through it we drove, and were in the courtyard and front of the hospitable door of the Hotel of Two Towers.

The first thing a tired tourist does on obtaining a good room and performing his ablutions after a long railroad ride, is to test the cuisine of the hotel. At some Italian hotels, the perfume, as well as the use of garlic is intolerable, and it is necessary to forbid any flavoring with it, but in a house like this we were fortunate. The host set a table that was clean and well served, and his cooking was more English than Italian, for we had chops, yes, genuine chops, well cooked, eggs that were fresh, soup that was rich and not greasy, and bread that was sweet; the latter something to be thankful for by those who have endured the Florentine abomination. The refreshing effect of the viands of the Hotel of Two Towers, and the spacious room to which we were assigned, with its windows commanding a view of nearly half a mile of street directly in front, and the broad entrance to the great church at one side, coupled with the civility of the chief clerk, who spoke English, may have prejudiced me in favor of the house, for certainly it was one of comfort after the long railroad ride from Venice.

The hotel was built with those open piazzas or galleries, inclosing its court-yard, where carriages and post-stages drove in, and was probably the starting-point of the great *diligences* before the days of railroad communication. The weather was warm, and open windows the rule after the sun had gone down; and, as we sat at ours, and looked down from our three-storied height into the square below, we observed real activity begin. The street became more and more thronged with pedestrians; gossipy groups met as by common consent together in knots here and there before the great church. The proprietor of a wine-shop brought out half a dozen tables, and twice that number of chairs, and placed them on the pavement in front of his door; and ere long two white-jacketed waiters were flitting hither and thither among the groups that surrounded them, and the clink of glasses and glow-worm-like sparkle of lighted cigar-tips below told that the real business of the day was flourishing. There was a hum and chatter of voices of men and women; children raced and played in the cool evening air about the church-door; and the whole scene and its bustle and clatter contrasted strangely with the quiet that we had so lately left. There, when the sun went down, the liquid highway of the Grand Canal, which our apartments overlooked, gave forth no sound of pattering feet or noisy voices, except now and then as a dark gondola glided by with a gay party, whose tones were soon lost in the distance.

"I wonder what time these people retire to bed," thought I, as I rose from my couch after two hours' ineffectual effort to woo the drowsy god, owing to the clatter below, and, looking at my watch, found it to be past midnight. I looked out. The crowd had diminished, but there were still dark knots in the square. Only two or three of the wine-shop man's tables were now occupied, but the glasses had evidently clinked to some purpose, for the argument going on was fierce and vehement, with all that extravagant gesture that Frenchman and Italian throw into a discussion; and the rattle of tongues promised to abbreviate for me that necessary refreshment after a tiresome journey, a good night's sleep, so much that I began to question the judgment which located the hotel, wine-shop, and square in such proximity. The discussion at the wine-shop half an hour later culminated in a squabble, and the proprietor or police had to preserve the peace; the tables were taken in, and now all was quiet except the patter of feet of numerous pedestrians passing and repassing. It really seems as if the people in these warm climates are in the streets the most part of the night during the summer season (it was now June), and took their sleep during the day.

It was now two A. M., and young Verona was beginning to go home for the night. Either the young bloods of Florence and Verona break forth into music when *Bacchus pleni*, or when returning from opera or *soirée musicale* at these (to us) unseasonable hours, for they are all singing, loudly singing. These gay bloods sing not as a noisy fellow even, in America, but distance anything I ever heard in strength of lung and power of expression. This may be from the fact that some of them have trained musical instruction.

Fancy a young fellow with a powerful tenor voice passing through the quiet street singing at his highest register as if striving to drown an orchestra, and continuing on, his shouts reaching you nearly half a mile away after he has passed, only to be succeeded by three more, who arm in arm pass, roaring an operatic chorus as if their lungs and throats were of brass. Then come a couple more, one with a guitar, either going to or returning from a serenade, and improving the walk by a song, *fortissimo*. Indeed, it seemed to me these gentlemen of Verona thought that street singing, like street music, should be of the loudest possible description, as I tossed uneasily on my couch till tired nature at last succumbed, and I slumbered.

I was aroused by a peal and clangor of bells that brought me into a sufficient sense of wide-awakativeness that, as an American, I involuntarily listened for the firing of cannon and explosion of fire-crackers, which " usher in " Independence day; and then, as none came, I recollected I was in this land of bell-ringing, as the clangor went on for ten minutes or more, and found on consultation of my watch that they were ringing for five-o'clock mass. I had enjoyed two hours' slumber only. At length the din ceased, and, dozing off again, I was once more roused, half past five; and so on with this infernal din, until seven o'clock. The incessant clangor of bells is one of the nuisances in Italian cities, especially at early morning, if one is easily roused and desires rest, but, like some other annoyances, soon come to be disregarded as one gets thoroughly seasoned as a tourist.

The Montagues and the Capulets! We thought of them as we halted and looked about in a quaint, almost deserted old street that in the quiet sunshine seemed like one of those scenes set on the theatrical stage, where the combat of Mercutio, Tybalt, and Romeo took place.

" Would Monsieur like to see Juliet's house ? "

" Certainly ! Drive us to Juliet's house, to Juliet's balcony."

We remembered that " the orchard walls were high and hard to climb," as the fair Juliet had told her lover, and called to mind the engravings of Italian terraced gardens with plashing fountains, flower vases, and marble steps. We thought of the balconied window of the marble palace from which the fair Juliet looked forth upon the quiet night, and 'neath which Romeo, " who with love's light wings did o'er-perch these walls," had sworn by " the moon that tips with silver all these fruit-tree tops."

So when our carriage drew up inside an old inclosed street or court-yard, shabby and dirty, and the driver pointed to the carving of a cardinal's hat over an archway as part of the armorial bearings of the Capulet family, we had the impression from the surroundings that we had halted in an old stable-yard, or opposite a third-rate Italian inn.

This old brick or stone edifice, with two dirty, lounging men smoking in the shade of an angle of a staircase, and a slattern, sore-eyed woman with a baby in her arms, who came and asked alms of us, an old ruined cart, and a heap of rubbish for surroundings, — and that old rounded window, — Juliet's balcony! — a flannel shirt was hanging out from it to dry, — and the smell of garlic, too — faugh! How glorious garden, perfume of flowers, plashing fountains, and fragrant orchards vanished like a vision of romance as they were, as our carriage rolled out of the Via Capello, and we rode to the garden said to contain the gentle Juliet's tomb.

There is not quite so rude a shock to the imagination here. We halt beside the dead wall of a large garden, and an old woman coming from a house near the gate, unlocks it, and we follow her along the long broad path at one side of the garden, above which a pleasant shade was formed by overarching trellised grape-vines. Turning at right angles from our path at the furthermost corner of the garden, we reached a sort of cheap, two-story brick shed. Three simple arches formed the lower story, the middle one forming a door, open except a protection of light iron grating, and contained what we were asked to believe was the sarcophagus of Juliet, and which looked like an old shoe-shaped sort of stone trough, the length of which suggested that the gentle Veronese must have been short in stature.

The garrulous old woman, our guide, told us this chapel was not the real location of the tomb; but leading us to a spot in the centre of the garden, said here stood the tomb of the Capulets, and plucking a bit of geranium from the spot, stuck it in my button-hole. Here we were told Juliet's sarcophagus long stood as a washing-trough till the continued visits of tourists gave it such value that it was removed and enshrined as we saw it.

Whether we have stood upon the spot occupied by the much-mentioned Tomb of the Capulets we are doubtful; but, if an imaginative mind desires to have the dream of romance that has been incited by one of the most charming creations of the bard of Avon taken out of it, one cannot have it more effectually done, or his sensibilities receive a ruder shock, than starting for picturesque mementos of this romantic love story, and encountering what is pointed out as all that remains of it in Verona.

The dream of youth, the hopes of years, the keen delight of anticipation and desire, ended in fruition when I stood in the centre of the vast arena of Rome's Flavian Amphitheatre, and repeopled it with the hundred thousand eager and expectant spectators, as thoughts flew back to the past; while a visit to the Amphitheatre in Verona took more of a practical than an imaginative turn, for here the general features have been carefully and sacredly preserved. The ravages of the earthquake and the never-failing tooth of time have told upon the structure, but the great tier upon tier of marble seats still remain, with the vaultings of Roman brickwork beneath them perfect and entire, and the building has been carefully protected, and from time to time restored at various points.

You may go down to the arena and to the arches, and see where were the wild beasts' dens and the gladiators' entrances, pass round and examine the admirable arrangements for entrance and exit of the audience, walk through corridors and up staircases, and, having fresh in recollection the ruins of the Roman Colosseum, may be able to fill out the wanting fragments in that vast ruin. The founder of the latter is known, but the founder of the Veronese

Amphitheatre, or the year in which it was erected, is unknown: it is only supposed to have been built about A. D. 85.

The theatre is built of Verona marble, formed a grand circle of fourteen hundred and thirty feet, and was originally about one hundred and twenty feet in height from the pavement. There were originally seventy-two arches of the outer ring (eight less than in the Colosseum), but, notwithstanding all the care that has been taken to preserve the structure, dating back to edicts in 1228, but four of the original outer arches, according to a guide-book I found at my hotel on returning, have been preserved. If this be so, what I took for the real outer row must have been mainly restorations.

There was one set of arches, however, that there was no disputing the antiquity of, and that was the only remaining four of the topmost tier that ran its graceful circle round the whole structure, a hundred feet above the pavement. This fragment was all that was spared by the earthquake that toppled the rest to the ground nearly seven hundred years ago. But over this, according to historical authority, there was a fourth story of lesser arches going completely round the building, so that the whole structure must have been at least one hundred and twenty feet in height.

Inside, and we have the grand entrances and tiers of seats preserved or restored so completely that quite a correct idea may be had of what the structure really was in its prime. We climbed to the top and looked down into the arena, an ellipse two hundred and sixty-three feet long by one hundred and forty-six feet wide, surrounded by its rings of marble benches, of which I counted forty-two, one above the other to the top, and was informed that there were two more rows sunk beneath the present level of the arena; and, when we descended, the guide showed us, by means of an aperture in the present flooring, through which he thrust a pole, that the real arena was several feet below the present surface. We were also shown the ruins of an old aqueduct, used, it was said, to flood the arena when naval spectacles or combats were to be presented. The ancient benches in the auditorium appeared to have been vast blocks of marble, accurately cut and jointed into perfect rings of masonry, but the restorations are of stone, of a more perishable or flaky nature. Each row of seats was about one and a half feet in height, and of the same breadth, with about a foot and a half space allowed for each spectator; of course, no backs to any seats, unless, perchance, curule chairs, or other movable seats, occupied the podium for ædiles, prefects, consuls, and other privileged patricians.

At one end, railed off, a portion of the arena was occupied, when we visited it, by a temporary structure, which had a small stage before it, upon which, we were informed, an exhibition of jugglery and gymnastics was to take place; and the audience of about two hundred persons were sitting upon the same stone seats from which, a thousand years before, their ancestors looked down upon the fierce contests of furious beasts or still more cruel gladiators, who fought each other with deadly fury. This audience, of two hundred spectators or so, looked absurdly small, gathered, as it was, at one end of the great ellipse, — something like a little cluster of flies at the corner of a table-cloth, for the capacity of the interior is for about twenty-five thousand spectators. So, while this little knot were patiently listening to an orchestra of three pieces that was industriously playing a preliminary overture, we turned and took such a view of the city as we could from the topmost tier, and looked down into the adjoining square, laid out in such fanciful figures as to remind one of a kaleidoscope, and, after one more farewell sweep of the eye over the grand ellipse of the interior, descended.

A short drive brought us to a narrow thoroughfare, in and near which stood the monuments of the Della Scala family (Scaligeri); and one circumstance that redounds to the credit of the Veronese, or maybe to that of their enemies, is, that these sumptuous monuments to the lords of Verona have been so well preserved as they are, notwithstanding they are in the heart of the city, and some of them have stood in a narrow and crowded thoroughfare for more than five hundred years, that has been the scene of frequent conflicts. The monuments are very elaborate. That which first claimed our attention was, of course, that of *Can Grande*, which signifies the Great Dog, though, for what reason he was called by that canine title, history is silent. Nevertheless, it was he that afforded the poet Dante protection, and the poet immortalized him in the seventeenth canto of his "*Paradiso*," referring to his as —

" ... the great Lombard's courtesy, who bears
Upon the ladder perched, the sacred bird; "

and in a dozen or more lines, which, as all the guide-books quote, I will not; but which lines have done more to preserve the "great Lombard's" name since his death, in 1329, than his costly monument, which forms a sort of portico, as it were, to the Church of Santa Maria Antica.

This monument, or portico, consists of three sections, supported by handsome columns, with elaborately wrought capitals. First are figures of dogs, with the ladder and shield, — armorial bearings of the Della Scala family. These uphold the sarcophagus, upon which is stretched a full-length, recumbent figure of Can Grande, with sword girt to his side. Above this rises a pyramid, upon which is his sculptured representation on horseback, and in full armor.

The Tomb of Martin II. is also quite an elaborate piece of work, the large block of marble which supports his funeral urn being upheld by four columns, each with an architrave of nine feet. Four other columns uphold a canopy above this, which cover the urn; and above, he is sculptured as large as life, on horseback.

That which appeared to me as the most beautiful of all these monuments — and there were, I think, six or seven of them in all — was that of Can Signorio, who, notwithstanding he was the murderer of his two brothers in the twelfth century, is honored with a most sumptuous mausoleum. Notwithstanding the low state of morals in Italy at that time, this, in a measure, may be accounted for when we find that he had it designed himself previous to his death, and determined that, in sumptuousness of design and execution, it should surpass that of any of his predecessors. Six elegant columns support the first or lower section, and it is composed of four different sections, one above the other. Among the different sculptured figures supporting some of these different divisions, I noticed those of Faith and Charity, and other allegorical representations of virtues; also, six knightly figures, upon as many pilasters about the monument. The recumbent figure is on one of the divisions of the structure; and the whole is surmounted by a handsomely sculptured life-size equestrian figure.

The inclosure here is the old cemetery of the church, and was the family burial-place. The iron fencing, or rail-work surrounding the tombs, is pointed out to visitors as being extremely rich; and it is, as a specimen of iron skilfully wrought by handwork, graceful and flexible, the design being the ladder (*scala*) of the arms of the family, intermingled with quatrefoils and delicate tracery.

From these tombs we whirled away through quaint old streets, and emerged into the Piazza dei Erbe, a vegetable market place, noisy with the clatter of market-women, and surrounded by several quaint old Gothic buildings, and having at one end a tower erected by the same Can Signorio whose tomb we had just left, and in which he placed the first clock put up in Verona. Many of the other curious old buildings doubtless had interesting stories connected with them, if we could have found them out. One was a merchants' Exchange, built in 1301. There stood also in this square the pillar which once supported the Winged Lion of St. Mark when Verona was subject to Venice, but which was removed from its lofty pedestal in 1799.

Our drives about the city took us beneath some of the old Roman arches, one being called the Porta dei Borsari, which extends directly across one of the principal streets, — an ancient double gateway, which, from inscriptions upon it, appears to have been built in the reign of the Roman Emperor Gallienus, about the year 265. For more than six centuries has this handsome marble barrier — for it is singularly rich in ornament — stood here across the public highway. Each of its gateways has Corinthian pilasters upholding a light pediment, and above are two stories, with six small, arched windows in each. The various flutings, columns, and curious ornamentations of the structure, which are numerous, must afford an interesting study to those architecturally inclined.

Verona is a Gothic old city as regards architecture, and full of curious and interesting streets, squares, and churches. Strolling along during the afternoon, I came to a street named after the great Italian poet Dante, and it carried me into a broad, rather quiet square, or what would have been quiet, had it not been for the groups of children, who seemed to resort there for an evening's romp. One pompous, uniformed official, with a large, ornamented cane, stood watching the proceedings; and he, I found, was a policeman.

The square was surrounded by lofty old buildings, formerly the dwellings of the lords of Verona; and our theatrical scene-painters ought to get sketches of it as a good scene to transfer to canvas. In fact, Verona is rich in picturesque, theatrical scenery-looking streets, with quaint architecture and coloring, light, and shade; and even the dinginess that reminds one of the worn side-scenes and serviceable flats that answer equally well for a "Street in Lyons" in the drama of "The Lady of Lyons," a "Square in Mantua" in "The Wife," a street-scene in "Romeo and Juliet," or similar scenes from a dozen other plays one might mention. In the middle of this square stands a beautiful colossal statue of Dante. He is represented as looking towards the house in which he was received, during his exile, by Can Grande.

One of the most conspicuous buildings upon this square, which is called the Piazza dei Signori, is the Palazzo del Consiglio, whose columns, pilasters, and the statues that surmount it, show it to be a pile of no ordinary merit. The statues are said to be those of celebrated men born in Verona; and there is a saying that every man of any note in ancient time, who is recorded as ever having visited Verona, is now claimed by the Veronese to have been born there. This palace was erected in the fifteenth century, and was designed by Father Giocondo, who, besides being an excellent scholar and contributing much to literature, was one of the best architects of his times. The Campanile, in this square, is a splendid specimen of brick masonry, soaring three hundred feet into the air.

We did not go over the Castle Vecchio, which stood near the swiftly flowing river Adige, but contented ourselves looking at the exterior of this picturesque and battlemented old relic of the Middle Ages; but the turreted and battlemented bridge — this must not be left out of our experience. This, too, with its ancient brick arches, is an exceedingly picturesque object, and one of its arches makes a span of one hundred and sixty-one feet. It was built in 1355, and from it we enjoyed some fine views up and down the swiftly flowing stream.

Travellers who are interested in visiting churches will find enough to claim their attention in Verona, and to use up no inconsiderable portion of time, for there are said to be over forty different churches here. I can confess to but three, and these were inspected almost as hastily as the director of an American charitable institution goes through it on the annual visit of the Board.

The Cathedral, they pretend to say, was built by Charlemagne, but the guide-books and other authorities place it as an edifice of the twelfth century. As far as quaint and curious antiquity of some parts of it is concerned, one might readily believe it to have been built in the time of Charlemagne, but portions are known to be, and can be readily recognized as additions and productions of a later date.

One of the chief exterior attractions which everybody goes to see is the ornamented porch at one of the entrances, where, besides the arches and columns supported by griffins, there stand, on either side of the door, sculptured representations of those noted paladins, Roland (or Orlando, that being the Italian form of the name) and Oliver. In his right hand Roland holds his celebrated sword Durindada, which, it will be recollected, the fable says he won from a Saracen warrior, and that it once belonged to Hector of Troy. The sculptor has cut the name of the sword upon it, that its character may be fully understood by the visitor. One of the noted warrior's legs and feet is in armor, and the other bare. Oliver, on the other side of the entrance, is also an armed figure; and he bears in his hand, not a sword, but a club, to which is attached a round, spiked ball, something like a weapon with a longer handle I remember to have seen at the Tower of London Armory, and called there, I think, the "morning star," and calculated, when swung by a stalwart arm, to make the owner of the head it might encounter "see stars," if it did not let daylight in.

They point out to you, among the sculptures over the door, that of a hog dressed as a monk, and standing upon his hind legs with his fore feet planted in an open book, as if officiating at some ceremony, — a satire in stone work; and upon a porch on another side of the church are ranges of columns, upon which the sculptor has seemed to revel in carving burlesque and satirical work in his art, of grotesque heads of imps or saints, beautiful tracery, and ornament intermingled as if working with freedom to show what could be produced from his chisel.

I will not tire the reader with a description of the interior, where is the beautiful picture of the Assumption, by Titian, a fine one of the Adoration of the Three Kings, besides many rich and curious chapels of old Verona families, with pedigrees running back I don't know how many hundred years. Some of these chapels are extremely rich and elegant in their decorations, notably so that of the Maffei family. We might, if we had a permit, we were told, have gone into the great library, which is entered from the cloisters of this church, — a collection rich in ancient literature, containing manuscripts written in the fourth and fifth centuries. Many of the manuscripts in this collection were discovered to be palimpsests of great value. But we must confess to doing Verona hastily; for the fierce heat of an Italian sun was making itself felt, and the season well advanced, and we were anxious to move towards a region of cooler atmosphere.

The river Adige sweeps round the city of Verona, dividing it into two parts; and its rapid stream keeps in motion water-mills, which are built on rafts, and anchored in some manner at midstream.

The Church of St. Anastasia, close to the entrance of our hotel, we visited one afternoon, delighted to get into its cool interior from beneath the rays of the sun. This old church, Gothic in its style of architecture, was built by the Dominicans in the thirteenth century. It is about three hundred feet long and eighty wide, and has a floor inlaid with various-colored marbles. It is filled with side-chapels and altars; the chapels, as usual, of noted Italian families, and rich in sculpture, paintings, and decorations. There were the St. Germigrano Chapel, with a fine old tomb of Gothic design and elegant frescos; the Pellegrini Chapel, with a curious set of terra-cotta figures, representing scenes in the life of Christ; the monuments to members of the family, and frescos with figures which, we were given to understand, were portraits of some illustrious members of the family, whose dust mouldered in the vaults below; the

Chapel of the Fregoso and Lazize, with beautiful altars and ancient frescos. There were several monuments to Italian authors, mathematicians, and scholars, and paintings that bore names that I confess I had, alas! never heard of before; some of the latter, rich masses of coloring, and with those grand effects of grouping, light, and shade, that the old masters excelled in, and others the hard, stiff representations of saints and martyrs that the tourist becomes wearied of from frequent repetition.

Our railway ride from Verona to Botzen carried us first across a bridge over the rushing Adige, and then past a great defile with huge walls rising on either side, not far from the field of Rivoli, one of Bonaparte's earliest victories. We gradually leave what is known as the Valley of the Adige, and finally cross the frontier, and are in the Tyrol; and, having been whirled through little towns whose names I cannot remember, and past an old castle or two that I have forgotten, at last pull up for a brief halt at the station in Trent, a fine old place with walls and towers, and one of the principal cities of the Italian Tyrol, on the banks of the Adige.

We leave Trent behind, and after a short ride over another bridge, we have crossed and recrossed the Adige two or three times in our journey, and had it in sight, as the road seems to run in its immediate vicinity, the whole distance to Botzen. We ride through the porphyry region of hills, from which that stone is taken, cross a final bridge which we are told is over the Eisach River that runs into the Adige, and halt for a night's rest at Botzen, before going on to old Innspruck for a rest and cool-off.

Botzen appeared to be a picturesque town, with quaint streets, having arcades under the buildings, a church with a curious old red spire, and here and there the streets cut by canals of running water; but the water from above came down in a brisk shower on our arrival, and we were glad to seek shelter at once, passing on our way a procession of little boys returning from school, headed by a priest, who were taking their drenching with much apparent enjoyment.

A good dinner was had at the Hotel *Kaiserkrone* (Emperor's Crown), which the guide-books set down as "comfortable but dear;" and another hint which they give, which those who use light wines will be grateful for, is to try the Terlaner wine, which is a fluid of rare excellence, and can only be had in this immediate vicinity. It is pure and light in its character, of delicate flavor, which for some reason it is said to lose on being transported to any distance.

I had promised myself a good night's rest at Botzen, at a good hotel, and in a town, as it looked to be, the very spot to enjoy dreamy musings and sound slumbers.

A picturesque church-steeple was pointed out to me from my chamber-window by the officious *valet de place*. He had called to proffer services, and was sorry I was not going to stay the next day, and go into it and see some old carved font or pulpit, or go to the old castle built by the Archduke Sigismund in 1473. But I remembered that old steeple, for at four o'clock next morning began its jangle of bells, and again and again their brazen clangor was repeated every half hour, rendering slumber impossible, and, as I threw open my window-blinds to breathe the fresh morning air at half past six, just after the peal at that time had ceased, I saw the bell-ringer leaning out of a window from the bell-tower of the steeple getting cooled off after his exertions. The only revenge I could take upon this tintinnabulator was to shake my fist at him, which act seems to have encouraged him to renewed exertions, judging from the rattling peal he rung out half an hour later.

From Botzen to Innspruck by rail by the Brenner Pass carried us through some romantic scenery, but really the way to enjoy the scenery of Swiss or Tyrolean mountain-passes is to travel by private post-carriages. The Brenner Pass is one of the least interesting, however, of the Alpine passes, and the road being lowest down is open at all seasons of the year; so we comforted ourselves with this assurance and the knowledge that numerous other experiences over mountain-passes by other methods should be an excuse for adopting that annihilator of time and romance in travel, the railway train.

We left Botzen behind, whirled through a great tunnel twelve hundred feet long, cut through porphyry rock, and passed by views of a beautiful country with a background of precipitous crags and mountains. The railway follows along, for some distance, the river Eisach, in a narrow ravine, with high porphyry cliffs on either side. Then we pass the Castle of Trostburg, a picturesque little structure perched on an elevation high above the road, and various other ruins or fragments here and there amid the rocky fastnesses, but few of which the tourist will remember unless he make industrious use of pencil and note-book. I have in mind the richest monastery in Tyrol, said to be in a little village that looked hardly big enough to support the church which stood guard over it like a giant with a flock of lambs at his feet. Then we ran over a flat expanse of country, said to be the scene of one of Hofer's victories, and see a castle called Reifenstein, that some old fellow lived in who was a wonderful huntsman or sportsman; — fill out any Tyrolean legend of a marvellous rifle-shot, and revelry in the castle hall, and you will probably have the story. Not more than five or six miles further on, and a good-natured German *compagnon de voyage*, who speaks English, points out an old stronghold known as Raubenstein, or Robber's Nest. In fact, that was really the character of half these old castles in the feudal ages, whose owners lived by levying contributions on neighboring provinces or passing travellers.

We made a brief halt at Brenner, a station which is said to be the highest point reached by the railroad, being about forty-eight hundred feet above the level of the sea. Here they point out two little streams, one of which is a noisy and bustling little waterfall or cascade, and is said to be the beginning of the river Eisach, whose rapid flood we crossed once or twice at the commencement of our journey; and the other a small stream that begins the river Sill. The Eisach flows southerly, and pours its tribute into the Adriatic; and the Sill north, into the Black Sea. As we approach Innspruck the scenery becomes more romantic and beautiful; the great mountains soar into the air, their sides streaked with snow, or glittering with silver rivulets that pour down from far above; the train thunders through great ravines, with rocky walls on either side, or crosses from one to the other on the high stone bridges that span them, and beneath which the river Sill rattles in sparkling foam; then we emerge in sight of towering mountains, lifting their great frontlets up, up to the very sky above. The Alps! The Alps! And, as the tourist

> "Hails in each hill a friend's familiar face,
> And clasps the mountain in his mind's embrace,"

he hardly thinks to bestow a glance, just before he reaches the Innspruck station, at a distant hill to which his attention may be called as indicating the point where Andreas Hofer, the Tyrolean patriot, with his army of peasantry, defeated the soldiers of France and Bavaria. But of him anon; for we left Botzen at 10 A. M., and now the dial points 5 P. M. as we roll into the station at Innspruck. So, though it may be quite suggestive that we have been through the pass traversed by the young Roman general Drusus with his legions, twelve years before the Christian era, who, though only in his twenty-third year, defeated the tribes of Brenni and Germani, and completely subjugated the Tyrol, was welcomed back in triumph to Rome, and that his was the ruined triumphal arch that we have stood beneath and which St. Paul must have passed when he entered the imperial city, — though these suggestions may arise, there arises another that the tourist too often finds will not be put aside, and that is one of hunger and the dinner-hour.

We drive through the clean, broad, well-kept streets of Innspruck, emerge into a broader and wider one which has a monument in the middle, a church at one end, and a triumphal arch at the other, and the two principal hotels (the Golden Sun and Hotel Austria) on either side. We choose the latter, and find ourselves in an excellently managed house, with spacious rooms kept faultlessly clean, a *table d'hôte* excellent, and attendance that is prompt and efficient.

Our rooms look out upon the broad street known as the Neustadt, according to the guide-book. In the centre of the street is a monument that none of the guide-books mention; it is formed of a white Corinthian pillar resting upon a red pedestal some twelve feet in height, which in turn rests upon a base consisting of three broad steps. In the pedestal on sunken panels are bas-reliefs of religious and allegorical subjects, and upon it, at the base of the Corinthian pillar, stand life-size figures of St. Vigilius and St. Cassian (two apostles of the Tyrol), and St. Anne and St. George. The top of the pillar is surmounted by an effigy in honor of the Immaculate Conception. On the steps at the base of this monument, at noon, would four or five little apprentice boys, workers somewhere in the neighborhood, rendezvous; and here their brothers and sisters, mites of four or five years of age, in coarse garments and wooden shoes, bring them their dinners, — a sort of porridge in an earthen pot, — which were eaten with gusto with an iron spoon by these artisans of twelve years old during their half hour's nooning. This monument, which is one of the most conspicuous features of the town, is built of the marbles of the country, and was erected in memory of a victory of the Tyrolese over the Bavarians and French in 1703, when a large portion of the Tyrol had been overrun, Innspruck taken, and when Maximilian of Bavaria was so confident of its entire subjugation, that he had ordered the *Te Deum* to be sung in the churches. But the Tyroleans, recovering from their first surprise, roused the whole country by means of alarm-fires and messengers, and the enemy were caught in one of the mountain passes, and completely destroyed.

This famous success is celebrated on the first day of July by a solemn procession round the square, which we were fortunate enough to see. The religious element predominated largely in the display. The procession issuing from one of the churches consisted of a band of music; monks bearing crosiers and gilded crosses; acolytes swinging censers of burning incense; barefooted friars who sang Latin chants; four uniformed officials supporting a canopy beneath which walked a mitred bishop whose magnificently embroidered vestments were upheld by pages who walked behind; young girls and boys, and men with uncovered heads; soldiers, and all the paraphernalia of pomp and parade the Church of Rome knows so well how to effectually display. They made the entire detour of the square, and when he who bore the host passed, with the monks chanting behind him, the crowd in the street uncovered their heads and fell upon their knees in silent adoration.

Standing in the middle of this Neustadt, the lofty mountains that tower all round above us, six to eight thousand feet high, seem close at hand, so close that one might fire a rifle-shot down into the square; but, though they appear thus to actually overhang the town, they are some miles distant. The town is really in the middle of a valley upon the banks of the river Inn, which joins its swiftly rushing current near here with that of the Sill. It is surrounded by natural beauties and romantic scenery, and is eighteen hundred feet above the sea-level.

The great mountains that form the walls of the valley in which the town is situated are a perpetual pleasure to the traveller who enjoys mountain views, and the varied pictures they present in the spring season, of their great patches of snow near the top, ribbons of water further down, and luxurious green succeeding beneath in the pleasant sunshine. A cooler atmosphere is experienced some morning, perhaps, and, casting the gaze upwards, we discover that a fresh white mantle has been spread during the night, and the advancing breath of summer is tempered by the cool blast of the snow-field till it gradually yields to the sun's rays, beneath which the little chalets, mountain paths, and verdure, and sparkling streams, come out in the clear atmosphere like a picture mellowed by the distance.

At one end of the street stands what is known as the Golden Roof, one of the sights of Innspruck. This is now an old post-house, or place for the starting of post-wagons; that is, the lower part of it, which is an open archway, and is a fragment or all that remains of a once princely palace. Above is a balustrade, with six coats of arms, or heraldic shields, of the provinces under Maximilian's government. Above this, in front of the second story, another balustrade, upon the six sections of which are carved figures in various fantastic attitudes; and above this, like a large-sized Italian awning, projects the "golden roof," an awning of gilt copper, eighteen or twenty feet wide.

The story runs that, in 1425, Frederick, Count of Tyrol, who dwelt here, annoyed by the sobriquet of "empty purse," built this "golden roof" at an expense of thirty thousand ducats, to show that his purse was not empty. The guide-book story, we may say, however, is not the true one; for Frederick was no spendthrift, but expended his means liberally for the people; and, to show the envious nobles who applied the nickname to him that, despite his self-abnegation and charity, he had means, he built his ornamental roof, this fragment of which is preserved in his memory.

Around in this vicinity are some of the older buildings of the city, projecting over and forming covered arcades like those noted in Berne, Botzen, and Verona.

At the other end of the Neustadt, which is a broad, handsome, and well-paved street, stands the triumphal arch of Maria Theresa, who arranged in 1765 that the marriage of her son (afterwards Leopold II.) with Maria Louisa, daughter of Charles III. of Spain, should take place at Innspruck. The inhabitants, appreciating this honor to their city, made numerous public improvements in preparation for the event, decorated the streets and public buildings, and erected this arch at the point where the imperial party would enter the city, which they did on the 15th of July, attracting a large and brilliant assemblage. The royal affianced ones were married August 5, and Innspruck had a month of gayety and festivity.

The arch is rather a clumsy-looking structure, consisting of one lofty central arch, through which passes the carriageway, and two lesser on each side for foot travel. Above the entablature, which is supported by two pillars and four pilasters, are two allegorical figures supporting the medallion of Francis I., and over the lesser archways medallions of other royal heads.

Passing by a shop-window one day, my attention was attracted by a small, handsomely finished oil-painting, that appeared to be a copy of the portrait of a beautiful woman. It was so pretty that I halted again on my return to gaze once more upon it, and finally became so much interested as to enter the shop and inquire who was the owner of those sweet features, when I found I had stumbled upon another of the celebrities of Innspruck, and was made acquainted with the main points in the romantic history of Philippina Welser, the historic beauty of the old city. The beautiful little copy of her picture is made from the original portrait, once kept at the Ambras Castle, which we straightway made haste to visit.

Philippina's father was a wealthy old burgher, but his daughter, though beautiful, was not eligible as a royal bride; but it chanced, when the Emperor Charles V. came into Augsburg, in 1547, that the young and handsome Prince Ferdinand II. rode by his side, and as the burgher's beautiful daughter leaned forward from her window to throw a wreath of flowers towards the emperor, the prince caught sight of her, and she of him, and it was a genuine case of love at first sight. But the course of true love never did run smooth; for the young lady had been betrothed by her father to the eldest son and heir of another rich old burgher in Augsburg named Fugger, who was anxious for the match, and old Welser having given his word, was sturdily honest and would not break it, even for a prince. The only thing left for the lovers was an elopement, which took place. It is said by some authorities that the young archduke's marriage gave offence to his father, who considered it degrading, and that it was not until twelve years after that the beautiful Philippina succeeded in so moving him by her beauty and pleadings that he consented to acknowledge her, and created her two sons margraves.

This story, however, is denied by other authorities, and is said to refer to the succeeding emperor, Maximilian II., who acknowledged the legality of Ferdinand's marriage on condition that the issue of it should not claim the rank of Archdukes of Austria. The offspring of this happy marriage was two sons, of whom one became a bishop and cardinal, and the other Margrave of Burgau; and his father left the latter this fine old castle, Schloss Ambras, where he and his amiable wife Philippina had passed thirty years of unalloyed happiness and wedded life,—a rare circumstance with royal couples, especially in a match of such description as this, so likely to provoke family jealousy.

The old castle was left to the son Andreas on condition that he would preserve the armor, books, manuscripts, works of art and *vertu*. On the death of the son the castle became the pleasure-seat of the royal family, was afterwards used as a barrack, but in 1842 was cleared out, renovated, and repaired.

It is but a short ride from the town, the last portion of the way being an ascent of the eminence upon which it stands. Schloss Ambras has anything but the appearance of a castle, lacking its round towers, turrets, and battlements, though the wall towards the valley has something of a fort-like appearance; but the building looks more like a big whitewashed factory, nunnery, or barracks, than a mediæval castle of the thirteenth century. The surroundings and walks, however, are very pretty, and the view from it grand, beautiful, and extensive. The whole valley of the river Inn, with its grand background of lofty mountains, is taken in at one sweep of the eye. The towns of Innspruck and Hall, and various little white villages here and there dotting the beautiful landscape, winding roads, and glittering river, — all form a charming picture. The castle is a great rambling mansion, with but little to interest the visitor. An ornamented cabinet and writing-desk, said to have been that used by Philippina, some curious old specimens of wood carving, a few specimens of arms and armor, and some old paintings, are shown. The collection of ancient armor that was formerly preserved here, consisting of suits owned and worn by various noble personages, kings, warriors, and knights, and authenticated beyond a doubt, was, to preserve it, removed to Vienna, where it is known as the Ambras Collection, and fills three large halls, being one of the most interesting collections of memorials of ancient chivalry and historical mementos of the manners of the middle ages in existence.

The chief interest in the old Schloss seems to be that it was the residence of this Philippina Welser, who, besides being a beautiful woman, was a model of domestic virtues, and as such was so endeared to the popular mind, that to this day her picture adorns many a peasant's cottage, and her story is one of the popular traditions of the Tyrol.

Returning home, we rode over a bridge spanning the Sill, which is a quiet little river in comparison with the Inn, a roaring, rushing stream, flowing with tremendous force, and fairly making the strong wooden bridge, built only for foot passengers, quiver, as we stood upon it one evening, enjoying the beautiful views up and down the river, and looking at the strollers on the banks. The *Hofgarten*, which is a sort of small *Champs Elysées*, and begins at one side of the royal palace, an uninteresting building, runs down to the banks of the river at this point, near the wooden bridge. Further down the river is a more substantial and modern chain-bridge, with massive stone structures for supports at each end.

Not far from the old bridge is the scene of one of the severest actions of the Tyrolean peasantry, under the command of Hofer, in their war for independence against the Bavarians and French. In and about Innspruck are the scenes of Hofer's memorable struggles; and carvings in wood, portraits, pictures, busts, and engravings of him are plentiful in the shops. The treaty of Pressburg in 1805 gave Tyrol to Bavaria, the allied troops under Marshal Ney poured in, the fortresses on the Bavarian frontier were destroyed, and Innspruck occupied. Early in 1806 Ney left, and the town was delivered over to the Bavarian government. The Bavarians appear not to have had the least idea of the characteristics of the inhabitants, for they made most obnoxious and unpopular laws, conflicting with the people's customs and religious belief, and in many ways made the yoke of their government excessively galling.

At last Hofer and Spechbacher, in April, 1809, drove out the Bavarians and beat back invading forces of superior numbers several times with great bravery. The achievements of these patriots were nullified by the Peace of Schönbrun, concluded October 25, of the same year; but the people, although desired by their sovereign, the emperor of Austria, to cease operations, could hardly be brought to believe that he really desired them to yield, but thought that he was forced to send them instructions by Napoleon, and so warfare was kept up by them in their mountain fastnesses. At last the French, by offering a large reward, succeeded through treachery in capturing Hofer, and after a brief trial he was condemned to be shot, and the sentence was executed in Mantua, the brave Tyrolean meeting his fate with the most undaunted courage, refusing to have his eyes bandaged, and himself giving orders to the soldiers to fire upon him as he stood before their levelled muskets on the 20th of February, 1810, and fell at the age of forty-five years.

The Museum is planned with a design of exhibiting the productions, manufactures, mineral and vegetable products of the Tyrol, as well as specimens of its literature, natural history, and fine arts. It is really a strictly national exhibition, and as such is interesting to tourists who will spare the time to visit it.

Upon the lower floor were minerals, marbles, and various ores found in the mountains, and we saw among the latter some fine specimens of gold and quicksilver. Splendid specimens of marble, porphyry, malachite, and curious minerals, were also displayed here. But a treat to the botanist was the beautiful herbarium, which contained a complete collection of the rich flora of the country, and all the varieties of the graceful, delicate, and beautiful flowers and blossoms which in spring and summer enchant the traveller with their beauty, or interest him in their curious forms and hues, as he journeys over the mountain passes. Among the exhibits of products and manufactures were beautiful specimens of salt from the salt mines of Hall, and models of machinery used at the mines, also silk and worsted work, and a variety of the wonderful wood carving from a part of the Tyrol called Grodnerthal, where this art is carried to a great degree of perfection. Some of the figures excel statuettes in detail and effectiveness of execution.

The reproductions in wood carving of the bronze figures of King Arthur and Theodoric, which stand in the Franciscan Church, are done with great fidelity, and command a good price in the shops from strangers as curiosities. I have before me, as I write, the figure of King Arthur, cut from some ordinary wood of the country (said to be apple-tree wood). Although but ten inches in height, it is in excellent proportion, a knight in full armor, outer armor, under-shirt of chain mail, with the links perfectly wrought, sword and sword-belt, gauntlets, helmet with movable visor, and collar of an order of knighthood, all elaborately carved.

Another curiosity seen only here in Innspruck are paintings upon spiders' webs. These webs are nearly the size one sees spangled with raindrops in the grass on a cloudy morning, where they look vastly prettier: by some process the webs are made to receive delicate colors, and by the combination of web and painting to present effective landscapes and even portraits of Philippina Welser, Hofer, and various saints, without injuring the fragile canvas. The web may be of some extraordinary species of spider, or, more probably, prepared in some peculiar manner, for the artist, for the process of the production of these pictures is said to be a secret in the possession of one family, who have held it for several generations. Among the manufactured articles were specimens of cutlery, iron-ware, and tools — some rather curious and clumsy-looking ones — that come from a portion of the country where the inhabitants are nearly all blacksmiths and tool-makers.

In the library, they have, among other literary treasures, several fine illuminated manuscripts from the patient fingers of the old Carthusian and Dominican Monks of three or four hundred years ago, and some early works struck off from one of the early printing-presses, which was brought from Schwatz, another Tyrolean town, and set up in Innspruck in 1529. They also have here a letter written by Lord Bathurst, which he sent with thirty thousand pounds from the British government to Hofer and his patriotic countrymen to assist them in their efforts against the French; but all too late, as it did not reach its destination until the struggle was entirely over.

Among the more modern manuscripts the old custodian showed us, with some degree of pride, an extract from

Longfellow's poem of "Excelsior," with the poet's autograph attached, and further informed us that he had, when the poet visited the Museum, a discussion with him as to the proper use of the word, he, the custodian, contending that the word as used by the poet was an adjective, whereas it should have been used as an adverb, and been "Excelsius." Mr. Longfellow, he informed us, admitted in some respects the justice of his criticism. One may readily imagine that, when a poet's works have so wide a reputation that he finds extracts from them repeated by heart among the Tyrolean mountains, or, as they are, inscribed in Chinese characters upon the door-posts, in the Celestial Empire, while his lyre is still in tune, he may feel gratified enough to bow to criticism and critics like this with unruffled composure.

The relics of the brave Hofer, which all visitors look upon with interest, are a letter written by him shortly before his death, his rifle, his braces and belt, and a medal that he wore around his neck when he was shot. The custodian was eloquent over his patriotic countryman, whom all accounts agree in recording as a man of rigid honesty, truthfulness, and humanity, and his brief career of command as being unstained by a single dishonorable act, or unworthy deed.

The Franciscan Church, or *Hofkirche* (hoafkeercha), as they call it here, signifying the court church, a building not at all remarkable for architectural beauty, was begun in 1543, and consecrated in 1563, and is, with its contents, the chief and great attraction to tourists. Indeed, the great tomb of Maximilian I. in this church is one of the most magnificent and elaborate monuments in Europe, and the twenty-eight colossal bronze statues that adorn the aisles are curious and wonderful specimens of art.

But we will first turn our attention to the Tomb and Monument of Hofer, which is directly at the visitor's left on entering the church. It consists of a square sarcophagus surmounted by his full-length marble statue, which was cut from Tyrolese white marble by a Tyrolean sculptor. He is represented in Tyrolean uniform, has the broad belt, short breeches, long boots, and frock; one hand grasps the end of the carbine swung at his back, as though about to bring it forward, and the other holds the staff of an unfurled flag, while his Tyrolean hat is thrown down upon the bank at his side. Upon the front of the sarcophagus is a bas-relief representing the Tyrolean patriots surrounded by their countrymen swearing fealty to their flag. The pedestal bears the inscription in Latin, signifying "Death is swallowed up in victory;" and one in German, which translated is, —

"The grateful Fatherland to its sons fallen in the struggle for freedom."

The great cenotaph of the Emperor Maximilian I. occupies the principal portion of the nave of the church. It is a monument thirteen feet long, six feet in height, and seven in width, composed of different-colored, highly polished marbles, and supported on three red marble steps. Upon the top of the monument is a colossal kneeling statue in bronze of the emperor in full costume, and quite elaborate as a work of that description; but the great wonder of the monument is its sides and ends, which are divided into twenty-four different compartments of fine white Carrara marble tablets, upon which are executed as many different scenes in the emperor's life in bas-relief of wonderful execution. The amount of labor, artistic skill, and patience that must have been betowed upon these pictures in marble (for they can hardly be called sculptures), is astonishing.

They represent sieges, processions, treaties, battles, marriages, and assemblages; and in each tablet, although it is filled with figures, all the details of costume, grouping, architecture, &c., in the scene are given with astonishing distinctness, and approaching in minuteness that of a cameo cutting. Being faithful representations of the architecture, manners, and costumes of the period, they are of high historic value.

The monument itself is surrounded by an iron railing, through which you can look at these wonderful carvings, but the silver key unlocked this for us, and we enjoyed several long and close inspections of this marble lace work, and furthermore the advantage of seeing it just after it had been thoroughly cleansed — a long and laborious work, only performed at intervals of many years. The tablets were therefore fresh and white as if just from the hands of the sculptor, and, though each is but about twice the size of a sheet of letter-paper, they presented as graphic a story in stone as could well be rendered by sculptor's chisel.

Among the most interesting was a representation of Maximilian entering the city of Vienna in 1490, in which he is represented in the foreground, surrounded and followed by a crowd of knights, courtiers, and men-at-arms, both on foot and on horseback. I counted twenty-eight figures in the foreground, all of course of Lilliputian size, but with helmets, weapons, armor, and even features faithfully cut and finished in detail, many of the heads being portraits. In the background was seen the city with its fortifications, steeples, and conspicuous buildings, and the long line of victorious troops entering it.

When it is considered that there are faithfully rendered upon these small figures such details as the ornaments upon the emperor's helmet, the tassels of the horses' ornamented bridle-reins, the ribbons at the courtiers' knees, chain-links in the armor, spurs at the heel, and even hairs of the head and beard, the reader may imagine with what minute accuracy they are given, and that to be enjoyed they should have long and careful examination. I will not say how long a time I spent kneeling upon the steps of the emperor's tomb, looking at these wondrous tablets; but suggest to those who visit it to do as I did, go more than once, and at hours when but few visitors are likely to be present, satisfy the custodian, which can be done by a moderate fee, and then inside the grating you may look them over at your leisure.

I have never seen anything in bas-relief that equals the superb pictures carved on this splendid mausoleum, and description is utterly inadequate to give the reader a proper idea of their excellence and beauty. I ought to have mentioned that the artist has in the battle-scenes represented the arms and costumes of the different nations correctly, and in his representations of Maximilian, who figures in each tablet, preserves the emperor's likeness throughout, differing only in age. For instance, in the scene representing the marriage of the prince when but eighteen years of age, in 1477, he will be found presented youthful as he was, but may be recognized in some of the other scenes as the same person come to man's estate. Another instance of the minuteness of detail before mentioned in these carvings, may be seen in that representing the prince's marriage, where the pictures are represented in bas-relief hanging on the walls of the apartment in which the ceremony was performed.

These sculptures were begun in 1561 by two brothers, Arnold and Bernhard Abel of Cologne, who both died two years afterwards, having completed but three tablets. The work was then taken up by a sculptor named Alexander Colin of Mechlin, aided by a great number of assistant artists, and was completed in 1567.

Each side of the church, up and down its aisle, upon their pedestals between the red marble columns of the church, stand twenty-eight colossal bronze figures of emperors, kings, princes, empresses, and other notable historical characters of Europe, three centuries ago, admirably modelled, faithfully executed with all the details of armor and dress that belonged to the period in which they flourished. This company of giants of the past, having assembled as it were to do homage at the emperor's tomb, cannot fail to impress the visitor with a certain feeling of awe as in the twilight of afternoon he sees them standing motionless and silent, keeping watch and ward by the tomb of "the last of the knights," as Maximilian is sometimes called.

These figures are each eight feet in height, and valuable, many of them, as being correct representations of the costumes of the sixteenth century. The coronation robes with embroidery, figures upon the vestments, the dress, accoutrements, arms and armor, drapery, and trimmings of both male and female figures, are marvellously well executed, and combine to render them some of the most remarkable works of their age.

Another thing that was gratifying to me, as a curious and prying American, was the freedom with which we were permitted to examine these remarkable figures. Perhaps it was because they were too heavy to be carried off, and too hard to have fragments broken from them by vandal hands, but the privilege of closely examining and freely handling them was permitted without restriction; so that we took hold of and admired the figured robe, unbending to the touch, but richly ornamented as from the loom, of Mary of Burgundy, the emperor's first wife; examined the curiously wrought overcloak and under-robe, in rich embroidery of Frederick I., Maximilian's father, who reigned from 1415 to 1495, or the clumsy figure of the Duke of Burgundy, an ancient ancestor of the emperor (640), a thick-set individual with clenched fist and arm in thick fluted armor, as if about to strike a body blow in a sparring match, and who, not content with shirt of mail beneath, wears heavy armor over it like a great surtout, and is crowned with a helmet heavy enough to weigh down a giant.

The two figures thought to be the best, and which are the most frequently reproduced in wood-carvings of various sizes by the Tyrolean wood carvers, are those of Theodoric, king of the Ostrogoths from 455 to 526, and King Arthur of England. That of Theodoric represents him in good-fitting undershirt of chain mail, with flexible sleeves and gauntlets, and a short surcoat of mail over it; his gorget and hood, of chain-mail, is crowned by a curious helmet, looking very like a grocer's tin flour-scoop with the handle upwards. He is leaning with his right hand upon a pole-axe, and his left rests upon his two-handled sword, hip-high, as he stands looking downward as in deep thought.

To my mind, by far the finest figure in the whole collection, and one which excels in gracefulness of pose, excellence of proportion, and spiritedness of attitude, is that of King Arthur of England. It is the very *beau-ideal* of the brave knight of ancient legend and romantic ballad, elegant and graceful in proportion, and richly clad in well-fitting armor, that sets off his athletic figure to advantage. The light undershirt of chain-mail, lower limbs in plate armor, a close-fitting surcoat richly ornamented with the dragon of St. George, and a collar of the order about the neck; head covered with a graceful helmet, a light coronet encircling its crest, and beneath the movable visor, when raised, the determined features of a brave man looking forth. The attitude of the figure is very graceful and spirited, the right foot firmly planted, the left leg slightly bent, the left arm akimbo as the left hand grasps the scabbard of the sword that hangs at his hip, the right hand half unclosed appearing as if just starting in action to draw the sword to combat with a defying enemy. The attitude of the figure is that of a knight just on the point of seeking his sword-hilt in answer to a challenge, and its admirable pose is in marked contrast with the stiffness of most of the others that surround it. The visor, or beaver, of the helmet is movable, and may be raised by the visitor exposing the bronze features, or left down with its crossed bars concealing them.

The names of these worthies in bronze are all recorded in the guide-books, so I will not enumerate them here, save to mention that among them, besides those mentioned, are old King Clovis, Godfrey de Bouillon the Crusader, and Charles the Bold, of Burgundy. There are twenty-three other bronze figures of small size, originally intended to adorn the tomb of Maximilian, that are kept in an apartment adjoining the church, gained by a short staircase, and called the Silver Chapel from the fact that it contains a statue of the Virgin, and an elaborate altar-piece of elegant bas-reliefs in solid silver. These figures are those of individuals connected with the house of Hapsburg, and distinguished for the sanctity of their lives or deeds, and probably each for that reason having the title of saint prefixed to his name.

The Silver Chapel was built by Ferdinand II., Archduke of Austria and Count of Tyrol, to satisfy the devotion of his wife, the beautiful Philippina Welser, before mentioned in these sketches, to the doctrine of the Immaculate Conception. In this chapel she used to offer up her devotions, and after her death, in 1580, it was made the place for her mausoleum, which is an altar-shaped tomb, with her recumbent effigy upon it in marble, a figure of great beauty, above which is seen the Angel of Death extinguishing his torch. The upright slab in front of the tomb is divided into three sections, and upon each side are allegorical figures, representing works of charity and mercy, and in the background Innspruck as it was in her day. The middle section contains an inscription recording the gentle lady's piety and good deeds. Ferdinand's monument is in the form of an arch, twelve feet high, and nine feet in width. It is of white and black marble, and near that of his fair wife. Upon it rests his marble effigy with upraised hands, and around the arch are emblazoned shields bearing the arms of the different branches of his house. Upon it are four elegant bas-reliefs in white marble, similar in character to those on the tomb of Maximilian. They are all executed by the same artist, Colin of Mechlin, and represent remarkable events in Ferdinand's life.

I have given so much attention to the Hofkirche that I shall not fatigue the reader with especial descriptions of the others, which contain but little of interest, comparatively speaking, after one has visited this. The church and monastery of the Order of Servites, at the end of the Neustadt, contains some good pictures by native artists, and fine frescos in the roofing; and there is another church known as the *Dreiheiligkeitskirche*, — think of that for a word of learned length and thundering sound, which, translated, signifies "Holy Trinity Church," — an edifice built by the burghers of Innspruck for the Jesuits, in 1611, as a token of gratitude for the staying of the ravages of a terrible epidemic, in which is an altar-piece representing the three — let the reader take breath for another long name — *Pest-Schutzheiligen* — "patron saints against pestilence." This church is of the best architectual design of any in Innspruck, and from the balcony around the lantern of its cupola, which is two hundred and fifteen feet from the ground, the spectator may enjoy a fine view of the whole valley of the river Inn.

Then there is the *Pfarrkirche*, containing much beautiful marble work of the marbles of the country, with which it is lavishly decorated, and frescos in the roof representing deeds in the life of St. James, who appears mounted on horseback; and here is told a new version of the familiar story of the artist, who, as he was engaged on his lofty platform in the cupola, putting the finishing touches to the saint, walked backwards to observe the effect of his work, and, as he reached the edge, instead of a friend daubing his picture and causing him to rush forward from the brink and the danger of a fall, the saint in the picture stretched out his arm, and with his strong grasp seized, held, and saved the artist from being dashed down upon the pavement far below — a case of gratitude on the part of an artistic production that will be thought remarkable, to say the least.

Innspruck, which is the capital of the Austrian Tyrol, has a most interesting history, and has been the scene of many notable royal receptions, marriages, fêtes, and visits, and also some severe contests in and about its immediate vicinity. It is a pleasant and agreeable place for a week or two of rest for the tourist, especially in the months of June and July, the hotel accommodations being good, the town quiet and clean, and the rides in the vicinity romantic and pleasant.

CHAPTER XV.

FROM Innspruck to St. Moritz, in the upper Engadine, they manage to make about a three days' journey by posting, and this mode of travel is the most interesting and agreeable method of going from point to point in the Tyrol. All the romance and charm, the adventure, and most of the novelty, are lost when the railroad tunnel is used instead of the mountain zigzag, as I found on my second passage of the celebrated Mount Cenis, where a whole day's charming sight-seeing, of invigorating atmosphere, and glorious mountain views was exchanged for an hour's dark transit in a close railway carriage.

However, in the trip we were now about to take, post-carriages were the only conveyances. As these carriages can easily carry four persons, and as there were but two of us to go, I waited, and sought in the opposite hotel, "The Golden Sun," for companions to share the carriage and the expense of the trip; but there were none there, and, at our own, two Americans and two English people went off in an opposite direction, while another English party, gentleman and wife, attended by their servant, although sitting near us at dinner, passing us daily in the hotel, and at places of interest in the town for more than a week since their arrival, had, with true British reserve, never addressed a word to us. Never been introduced, you see. Of course, one couldn't have the audacity to address them proposing travelling companionship! We asked the landlords to inform us of any traveller or travellers desiring to make the trip, but as usual they heard of no one.

I found a jolly young Tyrolese, however, whom I had seen lounging round the stables, and contrived to learn from him that he wanted to get to the very next town I desired to reach. His post-chaise was a fine one, and his dapple grays sound and strong, his price some eight dollars less than mine hosts had indicated; so I waited no longer, but closed with him, and ordered the landlord to fill out a written contract for the same for him to sign, in which was expressed the time to be occupied, the stops to be made and where. I was somewhat startled when the post-driver came to sign his name — Franz Hell; but his name was far from being indicative of his character.

The British guest I observed at breakfast, on the morning of our departure, making the most ample preparations of cold fowl, sandwiches, and cold meat packed in a tin box, and overheard him observe that they must "provide against these beastly Tyrolean inns after leaving h'yar," — a warning I took heed of myself; and, having in mind former experience of acid wines, sour bread, and bad water, added some sandwiches and two or three bottles of claret to my own provision for the journey.

Our carriage stood opposite the hotel, and the horses rattled their harness trappings, anxious to start, as we descended the staircase, and found our Englishman telling the landlord that it was an hour too early.

"But this *voiture* is for Monsieur," said the host, indicating myself.

"O, ah! beg pardon; but the fellow said it was a carriage going to St. Moritz."

"And I *am* going to St. Moritz," said I.

"Really! Most extraordinary thing! I've engaged carriage for same route half an hour later."

"Monsieur's carriage will be ready in half an hour," said the landlord, bowing. Wily host; he had kept the fact that both guests were going over the same route from each, and ourselves for a day or two looking for companions till at last each took separate conveyances.

However, it is doubtful if the Englishman would have joined us; but, as he found we were to precede him on the road, he politely requested us to order rooms for him after we had selected our own, and was, as all well-educated English gentlemen are, a most agreeable and courteous travelling companion and friend after the outer crust of reserve had been fairly broken.

We left our clean and comfortable hotel, passed over the bridge above the rushing and roaring river Inn, and once more were on the full trot on the post-road on a fine summer's morning. Away we rattle along past the shooting-ground, and leave the river at our left, but the valley and ravine gradually narrow, and, after a ride of half a dozen miles or so, we are pressed back towards the river again by the rising precipices, until at last the great perpendicular *Martinswand*, as it is called, pushes the road to the very bank.

This Martinswand is one of the celebrities of the country. It signifies "Martin's Wall," and is an almost perpendicular precipice eighteen hundred and thirty feet above the road, on which we stand to look at a sort of cave or crevice in it, which is over seven hundred feet above our heads.

We can see a crucifix that is set up there opposite the hole in the wall, and the story is that the Emperor Maximilian, trying to descend, found himself at a point where he could neither advance nor retreat. He succeeded, however, in reaching this hole, or chasm. Here he clung between heaven and earth, as it were, and after a long time was able to make known to his people where he was, by writing on his tablet, which he bound to a stone with his gold chain and threw down to those on the road below.

All, of course, was dismay and confusion. The priest

was sent for from the neighboring town of Zirl, who was to come and offer prayers for succor, or implore aid of the Virgin, or something of the kind. But, while the ecclesiastic was getting on his vestments and arranging the necessary paraphernalia, an effort of a more practical nature was in progress. A party of miners had assembled with ropes at the top of the cliff, but they were almost as hopeless as the spectators at the base, for the monarch was over a thousand feet below them. But one of their number, stouter and bolder than the rest, contrived to reach him, and bore him up after he had been in his perilous plight fifty-two hours.

The emperor was duly grateful. He caused the crevice that had sheltered him to be enlarged to a cell, and the miners to cut a path down to it for the use of those who should desire to make pious pilgrimages to the place, which is called the *Max-Höhle*, and a pension was settled upon his rescuer, Oswald Zips, of Zirl, which is said to be drawn by his descendants to this day. This incident in the emperor's life is said to have occurred on Easter Monday and the following day, in 1490, and is celebrated in Tyrolean ballard and story.

The following is the somewhat literal translation of an extract from a popular ballad describing the king's dangerous position.

>Here helped no spring,
>No eagle-swing,
>For under him lay the Martinswand,
>The steepest rock in all the land.
>
>A sound as of thunder roared at his feet,
>Where a tumult of men surged below him so deep,
>Above them all his Highness stands —
>But not raised in homage over the lands.
>
>On an airy throne
>Max is left alone.
>Forsaken and small, he shuddering thinks
>How to an object of pity he shrinks.

We took our noon rest at Telfs, and then pushed on over a beautiful drive of alternate ascent and descent until we reached Imst, our stopping-place for the first night, a pretty Tyrolean town of two or three thousand inhabitants, but where we found at the tolerably comfortable inn that Tyrolean-German was trumps and French at a discount; but, thanks to the perfect knowledge of the former tongue by the wife of our English *compagnon de voyage*, as we now felt we might call him, our wants were made intelligible.

From Imst we start off again over our romantic road, passing now and then crosses with rudely executed figures of the crucifixion by the roadside; some of them mere horrible caricatures, or shrines with the Virgin and child, at which little offerings of flowers or tinsel ornaments had been made. We reach Prutz, a little village in a flat, open space, and which I chiefly remember for its bad inn and insufficient lunch, which we were obliged to eke out from the supplies brought with us from Innspruck. We rattled away from here with good will, following the course of the river Inn, and now having those glorious views of mountains, distant and near, that are the charm of Alpine journeys. After passing through the little village Pfunds, and viewing the afternoon sun sparkling upon the snow-caps of the distant Œtzthal Mountains, and clattering over a wooden bridge beneath which the Inn rushes with all the force of an Alpine torrent that it is, we begin the grand ascent of the Finstermünz Pass.

This is another one of those splendid specimens of engineering and road-building that excites the traveller's admiration. The road is cut through solid rock, high above the back of the river; great tunnels pierced through the rock and zigzags carry you up, up, while the roaring torrent rushes below, or you pass between narrow walls of dark crags rising high on either side to emerge and catch delightful views of the valley, as your carriage winds slowly up the ascent over the smooth, well-built road, the driver on foot cheering his team and singing a Tyrolean song ; his peaked hat decorated, as I notice is a fashion of the Tyrolese, and one which travellers readily fall into, with a sprig of *Alpenrosen* or mountain wild-flowers.

Great gorges of wild, jagged rocks are in every variety of picturesque confusion ; waterfalls leaping from the mountain side rush madly down to swell the river below ; great slaty crags, inky as darkness itself, jut out black and terrible, and distant views of green hillsides, with the slanting afternoon sun resting upon them, and at the same time touching the patches of snow on the distant peaks, — all form one of those charming Alpine pictures that are long embalmed in the memories of those that have looked upon them.

Up we go through this cleft in the mountains, and halt, on the Fourth of July, for our late dinner and second night's rest, upon a rocky *plateau* six hundred feet above the river, at an inn known as the Inn of the Hoch Finstermünz, a well-built, well-furnished, and pretty little inn ; but at the time of our visit, under a financial cloud, owing to questionable transactions of a former landlord, who had absconded. The inn was now thrown open to catch what customers it might, and would accommodate but a dozen or so guests at most.

On this particular occasion, it being the national anniversary of our country, we commenced celebrating by a patriotic entry upon the travellers' register. The two best suites of rooms were secured for ourselves and our English friends, we four being the only guests that day in the house ; they consisted of two tolerably sized sleeping-apartments, both opening into a small dining-room, the windows of which commanded a superb view of the wild, romantic gorge and valley beneath, and a portion of the narrow string-like line of road we were to ride over on the morrow.

What would we have for dinner ?

" Everything — the best in the house."

They had " chops, potatoes, bread, tea, eggs, milk; Monsieur should have all."

So the dinner was ordered, and our English friend's carriage, but a short distance behind us, rolled up to the door while it was in preparation.

We both retired to cleanse ourselves from the stains and dust of travel, and finally, at the host's summons, gathered at the festive board. And such a dinner! I have endured a great many at public celebrations in my own country where the venerable fowls, saw-dusty Washington pie, and cinnamon-flavored ice-cream made one dread "the day we celebrate," but they must yield the palm to this banquet, three thousand feet above the sea-level. The chops, so called, might as well have been sole-leather, as far as any impression could be made upon them; the fried potatoes were saturated with garlic-flavored fat, the bread dark, hard, and sour, the tea vile. The banquet was sent to the postilions; and a dozen boiled eggs ordered, — they could get no grease or garlic inside their shells. The last of the Englishman's lunch stores were paraded, and my own last bottle of claret; the reader may be assured that no fragments were left of that feast.

At the dessert of dry biscuit and oranges, the American gave the first regular toast of the occasion, "The Queen." This was drank standing by the entire company. The next regular toast, "The President of the United States," was given by the Englishman, and received in like manner. The American then (as all Americans do) made a speech suitable to the occasion, which was frequently interrupted by applause and cries of "hear," "hear" from the English portion of the audience, and concluded with the strikingly original toast of "The Day we Celebrate," to which was added, "Peace and Fraternity between Great Britain and the United States." After the applause had subsided, the representative of Great Britain rose, and was received with great enthusiasm, especially as he announced that his servant had discovered in his travelling hamper a can of condensed coffee and a box of sardines. The speech that followed contained the most cordial expressions towards the United States, and concluded with the sentiment, "The Independent United States, may they endure as long as civilized man walks the face of the earth."

Other patriotic speeches were made, and the national songs of both countries given, and the company separated at an early hour, half past eight. Owing to the general fatigue of all parties concerned, further celebration was dispensed with, and it was found on retiring that, though the viands were bad, the beds were not, and a refreshing night's rest was enjoyed in the pure, cool atmosphere and quiet of this mountain region.

The sun rises early when you lodge high up in the mountains, and it is a grand sight to see him rise, sending the wreaths of mist whirling up hillsides and ravines, his rays sparkling upon the edges of ragged cliffs ere he mounts above their rocky screens, and at last shooting his gleaming arrows of light right down into the dark gorge, and turning the spray of the mountain torrent into diamond dust. The morning air is cool and sharp, though it is July, as we walk out from the hotel and look from the little rocky platform upon which it stands far down into the deep ravine beneath us. Five or six hundred feet below where we stood, ran our old friend the river Inn, forcing his way through the narrow cleft in the mountains; across the stream was a little wooden bridge, with a stone tower on the opposite side, and on the side towards us was a little group of three houses, a little church, and a mill. Along the banks of the river we could trace the windings of the old road, and from our hotel-door, stretching to the left, the new one.

We were agreeably surprised in the morning by an improved bill of fare at breakfast, the parties in charge of the house and the Englishman's postilion having been on a foraging excursion during the night. An improvement in the way of fresh milk, eggs, and sweeter bread, was welcomed with sharpened appetites.

Once more we were off. The road was now a succession of engineering wonders — beautiful views and grand mountain scenery that I have so frequently described. Tunnels ran through solid rock, and zigzags along the edges of precipices; profound gorges fall away deep, dark, and cavernous, and the trees beneath are diminished into shrubs by the distance, while the rough aspect of the rocks becomes softened from the same cause into picturesque groupings. The narrow defiles and road cut out from the edge of the rock, tunnels, and avalanche galleries, and the frequency of the dark, slate-like rocks, reminds one of the Via Mala Pass.

Coming through the Tyrol, one cannot help noticing what a love the people have for plants. In houses a little better than hovels, where the women were barefooted, and the children's faces seemed not to have been on visiting acquaintance with soap and water for a fortnight, a neat little shelf would be seen placed at the window, which would be filled with several varieties of geraniums, double clove-pinks, and other plants that must have been rare in this locality, while in the better class of houses the little garden would be tastefully arranged, and cloth-of-gold roses, rose peonies, and damask roses bloomed in profusion.

Our ride, after leaving the Finstermünz Inn, carried us past a beautiful waterfall, and soon after we came to the fortifications that guarded the entrance into Switzerland. The narrow road was spanned, or rather commanded, by a stone fort as solid as if hewn out of its rocky walls — as a portion of it is. The grim cannon pointed down directly at us, and indeed it seems as if a single discharge would have swept every square inch of the road as we mounted towards their muzzles, and passed through the guarded gateway from Tyrol into Switzerland. A sharp turn, a ride across a comparatively flat piece of country, and then we begin a descent of zigzags till we reach Martinsbruck, where we halt for rest.

As the traveller advances into the upper Engadine valley,

he cannot but be struck by the marked improvement in the appearance of the people the moment the Protestant and Romansch succeed the Roman Catholic villages. The rude crosses and roadside shrines in glaring colors, the ragged people and the beggars, are succeeded by a thriftier, better clad, and more intelligent-looking community. The difference and the change after passing from the boundary of the Tyrol will be noted at almost every village the traveller passes.

We go through Strada, with its little stone houses, with deep-set windows, and finally reach a place called Remus, where a bridge of sixty-six feet span leaps a tremendous gorge, at the bottom of which roars in feathery foam a rushing torrent, and round and about is every variety of wild and picturesque scenery, including the remains of an old feudal castle perched high above us in its rocky eyrie. We halted here, and as usual did homage to nature in our admiration of " cloud-capped towers," rugged crags, and light and shade of sunrays and shadow that made portions of the view look like a great picture, as indeed it was, and none but God can paint such.

On through Schuls, a lively little village with very neat-looking houses; round and about it there seemed to be some cultivated patches, looking green and flourishing on the hillside in the afternoon sun, with the men and women busy at work in them ; and now we are driving down into a sort of sheltered valley which really has quite a home-like appearance, for all along the hillsides rise veritable boarding-houses, very like our own American ones, or summer hotels at popular resorts. We meet people out riding on horseback or in carriages in charming Parisian-got-up costumes for a watering place ; cultivated fields, well-kept gardens gay with flowers, a pretty bridge spanning the river, and a large, well-built, modern hotel, with beautifully laid-out grounds, as our driver starts up his horses into a brisk trot ; and, with the usual flourish and fusillade of whip-snapping, brings us up at the entrance of the *Kurhaus*, or hotel at Tarasp, where we are to pass the second night of our journey.

This hotel was indeed a charming contrast with the one of the evening previous. It has been established at this point, on the banks of the river, near a mineral spring which is said to possess certain medicinal virtues; and arriving as we did in the height of the season, when several hundred guests were present, we were fortunate in obtaining excellent rooms for the night. The scenery is charming about here, the hotel, at the time we visited it, excellently kept, except, if it be an exception, on calling for butter at the great *table d'hôte* at tea, we were told that it was not permitted, this being a Kurhaus for parties being treated for their health. Three kinds of preserved fruit, excellent bread and honey, and cold meat, were allowed, and I don't know how many other good things, but butter and pastry were forbidden, and could not be bribed or begged from the servants.

We left the elegant hotel of the Tarasp Springs behind us as we proceeded on our journey, a charming drive, with beautiful Alpine scenery all about us, and the rushing river Inn still our companion. We soon note a better class of people and a better class of buildings in the villages, and also a different kind of language from what we have encountered before, for we are passing through the country of the descendants of the Romans, who fled here 587 B. C. to escape from the Gauls, and who were the first inhabitants of the Engadine Valley, their language, the Romansch, a queer sort of dialect. The beggars, squalid huts, and numerous praying stations and roadside crucifixes are left behind, and at each village, beside the chalets of the poorer class, are generally some two or three big (for these latitudes) Swiss houses, strongly built of stone, somewhat after the pattern of their humbler neighbors, but with pretentious entrance, large garden brilliant with flowers, and inner balcony of carved wood brightly painted; cleanliness, whitewash, and paint, their summer dress, making them conspicuous.

These are mainly residences of those who have returned to their native villages with small fortunes made as keepers of hotels, pastry cooks, waiters, confectioners, glass-blowers, and followers of other occupations in the continental cities, the Engadine Valley being noted for the number that it sends out that take up with these occupations, and who possess so strong a love for their native villages, notwithstanding the inhospitality of the climate, which gives scarcely more than three months of mild weather, that they return thither to enjoy their prosperity.

Twisting in and out the mountain roads, we pass the village of Ardetz, which is said to have been founded by the ancient Etruscans. The valley here is picturesque and beautiful, with its green slope down to the river veined with sparkling streams gliding down its side, while upon the heights, here and there, are the shattered walls or solitary tower of ruined old castles. High above pleasant green slopes on one side of the valley, rise snow-capped mountains, and dark, sombre forests clothe the heights of the other. We reach the little village of Lavin, a place that had recently suffered from a fire, but a Protestant and apparently thrifty place, which leaving behind we again meet the river Inn, have a beautiful drive through a pine-clad valley, and enter Zernetz, which presented a melancholy spectacle indeed, the whole village, with the exception of the church and two houses, being in ruins, having been destroyed by fire a few months previous, — a severe blow to the inhabitants, and exciting the liveliest sympathy in their behalf, contributions for them being taken up in England. The church, which was fortunately preserved, was built in 1623.

We rode through the silent and deserted little streets of shattered stone houses blackened with fire, and were stared at curiously by the inhabitants of the only two remaining ones as we passed them, and pushed on till we reached Samaden, the wealthiest town in the district; and here many of the retired innkeepers and pastry cooks before mentioned have built their pretty chalets. The street is well laid out; there are a banker, post-office, and telegraph office, and two large hotels. The Bernina Hof was a large and splendid house, filled with two or three hundred guests. It was kept as well as our great mountain and seaside resorts. Its balconies, upon which sat ladies and gentlemen at little tables, sipping their coffee after dinner, command a magnificent panorama, the Berniner Alps, their cold glaciers and sparkling snow-peaks soaring away up into the blue sky beyond the patch of green valley that lies between. All around Samaden is beautiful scenery and pleasant drives. Many of the houses about here have inscriptions in a curious mixture of Romansch and French upon them, generally brief extracts from Scripture. I copied one from a little church in a village between Samaden and St. Moritz, which read, "A DIEU SULET GLORIA ED ONUR," signifying, doubtless, To God alone is Glory and Praise.

The little *einspänner* — a calash or chaise — carrying two beside the driver, who is perched on in front, will carry you to Pontresina, St. Moritz, and other villages in the neighborhood, and to numerous romantic spots and stretches of scenery, while all around the vicinity in the summer season of the year the fields and hillsides are rich in the bright and curious flora of the Alps, affording a most interesting study for the botanist.

While our horses were resting here at Samaden, we enjoyed the unexpected pleasure of an interview with the Danish author, Hans Christian Andersen. The good-natured fairy story-teller, who was then sojourning at the hotel, on hearing that two Americans that had read his books would like to see him, came to us with extended hands of welcome, though just returned from a fatiguing excursion to the Morteratsch glacier. He had but recently returned from Italy, where he had been for his health, and had been staying here for a week's rest ere returning to Copenhagen. He was tall, thin, even attenuated in figure, his head small, but forehead high, which was the only point of beauty in his face, his nose being large and prominent, cheek-bones very distinct, and his gray eyes small, but they sparkled with a pleasant smile which wreathed his lips; and his simple manner pleased as a child to be praised, and his gentle tones made it easy to see why he was personally so prime a favorite with young people. He was pale, and appeared exceedingly feeble in health.

He was delighted as a child when told that his stories were read and admired by the children in America, and inquired if we had any storks there, and wondered how the children could understand some of his stories if they were not familiar with storks, as the boys and girls of Denmark, but that he had written some stories expressly for the children of America.

"Ah," said he with a sigh, "were I not so nearly done with life, I should like to see America."

I assured him he would meet a cordial welcome, especially from the little people.

"Give my love to them all," said he, "and tell them I enjoy telling them fairy stories; and stay, here is a little memento of our interview which you may show the children in Andersen's own handwriting;" and he wrote in Danish a sentence, beneath which he also wrote its English translation, —

"Life is the most beautiful fairy tale.
HANS CHRISTIAN ANDERSEN."

And then bade us good-bye.

Poor Andersen — but I will not say poor, either, for he was rich in the affection of all classes in his native land, as well as elsewhere, where his writings have been read. His death took place at Copenhagen two years after I saw him, and at his funeral the affection of all classes was shown by the immense gathering. The royal family were there, and the poor were present, and deputations from all parts of Denmark and other countries, and, as one writer expresses it, many persons were as much taken by surprise as they would have been if it had been reported that Æsop had died.

Away off at the left, as we leave Samaden, rises the high peak of Piz Roseg, whose icy point pierces the clouds twelve thousand feet above the sea-level, and you catch views of the Piz Bernina, twelve thousand five hundred feet, the highest peak of the Bernina chain. But twilight is approaching, the air chill, though in July, as we roll through two little villages close together in the valley after leaving Samaden and begin to wind up the hillside towards our point of destination. As we reach a bend in the road before entering a wood, the driver halts, and we look back to have a charming view of the valley of the Inn through which we have passed since leaving Zernetz. The road twists and winds about, and strings the two little villages of Cresta and Celerina, scarce a mile below us, upon its thread; five miles further on is Samaden, and Zernetz is at the end of the straight-line view, which is closed by a lofty mountain which rises behind it.

Up we mount, and with the setting sun enter the village of St. Moritz, nearly six thousand feet above the sea-level, a place which is said to enjoy nine months of winter and three of cool weather. The season for visitors is from the middle of June to the middle of September, and we had arrived at the height of it, so we were passed by parties who had been out to ride, to walk, and to ramble, returning homewards: Englishmen, with veil-wreathed hats and *alpenstocks*, young fellows with stout shoes and knickerbocker suits, who also have been climbing the neighboring mountains, and others whose dust-covered clothes and browned faces told of pedestrian excursions.

Every now and then an *einspänner*, reminding one of the

Canada caleche or Cuban volante, dashed past with its sturdy little horse, and pair of passengers behind, and we met ruddy-faced English girls in plain short merino dresses, broad hats and stout shoes, returning from their rambles. Evidently we were going to a popular resort if it *was* high up in the Swiss mountains; and so it proved, for the little village, which will number scarce four hundred of its own inhabitants, and not a quarter of that out of season, had now two or three thousand from various parts of the Continent, drawn thither for various reasons, chief among which might be mentioned that the mineral springs here are pronounced the best of their kind in Europe. They are a powerful chalybeate, strongly impregnated with carbonic acid and alkaline salts, and very efficacious for scrofulous affections, diseases of the stomach, and impaired digestion. This efficacy brings of course many exhausted fast livers here for the waters, and, there being among them quite a sprinkling of titled ones, the place is the fashion. Moreover, it is comparatively a new place, or was at the time of the author's visit, the gambling-houses of Baden-Baden having been closed, and pleasure-seekers hungering for a new sensation were making this the fashionable watering place; and a delightful and comfortable one it is during the hot season, to say nothing of the waters, the beneficial effects of which are indisputable.

We had directed our driver, on arrival at St. Moritz, to carry us to the grand hotel, the Kurhaus, the fashionable resort, built over the springs, about a mile beyond and below the village itself; and, having sent forward despatches two days in advance, looked forward confidently to a comfortable rest in comfortable rooms at the end of our four days' journey. So we rolled by "Badrutt's," or Engadine Culm, a big, square hotel, where the Countess of Dudley was staying, and groups on the space in front were looking down upon ourselves and other road-passers; and then we began to wind through the little narrow zigzag street of the town (built so as to shelter against the fierce winds of fall and winter) and past several pretty pensions or boarding-houses, to the great house which we could see resting in the valley below. The sun was setting behind the mountains, and the numerous guests thronging in to a late dinner, or early tea, as our dust-covered vehicle whirled through the ornamental driveway of the grounds and drew up at the principal entrance.

Here I descended, and was met at the threshold by the host.

Did Monsieur desire apartments?

Certainly he did, — his card, (presenting it;) he had *envoyéd un message* two days ago.

The host shrugged his shoulders; he had not an empty closet in the house.

"What, nothing?" and I took out a gold Napoleon in my hand.

The Frenchman's eyes glistened.

"*Ah, pardon, Monsieur, mais vraiment,*" he had nothing, the house was full, and he rattled off with such volubility and with so many shrugs and deprecatory gestures, that we were glad when the clerk, who spoke English, put in an appearance.

In response to our assertion that we had telegraphed, he asked me to look in at the telegraph bureau, near which I was standing, and there, at the side of the instrument, were a score of messages beside my own — " and all these, received before Monsieur's, must be disappointed."

It was true; the place was crammed, and we were late comers, and must find quarters elsewhere.

The great Kurhaus had been enlarged the last season, so that at the time of our arrival it held more than five hundred guests, but the new accommodations were all taken; so we must turn and climb the hill that we had just descended, back to the village with our tired horses, and seek accommodations where we could find them.

The English-speaking clerk was good enough to give us a hint, which we were not slow to act upon, which was to go to the *Pension Suisse*, and take the best engaged rooms that were not yet occupied, "agreeing" to vacate at "immediate notice" in case of arrival of parties who had engaged them.

The Pension Suisse was a neat little hotel in the village; the host had no rooms in the house itself, but, sure enough, in its dependency, the Flugi-Engelberg directly across a roadway, were two nice rooms, saloon and sleeping apartment, which were reserved for some distinguished party, and if Monsieur would take them for a week and submit to be moved in case my Lord and Lady Nozoo should arrive, then he could be accommodated.

Monsieur and madame, fatigued and dust-covered with four days of post travel, were but too happy to obtain such comfortable accommodations as these proved to be. The little Pension Suisse contained about twenty rooms, was beautifully clean and well kept; the reputation that the Engadine has of furnishing pastry cooks, waiters, confectioners, café managers, &c., for the Continent, was borne out by the cuisine here and a specimen of a tiny confectioner's shop under the hotel, in which barely half a dozen customers could get in at once, but where the *l'eclairs*, cream cakes, bonbons, and pastry were not excelled by the best in Paris and Vienna.

The dining-room, with its *table d'hôte* and little tables for dinner *à la carte*, overlooked the quaint little zigzag Swiss street, up and down which went goats and cows and *diligence*, *einspänners*, Tyroleans, and tourists, a curious medley, during early hours of morning and evening.

Our lodgings were in the Dependence, a solid stone mansion of two stories in height, situated upon the verge of the hillside at the end of the village nearest the Kurhaus, and commanding a wild and romantic Tyrolean view. First, sloping downward from beneath our windows, extended a bank of verdure, crowded with fragrant wild-flowers; beyond lay a placid lake of emerald green, about two miles in length by a mile in width, calm as a mirror, and reflecting the lofty peak that seemed to rise from its opposite shore and pierce the sky ten thousand feet above, but which was really miles beyond its verge. The mountains opposite were beautifully green, with verdure at their base; then above, as it gradually disappeared, there came into view the numberless silvery and flashing, ribbon-like streams and cascades that flowed downwards from the glaciers and vast snow-robe that enveloped the whole range of lofty peaks high above and before us. The lofty mountains and their snow crown are mirrored in the lake below them by day; at early morn the sunrise upon their glittering heads is a glorious sight; and at moonrise, with the stars shining in the deep blue of the heavens, the moonbeams bring them out with a strange, weird effect of ghastly white.

Far beyond us, some two hundred feet below the level of the plateau on which our little hotel rests, at the end of the deep, emerald green of the lake, and in a sort of flat, scooped-out valley, which would be close and hot, if there could be such a thing in this altitude, rests the great hotel, a huge, white structure, with wings and L's, — a village in itself, — which, seen with its glittering lights across the lake at night, reminds one of a New-England cotton factory. This beautiful lake at the mountain-base, — a natural Alpine mirror, and doubtless principally an accumulation of glacier-water, — nevertheless furnishes delicious trout, which often grace our breakfast-table.

Round and about its margin Tyrolean washer-women gather, kneeling on their little board platforms, and washing in the cold water all day long, keeping up a healthy circulation of the blood by the vigorous manner in which they beat and assault the clothes under ablution. At one end, towards the village, the waters of the lake tumble over in a series of pretty cascades, forming a portion of the source of the river Inn; and on the romantic wooded banks here, the devious walks, shaded by forest-trees, form a most enchanting lovers' promenade.

There are two winding roads down to the Kurhaus, — the one near the lake, which carries you through a newly started village (by this time possibly completed) of carpenters and masons, erecting another hotel, handsomely built of stone, of about one hundred and fifty rooms, fronting the lake, and also several lesser buildings and dependencies, showing the rapidity with which St. Moritz has recently grown into public favor. The other, or upper road, is less steep and less direct, and that generally taken by the *diligence* and other vehicles, and leads past a tiny English church, that might hold, possibly, a congregation of seventy-five persons.

The extended arms of the hotel embrace a handsomely laid-out park, and walks in front of it; but in the middle of the day in July, when the sun beats down fiercely, one is glad to get into the friendly shade of the house or bathroom corridors. A long, covered passage, or promenade, leads from the hotel to the springs, or, as the English always unpoetically designate the place, " the pump-room," where the water is served, morning, noon, and evening, to drinkers. There is an array of mugs here in their racks, labelled like those in an American barber's shop; tumblers and glasses, some with crests and initials, also decanters and bottles belonging to the drinkers, who come down in force in the morning when the band plays, and fill the broad hall that surrounds the springs, as they promenade, glass in hand, clad in elegant *néglige* morning costume, listen to the music, and chat with each other.

The scene then is a gay one : ladies in ravishing costumes, in delicate morning hats and dainty slippers, some pale-faced and thin, others rosy and healthy; old dowagers, mere shadows in muslin and diamonds, here in the vain hope that they may find in this the fountain of youth they have vainly sought all over the Continent; the really ill, with marks of suffering in their worn faces and exhausted frames; men in velvet morning dressing-suits, slippers, and embroidered caps, to whom a three months' banishment from fast life and the same amount of hard labor and plain food would bring more health than any spring-water in existence; exhausted old titled *roués*, with eye-glasses, and in costumes twenty years too young for them, some hobbling painfully along by the aid of a cane, and others leaning upon the arm of a liveried *valet*; overfed Englishmen or Germans under diet to get their bursting skins down to reasonable dimensions, and turgid livers into decent working order; fat old dowagers sitting in the window recesses, holding their glasses of water suspended beneath their lips, as they gossip over it with each other, as at a tea-drinking.

Then there were scores of young people and young lovers, — some who had come because it was then a new place, and the fashion; others who had come down with uncle Joe, who wanted to try the water a week or two for his gout; and the two sisters, Blonde and Brunette, who had come with mother for her neuralgia; and the others who had come with their father, an old Indian officer, whose yellow visage told of curry-powder and a liver that bothered him. There was the usual sprinkling of titled individuals, and, as is usual in such places, those making the greatest parade were likely to be the most impecunious.

The band played, and the groups sauntered about: here a pair was followed by a liveried servant to replenish or take the cup when emptied; others repaired to the basin of hot water to heat their draughts to a certain temperature; and others, having drank, lounged round the long bazaar of a dozen stalls, or ornamented booths, where Swiss girls sold carved wood-work, trinkets, jewelry, laces, wrought handkerchiefs and embroidery, for which the neighboring country is celebrated; crystals, photographs, pictures, glass-work, and other attractive fancy goods.

There are fifty or sixty bath-rooms, where those who desire to be treated in that manner, have opportunity to make use of the waters. A young English physician, who came up here without practice for a summer excursion a few years since, before the place was so much frequented, was interested in an analysis of the waters, and, on his return to London, wrote a pamphlet, or book, upon the subject. It was favorably commented upon; and the next season, when he went for his succeeding summer vacation, his pamphlet was placed on the bookstall here, it being the only description of the springs and their properties, the guide-books hardly mentioning them. Visitors bought it; and finally, an old lady, being ill, sent for him, was relieved, praised his treatment, and it came to be understood that the St. Moritz waters should be drank according to medical advice. The young physician managed his business well, enlarged his pamphlet into a book, took rooms *en suite*, and established himself at the Kurhaus as *the* principal physician, numbering his patients by hundreds, and, taking the tide at flood, it is rapidly leading him on to fortune.

There are billiard and reading rooms attached to the hotel, for those who stay indoors, while, outside, the numerous rides and rambles in easy reach render the place particularly attractive. There is a beautiful walk, which can be accomplished in about an hour, through the neighboring forest to a high point that commands a view of great beauty, including several mountain lakes; excursions to the neighboring villages, valleys, passes, and glaciers can be made from here; an ascent of the Piz Nair, an elevation of about nine thousand three hundred feet, which is not very difficult, and can be accomplished in about three hours from St. Moritz, and from which a superb view of the snow-capped Bernina chain may be had.

One of the pleasantest of these excursions is that to the neighboring village of Pontreseina and thence to Morteratsch Glacier. In an *einspänner*, myself and companion rode a delightful drive to Pontreseina. It was about the middle of July, the temperature being that of an English May morning, or the early June of New England. What harvest there is here in the Engadine is late, and it had not yet been gathered in; the fields were a perfect wealth of wild flowers, the air heavy with their perfume, and, as we came to the village itself, after a ride of about five miles, the gardens of the people were rich in flowers of every hue. Indeed, the place might be said to be noted for the floral taste of its inhabitants; and this, let it be remembered, in a place about six thousand feet above the sea-level, — a higher altitude than Mt. Rhigi, described in the author's former work, and in a locality where grass is of that value that dried moss is used as the bedding for cattle.

At Pontrescina we pulled up for a brief rest at the Roseg Hotel, and also to enjoy from its balconies a panoramic sight of the Roseg Mountain and its great glacier, which is spread out in full view here (even as the Jungfrau is before the windows of the Hotel Victoria, at Interlaken), for it is but three miles distant; and here in this village gather those enthusiastic tourists who are so fond of glacier excursions and mountain-climbs, for there is an abundant opportunity in the vicinity to enjoy them without any great risk.

After enjoying our mountain view of Roseg and Bernina and other peaks and points, and the broad expanse of snow and ice elevated far above us in the blue sky, like a great, white-covered altar to the Most High, we left the village behind us, coming to a most beautiful waterfall at the roadside, — a tumbling, rattling cascade, bursting out of the Languard valley, white with foam-wreaths, — a genuine Alpine torrent, a view for a painter, having the conventional, picturesque old saw-mill and distant Swiss chalet, and two peasant figures in red dresses and blue yarn stockings, in the foreground. Near here the Bernina Pass begins, and winds about its course of ascent above us: we are still in the midst of romantic Alpine scenery; for, turn which way one will, the lofty peaks, picturesque crags, or wooded heights meet the view, and the air is filled with the rush of brawling brooks.

We turn off from the main road, ride through some rough land, as far as passable for our vehicle, and halt; the driver is to wait till our return, as we proceed over the little foot-path to visit without a guide the Bernina Brook and the glacier. We plod along some distance, and wonder whether we are right or wrong, and with that uncertain feeling of what if we were to lose our way in this wild mountain region of a foreign country; but the path is well worn, though the country is wild and picturesque. We round a turn in the path, and in a nook find a rough little chalet of two rooms, one of which answered as a refreshment room for the sale of a very limited stock of refreshments, — a few bottles of claret, the inevitable show-card with the pink, triangular trade-mark of Bass & Co., announcing pale ale of their brewing, and a few biscuits. Attached was a little wooden pagoda and a sort of garden, with two or three tables for the use of customers.

The only occupants of the place were a woman and a little child; and in answer to our signs, the former, with smiles and pantomime, indicated to us to go on, and went forward herself to open a sort of gateway to the right path, placed there evidently for a slight fee, which she smilingly and gratefully received. We soon reached a rustic bridge, in a narrow, rocky gorge, scarce twenty feet in width: from high above, down the irregular chasm over the jagged rocks, leaps and rushes, tumbles and roars, the waterfall. It is dark, shady, and cool here, although mid-day, and the showers of mist fly into our faces,

From the side of the bridge we observe a foot-path, steep, to be sure, but worn by climbing feet; we catch at shrubs and trees, and ascend to see the source of our glorious waterfall, and at last reach the summit, when, lo! here comes down another still above us, even more magnificent, precipitating its flood, with the roar of a true torrent, into a great rocky basin, whose overflow is the fall below us. A rest here, and enjoyment of a look-up at this superb cascade and down at the one left, we take our mountain-path again, and still higher encounter the third waterfall of still different and equally romantic and picturesque description. Yet higher, and we emerge from among the trees upon the rocky hillside, which is red with huge bushes of *Alpenrosen*, and rich in sweet-smelling purple and white flowers. The torrent, still some eighteen or twenty feet in width, as we follow it, is a succession of picturesque bends, rapids, cascades, and waterfalls over huge masses of rock, — a charmingly romantic place, — a Tyrolean edition of Trenton Falls in New York, except that it may be followed more easily, and the distant surroundings are more grand.

This beautiful Bernina Brook, as it is called, we followed up to the road or Bernina Pass, enjoying the numerous cascades, windings, and glorious waterfalls. Descending, we resumed our foot-path once more, meeting and crossing the water from the glacier towards which we were advancing.

Here it was at last.

We come first to a broad expanse of loose rocks, stones, and rocky shingle, in the centre of which rushed along the melted, bluish-gray glacier water from the great mass that had crept slowly forward to the valley. We picked our way up to its very base, a great wall of a mixture of ice and sand, gravel and stones, sixty feet high : the chill of its shade was sensibly felt after the heat of our pedestrian excursion. The dirty gray of the exterior of a large portion of the end of glacier which may be approached thus, is unlike its unsoiled purity thousands of feet above. But, approaching to the point from which poured forth the melted torrent that went forward as a contribution to the river Inn, we could see within the well-known caverns of clear blue, pitiless ice, seamed with clean cuts and fractures, bluish green as bottle-glass, and chill as the frozen ocean.

By the side-path we climbed up, and went far enough to

say that we had stood upon the Morteratsch glacier, and had pelted one another with snowballs gathered at its verge in July ; but the fatigue of the ascent, as well as the great yawning fissures that seamed the surface, deterred us from any excursion upon it, especially as we were without a guide to direct our footsteps.

It is a fact that, rapidly as one may come down hill on these Alpine excursions, he is pretty apt to discover that he needs some strength for descent as well as ascending, and also that in most cases very little is left. Such was our case in returning from the Morteratsch glacier, so that, after passing the rustic bridge of Bernina Brook again, and reaching the little chalet that we had passed, we sank down in the rustic chairs of its ground with a sigh of exhaustion, thirsty and heated.

The tumblers of milk brought were fresh, rich, and invigorating ; it must be that the rich herbage that I have referred to at this season in this region imparts a corresponding richness to the milk. With a half hour's rest and our refreshment here at the chalet, we were sufficiently invigorated, and soon on the way back to where we had left *einspänner* and driver some hours before. The latter, who was comfortably snoring beneath his vehicle, was roused, and his horse was again harnessed, and we rattled back through Pontrescina, on for four miles, and up the wooded height to our little hotel at St. Moritz, in season for the *table d'hôte* dinner, at 5 P. M.

From St. Moritz to Coire, where we desired to take to the rail again, is a two days' posting journey over wild and romantic mountain passes. But, invigorated by a week's rest at our little mountain retreat, we were ready for the journey. Accordingly the inevitable post-carriage was duly secured, the contract drawn up by the English-speaking assistant of the host of the Pension Suisse, whose use of the language betrayed an occasional refreshing of memory at the dictionary, as for instance when he informed us that the driver had gone to "charge" the luggage, which I ascertained was his English for "load" the luggage, and that the carriage would go "down stairs safely," meaning down hill easily, a sort of pigeon English probably acquired at hotels.

The luggage having been duly "charged," the hotel-bill of three dollars and fifty cents per day each was paid, — a high price for Switzerland, but we were at an expensive place in the Canton des Grisons, at the height of the season, which is very short, and at a resort that is considered very fashionable. These details having been settled, the well-appointed post-carriage, with its Tyrolean decorated harness, and dapple-gray horses, driven by Tyrolean driver wearing pointed hat decorated with flower sprigs, came up to the door with the usual whip-crack salute, and, as is customary, landlord, landlady, and gentlemanly English-speaking assistant were at the door to speed the parting guests.

The white-aproned host had learned enough French to say "*Bon voyage, Monsieur,*" the fat landlady courtesied and smiled, the English-speaking waiter raised his hat and said, "A pleasant journey, Madame and Monsieur, good-by I wish you," the driver started his team, and we cork-screwed up through the little zigzag street of St. Moritz till we left it behind and were upon the high road in the fresh morning flower-perfumed air, and descended the slope in a brisk trot on through the little villages of Cresta and Cellerina, back to Samaden, and on to a place called Ponte, turning off at which we entered fairly upon the Albula Pass. Now we began again the usual series of Alpine ascents, the air pure and bracing; the slopes about and around us are in their beautiful livery of green, and high, high above rise the glittering snow peaks.

Up, up, still up. Now we pass a sighing pine forest, now an open space brilliant with Alp roses and other wild flowers, finally reaching the rocks and green slopes which are above the trees, which now have diminished to bushes in size. As we near the summit of the pass, traversing a wild, rocky, barren waste, the snow, which we had seen far above us, began to appear in patches upon each side of the road, till at last, when we reached the summit of the pass, the carriage path was cut through a snow bank three or four feet deep, although it was the fifteenth day of July. The summit is desolation itself, and we wind through a perfect quarry of rugged, ragged, gray, storm-shattered rocks, and after passing these, the mountain sides are seen gashed with the avalanches of spring, which frequently damage the roadway.

Notwithstanding the snow in this portion of the pass, the southerly slopes in the vicinity appear for a few months to be a rich pasturing ground for herds which are driven up here to graze, the herdsmen living in rude hovels during the three months they are here. We saw hundreds of cattle feeding on the rich herbage, for the season for butter and cheese making was now at hand, and the tinkling of many bells on the lower hillsides was melodious as a campanalogian concert.

The verdure seemed to spring out of the mountain side directly the snow had melted and left it, and it seemed singular to see wild pansies blooming at one side of the road and a snow bank heaped up on the other, both scarcely thirty feet apart. Besides the cattle we observed a species of great, gaunt, reddish-brown, long-legged swine scattered about on the slopes, seeming not to thrive so well as the former, and from their uncanny appearance causing the spectator to mentally resolve never to taste pork in the Tyrol.

Grand as ever is the glorious mountain scenery, a new phase of that often described by the author, but ever novel, never tiresome, always grand and magnificent. The air was thin and bracing at the summit of the pass, and made the nerves of my face thrill as with neuralgia; but though we were up some seven thousand feet above the sea-level, ambitious youths, "'mid snow and ice," could with propriety shout

"Excelsior," for far above us, five thousand feet into the air, rose lofty peaks of barren rock, or enveloped in their robes of snow which sparkled like frosted silver in the sunlight.

Leaving the summit, we descended through grand notches and gorges by tremendous zigzags, often cut through solid rock, and protected towards the valley side by stone walls, till the scene of snow and ice, and the barren, stony wilderness of the summit, gave place to the beautiful view of the whole of the charming valley of the *Hinter-Rhein*, rich in green fields, picturesque chalets, graceful slopes, and rushing waterfalls. We halt *en route* to dine at Bergen, a little town in a green arena-like valley, surrounded by lofty snow-clad mountains.

After leaving here, we whirled round through the great ravine of the Bergen-Stein. This is a narrow wooded ravine, with a road blasted out of the face of the precipice, and which runs along high above the river Albula, which seems to have cut or worn itself a passage six or seven hundred feet below us. At times, in the turn of the road, we could by leaning over the cliff catch a sight of the angry torrent, foaming and boiling over its jagged bed of rocks, hundreds of feet beneath us; and again we could see naught but the profound chasm, which our roadway so far overhung as to conceal from view the torrent which we heard roaring far below.

It chanced that we were fortunate in the time of our departure, being a day behind a thunder-storm that had cleared the air and swollen the streams, and also sent down some avalanches of earth and stone. One from a mountain side a mile off had delivered a contribution of three feet in thickness across the road, which laborers had but just shovelled away ere we reached the spot. We have left the wild chasm and ravine-like passage of the Bergen-Stein behind, pass through a little village called Bad Alvenue, where English and other invalids come to make use of the sulphurous springs, and still descending by the river-side, run into the picturesquely situated village of Tiefenkasten, with its pretty cascade tumbling into the Albula River, and its old ruined castles in the distance on the hillsides, above its resting-place in the hollow of the hills.

Coming down from the wild Bergen-Stein ravine, we had one of those novel and interesting sights that are often witnessed in the Alps, from the effects of atmosphere, clouds, or various changes of weather in these lofty altitudes. This was what is popularly known as a sun-shower, a light shimmering rain falling, and the sun shining brightly at the same time. Looking through this, the green hillsides and fields of the valley, populated with men and women who were scrambling to get their hay in, had an indescribably beautiful appearance; but, as we descended and rode out of the shower, the driver halted and called to us to look back, when, lo! the whole great gorge above us was spanned by an immense rainbow, one end resting on the barren mountain, and the other upon the opposite side among the larch trees, a gorgeous sight.

On we go, and about two hours after leaving Tiefenkasten are in the beautiful Schyn Pass (pronounced Shin Pass), an unromantic name for a most romantic pass, with lofty precipices, profound abysses, and splendid specimens of engineering skill throughout its whole length, — reminding one very much of the Via Mala in general characteristics. Some of the road is cut through a species of black slaty rock, and portions of it are damaged frequently by the storms of winter. We passed through one gallery and over one bridge by the side of an abyss which was entirely without guards, all having been washed away the previous winter with a portion of the roadway, which was supported by masonry; this latter had been replaced and strengthened, and a fresh barrier was to be erected.

After an enjoyable ride through this pass, we reached in the afternoon Thusis, the gate as it is called of the Via Mala

Pass, where we halted for the night, and after a good night's rest, despite a furious thunder-storm, we took a morning walk to enjoy the fresh atmosphere and romantic scenery before starting again on our journey. At a bridge that runs across the river Rhine at this point, there is a beautiful view of the valley.

The river Nolla, which flows into the Rhine at Thusis, has a most singular appearance. Standing on the Nolla Bridge, the river, which came rushing down over shelving layers of black, slate-looking rock, appeared black as ink, and as it flows into the Rhine, discolors that stream for quite a distance with its sable hue. This color is caused by the continuous washing of the porous slate banks of the river, converting them into a black paste, till the whole stream has the hue above described. A glorious view we took in on the Nolla Bridge, which afforded us a panoramic picture of a portion of the valley of the Rhine, with its barrier of lofty mountains. A huge gorge was seen with the river Rhine running through it on one hand, and on the other the rushing Nolla sending down its inky tributary stream. High over the banks of the Rhine, some six hundred feet above the river, are the ruins of the most ancient castle in Switzerland, Hoch-Realt, said to have been founded by Raetus, leader of the Etruscans, B. C. 587.

Leaving the bridge, we took a walk upon the commencement of the Via Mala Pass, whose huge walls rise perpendicularly over twelve hundred feet on either side. The roadway is cut in the solid rock, and far below it the river runs roaring through the deep and narrow gorge.

Having previously made the passage of the whole pass, we walked but a short distance — say about a mile and a half — to the first great gallery, two hundred feet in length, that penetrates the solid rock. But this is one of the finest portions of the pass, and tourists halting at Thusis, if not going over it, should make at least this pedestrian excursion of two or three miles, and they will be well repaid by the wild and grand scenery of this gloomy defile.

After refreshing our memories of a former visit to the Via Mala by this walk into its rocky fastnesses, and ourselves by an excellent breakfast, we were once more behind the post-horses, and soon left Thusis behind us as we dashed out on the Splugen road, passing through beautiful valleys with huge mountain barriers on each side, and various villages, till we came in sight of Reichenau, with the snow-clad Brigelser Horn towering above it. At this village there was pointed out to us the chateau in which Louis Philippe sought refuge in 1793. He was then Duc de Chartres, and arrived here on foot, stick in hand, and lived at the place for nearly a year as an usher in a school, giving lessons in French and mathematics, his secret known only to one person, — the head master of the school, — to whom he brought a letter of introduction, and during his exile here he heard of his father's death on the scaffold and his mother's banishment.

We cross the Rhine over a long single-span bridge, two hundred and thirty-seven feet in length, high above the river, and come into the prettily situated and pretty Romansch village of Ems, with its ruined castle, and leaving it behind, drive on out into the open country, passing within a short distance of a village called Felsburg, that is so near to the mountain side as to be in constant danger from avalanches. Indeed, it may be said to have had several warnings, as large ledges of rock and soil have slipped from the hill-side close at one end of the village, rushing half-way across the valley, — a sufficient bulk to overwhelm a large portion of the village, had it fallen there. We could see the great track of the earth and soil where the slide had taken place, and what remained above the village looked of treacherous and uncertain tenure. Some of the inhabitants have already taken the alarm and moved away, but a large portion of them remain, perhaps to experience the fate of those at Goldau.

We drew up at the Steinbock Inn in Coire at two P. M.,

parted with our post-carriage previous to taking the railway one next day, but employed the afternoon in visiting the upper part of the town or eminence upon which is situated the Episcopal Palace, and which commands a beautiful view of the surrounding country, the river Plessur, on which Coire is situated, and which flows into the Rhine, and the Rhine itself. We did not go into the palace, but accepted the services, proffered in pantomime, of a little Swiss boy to pilot us up the steep declivity to the Cathedral of St. Lucius, an edifice built in the eighth century, with curious old columns, resting on lions, and bearing sculptured representations of the Apostles in pairs, and containing a high altar most beautifully carved, and curious stalls and tabernacle, all made in the year 1491; also two or three noted pictures, one by Rubens and another by Holbein, and a curious gold and silver crucifix upon another altar, made during the twelfth century, the sarcophagi of some old counts and bishops, and antiquities which render the church a most interesting place to visit.

The Treasury, or Sacristy, of the church was in charge of a good-natured old priest, who let me have pretty much my own way among the rich church plate of antique workmanship of the fourteenth century, the relics, shrines, and other curiosities. A piece of the oldest silk in Europe, said to have been made in 513, was carefully preserved in a glass case; then there were old documents of King Otho, 888; of Ludwig, son of Charlemagne, 836; Charlemagne, 784; and others of the time of 849, 831, &c. The bones of St. Lucius, and skulls of other old saints, whose eyeless sockets were rimmed with emeralds and rubies, the custodian permitted me to handle at will, and also to closely examine the glass frame between which were the drops of blood of some other saints, nails from the true cross, and other wonders, which, having now become somewhat of a seasoned traveller, I neglected to make anything more than a general memoranda of in my note-book, knowing that all well-regulated cathedrals possess them.

But some of the most valuable articles in the treasury consisted of the large wardrobe of superb priestly vestments, the most ancient being those made in 1491; then followed those made in 1500, 1600, &c., down to our own time, enough to clothe fifty bishops. They were of the most elegant silk, velvet, and other stuffs I ever looked upon, loaded with the most magnificent gold embroidery, and heavy with bullion. One was shown me, of which the outer robe alone was valued at twenty-five thousand dollars, so rich was it in gold trimming and costly embroidery. In fact, the wondrous richness and beauty of these church vestments stowed away here in a Swiss cathedral was amazing. But Coire, it is recorded, is the oldest bishopric in Switzerland.

There is little else in Coire to interest the visitor.

From here we took rail for Munich, thence to Vienna, both of which having been referred to at length in a former volume ("Over the Ocean"), a description is omitted here.

How vexed we were, on arriving at Prague one hot summer's evening, to find no hotel omnibuses of any kind in waiting at the railway station, — nothing but a party of garlic-smelling coachmen bawling in a jargon we could not understand. There were seven of us, American and English, in the party, and we had concluded to stay over a day or two on our route to Dresden, and see what sights we might in that time; and out of the party we managed to get together enough of the proper language to engage coachmen to take us to a hotel. The first two houses tried were full; in the next we filled all the rooms remaining, and were congratulating ourselves, on assembling in the *salle à manger*, to find on the bills-of-fare handed us as we sat down to supper, a line stating that the proprietor, having resided in New York, particularly recommended himself to Americans and foreigners.

In whatever capacity he had served in America, it could not have been in hotel-keeping, as we found to our sorrow;

for the *cuisine* was barely tolerable, the sleeping-rooms vile, and the beds hard and uncomfortable; so that, after a sleepless night and bad breakfast, it was unanimously voted not to stay another night in Prague, but to take the first train, which left in a few hours, so that our sight-seeing was limited to a very brief space of time, which was devoted to a ride around through some of the principal parts of the *Altstadt* or old part of the city, which stretches along the margin of the river, and abounds in crooked streets, shops, and buildings black with dirt, age, and antiquity; and, as we glanced upwards, we observed that Prague seems to be built upon the sides of slopes or successive eminences, rising one above the other, crowned by the imposing palace or castle of the Bohemian kings, known as the *Hradschin*, upon the crest of a hill which overtops all the rest.

Of course we must visit that point; so we soon found our carriage whirling over a long and massive bridge, built in 1503, and spanning the river Moldau, which divides the old and new parts of the city, Altstadt and Neustadt, on one bank, from the *Kleinseite* (small side) and Hradschin on the other.

All along the battlements of this bridge stood colossal figures of various saints, — distressing-looking objects in ecclesiastical costume. There were twenty-eight of them in all, and the most celebrated is one in bronze with a five-pointed cross above him, with a metallic star at each point of the cross. We were halted to look at this, as it represents St. John Nepomucenus, and was erected in 1683 in memory of John something or other, whom the king threw over the bridge into the river at this point because the said John refused to disclose to him the confession made by the queen to him, which the king was exceedingly anxious to get hold of. John was drowned without betraying his secret, but such a chance for a Papal miracle was not to be allowed to pass, and so five stars are said to have hovered over the spot where the body of the drowned priest lay, until attention was attracted and he was drawn from the water and canonized as a saint, and his body put in a magnificent shrine in the Cathedral. We only had time to ride to a point near the new iron suspension bridge, which is erected a short distance above here. Between these two bridges the bank of the river has been laid out as a handsome promenade, affording a beautiful water view, and a handsome Gothic open monument stands there, in which, beneath the wrought stone canopy, is a bronze equestrian statue of the former Emperor Francis of Germany, from which the promenade takes its name, Francis, or, as they call it, *Franzens Quai*. The base of the monument is surrounded by allegorical figures, and the vicinity appears to be a very pleasant and attractive resort.

I was vexed indeed, when I came to consult my guide-book, and found what were the riches and curiosities of the Cathedral, and to reflect upon the historic associations of the city and its points of interest, which might at least have occupied me two days, that I had thrown aside the opportunity and had but an hour or so of rapid ride, for our trunks had been sent to the railway station, and tickets taken, after coming to the hasty decision to leave. Lastly we rode up to the Hradschin. Talk of riding up! I think I never rode up so steep a street before; it was almost at an angle of forty-five degrees,—and on arrival at the castle we had barely time to look hastily through a room or two, containing nothing extraordinarily attractive, and to survey the beautiful panoramic view of river, city, and country from its battlements, ere the enemy, Time, summoned us to descend in order to reach the station in season for the train.

CHAPTER XVI.

The Hotel Bellevue, in Dresden, is very pleasantly situated, and, thanks to advance despatches, we had delightful apartments, with windows looking out upon the River Elbe, up and down which went the little steamboats, — for it was the summer season, — and out to the floating bath-houses, moored mid-stream, continually went the row-boats with passengers.

In full view also was the noble stone bridge across the Elbe, connecting the old with the new city. A magnificent structure it is, fourteen hundred and twenty feet in length, and thirty-six feet in width, and has foot-pavement and iron balustrade on each side. It rests on sixteen arches, and is said to be one of the finest bridges in Germany. A friend called our attention to the piers of this bridge, the projecting portions of which, built in the usual form to resist ice or freshets, were on the wrong side of the bridge, — that is, point down with the flow of the tide, instead of against it. What may be the reason of this is a problem, unless the river ran in the opposite direction when the builders of 1727 restored the work of the old artisans of the twelfth century.

Our windows overlook the pleasant little garden at the rear of the hotel, fragrant with flowers and fresh with a plashing fountain; and we descend, walk across it, and take breakfast on a covered balcony almost overhanging the river, commanding a pleasant water-view, and a long beer-garden upon the banks a little distance further along, which is gay in colored lights in the evening. At the end of the great bridge, over which we can see the crowds continually passing and repassing, rises the lofty spire, three hundred and fifty feet above the pavement of the *Frauenkirche,* or

Church of our Lady, with its dome of stone, upon which the shot and shell of Frederick the Great rebounded harmlessly in his siege of the city in 1760. And this reminds me of the wondrous preservation of the crowning attraction of the city, the Dresden Gallery.

Founded in the beginning of the last century, it has remained unharmed and uninjured amid the innumerable conflicts that have since convulsed Germany, and often rolled almost up to its very portals. When Frederick the Great bombarded the city, and even battered down churches, he forbade the artillery to fire upon the Picture Gallery; and Napoleon is said to have also been so considerate, that none of the pictures ever made the journey to Paris by his order.

From our perch over the river we look, on the other hand, about half a mile down the Elbe to the beautiful railroad bridge, a structure with twelve graceful arches, each of one hundred feet span, its whole length being about fifteen hundred feet. Our first walk was over the old bridge, which is used for purposes of traffic, and it is a broad, spacious, and elegant causeway. One event in its history is that General Davoust blew up two of its arches in 1813 to cover his retreat.

After passing the bridge we soon came to a large open square, or market-place, in this *Neustadt*, as it is called, or new part of the city, and in the centre is a copper statue of old Augustus the Strong, on horseback, to whom be all honor for his cherishing, purchasing, and protecting works of art, the foundation of the grand collections that to-day make Dresden so celebrated in the world of art.

Not far from here is the building known as the Japanese Palace, bought by Augustus as a depository for various art collections, and which was one of our first sights in Dresden. It now contains a fine numismatic collection, a hall of antiquities, and a magnificent collection of porcelain. The antiquities, which are principally Roman sculptures and remains dating from the time of the empire, are of rather a tame and uninteresting character after one has visited the great galleries of the Vatican; in fact, there are but few pieces of remarkable or striking execution in the collection.

Modern busts such as those of Marshal Saxe, Cardinal Richelieu, and Gustavus Adolphus, though well executed, the tourist who has become familiar with sculpture galleries will pass by hastily. There was a beautiful group of girls and women, found in Herculaneum in 1715, in perfect preservation, which halted us at once to admire their beauty; also a fine marble figure of Venus, an athlete, a sarcophagus with bacchanalian procession on it, a statue in gray marble of a pugilist, Assyrian bas-reliefs from Nineveh, lions cut from Egyptian granite, Roman vases, and German antiquities.

The Royal Library, which contains over half a million volumes, occupies the entire upper part of the building, and is particularly rich in manuscripts and maps, containing no less than 20,500 of the latter, we were informed. There is in the grand or principal hall a great variety of curiosities and literary antiquities, over which we lingered with much interest. Beneath a glass case lay curious Runic calendars, written on boxwood, and made in the twelfth and thirteenth centuries; manuscripts in the handwriting of Luther and Melancthon; a tournament book of King René, of the fifteenth century, which was once the property of Charles the Bold. Albrecht Dürer's work on the proportions of the human figure, with his own original illustrations of the subject; volumes containing numerous beautiful miniatures (one presented over fifty of noted men of the fifteenth and sixteenth centuries, elegantly painted, the colors fresh as if laid on yesterday); a curious Mexican hieroglyphic document twelve feet long; elegantly executed illuminated missals and books on parchment, the letters and illumination as beautiful as the best press-work of to-day, and monuments of the artistic skill and patience of the sandalled brotherhood that produced them hundreds of years ago;

and besides all these, many specimens of the first attempts at typography and engraving.

But the collection in the Japanese Palace, which seems most to excite the admiration, is the magnificent collection of porcelain of East Indian, Dresden, Japanese, Chinese, French, and other manufactures, which is contained in the series of vaulted rooms in the basement story of the building, which are not very well lighted or adapted for the display. If a catalogue could have been procured, or the heavy, dull custodian have spoken French, or anything but German, we might have more thoroughly enjoyed this almost endless collection, which has been in process of accumulation for over one hundred and fifty years. Here were the specimens of the celebrated Dresden work, from the first attempts in 1709 down to the elegant workmanship of the present day; a bewildering series of all the different Chinese varieties, some of the old vases and bowls made in the time of Confucius, and others of the most fantastic and ugly patterns conceivable; blue china and curious antique Indian china that would make a collector crazy with delight; and of the small plates, bowls, and cups of Chinese and Japanese workmanship, many of surprising richness and beauty.

One could trace the improvement made in the manufacture of some of these collections, from rude attempts to elegant productions, though it must be confessed that the art seemed to have been pretty thoroughly understood by those whom we are accustomed to think semi-barbarous nations long before the more civilized. And even now, in strength of material, delicacy of hue, and novelty and originality of design, they in many respects excel.

After leaving this interesting collection, we drove to a neighboring street to look at the exterior of the house where Schiller resided from 1784 to 1786, and also another in which Körner, the poet, was born (1769). Both houses are indicated by marble tablets let into the walls, bearing inscriptions, and both are in a street named Körner-Strasse (or street), after the soldier-poet, whom the Germans seem to regard with sacred admiration.

Many American readers, not familiar with German literature, but who used John Pierpont's National Reader and American First Class Book in their youthful days at school, will remember extracts from the poet's "Lyre and Sword," such as the "Sword Song," the "Battle Hymn of the German Landsturm," and others. His most popular battle-songs were written in camp, while he was in the army fighting against Napoleon. As a soldier, he displayed great bravery, and was killed in battle, at the age of thirty-four, in a contest near Rosenberg, in 1813. We afterwards saw, in the Georges-Platz, a handsome bronze statue of the soldier-poet. He was represented standing, draped in his military cloak, with his left hand pressing his sword to his breast, while his right grasps a scroll of poems.

Coming back over the old bridge, we see directly before, in the Altstadt (old city), the Royal Palace and Roman Catholic Court Church, for the court is Roman Catholic, though the people are not so, as there are said to be not over eight thousand Romanists in the city, in which Protestantism flourishes sturdily, and will, as of old. Speaking of this Court Church, however, the music on Sundays is magnificent, and is one of the prime attractions to foreign tourists who are in the city on that day.

Fronting us, also in the Altstadt, as we recross the bridge, are the Museum, or Zwinger, which contains the celebrated Dresden Gallery; and, just at the left, after leaving the bridge, we came to the broad and beautifully laid-out promenade above the banks of the river, known as the Brühl Terrace. This terrace runs along for about one-third of a mile, and you mount to it from the street square by a very broad and elegant flight of steps. Upon these steps are four splendid groups of statuary, cut from sandstone, representing Day, Night, Morning, and Evening. This beautiful promenade, which is shaded with trees, is a favorite public resort, and crowded on pleasant evenings. At the farther end of it is one of the best beer gardens and restaurants in Dresden, the Belvedere, where you may enjoy the music of a full band for an admission fee of ten cents, and a large glass of beer for half that amount.

The Brühl Terrace reminds me of the illustrious Henri de Brühl, the favorite and all-powerful prime minister of Augustus III. of Saxony from 1733 to 1763; for his name, and that of his illustrious master are connected with the foundation of the greatness of that chief attraction of Dresden, the peerless Dresden Gallery. I approach this grand collection of art in these pages almost with fear and trembling, knowing that a mere tourist's sketch of this superb collection of masterpieces must necessarily be weak and inadequate in its endeavor to convey to the reader anything like a correct idea of their value and beauty as works of art.

There are collected, in this grand gallery, nearly three thousand different examples of the French, Flemish, Venetian, Lombardic, Genoese, Bolognese, Roman, Holland, and Spanish schools of painting.

Raphael's Madonna, in this collection, — one of the great works of art in the world, — has, as it should have, a room by itself, and is so perfect a work that no art education is required to enjoy it. This beautiful woman, holding a lovely child in her arms, with the beautiful Santa Barbara kneeling at one side of her feet, and a venerable old man (St. Sixtus) at the other, and with the two cherubs below, forms a group that is familiar to the whole world. But the surpassing beauty and heavenly expression of the Madonna's countenance, the loveliness of the child in her arms, and even the exquisite beauty of St. Barbara's face, and angelic countenances of the cherubs, have never yet been caught by copyists. They exist here only in the original of the great master, as does the rich coloring of the drapery, the celestial halo of the floating clouds, and the general happy combination of coloring, grouping, and finish that serve to make a perfect whole.

This work of Raphael belongs to his most brilliant epoch, and is the only oil-painting which, in conception and boldness of execution, reaches the character and grandeur of the celebrated cartoons. According to Vasari, it was painted for the high altar of the black monks of the Convent of St. Sisto, at Plaisance, and remained there until Augustus III., who had already admired it when, as electoral prince, he visited Italy, made an unsuccessful effort to purchase it. But it was not until forty years after his visit, in 1754, that, by the enterprise of an artist named Giovannani, who had made himself thoroughly acquainted with its beauties and its authenticity, it was purchased for this gallery for the round sum of nine thousand pounds.

Giovannani made the monks take down the picture, which had remained for two hundred years above their altar, and which had become dry and somewhat blackened, before he would positively decide to take it. Close examination revealed that but slight restoration would bring out all its wondrous beauties: a part of the drapery was bent back into the frame, and a portion of the infant's body stained with incense smoke, which could easily be removed. The principal injury, which was easily remedied, was the extreme dryness to which it had been subjected. The picture was secured and sent to Dresden as soon as the shrewd monks could have a copy made to take its place over their altar. It was not until 1827 that the picture, after arrival in Dresden, was carefully cleansed, and then the upper part of the curtain and aureole in the picture was, for the first time, discovered turned back beneath the frame. This portion was properly stretched, and the painting restored to its original dimensions.

It is said that, when the painting arrived at Dresden, Augustus was so impatient to see this much desired masterpiece, that he ordered it to be brought and unpacked at the royal castle. It was carried into the throne-room, or hall of audience, and on being unpacked the attendants hesitated about placing it in the best light, which was on the dais occupied by the throne itself. The king, however, moved the royal seat with his own hands, exclaiming, "Place for the great Raphael," an evidence of his royal devotion to art.

The Holbein Madonna, a picture which was originally painted by Holbein for a burgomaster of Basle named Meyer, and in which the artist introduced portraits of his patron's family, is another of the masterpieces of the Dresden collection. There is a dispute as to whether this is the original picture by Holbein or the so-called Darmstadt Madonna, now in the possession of Princess Elizabeth of Hesse, — this being said to be Holbein's own copy of his original, and by others *vice versa*.

Be this as it may, the Dresden picture is a beautiful work of art, rich in coloring and glorious in finish, notwithstanding two of the kneeling figures, at the right, seem like Turkish women half enveloped for a walk, the infant in the mother's arms puny, and far inferior in ruddy health and beauty to the one at the Madonna's feet, which is evidently a portrait of the sturdy old burgomaster's youngest; his heavy self kneeling close at hand.

This picture has quite a history, having passed through many hands after the burgomaster paid his thousand silver crowns for it, and was at last bought in Venice in 1743 for this gallery for a thousand sequins.

The masterpieces of great artists are so many, the collection of gems of art so rich, that one hardly knows where to begin, what to mention, or which to omit. Here we revel in an exceedingly rich collection of the Flemish and Dutch school of art. Old Brouwer's Dutch boors; Van Ostade, whose pictures almost smell of beer and tobacco; Gerard Duow's beautifully finished works. I will not say how long I stood gazing at his faultless and beautiful Praying Hermit, wherein the gray head and beard, the old brown robe, skull, hour-glass, and book, the bank of earth upon which they are placed, the vegetation, tree-trunk, and surroundings are so exquisitely finished and faithfully executed as to excite expressions of admiration even from the inexperienced.

Teniers and Snyders are here in abundance. Of the former I noted Peasants in an Ale-house, his Chemist at a Furnace, and A Village Fair. Then we had a host of Wouvermans, with that everlasting white horse in every picture; cows by Paul Potter; Cuyps; beautiful landscapes by Jacob Ruysdael; the deliciously finished details of Wilhelm and his son, Franz Mieris (one especially, of an old gamester, whom a girl with glass of wine in hand is embracing, is exquisitely finished); a girl bringing wine to a man seated at a table, and other figures, with a beauty of finish, detail, and color that Gerome and Meissonier to-day cannot rival.

The spectator may enjoy twenty specimens of Rembrandt, among which is his well-known picture of himself, with wife on knee and tall beer-glass in hand, so familiar from its reproduction in photographs and in paintings on porcelain, and distinguished for its richness of coloring of his own somewhat theatrical-looking costume, the pretty German face of his wife, and the faithfulness of the execution of drapery. Noah's Sacrifice, portrait of an old woman weighing gold, portraits of the artist, &c., are among his other works.

The Reading Hermit, by Salomon Koninx, which is frequently copied upon porcelain, is a wonderfully executed work of art: the aged, wrinkled brow, broad, massive, and thoughtful; the coarse, brown robe, the broad, snowy beard, the attitude, as he leans upon one hand, while with the other he supports the broad volume that he pores over, are all magically correct; you almost expect a passing zephyr blowing in at the cave opening will make the old recluse's snowy beard sway, or rustle the leaves of his massy volume, which look as if you could turn them over at will. The folds of the brown woollen robe can scarcely be counterfeit, for within half a dozen feet you cannot tell it from reality.

Ah! it is the work of these truly great artists, where harmony of composition, blending of colors, and grace of attitude combine to make the picture, and are coupled with such a thorough counterfeit of reality as this, that makes one think that such genuine art, such indisputable excellence, smashes to atoms all the fine theories respecting new-school daubs and obscurities, glaring effects, and color combinations, which must be viewed at a certain distance, or in certain lights, and which we are told to accept as high art under the pain of excommunication from the fashionable circles of the art patrons and art critics of to-day.

Another beautiful picture with which I was familiar from its frequent reproduction on porcelain was that of Vogel, of the two little children who had paused in their play to turn over and look at a picture-book of birds and animals. The sweet face of the youngster that is turned from the book towards the spectator, will linger long in his mind, with its childish, innocent beauty, more especially if the visitor have children of his own.

But what a wealth of pictures there is here by artists whose names are of world-wide celebrity, those of whom everybody has heard who has ever read a book or newspaper. Pictures, the copies of which you have seen in magazines and story-books when a boy, that you have seen as framed engravings, have looked at even in the family Bible, or which are familiar from numerous copies in every style; here they startle you with their original beauty, revealing the reason of their frequent and rough reproductions.

For here are the works of Raphael, Rembrandt, Rubens, Correggio, Angelica Kauffman, Snyders, Teniers, Ostade, Albrecht Dürer, Cuyp, Carlo Dolce, Paul Potter, Guido Reni, and others whose names are familiar as household words everywhere, and hosts of others familiar to art students and educated persons, and whose glorious works excite the admiration even of the uneducated who gaze upon them.

Like the Vatican, the Dresden Gallery is one of those sights that should be enjoyed leisurely and intelligently, the visitor looking over a section of it one day and returning in a day or two after to see more, taking it comfortably and enjoyably, or he may find that, besides a confused jumble of ideas, he also will have an aching head and fatigued limbs from the perambulation of its endless galleries.

It is, however, a succession of wonders and delights, and the general arrangement of the whole excellent and systematic. A long parallelogram is divided into twelve principal halls, with a grand rotunda in the centre.

These different halls are devoted to the different schools of art, and are lettered from A (which is devoted solely to Raphael's Madonna) to N. They contain large-sized pictures, but all along at one side of these large halls are a series of cabinets, or smaller apartments, containing lesser-sized paintings. There are twenty-one of these lesser halls, which are fair-sized apartments, and which, added to the others, make thirty-five rooms in all the visitor must traverse upon this floor, to say nothing of the corridors and staircases approaching or leaving it. Of the large halls, five are devoted to the Italian schools and six of the cabinets; one large hall to Spanish and Neapolitan schools; four halls and seven cabinets to the Netherlands; one to the German, &c.

These are on the main or first floor of the Gallery; but, leading from one of the halls of the Netherlands pictures, is a corridor by which you reach an adjacent pavilion containing three saloons of splendid pictures by living artists; and then we have the cupola saloon in the centre of the hall, adorned with elegant pieces of Flemish tapestry; and from this saloon a staircase ascends to another hall or upper floor, which the guide-book says contains "a few modern pictures and others of inferior value." But I found Angelica Kauffman's picture of a Vestal, the Disputation of Luther and Dr. Eck—a fine large painting by Julius Hübner,—and Paul Veronese's Europa on the Bull, and some others, which were only "inferior" on account perhaps of the greater wonders that were in the halls below.

It will be seen, therefore, that there are no less than forty different rooms full of paintings in the Dresden Gallery.

Besides those already mentioned, I find numerous gems of art marked with notes of admiration in my note-book, among which are some beautiful Correggios, including his Adoration of the Shepherds, and Madonna and Saints; Paul Veronese's Adoration of the Magi, and Christ bearing the Cross, a picture of great power; Titian's Cupid and Venus; Guido Reni's grand picture of Ninus and Semiramis; Correggio's exquisite Mary Magdalene; Claude Lorraine's coast views; Poussin's beautiful landscapes.

Teniers I have already spoken of. Here are his Boors at a Country Fair Drinking and Smoking; and there are scores of his and Wouverman's pictures in the cabinets that you may compare the one with the other at leisure, luxurious leisure among such pictures as these. Let the reader reflect, as he reads the few names given in these pages, what a wealth of art they indicate, and what a treasure-house of great artists we are in.

Here we pause in a room of pictures by Rubens and Van Dyck. Here is another with Rembrandt's portraits, and Snyder's Wild Boar Hunt; Van Dyck's Jupiter and Danaë, and his Children of Charles I. of England; Rembrandt's Feast of Esther and Ahasuerus; and Rubens' Diana and Nymphs returning from the Chase. Another hall shows us pictures by Holbein and Albrecht Dürer; another, Titian, Guido, and Caravaggio; and another, Ruysdael, Terburg, and Ostade; another with sixteen pictures by Gerard Douw, and another with the beautifully finished works of F. and W. Mieris.

The three halls of modern pictures contain many striking and beautiful paintings. Among them I noted that of the Saxon Grenadiers at the Battle of Jena, by Schuster, also his Battle of Borodino, both superb battle-pieces; two pictures by Dahl — Signing a Deed, and the Ferry; and a magnificent Spring landscape and Bridal Procession, by Richter. But, though the record of these titles calls up to the author a series of the most beautiful creations of the painter's pencil, it is only dull enumeration perhaps to the reader who has never looked upon them.

In the same building that contains the gallery of pictures is the Historical Museum, a magnificent and most interesting collection; and the Tournament Hall far surpasses the celebrated Horse Armory of the Tower of London. From the very entrance into this grand museum, you begin to study history from relics and mementos of the past. The great entrance-hall is furnished in the Renaissance style of the time of Augustus I., and hung with portraits of the Saxon princes, and contains curious antique furniture, great cabinets, and richly carved chairs and tables. Here in Luther's own cabinet is the old goblet from which he drank, and the sword that he once held in his determined grasp, and cups of curious and antique workmanship which belonged to, and have been used by, celebrated personages.

Then came a room entirely devoted to hunting implements. Here were the cross-bows and bolts of the fifteenth century, the tough boar-spears, and elegantly hilted and richly scabbarded hunting-knives, hunting-horns, and among these latter the hunting-horn used by Henry IV. of France; the falcon's hood, and the belts, gloves, bows and arrows of the archers. But the grand and magnificent display is the Tournament Hall, where, seated upon their motionless steeds, are the richly armed figures of the old warriors of two or three hundred years ago. The wondrous finish of some of these suits of mail is fairly marvellous, and suggests that the jeweller's art must have been united with the armorer's to produce it, so exquisitely are the inlaid damascened and chased designs wrought.

Another thought that is suggested on examining these figures is, the prodigious amount of muscular strength and endurance it must have required to bear about this weight in battle, and the impediment it must have been to rapid movements. Doubtless some of the armor displayed here is the show or parade suits of the princes who owned them, but a large portion of it has seen actual service in the battlefield as well as the tournament lists, as is well authenticated.

One suit of armor of solid silver was most elegantly wrought, and was made in Italy for the Elector Christian II., who died in 1611; another suit, magnificently decorated, was made for the same prince in Augsburg, and is a splendid piece of workmanship. Then we have the armor of Gustavus Adolphus; two elegantly gilded suits of armor of Prince Christian, who died in 1630; the elegant armor of the Duke Charles Emmanuel of Savoy, who died in 1630; and exquisitely wrought suits of Milán steel, made as light as such metallic clothing could be, and shield the wearer from sword-cut and lance-thrust. There were numerous figures whose names were as novel to me as those of the Norse chieftains, which were labelled as having fought in their suits on long since forgotten battlefields, and the dints of the contest were still visible.

Here, in the next apartment, a long hall called the Saloon of Battles, are arranged in chronological order the armor, weapons, and other paraphernalia of war used by the Saxon princes and great generals; and here I saw the armor of that brave King of Poland, John Sobieski, which he wore at the raising of the siege of Vienna in 1683; the swords of Peter the Great of Russia, Frederick the Great of Prussia, and Charles XII. of Sweden, and Augustus the Strong of Poland; Frederick the Great's hat, Napoleon's boots, shoes, and pen; and a weapon of a more peaceful power, Thorwaldsen's chisel.

As an evidence of the strength of that stout old chieftain, Augustus the Strong, they show us here a horseshoe which he broke in halves by twisting it in his more than iron grip.

Here is the sash that was worn by the Elector Maurice in the battle of Sievershausen in 1533, where he was killed — and the stains of his blood are still visible upon it; pistols that were used by Charles XII. of Sweden and Louis XIV. of France; a perfect series of fire-arms from their first invention down to the present time, including the old arquebuse and a great variety of curious and richly finished pistols, including our old friend, the revolver, of a hundred years or more ago; the great scythe-sword used by the Poles in their memorable struggle; curious arms and trophies of various kinds captured by the Saxon troops in different memorable battles, including a Moslem tent of a Turkish commander, and the horse-tail standards, cimeters, and shields taken from the Turks.

In a Saloon of Costumes we saw the robes and regalias of the old kings of Poland, which were most gorgeous in gold embroidery and jewelry; also coronation robes worn by various princes. The shoes worn by Napoleon at his coronation, and a sumptuous saddle that once belonged to him, are among these relics.

Of swords there seemed to be every conceivable pattern, short, long, broad, cavalry, and cimeter. There were those with their hilts wrought to a degree that suggested the Chinese ivory carving; others fairly crusted and blazing with diamonds and precious stones; scabbards of gold, silver, and more serviceable leather or iron, — a museum of swords, rich, rare, curious, and historical.

But we have not yet done with this grand collection of art, antiquity, and science, the Zwinger, in which most of the noted Dresden collections are placed.

Besides those already mentioned, there is the natural-history collection, which, though now small, will soon be one of the most interesting of its features. The collection of stuffed birds here is very fine, and so is that of every species of butterfly and moth. This is succeeded by a hall devoted to minerals and fossils, in which there is a fine display of ores of different kinds, geological specimens, and curious fossil birds, fishes, and plants, which have been discovered from time to time. A mathematical and medical museum contains many curious scientific instruments and apparatus, some of which are of memorable historic interest, and others showing their earliest invention and progress that science has since made.

Although a Saxon king to-day would make but a poor display in the comparison of his income list with that of the other monarchs of the old world, his collection of treasures, kept intact and handed down since the reign of Augustus the Strong in 1724, would indicate more gorgeous possessions than any other, and rival those which we have read of as belonging to East Indian princes.

For when one fairly gets in among the wonders of the celebrated Green Vaults, it really seems as if the workshop of the fabled gnomes had been opened to view, such is the wondrous wealth of gold and gems and precious stones there displayed, and not only of value in themselves, but made more so by the curious and ingenious workmanship that has been bestowed upon them; and as you pass from room to room, and from cabinet to cabinet, where curious-shaped pearls are used to represent grotesque dwarfs, and rubies and emeralds are wrought into Lilliputian figures, great ostrich-eggs into artistic drinking-cups, and whole fortunes of diamonds twisted into glittering and flashing semblance of feathers, plumes, and flowers, you can but, amid continuous exclamations of wonder and admiration, find that the thought will continually intrude itself, as to whether the years of patient labor required to produce these results might not have been better expended, or whether this wondrous collection of wealth might not be used to more advantage and service to mankind.

The royal palace which contains the Green Vaults is an irregular old building inclosing two quadrangles. It was founded in 1534, and in the eighteenth century was enlarged and improved by Augustus the Strong. In fact, it seems as if one could scarcely look up any authority of museum, palace, science, art, or advancement here that this grand old Augustus in his time did not put the impress of his encouraging influence upon.

At one end of this palace is a fine tower, said to be the loftiest in Dresden, over three hundred and sixty feet in height, which I should have liked to ascend; but from some blunder of my ticket of admission, or from the lack of my knowledge of the tongue of the country, or the custodian's lack of understanding of English and French, we were unable so to do, and contented ourselves with viewing the magnificent frescos in the throne-room, which represent different scenes in the lives of great lawgivers, commencing with Moses and his tables of stone, and coming down to Maximilian I.; and the splendid state ball-room, which is decorated with frescos of the heroes of Greek and Roman mythology and classical history.

The Green Vaults we found to be on the ground floor of this palace, probably so called because they are not green, but were once decorated in that color. They consist of eight different rooms, in which are collected a most wondrous assortment of curious riches — among them splendid carvings in precious metals. A statue of St. George, cut from a solid piece of cast-iron, is a curiosity, although iron may not be classed as a " precious " metal; but in the same room are bronzes of rare and beautiful workmanship, among them one by John of Bologna, a crucifix of most artistic design and finish, also groups of the Rape of Proserpine, Bacchus and Children, and statues of Louis XIV. and Augustus the Strong, and numerous other elegant figures and groups.

There is a room entirely devoted to the ivory collection, which contains some of the most wonderful specimens of carving in that article I ever looked upon. One is an ivory cup, only sixteen inches high, which is one mass of intricate carving, which must have been the labor of years, for upon it are more than one hundred distinct figures carved, representing the Foolish Virgins, lamps in hand; Lucifer and his angels being hurled down from Heaven in every variety of attitude; and the very features in the faces of these figures are wrought out so that an expression is visible in each. A wondrous crucifix, wrought by Michael Angelo; a battle-scene, carved by the cunning chisel of Albrecht Dürer; elegant vases carved with figures in bas-reliefs; hunting-cups, with scenes of the chase beautifully wrought upon them; elegantly carved sword or dagger handles; groups of the Battle of the Centaurs; Hunting the Stag; the Crucifixion, &c.

Another room was rich in elegant Florentine mosaics; carvings in amber of crucifixes; angels, Madonnas, and curious figures of animals and flowers; exquisite paintings in enamel, including a beautiful Madonna and Ecce Homo; wondrous work in coral, of birds and flowers and heads; a magnificent chimney-piece of Dresden china, which was elegantly adorned with various precious stones, agates, chalcedony, and rock-crystals. Others contained great ostrich-eggs fashioned as cups, and set into pedestals, with tracery and pictures wrought upon their sides, some in a framework of delicate tracery of gold that sparkled with diamonds, rubies, and emeralds; nautilus-shell cups, their sides brilliant with the hues of the opal, set in elaborate framework of the goldsmith's art, a choice design upholding them, as ship or vase or drinking-cup, according to the fancy of the designer; drinking-cups fashioned by the artificer into griffins or dragons, and seemingly into most inconvenient shapes for use; and two goblets actually cut out of antique gems, and valued at ten thousand dollars the pair.

Here, in one of the rooms devoted to gold and silver ornamental work, we saw a pitcher and cup wrought by Benvenuto Cellini; splendid gold and silver wrought plates, goblets, pitchers, and cups in exquisite design; and in another room, cups of agate, jasper, chalcedony, great vases of pure and beautiful rock-crystal, a large globe of rock-crystal, and the largest pearl in the world, which is the size of a hen's egg, and wrought into the shape of a fat-bellied court dwarf.

A display of jewels of rare value, and the magnificent regalia of Augustus II., King of Poland; a collection of Dresden porcelain, with curious carvings in ebony and other woods, occupied another room, — a perfect museum of astonishing workmanship.

Another feature of the Museum was a curious collection of caricatures of men and animals, made from pearls and other precious stones, — a man, for instance, with body of glittering ruby, a quaint-shaped pearl forming his face, and two sapphires his legs; a great pearl forming the body of a dog; a monkey, with eyes that flamed in rubies and diamonds, and a body that was of emerald; curiously shaped pearls, sapphires, agates, or other precious stones, that would make you laugh to see how these natural shapes had been adapted to cause them to become pot-bellied little old men, red-bodied hunchbacks, or green dragons with ruby heads and diamond eyes, or deformed dwarfs, whose bodies were worth a small fortune; serpents that flashed in all the colors of the rainbow, and peacocks that unfolded most attractive tails.

The further we penetrated, the richer and more wondrous grew the wealth. Suits of armor that flashed with diamonds and precious stones; regalia that was heavy with rubies, emeralds, diamonds, pearls, and sapphires of marvellous brilliancy; plumes of diamonds, and necklaces of emeralds and pearls; one grand necklace of great diamonds, being valued at seven hundred and fifty thousand dollars; swords that in drawing you might grasp a hundred and fifty thousand dollars in the great, flashing diamonds that studded the hilt; the electoral sword of Saxony; daggers that rivalled the most wondrous worn by Eastern princes, and costly jewels that were enough, it seemed, for a nation's ransom.

In the room, the last of the series, diamonds seem to be shown in masses, and other precious stones to be a drug; and here are many of the most rare and interesting specimens of jewels: the largest onyx known, — seven inches high, and two and one-half broad; opals of a size and blaze that were fairly amazing; the largest sardonyx known, which is six and a half inches long, and four and a quarter broad; Peruvian emeralds, presented, in 1581, by the Emperor Rudolph III.; splendid sapphires, one of very large size, the gift of Peter the Great; a black diamond, a very rare and curious gem; two rings that belonged to Martin Luther; ·the crown-jewels, including one remarkable green diamond, which is used as an ornament for the hat, and weighs one hundred and sixty grains, and is worth half a million dollars.

Elegantly wrought works of the goldsmith's art are also displayed here, among which is a costly lamp, upon which is displayed the myth of Acteon and Diana; beautiful vases and drinking-cups, too elegant to use, being simply specimens of rare artistic workmanship in the precious metals. Some were mere contrivances, designed, it would seem, to prevent persons from drinking from them. Many of these were wrought, in 1705 to 1728, by a celebrated Saxon artificer (Dinglinger), who was the Saxon Benvenuto Cellini.

But the crowning wonder in the Green Vaults is the costly toy entitled "The Court of the Great Mogul," which represents the Great Mogul seated on his throne in state, surrounded by his guards and courtiers, receiving and giving audience to ambassadors, and awaiting the approach of troops and subjects, who are seen advancing to do homage or bring gifts or tribute. The space occupied by this court and the actors in it is about thirty-six by fifty inches in space; and the number of figures, none of which is taller than one's little finger. is one hundred and thirty-two, all of gold, diamonds, and precious stones.

The tent over the Mogul's elegant gold-enamelled and decorated throne is of gold,—the throne itself, the size of half a letter-sheet, a perfect blaze of diamonds, rubies, and emeralds. The figures are all elegantly apparelled with rich gold-enamel, rubies, diamonds, and costly chasings upon their Oriental robes; and the most delicate finish is visible in each of these little figures, even to the features of their faces and the sparkling of jewels on their sword-hilts. Some of the figures were cut jewels, and others had turbans of cut rubies and emeralds. Here approaching is an ambassador with his officers; in another place, a troop of horse; again, an Eastern dignitary, with elephant, Ethiopian slaves, and costly retinue; a party arriving in palanquins, a whole supper-party carousing at table, and a tiny band of musicians playing at full blast upon their instruments; troops of guards, properly posted; slaves, sentinels, and officials passing from point to point over the golden terraces upon their several duties. All are beautifully wrought in the highest style of the goldsmith's art. Twenty years' time, besides I know not what amount of money, was expended in this golden representation of Lilliput,—a curious, wondrous, and most costly, and, one cannot help saying, useless toy.

Fatigued with our examination of this Aladdin's cave, we were glad of a pleasant drive round the outskirts of the city, where were the residences of many of the better classes of people. The houses are generally surrounded by handsome gardens, and at one angle of the same a solid wall is built towards the road beneath broad, spreading trees that overhang it, or an arbor is trained above it. Here in this angle a little platform for tea and beer-drinking is arranged for the family, where, as they sit, their line of vision is just over the inclosure, so that they see all the passing without being too much exposed themselves. Many of these arbors at the wall-corners are elaborately and beautifully arranged, and shaded with beautiful running plants or ornamented with choice exotics, and, on pleasant summer afternoons, are almost always occupied by family groups.

The humbler classes in the suburbs, who have no such protection from the scrutiny of the passers-by, seemed to enjoy themselves equally well in the little garden plots in front of their houses; and it was a pretty sight to see the old artisan and his family grouped around a pine table, and taking their evening meal beneath a little bower of running vines and flowers, sitting in their rustic seats in a little garden hardly twenty feet square, gay with many-hued flowers, and a perfect model of neatness.

Good musical entertainments may be had at a very cheap rate in Dresden, — that is, if one will be content to take them as a larger portion of the inhabitants do, which is at the beer gardens in the summer season. At the Belvedere Restaurant and Gardens, on the banks of the Elbe, we listened to a very fine programme of music, performed by a full orchestra, the admission to which was but about ten cents. The sales of Vienna beer, light wines, and other refreshments to the four or five hundred persons who were present was, of course, the chief source of profit to the proprietor.

At this place, and also at a fine park called the *Grosser Garten*, we met groups of people of the first respectability around the tables, sipping their beer, applauding well-played compositions heartily, and at the intermission walking about and visiting each other at their different tables, as is done at different boxes at the opera-house. The waiters at these beer-gardens literally have their hands full; for they will carry a wonderful number of beer-glasses at once, and take an innumerable number of orders at a time, the latter being given and executed at the close of the performance of each piece.

Dresden is full of these pleasure and beer gardens, and some are pleasantly situated on the river-banks, and, besides the music, give exhibitions of fireworks on certain evenings; or the visitor may, during the day, enjoy the cool breeze and pleasant views which they command. The American visitor in Dresden may be certain of finding a very liberal representation of his countrymen in the summer season at the evening concerts at these places.

As it is pleasant in the summer season here, the living comparatively cheap, the surroundings of the city pleasant, music cheap, excellent, and plentiful, and the city decorous and quiet, and said to be one of the best places to study the German language in, it has quite a large population of American and English residents. As usual, however, I was informed by one of my countrymen that the Americans had, by their prodigality of expenditure, been the means of raising the price of living, within the past few years, as well as that of articles which tourists most do purchase; and even in some of the beer-gardens, the sharper sort of waiters have now the trick of charging the newly arrived American, whom he may detect as such, a trifle more than the regular rate for his glass of beer, a trick he would not dare practise on a regular *habitué*.

There seems to be but very little business enterprise in Dresden; all transactions of that nature being carried on in a slow, phlegmatic, Dutch sort of style, as if time was of no account, which is exceedingly exasperating to the electric American. This may be the reason that many tired ones, who have come to Europe for rest from business, halt here for the season.

Dresden porcelain, so celebrated the world over, is made at the Royal Porcelain Factory, founded in 1710, at Meissen, a short distance from the city, where six hundred workmen are kept employed; but we did not visit it. Scarce any tourist leaves the city, however, without buying a specimen of painting on porcelain; principally copies of popular and celebrated pictures in the gallery, such as "The Chocolate Girl," "The Madonna," Salomon Konincx's "Reading Monk," Gerard Duow's "Praying Hermit," "The Three Children," by Vogel, &c.

Very beautiful water-color copies of the Madonna are made here; but, as poor and cheap copies are also made, visitors who purchase either porcelain or other style of copies of pictures should be good judges, or purchase at reliable places, lest they be imposed upon. Some of the artists who copy pictures on porcelain will propose to take orders of the visitor and forward him a copy to Paris or London, — a risk which should seldom if ever be taken, and especially no money paid in advance for such work; for these artists rival the Paris shopkeeper in the matter of promises, which, they evidently consider, are only invented to be made, not performed.

We sought the Hotel du Nord, in Berlin, where we had very tolerable accommodations at fair prices. It is situated on the street known as *Unter den Linden*, which is a broad, grand avenue of one hundred and sixty feet in width, and, as is well known, takes its name from the double row of linden-trees that are planted along it, and which, from the frequent references made to it by newspaper correspondents, the style in which authors emphasize the "linden" part of it, and the unctuous manner in which those who spoke of it rolled out the words "Unter den Linden" from under their tongues, had been pictured in my imagination as chiefly remarkable for the elegance of form and umbrageous shade which these beautiful trees would present; but, alas! for imagination, the reality presented only a lean array of trees, sparse in foliage, and nothing to compare to the linden walk on Boston Common, the elegant elms of New Haven or Portland.

As far as the linden part of the street is concerned, it is scarcely up to mediocrity; but it is in the busiest and best part of the city, contains grand hotels and shops, beautiful palaces, and statues, including that of Frederick the Great; and, crossing it at right angles, are many of the other broad avenues of the city, down which the spectator, as he passes them, has a good view of the busy scenes that are transpiring.

The celebrated Brandenburg Gate, which is a sort of triumphal arch between the city and the great pleasure park of several hundred acres, known as the *Thier Garten*, is at one end of this grand avenue, and the Royal Palace at the other, while at the finest point in the street, near the great public buildings, is the magnificent bronze statue of Frederick the Great, familiar to all Americans who have visited the American Centennial Exposition at Philadelphia, where so many bronze copies of it were on exhibition in the German department.

The statue of Frederick the Great, being but a few rods distant from our hotel, was the first sight that we turned our attention to. It is a magnificent monument in bronze, the pedestal surmounted by an equestrian figure of the monarch.

Baedeker's guide-book says, "The Great King is represented on horseback, with his coronation robes and his walking-stick, in bronze." If Frederick's coronation robes were a close-fitting military frock, and a military cloak, fastened at the neck, and falling back from the shoulders, then this description is correct; for in this way the figure is clad, the high military boots, small clothes, sash, and well-known cocked hat completing the costume.

The monument is in all forty-two feet in height, its pedestal divided into three sections. The first above the foundation-stone, which is of polished granite, contains the inscription, and the names of distinguished men of the time of the great monarch. Upon the top of this, which is not covered by the second section, — which is smaller, and leaves a broad shelf or platform all around it, — are large bronze figures, of life-size, of contemporaries and distinguished military officers of the king, as Prince Henry of Prussia, Generals Zieten, Seydlitz, and others, — the figures at the corners being equestrian.

Upon the sides of the second section are also figures of distinguished men, sculptured in bas-relief. Above this is the third section, supporting the platform, upon which stands the great equestrian figure. This block is ornamented on the sides and ends with allegorical and other figures representing scenes in the king's life, and illustrating his love of arts, arms, and music; and at the four corners are the figures of Justice, Strength, Wisdom, and Moderation.

Berlin seems to be partial to statues, for all along *Unter den Linden* are statues of her celebrated men, the military element predominating, and the exteriors of the palaces and museums are adorned with groups in marble or in bronze. A little further along, and we come to the palace bridge, or old *Schloss-Brücke,* as they call it, which crosses an arm of the river Spree, upon which the city is located. On each side of this bridge are four groups of marble statuary, larger than life, illustrating military life, and I suppose designed as an incentive to the Prussian military spirit.

In the first group, Minerva is exciting the youth to the profession of arms, by exhibiting to him a warrior's shield, on which are inscribed the names of Alexander, Cæsar, and Frederick; in another, she instructs him in the use of arms, and is teaching him to throw the javelin; in another she presents him with a sword; and in the fourth she crowns him victorious. The other groups represent her protecting the warrior, encouraging him to action, raising him when wounded, and conducting him in triumph.

Between Frederick's statue and the bridge just described I paused to look at the bronze statue of General Blücher, with two other generals, one at his right and one at his left, all over life-size; and in front of the guard-house are placed statues of Bülow and another general, both very well executed in bronze, and the pedestals ornamented with handsome bas-reliefs; while beyond the bridge, in the *Lustgarten,* — a two hundred and fifty yards square inclosure, — is an equestrian statue of Frederick William III.

This inclosure is bounded by the Royal Palace on one side, the old Museum, the Cathedral, and the arm of the Spree just spoken of, on the others.

The old Museum front presents a beautiful Ionic portico, about two hundred and seventy-five feet in length, with a double row of handsome pillars of that order of architecture, eighteen in number. Above them, upon the cornice they support, is a row of eagles with half-spread wings; and high above these, on the corners of a central dome, two groups of statuary, — "the *Dioscuri*" is what the guide-book calls them, and which the reader who is not versed in Greek and Roman mythology (as is the condition of more than two-thirds of those who use guide-books), will ascertain, on overhauling his classical dictionary, means the well-known mythical heroes, Castor and Pollux. Castor was famed for his skill in managing horses, and Pollux for boxing; so one may presume that the statues must have been designed for the equestrian brother, as they represent athletes beckoning or holding up their arms to rampant horses.

But if the traveller has been at Rome, he will recognize them as copies of the two groups on Monte Cavallo, or Quirinal Hill, which are supposed to represent Castor and Pollux, and to have been sculptured by Phidias and Praxiteles. Indeed, a later edition of one guide-book seems to recognize this error of supposing all travellers to possess a classical education, and calls the statuary "The Horse-tamers of Monte Cavallo."

At each side of the entrance of the old Museum are two splendid bronze groups: one a horseman engaged in combat with a lion that he has thrown to the ground, and is about to transfix with his spear; and the other an old and familiar acquaintance that figured at the first Crystal Palace Exhibition in London, — the Amazon on horseback, defending herself against a tiger, by Kiss, — a beautiful and effective group. In front of the steps of the Museum is a huge granite basin, which fairly rivals some of the great stone vases of the ancient Romans, which are preserved in the collection in the Vatican, for it is twenty-two feet in diameter, and weighs seventy-five tons. It was cut from a single large bowlder, and brought to Berlin from a spot thirty miles distant.

Two more large groups of "horse-tamers" are posted at the entrance by which the public are admitted from the *Lustgarten* to the Royal Palace; and one of the most spirited groups of bronze statuary in Berlin, I think, is that of St. George and the Dragon, a colossal group in bronze, by Kiss, in the first great court-yard after entering at this portal.

It represents the valiant English champion, not in armor save coroneted helmet, which gives opportunity for the sculptor to show the contour of an elegantly moulded form, seated upon a rearing horse. With left hand he bears the banner of the cross aloft; the right is swung up, grasping the trenchant blade for the downward cut at the monster that is partially prostrated beneath his horse's fore feet, but which rears its terrible form, the scales upon the neck rising with its anger, and its horrid claws uplifted to drag the rider from his seat. The figure of the dragon, with its demoniac wings, scales, and long, serpent-like tail, with its fold catching around one of the horse's hind legs, is the best reproduction of the mythical monster that I have ever seen. Certainly it is a most elaborate and finished piece of work, while the figure of the horse is excellently done; and St. George, with noble and determined countenance, sits the steed like a bold rider, and wields his sword like a brave warrior.

Just before passing over the *Schloss-Brücke* (palace bridge) above mentioned, we see the Grand Opera House, along the roof of which is a perfect string of statuary; and in the tympanum, which is a sort of flat, triangular space inclosed by the cornice, supported by four pillars above the main entrance, is an appropriate group, which is cast in zinc. They represent the Muse of Music, the Tragic and Comic Muses, the Dramatic Poet, allegorical figures of Painting and Sculpture, a Terpsichorean group, and the Three Graces.

The reader will observe, or he who has ever been in Berlin, that I am taking the usual first walk of every newly arrived tourist who settles himself upon *Unter den Linden*, that is, a saunter up and down that splendid avenue, to get the bearings and distances, and see the beautiful buildings and their exterior ornamentations, and the statues that abound in the city, before entering the picture-galleries, museums, or shops. So I went to the other end of the famous street to see the Brandenburg Gate, which is at the opposite point from that which I have just been describing.

This structure is modelled after the Propylæ, an entrance to a grand temple or sacred inclosure at Athens. It is a splendid structure, seventy-five feet in height, and two hundred in width. The central entrance is reserved for royalty only, and the structure is supported by elegant Doric columns. There are four other entrances; and the top is crowned by a group, in copper, of Victory in a chariot drawn by four horses, which is celebrated as having been carried away by Bonaparte in 1807, but brought back in triumph in 1814.

Near this gate is the fine square known as *Pariser Platz*, named in honor of the victories of 1814; and about here are several beautiful buildings, among them Blücher's Palace, presented to him by the city as a testimonial for his arriving at Waterloo before night, and thereby gratifying Wellington's wish on that memorable day, "that night or Blücher would come;" the residence of Marshal Wrangel; and the palaces of the French embassy, Count Boitzenberg; and various public buildings.

By the time one has reached the Brandenburg Gate, making the pedestrian tour that I had, in this first examination of *Unter den Linden*, he comes to the conclusion that there is much here to see, and that Berlin is a large city. One fact which struck me as singular is, that so little stone is used in the construction of buildings. This was found to be accounted for by the fact, that there are no good stone quarries in the vicinity of Berlin; hence brick and stucco work is extensively used, which lacks that solid and substantial appearance which one looks for in large buildings. Berlin is said to be situated in the midst of a dreary plain of sand, that is destitute of either beauty or fertility, and a writer has described it as "an oasis of stone and brick in a Sahara of sand." But there is more brick than stone.

The city of Berlin ranks fourth among the capitals of Europe, and contains nearly a million of inhabitants, of which twenty-three thousand are soldiers, twenty thousand Roman Catholics, and sixteen thousand Jews. When Louis XIV. was weak and despotic enough to revoke the celebrated Edict of Nantes, as he did in 1685, and drive four hundred thousand Protestants out of French dominions, who would rather leave the country than conform to the established religion, France lost by the act her best merchants, manufacturers, and skilled artisans. The loss to the nation was immense, and the gain, to Prussia and other countries that received them with open arms, correspondingly great. Berlin especially profited by this emigration, and there are still among her inhabitants over six thousand French Protestants, descendants of the exiles who left their native land and sought asylum here by reason of the French sovereign's infamous decree. The surface of the city of Berlin is as flat as Philadelphia, but is not laid out in such painfully parallelogramic regularity as the American city. Its streets are broad and generally well kept, and there is but little in their general features to remind the American that he is in a foreign country.

The streets are all "strasses" (*straassers*, as you must learn to call them), and you will find in the old part of the town the *Königs-Strasse*, or King's Street, a busy and bustling scene of trade. Here is situated the Imperial Post Office; and, opposite, a splendid brick edifice, the *Rathhaus*, as Baedeker's guide-books call it, neglecting to translate it into English as the City Hall. It is built of granite and brick, and has a frontage of three hundred and twenty-five feet, a magnificent portal, and a great tower which is two hundred and seventy-six feet in height. I sauntered in without guide, and up its staircase to a grand corridor, the vaulting of which was spangled with stars, and the glorious stained-glass windows rich with the armorial bearings of nearly one hundred different cities and towns; and entered the magnificent saloon devoted to the library, the vaulted ceiling of which is upheld by fourteen columns and twenty pillars. The books are in bookcases, the doors of which are ornamented with medallion portraits.

There is another elegant hall here, which the guide-book, presuming that all travellers understand German, calls a "*Festsaal*," and which a German friend tells me signifies Banquet Hall, which has a superb ceiling in fret-work, broad oaken doors elegantly carved, and magnificent candelabra. Near by is the Town Council-Chamber, which is elegantly decorated; and the Magistrate's Saloon, which is adorned with fine full-length pictures of the kings of Prussia. The grand tower of this building is said to command a fine prospect; but the author, having had considerable pedestrian exercise in the lengthy streets of Berlin, resisted the courteous invitation of the custodian to ascend.

Other interesting streets, which my pedestrian rambles brought me into one day, are the Leipziger-Strasse and the Friedrichs-Strasse, the latter the longest street in Berlin. This quarter of the city, called the *Friedrich Stadt*, is that most visited by tourists, is the best and most regularly laid out, and contains the finest shops. And, speaking of shops, Berlin is the headquarters for amber ornaments. There are quantities of amber used in Vienna and other cities for mouthpieces for pipes; but Berlin is where the tourist can make his purchases most to advantage. In the shop-windows, elegant necklaces, chains, bracelets, brooches, cigar-holders, mouthpieces, and even candlesticks and vases of it, were exhibited, some of exquisite and delicate straw color and translucent. This is the "earth amber," and is the most valuable. Amber varies in delicacy of tint like coral, the palest and lightest of yellow being the most expensive, and the latter, of the purest description, can be found in beautiful designs at the Berlin shops.

In America, we are all familiar with Berlin worsted work. The worsted was in old times called "crewel," to distinguish it from worsted yarn. Here the fine, delicate work called single stitch, especially in delicate designs of flowers, and even copies of paintings for screens, which are wrought with great beauty, may be purchased at a price which to American ideas is a very low figure; and American ladies, consequently, come away laden with it; while the beadwork, which in America is sold with Berlin work, and which some of my lady friends expected also to find here, they were disappointed in not being able to obtain, that class of work being found in its perfection in Frankfort and Munich.

The Leipziger-Strasse, above mentioned, is also a fine avenue, running parallel with *Unter den Linden*, and is a busy street full of shops, containing, among other attractions to shoppers, the show-rooms of the Royal Porcelain Manufactory, filled with beautiful specimens of this attractive merchandise, which fairly rivals the Dresden work. It is a museum of samples of the best work from the royal factories. Strolling down this street, the pedestrian will see sculptured in sandstone, in front of the Prussian War Department, figures of an artillery-man, a light horseman, cuirassier, and grenadier.

Wilhelms-Strasse (William Street, the translation of many of these street names is so obvious that it is hardly necessary to give them) is quite an elegant avenue. It leaves *Unter den Linden*, and, with Friedrichs-Strasse and a street called Linden-Strasse, terminates in a grand circular "*Platz*" known as the *Belle Alliance Platz*, named in honor of the alliance against Napoleon, and containing a magnificent monument erected in honor of the peace of 1815, called the Column of Peace, which was raised in 1840 to commemorate a peace that had lasted a quarter of a century. It is a splendid column of granite, with marble capital, surmounted by a figure of Victory, with the wreath in one hand and the palm of peace in the other. The Wilhelms-Strasse, near the *Under den Linden*, is considered the most aristocratic quarter of Berlin, containing, as it does, the palaces of Princes Alexander and George of Prussia, residences of the Minister of the Household, Chancellor of the Empire, Minister of Justice, and other distinguished personages.

At one side of this avenue there opens a handsome square called the *Wilhelms-Platz*, which is elegantly laid out with flower-beds, and contains six handsome statues of distinguished generals in the army of Frederick the Great, who served with him in his most memorable campaigns.

Perambulations through Berlin streets rendered a ride out to the *Thiergarten* (garden of animals) a pleasing variation. This is the great pleasure-ground and park of Berlin, and is two miles in length by about one in width, elegantly laid out and finely shaded by grand old trees, and containing artificial ponds and streams, some of which — owing, I suppose, to the sluggish current of the river Spree, upon which they must depend — seemed to be mere pools of green, stagnant slime; but the rustic roads and paths were pleasant and romantic, and were decorated here and there with statues, while along its borders are some of the most elegant residences in the city. At one extremity of the garden is the Zoölogical Collection, a remarkably fine one, excellently arranged, and containing at the time of the author's visit an extensive collection of wild beasts in good condition.

Driving from the Zoölogical Gardens, we rode out over the Charlottenburg road to that town, to visit the beautiful

Mausoleum of Frederick William III. and his queen Louise. This is a Doric structure in the palace garden, a beautifully laid out spot, and is approached through an avenue of sombre pines. The interior of the mausoleum is sheathed with rich marbles, and in the centre are the marble sarcophagi of the king and queen. They have richly ornamented pediment and cornices, the ends being supported by an eagle, the royal shield with eagle and crown placed at the sides, and handsomely carved pillars at the four corners. Upon marble couches at the top rest the recumbent figures of the royal pair, most beautiful specimens of artistic sculpture.

Queen Louise, who died at the age of thirty-five, is represented as lying with a loose sheet thrown over her figure, while her head, with the tiara which sets off her beautiful face so well, rests on the pillow, and her hands are crossed upon the breast. It is an exquisite representation of this beautiful woman. Her full-length portrait is in the Royal Palace at Berlin, and will none the less fail to excite the spectator's admiration. All the details of this fine sculpture are so faithfully executed, that, in the subdued halo of delicately purpled light that falls down upon the figure like an atmosphere which is perfumed with a faint fragrance of flowers, the spectator is half in doubt if the careless folds of the translucent drapery, which reveals even the shape of the nails upon the feet and the graceful contour of the body, will not be blown aside by the gentle breeze that sweeps in from the garden. The king's figure, also recumbent, is in military uniform, and folded in his military cloak, and is a splendid piece of workmanship.

Both of these figures were executed by the sculptor Rauch, who is to Berlin what Schwanthaler was to Munich, or Thorwaldsen to Denmark. His works and designs are among the most prominent in Berlin, and Queen Louise was his royal patron when living. This statue of her is said to be his masterpiece, and he spent fifteen years completing the two figures.

At the side of each sarcophagus stands an elegant candelabrum; one is ornamented with sculptured figures of the Three Fates, by Rauch, and the other executed by Tieck, with the three Horæ, — goddesses who gave to a state good laws, justice, and peace. Around the cornice of the temple are appropriate extracts from Scripture. This royal pair, who possessed many excellent traits of character, and were thorough Protestants, died sincerely lamented by the whole nation.

CHAPTER XVII.

It will require some patience, if the tourist has already visited the Vatican, the galleries of Dresden and Munich, and maybe some others, to give the museums at Berlin the attention they deserve: first, because the collection of paintings is not equal in extent, value, or historical celebrity to those we have already seen; and, secondly, because in the Museum of Art and Sculpture the objects are but different specimens of those we have already seen elsewhere, or casts of great original works of antiquity. This last feature, however, is by no means to be despised, and *good* casts of the great works of sculpture in the world are, as is well known, of genuine service to the art student, and also even to the mere curiosity-seeker or casual visitor, as an educator of the taste and the eye, so that when he looks upon the grand original he is the better prepared to appreciate and enjoy it.

The museums in Berlin are known as the Old Museum and the New Museum. The old is comparatively a modern affair, as it was finished in 1828, in the reign of Frederick William III. It is connected with the New Museum by a passage gallery. The entrance and front of the Old Museum are adorned by Kiss's statue of the Amazon attacked by a Tiger, and the Horseman and Lion I have already described; but after passing up the grand flight of steps we come to the grand portico, which is elegantly decorated with wall-paintings of mythological or allegorical subjects.

At one side is Uranus, represented as seated, with the stars as graceful couples dancing about him, while a great rainbow spans the sky; and the zodiac with its twelve constellations stretches around. Then we have representations of Jupiter creating Light; Prometheus lighting his Torch by Jupiter's lightning-flashes; Art, Love, and Labor; War with his spear, and Peace with her palm; Nymphs welcoming the approach of light; Venus, the star of the morning, preceding the Sun; and the great Sun-god himself in his chariot rising from the sea.

Turning to the right, we find that the artists have made human life their subject in its four epochs, as represented by the four Seasons. Spring, the first, shows us a sibyl writing; pastoral tribes and herds; the Muse and Psyche stringing the poet's lyre, &c., — a well-executed fresco, but showing a poverty of illustration of so prolific a subject. Next is Summer, the noon of life, which is represented by the harvest; a nymph offering a cup to a warrior; Pegasus springing from the top of Mount Helicon; a youth and maiden, nymphs and poet; shepherd playing on a flute, showing, maybe, artistic skill, but requiring a stretch of imagination or very thorough artistic education to satisfy one that it is a good allegory of life's noon or summer as it is set down to be.

Autumn, or Evening, is represented by the vintage; young men gathering grapes and pressing them under the direction of an old man; a mother with her child at the fireside; art developed by the sculptor; heroes returning victorious, &c. Winter, or Night, shows us the Muses dancing before Old Age; an old man studying the starry heavens; a sailor pulling his boat out to sea, encouraged by the Muses;

and farther on we have the grave with mourning relatives, and beyond that, genii of light, hailing a new day.

Beneath these extensive allegorical representations, which are from the pencils of Stürmer, Schadow, and other eminent artists, are fourteen pictures of the Myths of Theseus and Hercules, including representations of the familiar stories of Theseus killing the Centaur, Hercules killing the Nemean lion, fetching the Hesperidean fruit, and subduing the horses of Diomedes.

But let us go inside the Museum, which is done by ascending a grand flight of steps or staircase leading from here to the vestibule. Here stands a metal copy of the great Warwick vase, on the right and left of which are two granite pillars, one having the figure of Victory and the other Apollo on its summit. The walls are decorated with frescos representing barbarous and peaceful life. After leaving the vestibule, the visitor finds himself in the grand rotunda of the museum, a large circular hall fifty or sixty feet in height, and crowned by a glass cupola. Between the columns which uphold the gallery above, are eighteen ancient statues of Jupiter, Æsculapius, Minerva, Juno, &c., and two great bathing-tubs from the Baths of Diocletian at Rome.

Crossing from here, we enter a great gallery of sculpture, known as the Gallery of Gods and Heroes. This, although it contains upwards of a thousand specimens, will interest those who have visited the Vatican at Rome but little, as there are but few figures that are of any great celebrity or value. Notwithstanding this, as specimens of ancient art and antiquity, the visitor will probably find much that is worthy of notice. Among those that I find pencilled down in my note-book are a figure of a girl sitting and playing with dice; two superb figures of athletes in the attitude of shooting, and an exquisite figure of Apollo and four of the Muses; the figure of Polyhymnia, a beautiful draped statue; a bronze figure of a boy praying, which was found in the river Tiber and purchased by Frederick the Great for seven thousand five hundred dollars; Apollo and Mercury; Cupid bending his bow; Bacchus with his panther; Roman Gladiator; Satyr and Hermaphrodite, and several fine busts of mythological deities. Opening out of the great Sculpture Hall are two lesser ones: the Greek cabinet, and the Etruscan-Roman cabinet.

The walls of the Grecian cabinet are adorned with paintings representing Greek life from birth to the hour of death: the plays of the child, sports and joys of youth, occupations of man, and lastly the funeral procession, succeeded by the barge of Charon ready to convey the soul across the river Styx. This cabinet contains some fine specimens of Greek sculpture and antiquities. The Etruscan cabinet has its walls painted in imitation of the walls of the tombs at Tarquinii, and contains many interesting remains of Etruscan funeral monuments, such as coffin-chests, one of alabaster on which was sculptured a battle-scene; a sarcophagus with a representation of Achilles mourning, sculptured upon the top; altars and Roman remains of similar description.

Opening at one end of the Hall of Gods and Heroes is the Hall of the Emperors, so called for its containing a large number of busts and figures of Roman emperors, such as Cæsar, Vespasian, Vitellius, Tiberius, Caligula, &c.; in fact, it seemed as if the whole line of Cæsars and Roman emperors were here. There was a grand colossal head of Vespasian; Trajan represented as Jupiter; Marcus Aurelius as a ploughman, with a team of bulls; Commodus; a red jasper bust of Titus; Scipio Africanus the Elder; Crispina, the wife of Commodus; Marciana, sister of Trajan; and Plautilla, wife of Caracalla, — more than a hundred figures in all.

At the opposite end of the Hall of Heroes opens the Hall of Greek, Roman, and Assyrian sculptures. Among the Greek and Roman objects are an antique copy of the celebrated figure in the Capitoline Museum of a boy extracting a thorn; a porphyry statue of Vespasian; Faun with young Bacchus; an athlete in black marble; a head of Medusa, &c. Of the Assyrian works there are the great gray marble or alabaster slabs from the walls of the royal palaces of ancient Nineveh, which were erected about 800 B. C. These are covered with figures representing religious ceremonies, warlike and hunting scenes; also figures of demons, priests, kings, and eunuchs. One represents two eunuchs, with the riding equipage of the king; another a procession; a third a collection of warriors and eunuchs,—all interesting specimens of Assyrian decoration.

Having seen thus much of the antique, we turn to a hall opening out of the Hall of the Emperors, which contains a very pleasing collection of mediæval and modern sculpture, including what is said to be the best existing likeness of the Emperor Napoleon I., a statue of him as a Roman emperor executed by Chaudet, also the first original of Canova — a Hebe.

Descending to the next story, let us visit what is known as the *Antiquarium*, which is a most interesting portion of the Museum, especially to students. This is divided into collections of gems, coins, antique objects of metal of household and daily use among the Greeks and Romans, terracotta articles, and a splendid collection of antique clay vases, containing about two thousand specimens. These clay vases and vessels are chiefly from central and lower Italy, and from Greece and the Greek islands. They were generally those placed as gifts for the dead or in their honor in the tombs, where they were arranged about the corpse. These vases are important on account of their variety of form and grace of model, and also as being the only remnants that have been preserved of antique paintings.

Here are, for instance, vases whose models are used in our own time, but which were moulded by the potter's hands four centuries before our Saviour came into the world.

These beautiful vases, with figures telling the stories of Grecian mythology, are from the artistic touches of the workmen of Corinth, where the art twenty-five hundred years ago attained its highest perfection; and the perfection of Greek art is also seen in the black vases with red figures representing festal processions, battles, and the chase.

I cannot enumerate even the principal objects in this extensive collection, so many surprise you as works of ancient art by their being so similar to modern productions. Here are some amphoræ (vases with two handles), with paintings of the Judgment of Paris, the Deliverance of Prometheus, Hercules and Lion, and Bacchanalian revels. Another collection of red figures in a background gives us pictorial representations of the Rape of Europa, Hercules in the Garden of the Hesperides, and Apollo with the Lyre. A third collection of very large-sized vases had among them those decorated with figures of Apollo and the Muses, Vulcan and his Forge, the Education of Achilles, Hercules and Omphale, &c.

The collection of antique objects of metal is an exceedingly interesting one, and belongs, with a very few exceptions, to the classical nations of antiquity, Greeks, Romans, and Etruscans, and gives one something of an insight into their domestic life, religious ceremonies, and customs of war.

As mentioned in my inspection of the Etruscan antiquities at Rome, the articles of ancient jewelry and ornamentation show a refined taste in art upon which very little advance seems to have been made, as our artists and jewellers are using the same patterns and models to-day. Indeed, it seems artistic taste was consulted even in the production of such articles of household use as saucepans, lamps, and shovels. This collection also contains an interesting variety of ancient weapons of war, such as helmets, swords, daggers, and shields, the originals of what you see in Flaxman's illustrations of Homer.

A fragment of Etruscan gold cuirass; a victor's laurel wreath, thirty leaves wrought in pure gold; a beautiful wreath of golden olive-leaves (just think of these specimens of the jeweller's art two thousand years ago); a diadem and bracelets of gold; a necklace set with two hundred and eighty garnets; engraved gold bracelets; a clasp of gold and crystals; a silver ring, with the head of the Emperor Alexander Severus cut in onyx; silver drinking-goblet; the Three Graces in pressed silver, and numerous rings, bracelets, and necklaces of great beauty of design and elegance of finish.

The articles of household use and weapons of war, which are of equal, if not exceeding, interest to the gold and silver ornaments, are chiefly of bronze, iron, and lead. Here are chandeliers or candelabra formed like little trees; an ash-pan with a figure of Apollo for its handle; plates; toys with artistic handles; spoons; and the medicine-chest of a Roman physician, on the lid of which is the figure of Æsculapius inlaid with silver, and inside of which are curious antique medical and surgical instruments of the owner's time.

Of the less precious metals the articles were very interesting. Here, for instance, was the round shield and breastplate of an Etruscan warrior; swords of various forms, and some of graceful and beautiful design; harness for chariot and horses; dishes, basins, scales and weights, bolts and locks, tankards and drinking-cups.

There was a curious collection of Etruscan mirrors of polished metal adorned with inscriptions, images of gods and heroes, and scenes of practical life. There are one hundred and forty of these mirrors, and the workmanship upon some of them is elaborate and artistic.

The Collection of Gems concludes the rooms devoted to the Antiquarium. This was quite a collection in the seventeenth century, and was added largely to by Frederick the Great as well as his successors, so that now it contains over five thousand specimens, of which more than one quarter are gems set in gold rings and medallions.

The art of cutting precious stones reaches back to remote antiquity: the Hebrews were familiar with it, and, as is well known, the ancient Egyptians and Babylonians cut hieroglyphics into stones, or carved the *scarabæus* (sacred beetle) from stone, to wear as amulets; and among the Greeks it was a cultivated art, attaining its highest perfection in the time of Alexander the Great, and in his reign and those of his successors, gems were worn as ornaments.

The rarest of the ancient gems in this collection are exhibited in glass cases, and others are kept in presses which are accessible to the student or antiquarian who may desire to examine them. They are divided into various classes. First is the Egyptian or Oriental style, from the finest period of Egyptian art down to A. D. 300, and commencing with an excellent cutting of a sacred falcon, with Osiris' crown cut in sardonyx, and including cuttings in agate, carnelian, and jasper. Then came Grecian and Etruscan gems, among which were cuttings in carnelian of Cadmus fighting the Dragon, and Neptune and his Dolphins in amethyst. Then the Greek and Roman gods; cuttings dating from three hundred years before to three hundred after Christ, including a splendid head of Jupiter in carnelian, head of Ceres in agate onyx — Actæon surprising the bathing Diana, Genius of Youth in lapis-lazuli. There were also other classifications, including representations of Greek and Roman heroes, historical representations, animals, &c.

In the collection of antique cameos was an onyx eight and a half inches long and seven broad, on which was cut an apotheosis of the Emperor Septimius Severus, and which was purchased for this collection for nine thousand dollars. Another onyx, illustrating the birth of one of the Cæsars, found in a Roman tomb near Cologne, was sold by the finder to a German jeweller for about seventy-five cents (our money), but the king subsequently caused him to be paid one thousand dollars for it.

In the Hall of Gems, the antiquarian or numismatist will have a rich treat in the inspection of the Collection of Coins, which number nearly one hundred thousand, in gold, silver, and copper. Of these, forty thousand are antique pieces, principally Greek and Roman coins, the Greek coins being arranged geographically and the Roman ones chronologically. The visitor who desires to inspect intelligently this collection of gems, vases, or indeed any of the treasures of the Antiquarium, will find it necessary to purchase one of the little local guide-books, translated into English, as the regular guide-books give scarcely any particulars of the different objects, passing them by as "a suite of rooms containing terra-cottas and vases," "bronzes, weapons, statuettes, and domestic utensils of the Greeks and Romans," "Cabinet of coins and collections of gems."

The reader, if at all enthusiastic in any of these different branches of antiques, may form some idea of the priceless value as well as the great interest of the collection from the few prominent objects hastily made note of by the author in passing. That which is but apparently a collection of rudely cut pebbles becomes of absorbing interest when a descriptive catalogue spreads them out as the seal-rings of the Pharaohs and the ornaments of Roman emperors and Grecian warriors; and the battered discs of copper, gold, and silver, which might have been hastily passed or never sought out, we look upon with curiosity as the early bronze circulating medium of ancient Rome, the gold of Greece, or the golden money of the Roman empire.

Many of the earlier coins in the numismatic collection are stamped with simple emblems, and at a later period with representations of the gods, and finally with effigies of the kings or emperors. Alexander the Great was the first among the Greeks who stamped his own effigy on the coins, and Julius Cæsar the first among the Romans.

Among the oldest European moneys exhibited here are the coins of Etruria, Spain, and Italy; coins of the tyrant Hiero II. of Syracuse, who reigned two hundred and fifty years before Christ; a fine collection of Grecian gold and silver coins stamped with the effigies of the Macedonian kings, such as Philip II. and Alexander the Great; and one with the head of Mithridates VI. upon it. A collection of curious Indian coins is shown, dating two hundred years before Christ; also Persian royal coins, and Egyptian.

The collection of Roman coins is particularly rich and interesting. The most ancient Roman coin is the "*as*," which was made as early as the reign of Servius Tullius, five hundred and forty-six years before Christ; and of this coin, which is in bronze, there are three or four; also two or three specimens of the half *as;* then came the coins — gold, silver, and bronze — of the Roman Republic, over one hundred different specimens, stamped with representations of gods and heroes. Then a magnificent collection of imperial Roman coins, three hundred and seventy-five in number, stamped with the effigies of the emperors and their relatives. The series begins with coins of the reign of Julius Cæsar, and terminates with those of Constantine XIV. in 1453.

In addition to these there are coins of the Middle Ages and modern times; a collection of six thousand specimens of Oriental coins, including Mohammedan, Chinese, and Japanese specimens; and a collection of seven thousand medals, which I will not fatigue the reader with more special description of. Sufficient allusion to this department of the Museum has been made to indicate to the visitor interested in the objects mentioned what he might perhaps otherwise pass by unnoticed, but which he may see very thoroughly on application to the custodian, many of the coins being only accessible in that manner. The same is the case with a portion of the Collection of Gems.

Another picture-gallery journey is now before the visitor, but the collection, although a very fine one, is not equal to several other great galleries in Europe, and is often rather hastily passed over by American visitors. The gallery in the Old Museum, which is upon the upper floor, and entered from the rotunda, is divided into thirty-seven apartments, and the classified into different schools of art. Thus, we have Italian schools — first, those of the fifteenth century (epoch of culture); and this includes the Lombardian, Tuscan, Bolognian, and Umbrian schools. Then the Italian schools from 1500 to 1550 (to the "highest bloom" of the art, as they specify it); then from 1550 to 1590 (epoch of decay); then from 1590 to 1770 ("after bloom and decay"). The Dutch, German, and Netherland schools are similarly arranged.

After one becomes familiar with picture galleries and art collections abroad, he will be continually finding reproductions of old acquaintances in the way of statues, pictures, and celebrated works of art. Thus, upon entering the great rotunda here, he will find hung upon the walls the familiar scenes of Raphael's cartoons which he has seen upon the famous tapestry in the Vatican, if he has visited Rome, and also again at Dresden. This tapestry, however, is celebrated as having been woven at Arras in the sixteenth century, for that royal butcher, Henry VIII., and has been in the possession of the Emperor Charles I. and also the Dukes of Alva, and was bought by Frederick William IV. for this collection in 1844.

Passing from the rotunda to the different rooms, we see in the first room the Venetian pictures, the best one being that of the body of Christ, supported by two weeping angels. The pictures in the first room are principally religious subjects. Through second, third, fourth, and fifth rooms you see Madonnas, saints, and virgins till you tire of them; and, at the sixth, you come to pictures by Titian, the most beautiful being the portrait of his daughter Lavinia. Chess Players, and a Venus, by Bordonne, in this room, are beautiful works; but the other succeeding rooms are prodigal in sacred subjects, including a Madonna, by Correggio; Adoration of Shepherds, by Ferrari; Madonna and Child, by Raphael; and a beautiful picture of John the Baptist in the Desert, by Salviati, painted in the sixteenth century. In the seventeenth room I found a landscape, by Claude Lorraine; Spanish Woman, by Murillo; Shipwreck, by Salvator Rosa; A Girl, by Greuze, and The Entombment, by Caravaggio.

What is considered the great work in the collection in the Old Museum are twelve paintings on six panels, which were executed for two distinguished families for an altar-piece in their chapel in the Church of St. John, at Ghent, by John Van Eyck and Hans Holbein, pupils of Albrecht Dürer. These panels are interesting as having a story. There were thirteen of them originally, and they were stolen from the church by the French; the six that are here were purchased of a dealer, into whose hands they fell, for one hundred thousand thalers, or about seventy-five thousand dollars of our money. The pictures represent the just Judges, the Champions of Christ, singing and playing angels, hermits, and pilgrims. When this altar-piece is closed, the pictures upon the reversed side, which are equally beautiful, are presented.

There are in this gallery of the Old Museum over twelve hundred specimens of pictures; and an indication of its value may be inferred from the fact that it contains, besides the works of artists already mentioned, specimens of those of Snyder, — Combat of Bear and Dogs; Ruysdael's landscapes and sea-pieces; Tenier's Peasants at Cards, and Temptation of Anthony; Cuyp's landscapes; Gerard Duow's beautifully finished figures; Rubens's Three Cavaliers; portraits, &c., — Van Dycks, Jean Mabeuse, Hans Holbein, and Wouvermans.

Leaving the Old Museum, you pass through a passage, or sort of arcade, which connects it with the new structure, and find yourself in a grand, lofty, circular saloon, called the Roman Cupola Saloon, which is elegantly decorated with large fresco paintings, the two principal of which are the Subjugation of Wittekind, King of the Saxons, by Charlemagne, and the adoption of Christianity as the religion of the state. These give you an introduction to Kaulbach's grand artistic creations (with which the visitor will soon be better acquainted), they being painted, after designs by the great artist, by Gräf and Stilke, and are filled with spirited figures illustrative of their subjects.

Passing from here, we enter the Mediæval Saloon, an apartment with nine cupolas, and decorated with portraits of the German Emperors, each surrounded with four-cornered pictures, representing German cities. This saloon contains casts of celebrated sculpture decorations in European churches of the time of the Middle Ages; and from it we enter what is called the Modern Art Saloon, the ceiling of which is elegantly decorated with fresco paintings, representing Industry and Trade, as the art of engine-building, forging iron and weapons, mining, painting, sculpture, commerce, agriculture.

We now come opposite the grand staircase of the New Museum, which occupies the entire height of the building, and is one hundred and thirty-two feet in depth, — a magnificent piece of work. A single flight of stairs, of Silesian marble, leads from the ground-floor to the first story, and then a double one from the first to the second story.

The copy of Old Father Nile (original at the Vatican), in the vestibule, the grand figures of the horse-tamers, and the four Caryatides, where the double staircases join, tend to give additional effect to this grand hall; but its chief and great attraction are the magnificent frescos, or mural paintings, designed by Kaulbach, which adorn it. These celebrated tableaux consist of six grand principal ones, filled with life-size figures, illustrating great epochs in history; and about them, in the intermediate spaces, are sixteen other pictures, the whole being surrounded by graceful allegorical arabesque, or frieze, also designed by Kaulbach, exhibiting the history and culture of mankind from Chaos to Humboldt.

These magnificent works of art, although modern, fairly rival some of the grandest works of the old masters: most of them are already quite familiar to Americans, from the excellent reproductions we have of them in engravings; but, to get the full effect of the artist's work, it is almost needless for me to say one should look upon the original pictures in this grand hall.

There is the familiar one of the "Age of the Reformation," with the noble central figure of Luther standing upon the topmost step of the altar, lifting with both hands his translation of the Bible high above his head. Near by is Calvin, also Zwingle, the reformer of Switzerland; and at different points in the great picture are Gustavus Adolphus, king of Sweden, in full armor; William of Orange, and Admiral Coligny (slain on St. Bartholomew's day); Wickliffe; Queen Elizabeth; Archbishop Cranmer; Copernicus, expounding his system; Galileo; Tycho Brahe, disputing with Kepler; John Guttenberg, holding his first printed sheet; Columbus, with his hand on the globe; Leonardo da Vinci; Shakspeare; Cervantes; Michael Angelo; and others, — all being portraits of celebrated persons of the fifteenth and sixteenth centuries, who contributed in any way towards the great movement of the Reformation, and forming a splendid pictorial historical group.

"The Crusaders before Jerusalem" gives that stanch old warrior of the Cross, Geoffrey de Bouillon, as King of Jerusalem, mounted upon his white charger, holding forward the crown of Jerusalem to the vision of Christ and the saints in the heavens, while he places the crown of thorns upon his own head. The friar, Peter of Amiens, kneeling, stretches his hands towards the heavenly group; slain Saracens, that have fallen before the crusaders' weapons, are upon the ground. Tancred and other knights, singers and minstrels, make up the composition.

The most classical and allegorical of the paintings is that of "Homer and the Greeks." The poet standing upright, lyre in hand, in a barge rowed by the Sibyl, is approaching the coast of Greece. Thetis and the Nereids are rising from the waves about his bark to listen to his singing; and on the shore are assembled Grecian artists, sculptors, orators, and poets, to welcome his coming, — Æschylus, Sophocles, and Euripides. In the foreground, on the beach, are Pericles and his pupil Alcibiades; behind stands Solon, with his law tablets. At the left is the Parthenon, in course of erection. Above, upon a rainbow in the clouds, are gods and goddesses of mythology, — Jupiter and Juno enthroned, Apollo, and the Three Graces. Beneath, the smoke from a sacrificial altar ascends to these deities, and around the altar a group of Grecian youths are dancing. Phidias, engaged in sculpturing the statue of Achilles, and other figures, make up the grouping of this great fresco.

The "Destruction of the Tower of Babel" is a grand work, where, from the clouds above, Jehovah is represented as looking down upon the ruin of Nimrod's Tower. The king himself sits upon his throne, defying the mightier Power, despite the pleadings of his wife, who clings to his knees. Idols are tumbling from their pedestals, the slaves of the Tower rising in rebellion and stoning their masters; the great Tower stands unfinished. Separated into three great divisions, the races emigrate, — the races of Shem, Ham, and Japheth. The tribe of Shem drives away its flocks, and is blessed by its patriarch, who stands with outstretched arms. The tribe of Ham represents the African races; and their priest, riding upon a buffalo, embraces his idol, while a woman kisses the hem of his garment. The Japhethites, founders of the Caucasian race, ride away on fiery horses, the first rider being said to represent the Hellenes, and the second the Germans.

The "Destruction of Jerusalem" is a familiar picture to-day in the windows of our print-shops, — the tall, central figure, the high-priest, piercing his bosom with a dagger, with his wife and children at his feet, entreating a like fate lest they should fall into the hands of the Roman conquerors.

The prophets who prophesied the destruction of Jerusalem are seen in the clouds above, looking down upon Titus and his legions, who are entering into the sacred city, whose burning temple and crumbling ruins show that the destruction foretold has begun; while the flying Jews, frantic women, helpless children, and priests, the wandering Jew starting forth on his endless journey, go to make up the grand effects of the picture.

The other great fresco is the spectral Battle of the Huns, and exhibits a splendidly grouped collection of figures in vigorous action, designed as an allegorical representation of Paganism against Christianity. Rome is seen in the background; in the foreground is the battle-scene designed to represent the spot where the devastating hordes met their first repulse at the battle of Chalons-sur-Marne, where the battle was so fierce that, as the legend runs, the dead rose in the night to continue it; and it is this scene the artist has represented. Warriors are arising, groping for and seizing their weapons; in the clouds above, upon a shield supported by his soldiers, is Attila, king of the Huns, "the scourge of God," brandishing his scourge in encouragement to his troops, while the Christians rally round the Cross, as their sacred symbol, or under the leadership of Theodoric, king of the Visigoths, rush bravely to battle with their fierce opponents. This grand battle-scene is thought by many to be the finest of the series; it may be for spirited action in the representation of the figures, but for quiet, satisfactory study, "Homer and the Greeks," and "The Age of the Reformation," will divide the student's attention.

Each one of these mural paintings about the grand staircase hall is surrounded by appropriate marginal paintings of small dimensions. That of the Destruction of Jerusalem has scenes from Jewish and Roman history; that of the

Battle of the Huns, scenes from Northern and Oriental mythology, &c. This superb approach to the interior of the New Museum is remarkably beautiful and appropriate, both in point of art and architecture.

I have referred to the Roman Cupola, mediæval and modern art saloons passed through on the route to the grand staircase. There are upon this same floor nine other halls devoted to the collection of casts of celebrated objects of antiquity. These halls are named from the nature of their contents: as the Niobe Saloon, which contains the group of the children of Niobe, taken from the tympanum of a temple of Apollo. This hall is superbly frescoed with Grecian battle and mythological scenes, and among its most prominent contents are copies of the Dying Gladiator, the Fighting Gladiator, and Quoit-Thrower, besides other copies which we linger over a few moments, as they serve more vividly to bring up the great originals before us.

Another saloon, known as the Greek Saloon, is rich in frescos, and contains ten fine wall paintings: such as a representation of Ancient Athens, the Acropolis, Sacred Grove at Olympia, Temple of Apollo, &c., which will bring back memories of school days and school studies in which the imagination had to paint these scenes, while the brain puzzled out the construction of the sentences that described them. This hall contains groups from the Temple of Minerva at Ægina, and sculptures from the Parthenon at Athens. A saloon known as the Greek Cupola Saloon is adorned with wall-paintings of Perseus rescuing Andromache, Theseus killing the Minotaur, and Hercules seizing the Arcadian Stag, and contains casts of Grecian statuary and other sculpture of an interesting character.

The visitor who has not made the grand tour, or visited the galleries of Rome and Florence, will go through these twelve apartments with more interest than he who has; but the latter should on no account omit them, as they contain very many extremely rare and beautiful objects, the collection being augmented each year.

Instead of ascending the grand staircase, which I have brought the reader before for the purpose of viewing Kaulbach's cartoons, we will descend to the ground floor for the purpose of inspecting the Hall of Northern Antiquities and Ethnographical Collection. The former hall is decorated with frescos of the gods and goddesses of northern mythology : Odin on his throne, and his wife Hertha, the northern Juno, coming down to earth in a chariot drawn by cows, scattering flowers and fruits in her pathway ; Frey, the god of gayety, riding on a boar ; Thor, god of thunder, flourishing his mighty hammer in a chariot drawn by goats. These paintings are on the walls on both sides of the hall and over the windows, and represent the principal points of northern mythology as laid down in the Icelandic Book of Heroes.

Starting from the entrance, the figures on the visitor's left hand represent the gods of Darkness and Night, and those on the right the gods of Light. The antiquities contained in this hall are of the stone, bronze, and iron periods, and such as have been found from time to time, I should judge, in and about Prussia or Germany, for the collection was not, at the time of the author's visit, either properly catalogued, numbered, or labelled ; and, although the guide-book gives but four lines to it, that is not always to be taken as an indication of a lack of importance or interest, in any gallery collection, locality, or sight abroad, as the readers of these pages have learned ere this. However, all we could ascertain was that the urns and ash-bowls on one stand were antiquities found at Altmark ; another was found near Berlin ; a collection of little pitchers (without long ears) was dug out in the Rhenish provinces. But a lot of vases, weapons, helmets, bracelets, battle-hammers, and household utensils, although carefully labelled with Dutch-looking characters as to where they were found, needed an antiquarian or expert to explain, to give most of them interest beyond that which otherwise would attach to a collection of old trash from household dust heaps.

The Ethnographical Collection is a collection of articles illustrative of the life, customs, and products of different nations, and is divided into five sections, Europe, America, Asia, Africa, and Australia. The American specimens are some of Catlin's Indian paintings, Indian weapons, garments, buffalo hides, moccasins, bows and arrows, porcupine quills, embroidery, and similar objects familiar to all Americans. A show of Peruvian relics, weapons, and utensils of Mexican and South American Indians and ancient inhabitants, is the South American portion. The Asiatic department contains the Chinese, Japanese, and East Indian curiosities with which all are familiar; and the African, the rhinoceros-hide shields, long spears, poisoned arrows, gourds, calabashes, carved clubs and paddles, and other objects that the African travellers tell about, and so on, — a collection of no great merit or interest compared with others we have to see.

The Berlin Museum, like others, has drawn on the oldest nation on earth for a portion of its attractions, and with no small degree of success, for the Egyptian Collection is quite an interesting one, and, moreover, the reproduction of ancient Egyptian architecture in the arrangement of the different halls, and the illustrative frescos upon the walls, heightens the effect. They also contribute a certain degree of instruction as good reproductions and illustrations of the subject.

The outer court or grand entrance to this Egyptian Museum is a faithful representation, on a reduced scale, of the Egyptian temple at Karnak. It is called the Colonnade Court in the guide-books, from sixteen pillars which surround it, which are also reductions of the pillars at Karnak. Above, on the ornamented cornice, is recorded by a modern Egyptian scholar, Professor Lepsius, in ancient Egyptian hieroglyphics, the fact that these monuments were arranged by Frederick William IV., in 1848. Done into English, the translation is as follows: —

"The Royal Sun Eagle, the Avenger of Prussia, Sun of Son, Frederick William IV., Philopator (the father lover), Euergetes (benefactor), Eucharistes (the gracious), loved by Tot and Saf, the Victorious Master of the Rhine and Vistula, the Elect of Germania, has caused to be erected in this edifice colossal figures, effigies, statues, and sculptures, stones, pillars, coffins, and many other good things brought from Egypt and Ethiopia."

In the centre of this atrium stands an altar, and on the right and left of it are two colossal ram sphinxes, with the sun disc between the horns; and farther on, at the continuation of the entrance hall at each side of the hypostyles, are two colossal seated figures in black porphyry: Rameses II., and another whose name I do not give, as, with the exception of his right leg and throne, he is entirely a restoration; while Rameses, or Sesostris, as he is sometimes called, who sits at the left, is the original sculpture of Egyptian chisels, with the exception of the beard and right hand, which have been restored. His name is inscribed upon his breast and throne. He reigned twelve hundred years before Christ.

All around the walls of this hall are stone tablets, found in the tombs of Memphis, which are adorned with hieroglyphical sculptures of religious and funereal rites, &c. The apartment also contains fine wall-paintings, for which the Berlin Museum is so famous. These were executed principally by celebrated German artists, and represent the grand works of architecture of the ancient Egyptians, such as the Memnon Statue at Thebes, Great Pyramids of Memphis, the Temple at Karnak, the Temple at Edfu, Temple in the Isle of Phylæ, and other scenes familiar to Eastern travellers and readers of books of Eastern travel. The ceiling is beautifully decorated with astronomical frescos.

The front of the hypostyle (covered colonnade) represents the doorway of the Temple of Rameses II., at Thebes; at its end, facing the visitor, is the colossal figure of King Horus. This apartment contains a curious and valuable collection of papyrus rolls found with mummies, which are decorated with pictorial representations inscribed with hieroglyphics, prayers, and other inscriptions. Here, also, are bricks made from Nile mud, and stamped with the name of the king in whose reign they were manufactured — a good way of handing one's name down to posterity.

We now enter what is known as the Historical Hall, a large saloon, with its walls decorated with paintings in imitation of the Egyptian wall-paintings, and representing battles, ceremonies, customs, hunting scenes, and historical events of that ancient people. Above the wall-paintings there is a frieze of medallions containing the names of the ancient Egyptian kings, from a very ancient one down to the Cæsars. In this hall are numerous glass cases containing ancient Egyptian amulets, gems, rings, bodkins, domestic utensils, and trinkets; also mummies of animals, birds, and crocodiles, heads, arms, and other fragments of human mummies, besides monumental stones and ancient sculpture.

A still more ancient collection is that shown in the Hall of Tombs, which contains monumental remains brought to Berlin by the Egyptian scholar before mentioned, Professor Lepsius, and which date from two to three thousand years before Christ. Here were two huge granite blocks, used for indicating the height of the river Nile, which were two thousand years old; an ornamental stone sarcophagus of double that age; fragments of tombs whose inscriptions prove them to have belonged to the time of King Cheops; stone tombs that have been restored, giving the visitor an idea of the ancient method of sepulture; and hieroglyphical tablets and stones sculptured with scenes of Egyptian life.

The Mythological Saloon is so called from its mural decorations representing the mythology of the ancient Egyptians, and the ceiling paintings representing month gods, zodiac, and constellations, and contains a rich collection of sarcophagi and mummies. At the right and left of the entrance sit statues of a lion-headed goddess; and the first sarcophagus we inspected was one of granite, the lid being a sculptured representation of the deceased. Then we came to a well-preserved mummy, which is kept in a glass case. It is that of a young girl, who, the inscription says, was named Hathor, and beside it is the sycamore coffin in which she was found inclosed. Among other interesting sarcophagi was a fine one of black porphyry, which had inclosed a famous Egyptian general named Pelisis, and another in granite of one named Nechtnif, whose commands had fought, bled, and died, as well as themselves, almost before,

"Antiquity appears to have begun."

Of the mummies, the two most interesting are that of one unrolled showing its armlets of gold, as when laid in the tomb, and another which was in a wooden sarcophagus. This sarcophagus was found at the Necropolis at Thebes, in 1822, and its occupant was a high-priest; and ranged round it are objects also found in the tomb, such as his staffs of office, offerings for the dead, representations of ancient Nile boats, which give us the view of the ancient navigation of the river four thousand years ago, that being the age of this sarcophagus and the objects that surround it.

Leaving the antiquities of old Egypt, we ascend to a series of five rooms, to which the guide-book gives three lines each, as containing "smaller works of art." Access is had to this portion of the Museum *via* the grand staircase and through a hall upheld by caryatides. The first apartment contains models, artistic and curious furniture, &c., which is displayed in four large and elegant glass cases. The models of celebrated buildings are finely executed, and must be especially interesting to a student of architecture. Among the most prominent were models of the convent church at Ratisbon, Cathedral at Freiburg, St. Isaac's Church, St. Petersburg, Pulpit for Cologne Cathedral, and the principal entrance to Strasburg Cathedral.

Among the curiosities of furniture, &c., we were shown

the camp-chair used by Gustavus Adolphus, King of Sweden, at the battle of Lützen; a cupboard that belonged to Melancthon; the last will of Frederick William III., wrought in silk; arm-chair of the time of Frederick the Great; and various elaborate and elegant articles of furniture, — among which was an elegant artistical cabinet in the form of a temple, with spiral pillars; an old church-pew of boxwood, with the figures of Faith, Love, Hope, and Patience carved upon it; cabinets of ebony and silver; curious old looking-glass frames that were elegantly wrought and carved; and a splendid cabinet of ebony and silver, which was made for Phillip, Duke of Pomerania, at Augsburg, in 1617. This cabinet rested upon four silver griffins, and was five feet high by about three and one-half in breadth, and surmounted by a representation of Parnassus and the winged horse Pegasus.

We next came to a niche which was rich in Prussian historical relics, which were excellently arranged for exhibition. The figures of Frederick the Great, King Frederick I., his father, and Frederick William I., his grandfather, known as the Great Elector, were represented by life-size figures, clad in the garments they wore while living. The custodian of this department, who was explaining to a large group of his countrymen, noticing our small party of foreign visitors outside the group, at once made way for us and invited us to a place of honor inside the guard-rail, that we might inspect closely and even handle some of the mementos of these great sovereigns; — he was a shrewd exhibitor, and probably argued, and correctly, that his palm would be liberally crossed for such voluntary courtesy. The figures were all artistically modelled, and the face of Frederick the Great was made from a cast of his face taken after death; his figure was dressed in full military uniform formerly worn by him, upon the breast the star of the order of the Black Eagle, and by the side the sword worn in many of his most celebrated battles. The custodian brought to us the helmet, or iron battle-cap, worn by Frederick the Great's grandfather,—a huge headpiece weighing twenty-one pounds,—and his great sword used at the battle of Fehrbellin, which was a weapon requiring a strength of muscle to wield that could be furnished only by that which could support such a helmet.

Among a curious collection of relics of Frederick William I. was a lot of tobacco-pipes used in the celebrated Tobacco Parliament, where all smoked; the king's and his wife's betrothal rings, his walking-sticks, and sword.

Among the relics of Frederick the Great were two crayon pictures made by him, his flute and sheet-music that he had to use by stealth when Crown Prince, under the tyrannical oppression of his half insane father, — some of the music sheets half consumed by fire, into which they had been thrust by his parent.

Then here was his magnificent military dress uniform of blue velvet embroidered with silver, his watch, his playing-counters, elegant walking-sticks ornamented with tortoise-shell and diamonds, his decoration ribbon, cocked hat — as marked an article of wardrobe as that of Napoleon, — snuff-boxes, sword, and arm-chair. A collection of historic swords included that of Charles XII., the Lion of Sweden; that with which Count Hardeck was executed at Vienna in 1595; another that did similar duty upon the neck of Duke Nicholas of Oppeln, in 1497; those of each of the Fredericks, of Prince Ludwig, of General Kleist, and other celebrated Prussians.

An interesting display of relics of Napoleon Bonaparte consisted of articles which were captured in his carriage at Genaape by the Prussians, immediately after the battle of Waterloo; among them were his pistols, portfolios, snuff-box, a hat, orders, and decorations. Two remarkable relics were the jasper sceptre of Charlemagne, and a box containing a fragment of the standard of Pizarro, the conqueror of Peru, this latter being presented to the Museum by Humboldt.

The saloon of majolica and glass contains a collection of that ware principally of the sixteenth and seventeenth centuries. Here we saw famous glasses of ruby hue; others adorned with portraits of Gustavus Adolphus and the Great Elector; the goblet with which Frederick III. drank brotherhood with Peter the Great; the clay drinking-jug of Martin Luther; curiously ornamented tankards, glassware, and decorated porcelain.

Then came a saloon of ecclesiastical works of art, in which were beautiful Byzantine crucifixes; a magnificent wooden cross of open work, most elaborately wrought, by Albrecht Dürer, on which over a thousand figures are represented; elegant altar ornaments; beautiful relic boxes, richly ornamented with precious stones; crosiers, candlesticks, and other religious works of art of great beauty. The colored-glass windows of this room have some fine painting; one window, the Kiss of Judas, dates about 1150, and another, Mary and John, about a hundred years later.

The principal saloon for the exhibition of small works of art of the middle ages, and down to the present time, contained a large, interesting, and very beautiful collection. There are more than five thousand objects in all; they are displayed in glass cases, over each of which is designated the century in which the objects in it were made. In one case was a magnificent collection of enamel works of exquisite design and finish; a dish with a representation of Daphne pursued by Apollo; medallions on which the combat of Satan and Michael was represented; and Bacchanalian representations of the history of Dido; Christ before Pilate, Christ at the Cross, scenes in the History of Samson; saltcellars with the labors of Hercules, and candlesticks representing the four seasons; boxes, cups, and medallions, upon which portraits, allegories, mythological scenes, revels, and armorial bearings succeeded each other in elegant profusion.

Next came a great case of the oldest carved works of wood and ivory from the sixth to the fifteenth century, and containing Oriental and German hunting-bugles of ivory, an ivory trinket box of the twelfth century, a book-cover with the life of Christ wrought upon it, an Oriental box of the eleventh century, &c. Other cases were equally rich in curious objects : such as a crystal vase with scenes cut in the setting, and handle wrought in gold, by Benvenuto Cellini; curious old watches, a set of the first manufactured, known as Nuremberg eggs ; a bowl of rock-crystal ; ostrich-eggs, and nautilus-shells as cups, richly ornamented. Amber work — a little spinning-wheel made of it — boxes, cabinets, and knife-handles ; a big silver gilt dish illustrated with scenes from the life of Moses ; a beautiful altar inlaid with amber. Coming down to the eighteenth century, numerous specimens of wood-carvings were exhibited, mosaics, gems, &c. One case contained a curious collection of weapons and musical instruments, hawks, hoods and bells for hawking, crossbows and belts, hunting-knives, battle-axes, daggers, and swords, with curious and elaborate handles, one sword-handle representing a combat of centaurs.

The Cabinet of Prints, or collection of engravings, which contain about half a million engravings and drawings in three rooms, is said to be admirably arranged for examination, but it is only open to the public on Sundays.

I must conclude my description of the Berlin Museum (which, lengthy as it is, has often from necessary condensation become almost a catalogue) by brief reference to two collections yet unnoticed. First, the collection of plaster casts, which are in a gallery over the Egyptian outer court, entrance being had from the grand staircase hall by passing under one of the great staircases, and which contains casts of a great many of the most celebrated Egyptian monuments, as well as Assyrian and Grecian sculptures and antiquities.

The second is a very rich collection of silver Roman articles found in excavating near Hildesheim, which is in the Antiquarian Collection, but might not be seen unless inquired for. It is called the Silver Treasure, and consists of a complete set of Roman drinking-vessels supposed to have been buried by the Roman general Varus. There are over forty different pieces, comprising beautifully wrought goblets, a large water-kettle ornamented with cupids, three beautiful bowls adorned with masks, others with bas-reliefs; also smaller bowls, plates, salvers, pitchers, and vases, all of great beauty of workmanship, and interesting as examples of the artistic taste of the age in which they were made.

Potsdam is by many styled the Versailles of Prussia, it being about twenty miles from Berlin, and its royal palaces and beautiful gardens especially built and laid out for the enjoyment of the royal family and court. Although a portion of it was done at a vast expense, especially the New Palace, as it is called, which was founded by Frederick the Great after the Seven Years' War in 1763, in order to show that his exchequer was by no means exhausted, the amount was a bagatelle compared to the millions which the Louises squandered in their luxurious profuseness at Versailles.

The best way to see the sights of Potsdam, is to take a carriage and English-speaking *valet de place;* which were attainable at the railway station in Potsdam at the time of the author's visit, and can generally be found there during the travelling season, when American and English tourists are likely to visit the place.

The rooms of Frederick the Great in the Old Palace, a suite of three or four which he occupied before completing the New Palace, are interesting from the fact that they have not been remodelled or their condition changed since their illustrious owner left them. One room contained a lot of old, torn, blue, silk-covered chairs, and a lounge, shabby enough indeed, but showing the condition to which the king had allowed his favorite dogs to reduce them. In fact, he was, if history does not belie him, more indulgent to his dogs than to his soldiers, for he had learned few lessons of forbearance from the cruel and rigid military school in which he was educated.

Here also I paused to lay my hands upon the ink-stained writing-desk at which the monarch had written for years ; and a square vacant place in the covering was pointed to us as a portion which had been cut away by Napoleon when he visited the place. Napoleon also took Frederick's sword, which formerly rested upon his sarcophagus in a vault beneath what is known as the Garrison Church, at Potsdam.

Here also is the king's bookcase, with a collection of French and German works, and his hat, snuffbox, walking-sticks, sash, music composed by himself, the music-stand that he had used when a boy, probably at the time when his brutal, half insane old father, ascertaining that his son wrote verses and played the flute, called him into his presence and ordered his graceful flowing locks to be cut and soaped in the most rigid military style.

The double-walled room, with the trap-door through which the table could be let down ready-set out with dinner for the king and those with whom he wished to dine privately, and his little sleeping-room, are objects of interest. The other apartments of the palace are such as I have frequently described, those most interesting being the ones occupied by Frederick William III. and Frederick William IV., which are kept as near as possible in the way that they were left. The garden near this palace, beautifully laid out, has numerous bronze statues and a big fountain, a great basin — a shell supporting Thetis and Neptune. The garden is a popular resort on Sundays, when the fine military band plays there, and a grand dress-parade of the troops takes place.

But the Park and Palace of *Sans Souci* will probably most interest the visitor. The designation of this, "Free from Care," or, as Carlyle translated it rather freely, "No Bother," originated from a remark that Frederick made when contemplating the royal burial-place near by : " Here I shall be free from care." The great fountain in this park throws a stream one hundred and twenty feet in height, and is surrounded by mythological groups ; all around in the vicinity are numerous other fountains, statuary groups, terraces, and beautiful parterres of brilliant flowers. A copy of Frederick's equestrian statue that stands in *Unter den Linden* is here splendidly done in marble.

Up a broad flight of marble steps sixty-six feet in height, and broken by six landings or terraces, we ascend to the dome-crowned palace above, the steps reminding us somewhat of the more magnificent stretch of similar ascent at the garden at Versailles. Like the other palace, the apartments here viewed with the greatest curiosity are those in which Frederick the Great lived, and where he died on the 17th of August, 1785. Frederick used three rooms for his private use — a reception-room, library, and sleeping-room. In the latter he slept on a small iron camp-bedstead.

There was no admittance to the apartments during our visit, however, as the Queen Dowager was at home, and curiosity-seekers and tourists were excluded. We therefore contented ourselves with a stroll through the Park, admiring some of its fine forest-trees, and noticing that it was not, as we say in America, "kept up" as is that at Versailles.

I had seen so many original pictures in the great galleries of Europe, that I confess to but a hasty glance at the collection of copies of forty of the best of Raphael's productions, in a beautiful modern-built building, over one thousand feet long, ornamented with niches and statuary on the outside, and not far from the palace, styled "the Orangery," perhaps because there were no oranges there except some orange-trees that were set along outside in huge tubs. It is but justice to say, however, that the copies of paintings were excellent ones, and this part of the establishment, which was on the ground floor, and entered by doors from the garden walk, was freely open to visitors.

A beautiful little reproduction of the Pantheon at Rome, which we were permitted to enter, in another part of the grounds, contained an elegant marble statue of Queen

Louise, of which the king is said to have remarked that it was not *his* Louise, and afterwards to have been more satisfied with the same sculptor's (Rauch's) work at Charlottenburg in the mausoleum previously described. A fine view is had down an avenue a mile in length, which crosses this park and terminates at one end with a triumphal arch, and at the other with an obelisk of red marble seventy-five feet high on a white marble pedestal.

We did not forget to go and look, while at *Sans Souci*, at the historical windmill so famous in story, which, when Frederick the Great was laying out the grounds, the obstinate owner sturdily refused to sell, and, on being sued by the king, beat him in a Prussian court of justice, and the king had to alter his plans of the grounds, leaving the mill out. Frederick then turned the case to account by building a new large mill for the miller as "a monument of Prussian justice," which is the one that is shown to the traveller. The present king was, a few years ago, waited on by the descendant of the former owner, who had experienced heavy losses, and desired to sell the mill. The king inquired into his case, and finding his story correct, furnished him with means to defray all his debts, and kept the mill intact and standing as an historical memento.

Babelsburg, but a short drive from *Sans Souci*, and a charming situation, was the residence of the present emperor while Prince Regent, just before his accession to the throne, and is a sort of Norman castle-looking place, built of dark stone and surrounded by beautiful grounds. Small in extent, but elegantly fitted up, it has a genuine home-like appearance, especially when we went into the king's writing-cabinet, where was his writing-table, crowded with documents and plans, two or three atlases, and much-used blotting-paper, paper weights, a couple of not very tidy inkstands, a paper-knife in an uncut pamphlet, two or three German newspapers, and a London *Times*. It was for all the world like a railroad president's private office from which he had stepped out for a moment. The old lounge behind the chair at the desk had a couple of much-used, half-rolled architect's plans lying upon it, and a little piece of half-finished ornamental needlework that some visitor, perhaps his daughter, had carelessly thrown down there at her last visit and forgotten.

In the king's chamber was his plain but comfortable camp bedstead, the coverlid surmounted by a Scotch plaid shawl; and by its side a wooden arm-chair made by the Crown-Prince Fritz, it being the custom that all the princes shall learn some trade, and be able to personally produce some article of it. This chair was one of the products of Fritz's skill as a cabinet-maker; and a specimen of the art-work of the Crown Princess, in the shape of a bust of her own cutting, stood upon the dressing-bureau, and a little sketch of her own painting was suspended on the wall.

The views from the windows of all the apartments are most charming, and include fine reaches of scenery through the dense foliage to *Sans Souci* and Potsdam, or take in, after a sweep of charming lawn, the beautiful Marble Palace in the distance.

The rooms of the Princess Imperial, who, it will be remembered, is Victoria, eldest daughter of the English queen, had a most charming and home-like appearance, unlike many other residences of royalty I had previously visited. Here was a charming sitting-room, elegantly fitted up, just such as an ordinarily wealthy person in England or America would have; a few choice pictures on the wall, two or three English magazines, among them *Temple Bar*, and a copy of London *Punch* on the table, and on a little tier of book-shelves a set of the old *Token* and *Oriental Annual*, which are so familiar as gift-books of thirty years ago. The disposition of the little flower-vases, arm-chairs, and other furniture had a decidedly English and American appearance, and the passing breeze that swept into the room was laden with fragrance of the flower-beds, upon one of which, as we looked from the casement, we discovered the name Victoria growing in gayly-colored flowers.

The beautiful Gothic dining-room entrance-hall, with its antlers, skins, — trophies of the chase, — the quiet, exquisite taste with which the various rooms were furnished with fine modern paintings, statuettes, and pretty vases, all suggested the residence of a gentleman of fortune and good taste, and was certainly a home, with home surroundings that ought to contribute to the comfort of its possessors, if any case can come to " the head that wears a crown."

The five palaces at Potsdam, and their beautiful surroundings, require much more time, to be seen thoroughly, than most tourists devote to them; and American residents at Berlin, who have opportunity to ride out again and again on pleasure excursions in this direction, find fresh objects of interest, which cannot be taken in on the one day's race round in charge of a *valet de place*, as laid down in the guide-books. Our stay was all too short in what is known as the New Palace, a superb structure at one end of the magnificent avenue that runs through the whole length of the Park of *Sans Souci*. This palace is said to contain two hundred different apartments. Those shown to visitors are magnificently decorated and richly furnished.

In the apartments of Frederick the Great, his study-table, the manuscript of his writing in French, his library, and a sketch of the ugly visage of Voltaire drawn by him, and articles that he used when living, are interesting relics to visitors. Another attraction is a grand saloon, the walls of which are entirely composed of different ores, minerals, metals, stones, crystals, shells, &c., of every conceivable variety, the whole lighted by huge and elegant glass chandeliers. They were arranged in the walls and ceilings in squares, rings, or diamonds, and very skilfully disposed. There were splendid specimens of copper ore in the rough, with here and there a bit of the rough mass polished; rich, cut agate, semi-finished in the same manner; sparkling, irregular masses of lead; elegant figures formed of the delicately tinted tropical mussel shells; jagged, irregular masses of iron pyrites; silver ore; the sombre coal, and its peacock-hued brother; brilliant coral, with its ruby red; and jet-black marble, contrasting with carnelian or porphyry. The effect of this large and lofty hall, when flooded with light from the crystal chandeliers above, must be magnificent, and remind one of a fairy grotto or mermaid's cavern.

Among the other apartments in this New Palace is a handsome little theatre, very richly decorated, which will hold an audience of six hundred persons; the great marble saloon, one hundred feet in length, so called for its being finished richly in that material; and the great ballroom, elegantly decorated, in which are several choice pictures by Guido and other celebrated artists. The visitor who has not yet become fatigued with viewing the works of the great masters in the picture-galleries, will find several in the drawing and ante-rooms that are shown to the public in this palace, — such as the Adoration of the Magi, by Rubens; a splendid Cleopatra, by Titian; and Giordino's Rape of the Sabines, and Judgment of Paris.

The palace known as the Marble Palace we contented ourselves with an external inspection of, and its beautiful grounds, known as the New Gardens; and at the elegant country residence, near the Park of *Sans Souci*, known as *Charlottenhof*, with a view of an adjoining structure, which is a reproduction of an ancient Roman bath-house, and contains a bath cut from jasper, and a beautiful marble group of Hebe and Ganymede; the interior being elegantly decorated with frescos, in antique style, and with bronzes, some of which were brought from the ruins of Herculaneum.

We could only look at, and wish also that time would allow us to ascend, the grand dome of the beautiful church of St. Nicholas, and enjoy the view therefrom; or to inspect the captured French battle-flags and eagles that hung as trophies about the walls of the Garrison Church; but the descending sun, and the hour of the departure of the railroad train, left no alternative but to drive rapidly past them on through the William Square, where stood Kiss's handsome statue of Frederick William III., inscribed, "To the Father of his Country," — on to the railway station, from whence we were whirled back in the train to the Prussian capital.

From Berlin to Hanover is about a four and a half hours' ride by rail. This city I made a halt at for a short rest previous to the long stretch of a whole day's journey by rail to Amsterdam. We reached this former capital of what was once the little Kingdom of Hanover, but is now a Prussian province, at about five in the afternoon; and one hardly needs to be told in the guide-books that the city occupies a position at the junction of several important railways, as he is sure to ascertain if he stops at any of the principal hotels that surround the great open semicircular space near the railway station.

This *Platz* is itself a noisy and busy place, with passengers coming and going from hotel to station, the rush and rattle of numerous arriving and departing trains, and the steam-whistles of locomotives at all hours, rivalling some of our American cities, and rendering sleep somewhat of a difficult performance, unless one is proof against noise. Then again we arrived the night previous to a grand leather fair, and every hotel in the place was filled with leather-merchants, and the pavement in front of hotels, restaurants, and *cafés* was thronged with them, exhaling clouds of smoke from their pipes, and discussing business. This part of the city and the vicinity is, however, the more modern, best built, and most frequented by foreigners.

Our investigations in Hanover were brief, and consisted first of a good look at a handsome equestrian statue of

King Ernest Augustus, king of Hanover, in cavalry uniform, in front of the railway station. We then took a stroll through some of the principal streets, almost at random. One of these rambles brought us into some romantic, quaint-looking old streets, near the market-place, where were a number of picturesque, Gothic-looking brick buildings, which we learned were of the time of the fifteenth and sixteenth centuries, and one, more curious than the rest, had a sort of projection jutting out from it, upon which were represented a number of Scriptural scenes. This a good-natured bystander, after some trouble, contrived to make us understand was the one we were seeking, the house of Leibnitz, the celebrated German scholar, who, it will be recollected, was one of the most remarkable specimens of universal scholarship on record, being eminent in languages, history, divinity, political studies, experimental and mechanical science, belles-lettres, and especially in philosophy, through which reputation chiefly, he lives in history. He was a native of Hanover, and died in 1716; and a monumental temple containing his bust is situated in the *Waterloo Platz*. His grave is in the *Neustädter* Church, in the immediate vicinity of the *Platz*. Not far from here is a handsome old city hall, built in the Gothic style in 1439, and the Market Church, with a steeple or tower three hundred feet high.

The palace here, which is situated on Lein Street, upon the banks of the river Lein, is not far from the principal square or park of the city, known as Waterloo Platz, which is handsomely laid out, its chief monument being the Waterloo Column, which is one hundred and fifty-six feet high, surmounted by a figure of Victory, erected in memory of the Hanoverians who fell at the battle of Waterloo. At the opposite end of this *Platz* stands the statue of General or Count Alten, who was the Hanoverian general at Waterloo, and died in 1840. Another fine statue is a colossal one of Schiller, situated on George's Square, which opens out of George's Street. This street, and Frederick Street, which opens out of Waterloo Square just described, are notably two of the finest streets in the city. On the latter is situated the theatre, said to be the finest in Germany. It will comfortably seat eighteen hundred persons, and the handsome portico is adorned with twelve statues of celebrated authors and musical composers.

A beautiful drive is that which is known as the road of the Avenue of Limes, from its being lined on both sides with trees of that description. This road leads to the *Schloss Herrenhausen*, or castle, which is noted as being a residence of three of the Georges, first, second, and fifth. The gardens, which are one hundred and twenty acres in extent, are elegantly laid out, but the buildings externally are quite plain and unpretending. Near here we were shown a large circular building with five towers, which is denominated the Tower of the Guelphs. This ride finished our day of rest, which was, on account of sight-seeing, postponed to the one succeeding, which was made literally so, as we resolutely abstained from further excursions next day, with the exception of an afternoon ride to the Zoölogical Garden, where, notwithstanding it was Sunday, there was an open-air instrumental concert. The grounds are very prettily laid out, and the collection of animals and birds is a very good one.

CHAPTER XVIII.

AMSTERDAM! Yes, we are in Holland, after nearly twelve hours of railroad journey, including stops, from Hanover. We passed Zutphen on our route, where Sir Philip Sidney received his mortal wound, — the scene of the story of his causing the attendants to give the wounded soldier the cup of water before himself; through Arnhem, a beautiful town surrounded by elegant villas and gardens, where Sidney died; to Utrecht, a bustling Dutch city, where we changed cars, and began to find everything around was wearing a decidedly Dutch look: quaint, antique brick houses and windmills came into view, and there was a general thrifty look to all the surrounding fertile fields.

The railroad carriage into which we changed was one kept free from smokers, and the notice to that effect proved that the Dutch took more pains to promulgate the fact, and appreciated better that all travellers did not understand their language, than the railroad managers in many other countries we had passed through; for the notice was in the following different dialects:

Niet Rooken.
Für Nichtraucher.
Defense de fumer ici.
No Smoking Allowed.

And this, in a land where nine-tenths of the male population are puffing like chimneys, is an appreciated boon to the non-inhalers of tobacco-smoke.

As we approach Amsterdam, the great windmills for grinding grain and for draining the land, the long reaches of flat country, dikes and fertile plains that must have been once, or would be now, the bottoms of great lakes were not the land wrenched from the sea, — sleek black and white cattle, and now and then a canal-boat in the distance, — tell us that we are fairly in the Hollow Land.

But a short distance from the railway station is the Amstel Hotel, a fine new building, constructed, as all the great hotels are getting to be in this age of steam and universal travelling, in modern style, and where travellers who have been annoyed and have experienced the discomforts of short beds, and great stuffed, down coverlids for top-covering in the German country inns, and have thanked their stars, as has the author, that he always had a good roll of Scotch shawls, will greet English beds, mosquito-nettings, liberal-sized washhand-stands, and other objects of familiar service to him, with decided satisfaction.

Our spacious room looked directly out upon the river Amstel, along which and the adjacent canal we could descry a row of Don Quixote's giants, the windmills, and also every variety of Dutch *treck-shuit,* or canal-boat. Windmills are decidedly a Dutch institution, have been used for hundreds of years in Holland; and some of those used for deep drainage, ranged along the side of a canal, with their huge revolving sails seen in the twilight against the sky red with sunset, are an imposing sight, and readily conjure up the simile of a long row of sentinel-like giants tossing up their huge arms in defiance. The smaller mills are cheaply made of wood like the little ones that we frequently see in America; but the larger, for drainage of land, or manufacturing purposes, have a substantial foundation of brick or stone, and on this stands the mill proper, covered with a heavy straw thatch, with its great hood and enormous arms, or sails, which sweep round a circle of over one hundred feet in diameter.

Some of these run huge gangs of saws that saw great logs nearly two feet in diameter; others are huge grain mills, — the runs of stone above, the granary storage-room, a stable, &c., being on the lower floor. The great pumping windmills will, in a fair wind, lift eight to ten thousand gallons of water per minute to the height of four feet. The foundation-story of these great pumping-mills is the habitation of the family whose head has charge of it; and inside is as charming and curious an old Dutch interior, with Dutch clock, brass-mounted presses, tiled fireplace, dark old dressers with quaint crockery, and old Dutch claw-foot chairs, as one would wish to look upon. When the breeze is fair, and you climb into the upper story, and hear the tremendous shudder which the great revolving wings communicate to the huge structure as they infuse life and vigor to the great shaft or spindle that passes down through the mill like its spinal marrow, and whirls round three or four runs of heavy mill-stones, or keeps the great gang-saws in steady motion, or the big wheel at its foot in one unceasing rush of water-gathering, you will realize that a Dutch windmill is a mechanical contrivance not to be despised.

The first walk or ride out in Amsterdam reveals to the visitor many quaint and curious scenes unlike those seen in any other European capital. Time has changed a great deal of that sleepy old romance which Washington Irving in his admirable sketches has thrown around everything Dutch, in the American mind. Though you are in the land of the Van Tromps, the Peter Stuyvesants, and the Wouter Van Twillers, you will look in vain for the steeple-crowned hats, the huge breeches, — ten *broecks*, ten breeches to a man, — or huge jackets, sleepy countenances, long clay pipes, and fat forms surrounded by leathern belts fastened with a big buckle, the small-clothes and rosetted or buckled shoes of the old burghers who dozed away their lives, as described in Knickerbocker's History of New Netherlands.

These, like the noble red man, the cocked hats and knee-breeches, live in the poetry of the past; yet the buxom forms of the Dutch maidens, the stout ponderosity of the men, the quaint old architecture of the houses, reminding one of the old brass-ornamented high chests-of-drawers that belonged to his grandmother, the scrupulous cleanliness of everything, and withal the great deliberation which characterizes all transactions, show that many of the old Dutch characteristics remain.

Some of the guide-books, as well as travellers who visit Amsterdam, are in the habit of styling it the Venice of Holland, or "Venice of the North," but the only similarity between the two cities is that both are built upon piles and are intersected by numerous canals. In Venice, however, a horse in the street would be almost as great a novelty as a Bengal tiger, and the busy squares or wide streets are the exceptions, while in Amsterdam both are plentiful. Great paved streets are noisy with huge drays and rattling vehicles, and in many of the thoroughfares you would not dream of the existence of the canals. The four grand canals are in the middle of very wide streets, with rows of trees, roadways, and foot-passenger ways on either side. These four are in concentric semicircles within the ramparts of the city, and are intersected by numerous others that run in every direction, the principal ones being bordered by handsome rows of houses and neat promenades. The grand principal canal, or great water avenue I might call it, down which I took a stroll, — the *Heeren Gracht*, — was four miles in length and shaded with beautiful elm-trees. Another of these broad semicircular avenues, the *Keizer's Gracht*, or King's, was one hundred and fifty feet in width, and a most elegant avenue. The lesser canals were, of course, the cross-water streets to these grand affairs, or short-cuts connecting one part of the city with the other; and the whole are said to divide it into ninety islands connected together by three hundred bridges.

The dissimilarity of Amsterdam to Venice is marked in the dreamy quiet of the latter, where no rattle of wheels or noise of traffic is heard, and where its light and graceful gondolas, tall marble palaces rising directly out of the water, its latticed iron bridges, and stillness that is broken rudely by a shout, the creak of cordage of a heavy craft, and general air of listlessness, contrast sharply with the roar and rattle of vehicles here; the forests of masts on the river, and the stubbed, thickset-looking canal-boats on the canals, beside which a gondola would appear as a gazelle next an elephant; in its great heavy warehouses filled full of merchandise, or the taking it in and out from luggers, or even great square-rigged ships, by means of huge, creaking cranes and hoisting-apparatus, and the solid character of the bridges, as well as the to me curious style of drawbridges. These bridges are attached by chains to a heavy framework of wood or iron above, the two sides of the frame looking like the walking-beam of a steamboat-engine, but the machinery of it is so nicely balanced that one man, or, at the heavier bridges, two men, pulling downwards at the rope that hangs opposite the chains, may easily hoist the bridge for the passage of the boats.

The necessity of these drawbridges upon nearly all the canals, arises from the fact that the Dutch canal-boats are all provided with masts and sails, and, unlike ours, depend upon the wind for propulsion, or, when that fails, the boatmen make slow progress by shoving their boats along with poles, or buckling themselves to the tow-rope. In the smaller family or market boats, it is not an uncommon sight to meet the woman with the loop of the tow-rope over her shoulders as she tugs along the tow-path, while the stout husband sits at the helm, steering the craft and comfortably smoking his pipe.

These canal-boats are much shorter than ours, and are oiled instead of painted, and, as a general thing, kept scrupulously neat, a large number of them being the constant residence of families who operate them. Some of the heavier description which I noticed, had their stern cabin-windows shaded with lace curtains drawn away with blue ribbon, and little vases of flowers set in the window-seat; while upon the deck, beneath the shade of a bit of canvas, sat the Dutch *vrow* in spotless cap, gold head-band and pins, kirtle, short dress, and worsted stockings, knitting away industriously as she enjoyed the cool evening air.

The varying crowd of canal-boats, with the loads of merchandise which they bring into the city; the broad masculine figures of the peasant women, with funny head-dresses; the lofty and narrow Dutch houses of red and yellow brick, with projecting gables, and sometimes sunk down at one side on account of the yielding nature of their foundation; the little shops where red-hot turf and boiling water are sold, the latter from shining copper tea-kettles;

and withal the spick-span cleanliness of everything, — are novelties that will be noticed by the tourist in his rambles about Amsterdam.

I was interested in watching the boatloads of cheese and dairy products that came lazily floating down the canals, some of them guided by women, in short woollen dresses, long blue worsted stockings, wooden shoes, and curious head-dresses, who put their shoulders against the padded end of a long pushing-pole, and worked their boats into position with full as much ease as the men. Indeed, except for their lack of beards and difference in dress, one would see but little difference in their coarse and masculine figures. The curious head-dress worn by the peasant women is a thin band of pure gold, two inches wide, that goes all round the head, and has side-pieces that come down at the temples back of the eyes, in the shape of rosettes or ornaments; and over this are placed layers of thin stuff or muslin through which the precious metal shines. These head-dresses are one of the necessities, it seems, of every woman, though comparatively expensive affairs, the cheapest costing forty dollars, and the better ones nearly a hundred. The poorest of the peasants, who cannot get one of gold, wear one of silver, but never, I was told, of brass or gilt.

The old Dutch houses in some of the more business-like quarters of the city are jammed together in picturesque confusion, and fairly bulge out with merchandise; but around all is prevalent the Dutch characteristic of order and cleanliness, which forbids the accumulation of heaps of rubbish offensive to the eye or olfactories. The wharves that I visited, to my uneducated eye, looked as if swept-up for Sunday: chains coiled up in place, anchors freshly painted, brass-work shining like burnished gold, the windows of the shops and houses along the water-front clear as crystal, the door-sills of wood white from polishing with soap and sand, or painted, that the stain of trade might not soil them. Upon the quay, where was pointed out to us the house in which the bold Admiral De Ruyter used to live, the houses, though right in the very atmosphere of tar, oakum, and ship chandlery, were as neat as a new Philadelphia block of houses after a morning's wash.

But if one wants to get an idea of the enormous trade of the country, let him go down to some of the great docks, with their crowd of ships of all nations, a perfect forest of masts. The great Custom House inclosure of bonded warehouses, or "*Entrepot Dok*," as it is called, is a wonder, in its way, and well worth the tourist's inspection. It is a vast inclosed canal, with a depth of water sufficient to admit steamers and great square-rigged ships, and has admirably arranged storehouses or magazines for different descriptions of merchandise. Here are piled up whole cargoes of coffee and sugar, vast heaps of corn, cotton, indigo, and rice; cordage and timber from Russia, tea from China, petroleum from America, English iron and tin, vast magazines of wines and liquors, — in fact, the enormous quantities of merchandise from every part of the world fairly staggers the beholder, especially if he has been wont to deem Holland a sort of insignificant little nation, and has it chiefly associated in his mind with the product of Dutch cheeses and Holland gin.

But here, with these vast storehouses bearing the names of Cuba, America, Africa, London, Smyrna, St. Petersburg, Odessa, Archangel, Hamburg, and a score of other producing ports, and surrounded by shipping from every part of the civilized world, with merchandise in mountains on every side, and hundreds of busy men, the moving to and fro of the great barges that are to take their vast loads down the Rhine, the Neckar, and the other watercourses, for distribution, he feels that he is in the presence of a great commercial and maritime nation.

The great dikes and canals of Holland, and their construction, is a subject that a volume could be written about, for they are a marvel and a wonder of engineering skill, and their improvement and construction to-day seem to be more closely studied than ever; and one cannot help questioning whether the vast expenditure which is going on will be repaid. An examination into the condition of the people, however, reveals no indication that they are seriously oppressed on this account, though taxation is said to be heavy; but they owe to a large degree the extraordinary fertility of their lands, which have been reclaimed from the sea, to the system of dykes and drainage; for it will be remembered that the draining of Haarlem Lake gave fifty thousand acres of excellent land to Holland.

And the pathway from Amsterdam to the sea is through one of their wonderful canals, — the North Holland Canal, which is directly opposite the city on the other side of the river Ij, — a canal twenty feet deep and one hundred and twenty feet wide. It is a wonderful piece of work. Its locks, made of huge timbers driven down through the mud into the firm sand far below, are the largest in Europe, and its sides are kept from being washed away by the numerous craft of every description that pass constantly through it by an ingenious arrangement of a thick growth of yielding reeds. This canal is ten feet below the level of the sea, and it runs on one level to Helder, a maritime town at the northern extremity of North Holland on the North Sea, fifty miles away. This great work was finished in 1825, at the cost of a million pounds sterling.

But, after nearly half a century's experience with this canal, the commercial activity of the people was such that it was deemed insufficient, and they determined to have a shorter cut to the North Sea, and at the time of the author's visit were actively engaged upon their new North Sea Canal. If the reader will look on the map, he will see that the narrowest part of the isthmus connecting the provinces of Northern and Southern Holland is at a point a short distance north of Haarlem, between two little stations on the railway, Velsen and Beverwijk, at one end of the Ij; through this narrow neck cuts the new canal to the sea, which is here not twenty miles from Amsterdam. Then this canal will go through the Ij (which, it will be remembered, is a sort of estuary or arm of the Zuyder Zee) directly to the city proper, and that portion of the Ij which is not needed for water commercial purposes was to be drained for cultivation; and thus Holland, while opening this great highway to the sea for herself, wrests a vast space already occupied by the waves, from them for agriculture.

This work on the Ij was in progress at the time of the author's visit, and referred to with great enthusiasm by the inhabitants; and well it may be, for it is one of the greatest works of the kind of modern time, as a few figures, obtained from authentic sources, will show.

The depth of water in the canal, in the enormous locks that separate it from the sea, is twenty-three feet; the width of its surface is over two hundred feet, and nearly fifteen thousand acres of excellent land will be gained by the drainage above mentioned. At the sea-shore, the great piers or jetties that shelter the entrance, run out three-quarters of a mile in length, and their foundations are thirty feet below low-water mark, and the wall is carried eight feet above high-water mark. The piers are built of great blocks of concrete, twelve feet long by four in breadth, and four feet thick. There is twenty-five feet depth of water between the piers at low tide. Close to the shore they are three-fourths of a mile apart, but the entrance out in the sea is but seven hundred and fifty feet wide. The whole work, it is estimated, will cost nearly three million pounds sterling. The North Holland Canal would admit vessels of but a thousand tons burden. This, however, will admit much larger, besides being a shorter route to the ocean. The merchant fleet of Holland is nearly two thousand vessels — an aggregate of half a million tons; its imports about twenty-five million dollars, and its exports one hundred and ninety million dollars.

It is well for some of us Americans, who like to boast of our enterprise and great public works, to look at what the people of this little kingdom are doing. Their sturdy perseverance and thrifty, constant industry rather belie the character popularly accorded them of being little else than smokers of long pipes, drinkers from deep flagons, and fat old fellows comfortably dozing away their existence. The Dutch have this advantage in their prosecution of agriculture: that, inasmuch as the rich farming lands have been reclaimed from water, they can easily, in dry times, by the same system of windmills, water-wheels, and ditches, irrigate them or add to their fertility; and the industry with which they have applied themselves to agriculture fairly rivals that which they displayed in their commercial operations, and has for years past steadily increased in importance. Indeed, they have become one of the most prominent of European agricultural peoples, and their rich fields and pastures reclaimed from the waters, sleek and well cared-for cattle, and heavy crops, are the admiration of visiting American agriculturists; and many of these steady old Dutch farmers, in their quiet villages, roll up good comfortable fortunes.

The traveller, among other curious things here in Holland, will notice the fire-buckets, as they may be with propriety called, which are used at breakfast and tea-time at the hotels to keep water hot for tea and coffee. A sort of metal bucket with blazing turf, upon which sits the burnished copper teapot, full of boiling water, is brought into the *salle-à-manger*, and they are placed at intervals for the use of eight or ten guests, so that perhaps there are half a dozen of them hissing in the room at once. This turf, of which one will find there is quite a large consumption among the Dutch for culinary and manufacturing purposes, is the product of their own peat bogs. The consumption is said to amount to millions of tons per annum.

Although there is in Holland "water, water everywhere," yet, owing to the absence of springs, there is said to be "not a drop to drink" that is healthful to the tourist. In Amsterdam filtered rain-water is used, and also water that is brought from a reservoir thirteen miles away, near Haarlem, but this is not recommended; indeed, one authority says, "Drink anything but water;" which may account for some American travellers' desire to test the drink of the country, and their orders for Hollands gin or Schiedam schnapps.

After we had enjoyed our ramble about streets and canals, docks and wharves, our *valet de place* was anxious we should see the Palace, a great, dreary-looking building upon a sort of square or market-place. The interior was a disappointment, as it was a damp sort of musty old place, with nothing particularly elegant in it except a few rooms in white marble. The most striking apartment was the Council Hall,— an apartment one hundred and twenty feet long, fifty-seven wide, and one hundred feet in height, in which were flags and trophies taken in various battles by the Dutch, and remnants of the flags of Philip the Second and the Duke of Alva.

The custodian especially directed our attention to Venetian glass chandeliers, and bustled round, opening closed-up shutters of darkened apartments in anticipation of a good fee; but we did the Palace hastily, for upholstery and great rooms, after months' experience in viewing them, become fatiguing, especially when there is but little historic interest attached to them. This palace is on the largest square in the city, which is known as the *Dam;* so called for being on one side of the most ancient dam of the city, which takes its name, it will be recollected, from the river Amstel — *Amstel-Dam.* The Exchange, opposite the Palace, is a handsome building, with a colonnade front and a huge glass-covered interior, in which the merchants assemble daily for the transaction of business.

The finest picture-gallery in Holland is that in Amsterdam, known as the Rijks Museum, which is celebrated as being a genuine national collection, four hundred and eight of five hundred and fifteen pictures being by Dutch masters; so that the art-lover who desires to study the old Dutch masters or the Dutch school can here have ample opportunity of so doing. The first room that the visitor enters contains two of the largest and most celebrated pictures in the collection, — The Banquet of the Arquebusiers, by Van der Helst, and Rembrandt's Night Watch. The former is a very spirited figure piece, and represents twenty-five arquebusiers the size of life, in various sitting and standing attitudes, about a bountifully furnished table. These figures are all portraits of men who more than two hundred years ago celebrated the conclusion of the Peace of Westphalia at a banquet, and the artist has thus preserved them for posterity, — a stout, hearty, sturdy-looking company; their rich velvet doublets trimmed with gold, the gusto with which some are enjoying their potations, and their free and easy attitudes, either sitting or standing, being remarkably well executed.

Rembrandt's "Night Watch," as it is called, is a large painting, eleven by fourteen feet in size, and the great master's largest, and by many deemed his most celebrated work. It represents a company of arquebusiers emerging from their guard-house, and one of its most remarkable features is the wonderfully effective manner in which the artist has managed the different effects of light and shade. The figures are of life-size, and the painting is hung so low as to nearly touch the floor, which adds much to its effect, inasmuch as the sturdy, armed figures seem to be advancing directly towards the spectator. The two figures of a captain and lieutenant in the middle foreground, clad, the one in a black and the other in a buff costume, are in full sunlight, and very effective, while behind, a figure of one of the guards adjusting his weapon, and the standard-bearer, are very finely rendered. The effect of the twilight or shade of the hall from which they are coming, and the setting sunlight without, is very well managed; and the admirable arrangement, natural and life-like attitudes of the figures, make them to seem verily as if they would step out from the frame in their quaint costumes of 1642, and, under the command of their captain, take an afternoon march to their several positions about the city for the night.

In this room are portraits by Van der Helst (artist of the first-mentioned picture), of Admiral Cortanaer, and others; and in the second room another picture by Rembrandt, of the five directors of the Guild of Clothmakers in 1661, also portraits. These directors of the old trade associations appear to have been as marvellously fond of having pictures painted of themselves as our city government officials of to-day in America are of being photographed in committees, for the next large picture I encountered was a fine one of the directors of a spinning-factory, five in number, painted in 1669 by Karel du Jardin.

Now, as the visitor ascends to the other rooms, he begins to find numerous gems of the art, such as Ruysdael's beautiful Waterfall, Jan Steen's beautiful picture of the Backgammon Players and Parrot, Hondekoeter's wonderfully correct picture of Ducks, Poultry, and Game, in which his skill at "feather" painting is strikingly illustrated. Then we come to the beautifully finished pictures of Gerard Duow, including his Evening School, — a painting in which the effects of the light and shade produced by candle-light are delineated with singular skill. It is but fourteen by twenty inches in size, and, according to one authority, was purchased for the Museum for thirty-seven hundred dollars, while another places the cost at double that amount. Then follow several Wouvermans, Ruysdaels, and Cuyps; Tenier's Guard Room; Ostade's Boors, smoking; Van Mieris' Poultry Dealer, and other beautifully finished works; a Landscape and Cattle, by Paul Potter, cost five thousand dollars; Snyder's Game and Fruit; a Magdalene by Van Dyck; in fact, a collection of old masters' choice works sufficient to make the eyes of an art-lover sparkle with delight.

There is another museum, that of Van der Hoop, consisting of about two hundred pictures left by a banker of that name, many of which are of rare merit, such as some beautiful examples of Jan Steen; the Jewish Bride, by Rembrandt; a wonderfully executed little painting of a hermit, by Gerard Douw, in which the great artist has put the most astonishing elaboration of details; portraits by Rubens; some of Ruysdael's superb landscapes; and specimens of Wouverman, Van Dyck, Potter, and other noted artists.

An excursion that every tourist who can, makes when he visits Amsterdam, is out to the Dutch village of Broek. We did this with carriage and guide, driving on to a boat that carried us across the Ij, after which we had a drive through a little bit of Dutch landscape and farming land. At one point we passed by the great dikes, high as the top of our carriage, that were keeping back the waters from the miles of fertile fields, which were plentifully stocked with sleek cattle. Then we passed little cross canals, which answered as country cross-roads, on which every now and then appeared a slow-going sort of little omnibus canal-boat, drawn by a single horse, conveying Dutch women with big baskets, or blue-bloused men with pipes, as passengers. Then we passed milkmaids with wooden shoes and snowy caps; then a family boat, slowly towed along by a couple of men; a hay-boat, that ever and anon had some of its contents scraped off into the water, which another little family boat not far behind, with a man, boy, and a woman as crew, economically rescued from the water as they came to it, spreading it out upon their deck to dry.

Upon some of these canals we noted what appeared to be a stagnant green slime covering the surface of the water, but which our guide informed us was " the richness and fatness of the land ; " and so indeed it proved, for we found the apparent slime to be green seed, growing as it floated upon the water. We halted to view a Dutch farm-house by the wayside, the home of a tolerably well-to-do agriculturist, I should judge by his surroundings. At any rate, the cow-stable that we were first ushered into was a new experience to those who had only been accustomed to see the manner in which these useful animals are cared for in a New England barn. It being summer, the animals were out in the grazing-lands for the season, and the quarters they occupied were in a sort of holiday attire. They consisted of a long, substantially built building of wood, the windows hung with neat white curtains. The interior beams and wood-work were either brightly scrubbed or whitewashed, not a cobweb or stain to be seen. The row of stalls that ran along the sides, the clean brick floor, whitewashed depressed stone gutter at the rear of them, and within some the fantastic arrangement of sand, which was drawn by a broom into various curious figures, were neat and pretty. In others, the beautiful arrangement of sea-shells and pebbles, and the display of curious old china delft-ware and pottery, would have made a collector of *bric-à-brac* crazy with delight, and cause the inexperienced visitor to turn to his guide, and ask if he correctly understood him to say this was a cow-stable, thinking that the word given might have been Dutch for reception-hall.

This well-appointed place, however, that we were inspecting, was really the cows' home from November to May, and the little apartments, with their curious museums of *bric-à-brac*, are at that season of the year the cows' stalls, but, according to custom, are thus treated in the summer, so that the place then becomes a novel sort of reception-hall. In the different stalls, besides china and shells, were curious old articles of furniture that had evidently been heirlooms in the family, such as old brass kettles that shone like burnished gold, antique snuffers and candlesticks upon an old black carved wood table, some fat old pewter or silver flagons, and long brass-hooped casks that looked like big black fingers with gold rings on them.

The flooring of brick, the ventilation and drainage, which

were perfect, depressed gutters for carrying away the droppings, and the brick drinking-trough that runs in front of the stalls for the whole length, and is supplied by a pump at one end, showed that the Dutch farmer understood the value of the animals who contributed dairy products, and spared no effort for their comfort, in which doubtless he found return in the quality and quantity of yield.

This farmer, like many others in the vicinity, was a large cheese producer, and his cheese-room was next this grand cow saloon, in fact opening out of it. We were shown into it by a buxom, round-armed Dutch woman. The making of cheese was not in operation, but we saw the big milk and curd tub, curd-knives, wooden benches scoured white, the well-known "pine-apple" and "cannon-ball" moulds, the press which takes in four to six of these moulds for their seven or eight hours' pressing, and finally were conducted to the magazine or storehouse of cheeses, where, after being salted, they are shelved to dry.

The cheese-factory room was faultlessly clean, the storeroom of cheeses, where serried rows of them stood in alcoves of shelves, like a library of cheeses, was spotless, dry, and well lighted. After being thus shelved, I was informed that they had to be turned in position every day for a month, and after that every alternate day for about the same time. Another part of the finishing process is once bathing them at a certain time in tepid water and drying in the open air, and also their being painted over on the outside with a thin coating of linseed-oil.

The process of making, before all this finishing, is equally careful and elaborate, and great care is taken that the apartments in which they are made and kept are preserved at a certain temperature, and perfectly clean and dry. The salting, moulding, curdling, and all processes are carried on with great thoroughness and exactness, requiring a degree of regularity, experience, and patience which, after one has it fully explained, causes him to have increased respect for the Dutch cheese and its manufacturers. The cheese product is something so enormous that it assumes the position of a great industry of the country, and fairly astonishes one who looks into the statistics of it for the first time: the province of North Holland alone is reported to produce twenty-six million pounds of cheese per annum, and it is exported to almost every part of the civilized world.

From the stables and cheese-making apartments we were invited into some of the rooms of the farm-house, in which dwelt the farmer and his family. Everywhere was visible the Dutch characteristic of neatness, showing that scrubbing, polishing, and scouring must occupy no inconsiderable portion of a Dutch housewife's time. Floors were white and spotless, window-glass transparent as air, brass work rivalled gold in brightness, and even nail-heads that were visible reflected back the light that fell upon them. The furniture in the apartments we visited — a parlor and sleeping-rooms — was principally rich, dark old mahogany, mounted with brass trimmings. Much of it was more than two hundred years of age, was admirably kept, and heirlooms in the family. A store of delft and curious old china teacups and tea-sets, plates, vases, and teapots, such as every Dutch family seems to have more or less of, was disposed about the apartment.

In the sleeping-rooms, seeing no beds, I was asked to guess where they were, but failed to do so correctly, for my conductor enlightened me by pulling at a sliding panel in the wall, which glided away and revealed three wide berths, or bunks, sunk in the place, one above the other, — a close, dark recess in which to sleep, and one in which I should imagine that it would be difficult to obtain the amount of fresh air during the hours of slumber to render sleep refreshing; but the Dutch, in-doors, seem to pay little regard to the admission of air, if one may judge from the windows of the rooms of their houses, which are rarely seen open, but generally tightly closed, even in warm weather.

Mounting our carriage again, we drove on through the flat country, with its canal and windmill landscape, to our destination, Brock, which has much celebrity as being one of the cleanest towns in the world. We halted at a Dutch inn just outside, for no vehicles or horses were admitted into this immaculate village, certainly not those of tourists. So after a lunch we entered on foot. The town contains about fifteen hundred inhabitants, and the streets are paved with yellow bricks, set up edgeways, or small stones in the same manner, and sometimes in various fantastic figures; they were all scrupulously clean as if just swept up, and I saw one of the street-cleaners at work. He was an old fellow who was seated in the middle of the street, and with a jack-knife cleaning away some moss and weeds that had made their appearance between the interstices of the pavement. The houses were of wood, with tiled roofs; they were nicely painted, and the little flower-gardens, front yards, and all appurtenances in apple-pie order, as if prepared for rigorous inspection.

The tradition is, here, that the front doors of the houses are never opened except for a wedding or a funeral. Some houses were painted white, some green, and others in fantastic hues that no one but a Dutchman or Cape Cod sea-captain would have thought of; but the matter of cleanliness and primness was carried to such an extent that the place looked like a toy village that had been set up for somebody's amusement. We visited one of the houses, a regular curiosity shop of old china, curiosities, and *bric-à-brac*, which is kept as a sort of specimen showhouse for visitors, and said to be the oldest house in the town, built in 1500, and one which all pay a visit to, as we found by the visitors' book of autographs, and where, besides inspecting the curious Dutch antiquities of tiles, china, furniture, plate, and utensils for a moderate fee, you could buy a little antique cup and saucer for a big price, or curious old silver teaspoons for a much larger figure; but nevertheless the collection was an interesting one of Dutch antiquities, which had formed the life-labor of the old couple — brother and sister — who exhibited them.

Their garden was another curiosity, where a giant growth of box-plant had been cut into the form of a peacock, bee-hive, chairs, a deer, dogs, and various other fantastic shapes, and, after a look at these and another ramble through the prim little town to a little toy-looking square, with a little stone public building set up in one corner of it, and past the red, blue, and green houses with their railed-in gardens, and by the little canal with its still water covered with green scum, we took carriage outside the limits, rode to the steam ferry, and were paddled back to Amsterdam.

The Hague, or 'S Gravenhage, we reached by railway journey via Haarlem, where the high-priced tulips came from during the tulip mania; and Leyden, which is one of the oldest towns of Holland.

The Hague, *La Haye*, or *'S Gravenhage*, the latter being the Dutch name, signifying the count's hedge or inclosure, was for hundreds of years the aristocratic city of Holland, and the favorite residence of the Dutch nobility. It is now the chief abiding-place of rich old Dutch merchants who have made their fortunes in Japan, Sumatra, Batavia, or somewhere else in the Dutch East India possessions, and come here to this most fashionable and handsome city in Holland to enjoy their wealth, and they do live here sumptuously and royally. The houses are large and elegant, many of them surrounded by beautiful grounds and gardens; the streets are broad and handsome, paved with brick, and some of them lined with beautiful shade-trees; and the city has every appearance, as it is, of being a handsomely built and well-governed European capital.

Established at the Bellevue Hotel, we make excursions into the somewhat homelike-looking streets, with their great shade-trees and clean pavements, and saunter through pleasant avenues, till we suddenly come to a handsome sheet of water in the middle of the town, on which black and white swans are sailing, and having a picturesque little island in its centre. This is known as the *Vijver*, or fish-pond, and round and about it is a very pleasant and much-frequented promenade; and not far from here, in a sort of open square, stands a handsome bronze statue of Prince William II., with four allegorical figures at the sides, representing Peace, History, Prosperity, and Glory; an inscription shows the names of Badajos, Salamanca, Vittoria, and other battles at which he was present.

Another fine bronze statue is that of Prince William I., who is represented standing with one finger upraised as if uttering his favorite motto, which is inscribed in Latin on the pedestal, a free translation of which is, "Calm 'mid troubled waters;" while another statue of Prince William I. on horseback adorns a space opposite the King's palace, its pedestal ornamented with the arms of the provinces under his sway. In the city park, known as William's Park, is a magnificent national memorial monument commemorating the restoration of Dutch independence in 1813, a tall column bearing a female figure which stands grasping a banner in one hand and a bunch of arrows in the other, while the lion of Netherlands is at her feet. The sides of the pedestal are beautifully ornamented with bronze figures of distinguished men, and bas-reliefs representing memorable events in the history of the country.

CHAPTER XIX.

THE Picture Gallery of the Museum at the Hague contains many fine examples of the old masters, and two that are great celebrities, namely, Rembrandt's School of Anatomy, and Paul Potter's Bull, a life-size cattle-picture. The study of art is now considered so necessary a portion of one's education that but few tourists will omit visiting the great galleries in the European capitals; and this, like that in Amsterdam for the study of the Dutch school, is one that should by no means be passed over. It contains nearly three hundred pictures. Among them are the productions of such artists as Snyder, Wouvermans, Rubens, Rembrandt, Gerard Duow, Van Ostade, Jan Steen, Van Dyck, Holbein, and Dürer. Look at this list of names, and see what an artistic treat is before the art lover in such a collection as this.

Many who have never seen Rembrandt's picture, The School of Anatomy, may have seen engravings of it. It represents an anatomist dissecting the left arm of a dead body that lies before him, and lecturing thereon to a group that stand about him. The figures are all of large size, and are eight in number. The lecturer, Nicholas Tulp, sits at the table, with one hand holding an anatomical instrument resting upon the subject, and the other upraised in the attitude of explanation. He has a broad-brimmed hat upon his head, but his companions are all uncovered, and the delineations of their heads and various expressions of countenance are magnificently done, more especially that of one seated, who is bending eagerly forward to examine the progress made by the demonstrator, and another immediately behind, looking over his shoulder. These figures are portraits of members of the Guild of Surgeons of Amsterdam; indeed the picture was originally painted by the artist for the Anatomical Institute of Amsterdam.

The representation of the corpse upon the dissecting-table is horribly real; and the surrounding figures, in their sombre black garments, and with their serious faces, so natural and life-like, have a peculiarly striking effect; and the whole scene possesses a sort of terrible attraction that draws the visitor to look at it, perhaps twice or thrice, after having concluded a first inspection, much in the same manner as one might be supposed to be attracted, by morbid curiosity, to take another look into a dissecting-room at which he had obtained a single surreptitious glance. There can be no doubt of the picture's being a most faithful representation; and, as an artistic production, the dullest comprehension cannot fail to acknowledge it at first sight. It was bought by King William I. for about twenty-five thousand dollars.

Paul Potter's Bull is simply a magnificently correct life-size painting of a young bull, whose clear, liquid eye, dewy nostril, and shaggy frontlet are so true to nature, that, after gazing at it a while, one would scarcely be surprised to see the young lord of the herd walk forth from the frame or stretch forth his shaggy head with challenging roar to another bovine champion. Besides the bull in this painting, there are two or three sheep, a cow lying down upon the green turf, and an old shepherd leaning over a fence, all being of life-size, and all of which will bear the closest inspection, — unlike many paintings of our more modern school, especially in America, which, we are told, must not be closely examined, but at a distance; imagination, effect of lights and shades, and other characteristics (which the author, who does not pretend to be an art critic, does not recall), giving the true effect to the composition. A large proportion of the great masters of the art, however, judging from their works, seem to have produced the effects themselves, leaving but little for the spectator to supply by either distance, light, or imagination.

Another picture, which has quite an artistic celebrity, is a beautifully finished one by Jan Steen, which is entitled "A Representation of Human Life," though why, I cannot imagine, as it represents about twenty persons, old and young, apparently in a public house, eating oysters. There is an old man dandling a child; a young woman cooking oysters on the half-shell; a party at table; man sitting at window, being offered wine by servant; children upon the floor; group in the background,—all finely executed, and the effects of light and shade most artistically managed, and details most carefully presented. This is said to be one of the best pictures of this artist, who, besides being a painter, was a tavern-keeper; hence, he enjoyed ample opportunity in studying the scenes of tavern-life, which he depicts with such genial humor and expression.

I halted opposite a beautiful picture by Van Ostade, which represented a wandering musician opposite a village ale-house, and entertaining six or eight persons,—which was wonderfully good, with its contrasted cool shade, warm, bright sunlight, and clambering vine over the inn-door, and beehives and foliage in the background.

Then, among other gems, was one of Snyder's vegetable and game pieces; a beautiful picture of a poultry-yard by Jan Steen, with ducks, pigeons, and fowls, girl and lamb, and other figures. Boys blowing Soap Bubbles, by Van Mieris, was a most exquisitely finished picture. Then there is a Stag Hunt, by Snyder; Carriage and Horses, by Wouvermans; Alchemist, by Teniers; a most beautiful picture by Gerard Duow, a perfect gem in finish and effect, called "The Young Housekeeper," of a lady with child in cradle and servant; Rembrandt's fine picture of Presentation in the Temple,—one of his earliest works; a beautifully painted Virgin and Child, by Murillo; Waterfall, by Ruysdael; portraits by Velasquez, Van Dyck, Holbein, and Albrecht Dürer.

The portion of the Museum devoted to curiosities contains a very large collection of relics connected with the history of the Netherlands, and an extensive and interesting display of curiosities from the Dutch East India possessions, also from India, China, and Japan.

The Japanese collection was particularly rich and interesting, containing domestic and warlike instruments, dresses, and costumes, tools, vases, and ornaments, beautiful porcelain curiosities, and figures fully clad in rich costumes, and representations of manners and customs of the people. A similar collection of Chinese curiosities filled a room; and among them were representations of a Chinese court of justice and execution, mandarins and other figures in full costume. Another room was devoted to costumes, weapons, implements, and other objects from the Dutch East Indies.

Among the curiosities are relics of William of Orange, the founder of Dutch liberty, who was assassinated, in 1584, at Delft, and the dress worn by him at that time is, of course, the most interesting. The armor of Admiral De Ruyter is here, and the *baton* of Admiral Hein, another stanch old Dutch sailor, who captured the Spanish silver-fleet in 1628, and brought about ten million dollars into the Treasury. Another relic of Dutch naval bravery is Lieutenant Van Speyk's sword, and fragments of his gun-boat, which, when it was driven on the enemy's coast in 1831, and he was surrounded by his foes and summoned to surrender, he blew up by firing his pistol into the powder-magazine. The bowl and wooden goblet of the Gueux, or "Beggars," the first revolutionary party in the Netherlands, who banded themselves together against Spanish rule, and sought the abolition of the Inquisitorial courts, are shown: each of the confederates, in token of his adherence to the band, struck a nail into this wooden goblet. Another goblet is shown that was used by General Chassé, who defended Antwerp against the French in 1832; gold chain and medal, presented to Admiral De Ruyter, and very many other relics, interesting as a national collection, or to those who are well read up in the history of the United Netherlands and the Dutch Republic.

A delightful drive is that to the Queen's Palace, or the "House in the Wood," as it is called, about two miles from the city. It is a very plain brick building, but surrounded by beautiful grounds. The apartments, which we were permitted to visit, were very interesting, and beautifully furnished.

The Orange Saloon, so called, is a superb eight-sided saloon, lighted principally from a cupola above; its walls are fifty feet in height, and covered with paintings illustrating scenes in the life of Prince Frederick William of Orange.

The Japanese Room was quite a wonder in its display of elegant Japanese work, all its fittings and furnishings being in that style. The walls were panelled in black and gold lacquer, and the centre of the panels filled with rich white silk, upon which were embroidered birds, flowers, plants, and insects, in bright colors, and in the most elaborate and elegant manner. Great chandeliers of quaint designs of gilt bronze hung down with a sort of Japanese cup-and-saucer arrangement for the lights, with gilded brass ornaments between. Superb Japanese vases and bronze figures were scattered about the saloon; the chairs were of black lacquer and gilt, with superb embroidered white silk cushions, in harmony with the wall-upholstery and curtains; rich porcelain, costly sofas, and lacquered inlaid tables, and silken hangings of the richest description, curiosities and wonders from the Mikado's empire, were scattered in rich profusion on every side.

The other apartments were beautifully decorated, and contained many fine pictures, to which we could give but cursory examination. Returning, we met the Queen's carriage, a heavy, gilded affair, without any attendants save coachman and footman; and the Queen, who was its only occupant, returned the salutation of our party with a pleasant smile and bow.

Coming back, we paid a brief visit to the Zoölogical Garden, which has but a small collection of specimens, and finished up the excursion with a drive in the beautiful park which is known as *Het Bosch*, — a favorite resort for the wealthier citizens, who enjoy its pleasant avenues as their carriages roll over the well-kept roads and beneath the shade of its stately trees.

We must not leave The Hague without visiting Scheveningen, the chief watering-place in Holland, and which is but about two and a half miles distant. Although there were three or four conveyances, such as omnibus, canal-boat, and, I really believe, a horse railway, we preferred, for comfort's sake, to take a private carriage.

The ride was a most delightful one, over a splendid road, which was macadamized, or, I may say more correctly, paved, with closely-set, small stones. It was shaded by magnificent trees, in double and sometimes triple rows, on either side; and you pass beautiful estates, picturesque country houses, and reaches of pleasant views, during the brief ride, while the well-kept, dashing equipages that are met remind one of the season at Newport or Saratoga, and that we are approaching one of the chosen resorts of fashion.

Scheveningen itself is but a fishing-village, located behind the dunes, or sand-hills, of the coast of the North Sea; literally behind them, for, as you pass through the village or beyond on the route to the fashionable resort itself, the beach is hidden, as is the sea, from view by the gradual rise of the ground, or sand-dunes. Arriving at the crest of these, and you come at once upon great modern watering-place hotels, saloons, restaurants, booths, and all those modern structures and adjuncts which one finds at fashionable seaside watering-places. At the great hotel of the baths, which is the property of The Hague, the crowd of visitors was immense, and the attendance as bad, and the prices as extravagantly high as they always are at such places, before a stranger gets acquainted sufficiently to command the first and accommodate himself to the second. The great, broad beach — a magnificent one for bathing — had a long line of bathing-machines ranged along like a halt of the baggage-wagons of an army, only they were wagons all with their shafts pointed shoreward, were roofed over, had a window in their wooden sides, and their rear end adorned with a great hood or screen towards the sea. These, as many are aware, are a sort of private bath-room on wheels, which is fitted up with pegs, mirrors, towels, soap, &c., and are drawn into the water to a certain depth, so that the occupants may descend easily from them, take their sea-bath, and return to the vehicle and dress entirely free from observation, and avoid that long, dripping walk from the waves to the bath-house, so dreaded in America by ladies who, when in full toilette, may excite admiration, but after a sea dip are anything but attractive.

Then there were whole regiments of bath-chairs, tall, covered, and shaded at side and top, made of basket-work, and each having a little footstool in front. In these comfortable seats, facing the sea, in bright weather, and shaded from the sun, sit visitors reading or chatting in groups, ladies knitting worsted work, and gentlemen smoking, or looking out to sea with glasses, or enjoying the air and the lively scene about them. While we were at the beach, a brisk squall set in, followed by a storm of rain, driving every one to shelter, and the rising wind sent in the dashing billows of the North Sea in great, tumbling, furious waves, high upon the beach.

We prepared with some regret to leave the Hollow Land, the country of dikes and dams, windmills, and cleanliness. Our first fifteen minutes' railway ride from The Hague carried us to Delft, on through Schiedam, with the black smoke of its gin-distilleries rising in the clear air, till we reached Rotterdam, through which we rode on our way *en route* for Brussels. Rotterdam, what little of it we had opportunity of observing, was similar in many respects to Amsterdam, although the cleanliness and order was not by any means so marked. The great canals, however, seemed to admit vessels of the heaviest tonnage to the very centre of the city, and their presence, receiving and discharging cargoes, as well as that of the numerous huge barges, filled with merchandise, in the canals, impresses the visitor with the commercial importance of the place. At Dort we had a good view of the town and its church, with its peculiar large square tower; and on arrival at Moerdyck admired one of the most magnificent railway bridges in the world, completed in 1871, to avoid the three ferries which travellers were formerly obliged to use. This superb structure is about a mile and two-thirds in length, crosses an arm of the sea at this point, and is upheld by fourteen magnificent arches, each having a span of three hundred and thirty feet. The iron bridge itself is upheld by fourteen stone buttresses, each fifty feet long and ten feet wide. At Breda we had an outside view of the Protestant church, which has a beautiful spire three hundred and sixty-five feet in height; and from here continued our journey by rail on to Antwerp, and thence to Brussels, the Paris of Belgium.

I was awakened next morning by the cheerful notes of a bugle, playing that old-fashioned melody, "The Mellow Horn," the words of which begin, —

"At dawn Aurora gayly breaks
In all her proud attire;"

and looking forth from my casement, saw the well-remembered English stage-coach, with its spanking team of grays, drive into the *Place Royale* and halt near the statue of Godfrey de Bouillon for a freight of passengers for the field of Waterloo, exactly as I had before seen it, and as though it were but yesterday, instead of six years previously, that I had looked upon the same scene, and figured as one of the interested actors in it, as I climbed to the roof, eager to visit the scene where the fate of the modern Cæsar was finally decided. But we are to rest here for a brief period; and the sights having all been inspected at a previous visit, there is but a lounge into the picture-stores and galleries, and an inspection there of the latest productions of Robie and Verboekhoeven; or the ladies to visit Julie Everaert's parlors at 4 *Place Belliard Rue Royale*, to look at and buy of her beautiful lace work, before we once more take train for the gay capital of France.

Arrived in Paris, and, as the reader has already inferred, our tour Abroad Again is over; and yet, much as has been seen, and described in these pages during the six months' experiences here set down, the lover of travel will doubtless, if he goes over the same routes and visits the same sights, experience in some degree the feeling of the author, who found the time far too short to see all as he could wish to see it.

The author has endeavored in this work, like his former one of a similar character, to give faithful descriptions of the sights and scenes in the various localities visited, and has supplied many details of information which he himself suffered from the want of while abroad, and which have been obtained in the preparation of these papers by the consultation of numerous authorities since his return. Especially was this the case in describing the Vatican and other museums, in many instances where neither guide-books nor local catalogue gave any information beyond the bare title of an object which often proved to be one which a few explanatory lines rendered extremely interesting.

The space of time occupied in making this tour may of course be materially shortened; indeed, some tourists accomplish a journey to nearly if not all the places that the author has described in the "Over the Ocean" and "Abroad Again" papers, which cover about thirteen months of diligent travel, in less than half that time. But it may well be questioned if the knowledge thus gained is of permanent benefit.

A journey to Europe the average American now puts down as one of the probabilities instead of the possibilities of his life, and the annual influx of American tourists has come to be so looked and prepared for of late years by the hotel-keepers and shop-keepers of the principal European capitals, that any diminution of the number of money-spending visitors is noted and felt. A question that is frequently asked by new tourists, and one that is in some respects difficult to answer, is, What is the best guide-book to use? The requirements of tourists vary so much, owing to differences of taste and education, that such as might be of value to one would be cumbersome to another. For practical usefulness and reliability as regards hotels, routes, charges, notable sights, &c., Baedeker's Guides I think to be the best of the foreign publications. Murray's are fuller in description, give criticisms, extracts from noted writers, and in that respect furnish material for callow correspondents to draw from for home letters, but they are cumbersome. Bradshaw's Continental Handbook is such a puzzle, that it is a common expression that you must have a guide to Bradshaw to understand it. Of the American guide-books of Europe, Fetridge's, published by Harper and Brothers, is rich in maps and other information, which is corrected yearly by the author. "The Satchel Guide," published by Hurd & Houghton, of Boston, also corrected every year, will however be found a model of compactness and correctness to those who desire to economize space. D. Appleton & Co., of New York, have published a series of good illustrated hand-books. These different descriptions are those now most used by travellers, although each year brings new competitors into the field.

That to see sights thoroughly, and especially thoroughly enough to make notes of them and write a book thereon, requires labor of no slight character, there is no denying. The Bard of Avon writes, however, "The labor we delight in physics pain;" so the pleasure of vividly recalling enjoyable scenes, years after they have been witnessed, for our own gratification as well as that of others, is the compensation in some degree derived for making a business of one's sight-seeing.

The author, in taking leave of the readers who have followed him through this second series of experiences, will feel more than gratified if he has succeeded in imparting information that will be of practical service to those about to make the journey, or if he has recalled pleasant memories to such as have visited the localities referred to in these pages. Or if he has been still more fortunate in enabling such as stay at home, to picture correctly in imagination the sights and scenes he has undertaken to describe.

THE END.

BOOKS PUBLISHED BY LEE & SHEPARD.

By the Author of "Abroad Again."

OVER THE OCEAN;
OR, SIGHTS AND SCENES IN FOREIGN LANDS.
By CURTIS GUILD,
Author of "Abroad Again," and Editor of the *Boston Commercial Bulletin.*

ONE VOL., CROWN 8VO. PAPER, —; CLOTH, $2.50.

This book has not only become a favorite among the reading public, but is now generally accepted as one of the best guides to Europe ever published. "Whether describing Westminster Abbey, or York Minster, Stratford-upon-Avon, or the streets of London; the wonders of the Louvre, or the gayeties and glitter of Paris; the grandeur of the Alpine passes; the quaintness of old continental cities; experiences of post travel; the romantic beauties of the Italian lakes; the underground wonders of Adelsburg, or the aqueous highways of Venice; — the author aims to give many minute particulars, which foreign letter-writers deem of too little importance to mention, but which, nevertheless, are of great interest to the reader."

"A Close Observer of the Manners and Customs."

"The utmost that any European tourist can hope to do is to tell the old story in a somewhat fresh way, and Mr. Guild has succeeded, at many points of his book, in doing this. He goes over the beaten track of Ireland, Scotland, England, France, Germany, Austria, and Switzerland, with a visit to Venice and Florence, a close observer of the manners and customs of the natives, and with a Yankee capacity for learning their ways and tricks. 'Over the Ocean' will be a pleasant refresher to those who have gone before, and a valuable guide-book to those who are to come after. Many of Mr. Guild's descriptions of scenery and sights are extremely graphic, and his hints to travellers are frequently very practical." — *Evening Bulletin, Phila., Pa.*

"The Most Perfect Pen-Pictures of Sights and Scenes."

"This is certainly a collection of some of the most perfect pen-pictures of sights and scenes in foreign lands we have ever read. The author carries the reader in imagination to the very scenes he himself has witnessed, conveying as vivid an idea of the places seen as could be conveyed to one who has never visited Europe. Many minute particulars are also given, such as foreign letter-writers deem of too little importance to be mentioned, yet which are of great interest to the general reader." — *Sentinel, Eastport, Me.*

"The Most Complete Book of Foreign Travel."

"There is no end to the books on European travel that have from time to time appeared, and they pretty much all go over the same ground, but in following Mr. Guild's narrative, one almost forgets that he ever read of the countries beyond the seas before, for the subject is presented in such a graphic and lively manner that the reader almost fancies that he is actually witnessing the scenes and experiencing the emotions portrayed and expressed by the writer. The volume is so minute in detail that it serves as a guide-book of travel, as well as one of entertainment. Valuable hints and information are given about the best hotels, and the names of shops in London and Paris are mentioned where Americans can find reasonable prices, &c. It is the most complete book of foreign travel that has ever appeared." — *Union, Springfield, Mass.*

"He has given Us a Life-like Picture."

"The habits of observation acquired by the author of this charming book, during many years' constant occupation as a Journalist, have proved so far a second nature to him, that upon whatever 'sight or scene' his facile pen was turned, he has given us a life-like picture. Europe 'is done' in a style that must serve as an invaluable guide to those who intend to go 'over the ocean,' as well as furnish every one with an agreeable book for a half-hour's entertainment." — *Citizen, Halifax, N. S.*

☞ *Sold by all Booksellers and Newsdealers.*

LEE & SHEPARD, PUBLISHERS, BOSTON.

BOOKS PUBLISHED BY LEE & SHEPARD.

New Editions of Favorite Books of Travel.

BEATEN PATHS;
OR, A WOMAN'S VACATION.
By Mrs. ELLA W. THOMPSON.
ONE VOL. 16MO. CLOTH. $1.50.

"The author seems to have hit upon just the most charming things to see, and carried to them a wealth of legend and romance and history which has enabled her to fill every storied scene with its own appropriate ghosts." — *New York Tribune.*

AN AMERICAN GIRL ABROAD.
By ADELINE TRAFTON,
Author of "Katherine Earle."

ONE VOLUME. 12MO. ILLUSTRATED. $1.50.

"A bright good-natured narrative of a European tour, which will be pleasant reading for all." — *Boston Advertiser.*

"The American Girl is a bright, merry-hearted girl, 'off for a good time;' and she and her readers are of opinion that the journey was a decided success." — *Liberal Christian, New York.*

GETTING TO PARIS.
A BOOK OF PRACTICE IN FRENCH CONVERSATION.
By FRANCIS S. WILLIAMS, A. M.,
Author of "English into French."

12MO. CLOTH. $1.75.

The first part of this book consists of conversations in English, connected with or arising out of the intended and accomplished journey of a well-to-do family from Boston to Paris. From the first announcement of the intention to travel, a continuous story, lively as well as instructive, is told in dialogue; that is, all the preliminaries of getting on board the Havre steamer at New York, the incidents of the voyage, the table-talk, the landing in France, the remaining journey, and the arrival at the Grand Hotel, Paris.

☞ The other half of the book is a translation of these dialogues into French. It is more amusing than many novels. Its advantage as a text-book is its conversational style and simplicity. The *Boston Traveller* says: —

"The book is good reading merely for a book. The facts of practical value are numerous. The preface lays down the rules by which the student and learner should be guided. *It is a charming book, and without being a novel, has all the interest of one.*"

☞ The book can be obtained in separate parts: English, $1; French, $1.

☞ *Sold by all Booksellers and Newsdealers.*

LEE & SHEPARD, PUBLISHERS, BOSTON.

BOOKS PUBLISHED BY LEE & SHEPARD.

A Great National Work.

THE COMPLETE
WORKS OF CHARLES SUMNER.

In Elegant Crown 8vo Vols. With Portrait, Notes, and Index. Eleven Volumes now ready.

PRICE PER VOL., FINE ENGLISH CLOTH, ... $3.00
"   "   "   HALF CALF, GILT EXTRA, LIBRARY ED. . . 5.00

(*Sold by Subscription.*)

This edition will comprise the ORATIONS, SENATORIAL SPEECHES, and the MISCELLANEOUS ADDRESSES, LETTERS, and PAPERS of Mr. Sumner through his whole public life, and will be one of the noblest contributions to our national history and literature ever published. It has peculiar claims upon the pride and patriotism of every American citizen, as THE ONLY AUTHORIZED EDITION of the works of the lamented Senator who was for so many years, identified with every important question relating to the nation's prosperity, honor, and existence, and who was, for almost a generation, the acknowledged leader in the cause of human rights. This edition will be elegantly printed, on tinted paper, at the University Press, from new type, will contain an exact portrait of Mr. Sumner, and will be furnished with a complete Analytical and Topical Index.

This great enterprise has received from prominent men in public life and in literary pursuits, a hearty indorsement which confirms the publishers in their long-cherished opinion that public sentiment demanded an edition like this, and that longer delay in the publication would have been a dereliction in duty to the country, and to the cause of human rights throughout the world.

The Standard Bacon.

BACON'S ESSAYS.
WITH ANNOTATIONS BY ARCHBISHOP WHATELY.

[NEW EDITION.]

This Edition contains a Preface, Notes, and Glossarial Index, by F. F. HEARD, Esq., of the Boston Bar. 641 pages.

STUDENT'S EDITION, post 8vo, $2.50 | LIBRARY EDITION, 8vo.
LIBRARY EDITION, 8vo, cloth, . . 3.50 | Half Turkey, gilt top, . . . $6.00
Half calf, marbled edges, ... 6.00 | Full mor. ant., gilt edges, 9.00

The first in time, and we may justly say the first in excellence, of English writings on moral prudence, are the Essays of Bacon. The transcendent strength of Bacon's mind is visible in the whole tenor of these Essays. They are deeper and more discriminating than any earlier, or almost any later work in the English language; full of recondite observations, long matured, and carefully sifted.

"Few books are more quoted, and, what is not always the case with such books, we may add that few are more generally read."— [HALLAM's Introduction to the Literature of Europe. .˙. .˙. "The best known and the most popular of all his works. It is also one of those where the superiority of his genius appears to the greatest advantage."—[DUGALD STEWART. .˙. .˙. Prof. Matthews, of the Chicago University, says "that, if compelled to limit his reading to one human composition, he would choose Bacon's Essays, with Archbishop Whately's Annotations."—[Interior, Chicago.

☞ *Sold by all Booksellers and Newsdealers.*

LEE & SHEPARD, PUBLISHERS, BOSTON.

BOOKS PUBLISHED BY LEE & SHEPARD.

UNIFORM WITH THE "BOOK OF AMERICAN EXPLORERS."

YOUNG FOLKS'
HISTORY OF THE UNITED STATES.
BY
THOMAS WENTWORTH HIGGINSON.

Square 16mo. 380 pp. With over 100 Illustrations. Price $1.50.

The theory of the book can be briefly stated: it is, that American history is in itself one of the most attractive of all subjects, and can be made interesting to old and young by being presented in a simple, clear, and graphic way. In this book only such names and dates are introduced as are necessary to secure a clear and definite thread of connected incident in the mind of the reader; and the space thus saved is devoted to illustrative traits and incidents, and the details of daily living. By this means it is believed that much more can be conveyed, even of the philosophy of history, than where this is overlaid and hidden by a mass of mere statistics.

"Compact, clear, and accurate. . . . This unpretending little book is the best general history of the United States we have seen." — *The Nation.*

"The book is so written, that every child old enough to read history at all will understand and like it, and persons of the fullest information and purest taste will admire it." — *Boston Daily Advertiser.*

"It is marvellous to note how happily Mr. Higginson, in securing an amazing compactness by his condensation, has avoided alike superficiality and dulness." — *Boston Transcript.*

AS A TEXT-BOOK IN SCHOOLS.

One of the most successful teachers in Boston says, "I am confident that the text-book has proved itself as reliable and comprehensive as it certainly is suggestive and entertaining. I know no book more helpful in promoting that crystallizing process in the student's own mind by which the accessories and details group themselves around the main facts and ideas of the narration. On this account, it is equally valuable to teachers and scholars, to the examined and the examiners."

This work has been translated into German, and has been received with marked favor. The Leipsic literary correspondent of the "New-York Staats-Zeitung" says, that, in its German version, it is pronounced exceedingly interesting (*höchst anziehende*); and predicts that it will inspire universal delight (*allgemeine Beliebtheit*) in German readers.

The Berlin "International Gazette" says, "Mr. Higginson has executed his task in a very clear and lucid manner, not making use of any hard aphorisms, so puzzling to the young, but placing himself on their level, and explaining every thing in so easy and gentle a manner, that he must be a very dull or a very perverse scholar, who does not find his attention riveted."

⁎⁎⁎ Sold by all Booksellers, and sent by mail on receipt of price.

LEE & SHEPARD, Publishers,
41 FRANKLIN STREET, BOSTON.

BOOKS PUBLISHED BY LEE & SHEPARD.

Just Ready.
A New Work by the Author of the Young Folks' History of the United States.

YOUNG FOLKS'
BOOK OF AMERICAN EXPLORERS

BY

THOMAS WENTWORTH HIGGINSON.

Uniform with the Young Folks' History of the U. S. One vol. Fully illustrated. Price, $1.50.

The YOUNG FOLKS' BOOK OF AMERICAN EXPLORERS is as distinctly a "new departure" in our historical literature as was its predecessor, the "Young Folks' History of the United States." The "Book of American Explorers" is a series of narratives of discovery and adventure, told in the precise words of the discoverers themselves. It is a series of racy and interesting extracts from original narratives, or early translations of such narratives. These selections are made with care, so as to give a glimpse at the various nationalities engaged, — Norse, Spanish, French, Dutch, English, etc., — and are put together in order of time, with the needful notes and explanations. The ground covered may be seen by the following list of subjects treated in successive chapters : — The Traditions of the Norsemen ; Columbus and his Companions ; Cabot and Verrazzano ; The Strange Voyage of Cabeza de Vaca ; The French in Canada ; Hernando de Soto ; The French in Florida ; Sir Humphrey Gilbert ; The Lost Colonies of Virginia ; Unsuccessful New England Settlements ; Captain John Smith in Virginia ; Champlain on the War-Path ; Henry Hudson and the New Netherlands ; The Pilgrims at Plymouth ; The Massachusetts Bay Colony.

Besides the legends of the Norsemen, the book makes an almost continuous tale of adventure from 1492 to 1630, all told in the words of the explorers themselves. This is, it is believed, a far more attractive way of telling than to rewrite them in the words of another; and it is hoped that it may induce young people to explore for themselves the rich mine of historical adventure thus laid open.

LEE & SHEPARD, *Publishers, Boston.*

BOOKS PUBLISHED BY LEE & SHEPARD.

"Such a Book as I should like to see in Every Family,"
Says the Superintendent of Public Schools, Boston, of

THE HAND-BOOK OF
ENGLISH LITERATURE.
By FRANCIS H. UNDERWOOD, A.M.
Author of "Hand-Book of American Literature."
CROWN 8vo. $2.50.

"Winning Golden Opinions"

Not only as the best text-book for schools, but as a book of **Elegant Extracts** from the whole range of English authors, beginning with Chaucer and ending with the popular writers of our day. The selections are accompanied by brief **Biographical Sketches**, which of themselves have been highly commended as models of condensation and brevity. Says a critic, —

"It is so fascinating as to fetter the attention of the general reader, and stimulate him to make a more intimate acquaintance with his mother tongue."

The extent of ground gone over is immense, and the arrangement of the various kinds of information given is made in the most convenient manner. An historical introduction gives a clear and succinct account of the origin and development of the English language. To those familiar with the sources of literary wealth the reading of a page will spur the memory to pleasant recollections; and for others who have neither time nor opportunity for extensive reading, a pleasant and easy way is given for acquiring some acquaintance with many literary styles.

☞ As a text-book for students, it is undeniably the best ever published.

"Much Superior to any previous Work of the Kind,"
Is the Universal Verdict on

THE HAND-BOOK OF
AMERICAN LITERATURE.
By FRANCIS H. UNDERWOOD, A.M.
CROWN 8vo. $2.50.

A Complete List of American Authors,

With specimens of their best efforts, covering a period of **one hundred and fifty years**, filling over six hundred pages of prose and poetry, giving as preface, a Biographical Sketch of the writer, and ranging over an almost infinite variety of subjects. The Biographical Sketches are immeasurably superior in value to anything of the kind heretofore published. They are admirable in their condensation, presenting in a nutshell, as it were, the points and peculiarities of the different minds, the complete portraiture of which is admirably proven in the selections which follow. These make the book a Manual of American Literature for families and the public, as well as a

Text-Book for High Schools.

It is a book in which there is a wider range of reliable information with regard to THE MEN WHO HAVE MADE OUR LITERATURE, and their specialties of achievement, than can be obtained from any other source.

☞ *Sold by all Booksellers and Newsdealers.*

LEE & SHEPARD, PUBLISHERS, BOSTON.

www.ingramcontent.com/pod-product-compliance
Lightning Source LLC
Chambersburg PA
CBHW021427300426
44114CB00010B/677